# HISTORY AND
# HUMAN SURVIVAL

HISTORY *and*

VINTAGE BOOKS

A Division of Random House/New York

# HUMAN SURVIVAL

BY ROBERT JAY LIFTON

ESSAYS ON THE YOUNG AND OLD,
SURVIVORS AND THE DEAD,
PEACE AND WAR,
AND ON CONTEMPORARY
PSYCHOHISTORY

# ACKNOWLEDGMENTS

1. YOUTH AND HISTORY. Originally appeared as "Youth
and History: Individual Change in Postwar Japan."
Reprinted by permission from *Daedalus*, Journal of the
American Academy of Arts and Sciences, Boston, Massachusetts, Volume 91, Number 1.

2. IMAGES OF TIME. Originally appeared as "Individ-
ual Patterns in Historical Change: imagery of Japanese
Youth." Reprinted by permission from *The Journal of
Nervous and Mental Disease*, 43:291–306. Copyright ©
1964, the Williams and Wilkins Company, Baltimore,
Maryland. Also appeared in *Comparative Studies in
Society and History*, July, 1964, 6:369–383.

3. YOUNG DEMONSTRATORS. Originally appeared as
"Japanese Youth: The Search for the New and the Pure,"
in *The American Scholar*, 1961, 3:332–344.

4. WHO IS MORE DRY? Originally appeared as "Who
Is More Dry: Heroes of Japanese Youth," in *The New
Republic*, 1962, 147:12–14.

5. THE HIROSHIMA BOMB. Originally appeared as
"Psychological Effects of the Atomic Bomb in Hiroshima:

The Theme of Death." Reprinted by permission from *Daedalus*, Journal of the American Academy of Arts and Sciences, Boston, Massachusetts, Volume 92, Number 3.

6. ON DEATH AND DEATH SYMBOLISM. Originally appeared as "On Death and Death Symbolism: The Hiroshima Disaster." Reprinted by permission from *Psychiatry*, Journal for the Study of Interpersonal Processes, 1964, 27:191–210. Copyright © 1964 by the William Alanson White Psychiatric Foundation.

7. ATOMIC-BOMBED CHILDREN. Originally appeared as "Accounts of the Unaccountable," in *The New York Review of Books*, February, 1963.

8. JEWS AS SURVIVORS. Originally appeared as "When We Dead Awaken," in *Partisan Review*, Summer, 1968, pp. 475–483.

9. AMERICA IN VIETNAM—THE COUNTERFEIT FRIEND. Originally appeared as "America in Vietnam—The Circle of Deception," in *Trans-Action*, 1968, 5:10–19.

10. REASON, REARMAMENT, AND PEACE. Originally appeared as "Reason, Rearmament, and Peace: Japan's Struggles with a Universal Dilemma," in *Asian Survey*, January, 1962.

11. WHAT AILS MAN? Originally appeared as "Man as Mistake," in *The New York Times Book Review*, April 17, 1968, pp. 3, 41.

12. WOMAN AS KNOWER. Originally appeared as "Woman as Knower: Some Psychohistorical Perspectives," in Robert Jay Lifton (Ed.), *The Woman in America* (Boston: Houghton Mifflin, 1965), pp. 27–51. Reprinted by permission from *Daedalus*, Journal of the American Academy of Arts and Sciences, Boston, Massachusetts.

13. PSYCHOANALYSIS AND HISTORY. Reprinted from *History and Theory*, 1965, 4:353–358. Published by the Wesleyan University Press.

14. COMMENTS ON METHOD. Originally appeared as "On Psychology and History: Further Comment." Reprinted by permission from *Comparative Studies in Society and History*, 1965, 7:127–132.

15. PROTEAN MAN. Reprinted from *Futuribles* series (French and English), Paris, Sedeis, January, 1967; and *Partisan Review*, Winter, 1968, pp. 13–27.

16. THE YOUNG AND THE OLD—NOTES ON A NEW HISTORY. Appeared in *The Atlantic Monthly*, September and October, 1969.

*For*
ERIK ERIKSON
*and*
DAVID RIESMAN

# CONTENTS

# HISTORY AND
# HUMAN SURVIVAL

# INTRODUCTION:
# ON BECOMING
# A PSYCHOHISTORIAN

The most certain thing one can say about man and his history is that he, it, and their relationship are changing. This is so because of the sheer velocity of historical developments, the enormity of the consequences of certain public acts and decisions, and most of all, the precariousness of our collective existence and the pressure of our need to understand and take hold.

Radical historical moments like ours—characterized by extraordinary intensity of change, inertia, and threat—call forth equally radical responses. This applies not only to social action but to modes of investigation as well. One example of what might be called investigative radicalism is the current intellectual effort, of which this book is a part, to apply psychological methods to the study of historical patterns, present and past. This psychohistorical approach, however, is more than a mere expression of social upheaval. It stems from a general uneasiness among practitioners of both psychology and history about the capacity of their traditional methods to describe and explain man during the latter part of the twentieth century. And a specific uneasiness about certain conventional stances of their professions (discussed in more detail later in this volume): the psychologist's tendency to eliminate history; and the historian's impulse to ignore, or else improvise poorly, psychological man.

Nothing in this volume is offered as a specific solution to our historical dilemmas. Nor is there suggested anything like a new philosophy of history, or for that matter a blueprint for the practice of psychohistory. But the essays do explore ways in which men and women—some of them exposed to the most extreme experiences of our extreme epoch—suffer, survive, adapt, and evolve new modes of feeling and thought, of rebellion, and of life. The essays also suggest systematic ways of studying and interpreting these diverse, and in some degree unprecedented, human developments.

The titles of the four sections—"Emergent Youth: The Japanese Example," "On Survivors," "Deceptions of War and Peace," and "On Contemporary Man and Woman"—reflect what may well be an impossible range of intellectual and ethical concern. But I believe that the far-flung subjects and themes treated are of the kind that merge within the contemporary psyche, and in fact have a great deal to do with shaping it. These themes come together, and reveal their essential unity in the last two essays—one depicting a concept of contemporary or "protean" man, the other concerned with young-old struggles to create a "New History." At issue in these selections from my shorter writings of the 1960s is not only the psychohistorical approach in general, but its applicability to present-day experience.

I have made no substantive changes in the essays, preferring that they remain true to their own history. But I have introduced each with a brief commentary in which I say something about what I think I was up to at the time, and about how it all looks to me now. The commentaries are a way of locating that area in which matters personal, geographical, and conceptual intersect—an area of great importance to all literary and scientific effort but generally ignored by psychological writers, at least in relationship to themselves. The focus is upon the interplay of the individual history of the investigator, the locale of his research, and the kinds of ideas that emerge—upon, in the largest sense, "place."

A number of us concerned with psychohistory have come to stress precisely this kind of self-location as a prerequisite for, and integral part of, the general approach. It resembles what the anthropologists speak of as disciplined subjectivity, and involves an ever expanding use of the self as one's research instrument. Rather than being weightlessly suspended in ahistorical-nonpsychological space, this "instrument" is subject to the gravitational pulls of its immediate setting and its prior commitments. Efforts to evolve a level of self-awareness that avoids both pseudo-detachment and indulgent confessional are still at their inception. Perhaps the only point in the essays at which I approach the ideal I am suggesting is the description (in Chapter 5) of my own protective response to atomic bomb horrors, a response I came to see as parallel to more extreme reactions of survivors themselves. The commentaries, then, delimit something of my own place within my investigations.

Concerning another aspect of self-location, I prefer to speak of psychohistory—rather than, say, social psychiatry—because it suggests an intellectual area of concern much wider than that of mental illness, even if, at the present time, as more of a vision of possibility than a comprehensive system of thought or, in an organizational sense, a "field." The boundaries set by traditional academic disciplines, and even by traditional intellectual callings, have less and less to do these days with real concerns or with affinities of one mind for another.

But those of us committed to evolving a specific body of theory find ourselves, undoubtedly more than others, preoccupied with two matters as fundamental as they are vexing: our relationship to the Freudian legacy, and our ability to devise methods of investigation that are both flexible (modifiable according to specific problems) and generalizable (applicable to varying kinds of problems).

The Freudian legacy is best viewed, I think, as an energizing paradox. Its fundamental visions—of the significance of man's unconscious life as well as of his individual
and collective past—provide the basis for psychohistory,
no less than for virtually all depth-psychological endeavor.
Yet these same principles, when applied with closed-system finality, tend to reduce history to nothing but recurrence (or "repetition-compulsion") and thereby eliminate
all that is innovative, or even accumulative, in the story of
man. Freud's work, then, is simultaneously a life-giving
source of breakthrough and the "dead hand" of the past.
The Faustian intellectual temptation is to eliminate the
paradox and make things very simple—either by direct
and uncritical application of clinical Freudian terms to all
manner of historical event, or else by making believe that
neither Freud nor the emotional turmoil he described has
ever existed. The alternative to these two unsatisfactory
positions is to confront and distill the intellectual power of
the Freudian tradition and at the same time free oneself
of its antihistorical bias. To do so (as I suggest in Chapter
13 in the review essay "Psychoanalysis and History")
requires not only new perspectives but a new level of
discourse more suitable to the idea of psychohistory.

Should this idea achieve its full power, it may eventually do so as a "revolution in the revolution" of the psychoanalytic movement. Or it may disengage itself from the
psychoanalytic revolution and create an intellectual terrain more fundamentally its own. Of course, psychohistory
may be destined for no such glory, and could end up as no
more than a rather interesting curiosity. But I think this
unlikely. The combination of current historical pressures
and of work already produced would seem to promise
something more—at the very least a reevaluation of
established ways of thinking about man and the record of
his existence.

Though I discuss questions of method in the essays
themselves, I would like to say something here of three
general approaches, which have evolved more or less in
historical sequence. Freud originated a kind of armchair

psychoanalysis of history: the application of a few specific principles of individual psychology (often psychopathology) to interpret great events and even whole epochs. The method has built-in absurdities, but in Freud's hands it could produce brilliantly provocative results. In the hands of less gifted successors the absurdities predominate. Erik Erikson held to basic Freudian insights but at the same time achieved a major breakthrough by focusing upon the *great man in history*, in a way that related individual psychological struggles to the major historical currents of an era. Beyond introducing the word "psychohistorical," Erikson has provided a model of man *in* history which has already had an important influence upon historians, political scientists, and literary biographers—not to mention psychiatrists and psychoanalysts, though the latter tend to receive their history grudgingly, and often through the back door of clinical reference.*

But the great man tends to be inaccessible, or if accessible not yet great; one must generally reconstruct him through records, or else (if he belongs to recent history) through interviews with surviving friends and followers. And there always remains some question about the extent to which any individual person can exemplify an entire epoch, especially during our own unprecedentedly diverse and fickle century. Hence the emergence of still another approach, that of *shared psychohistorical themes*, as observed in men and women who have been exposed to particular kinds of individual and collective experience.

This approach is influenced generally by Freud and specifically by Erikson, but I have tried to apply it more directly than they to contemporary events. I have done so

* Work by Abram Kardiner, Erich Fromm, and Otto Rank (to whom I shall return later in this chapter) has also been important. Kardiner's analyses of anthropological data taught a generation of psychiatrists important empirical lessons, but his method was essentially ahistorical, and therefore difficult to apply to complex, changing societies. Fromm has concerned himself more directly with the historical dimension, and his concept of "social character" has been useful to many; but he has neither deepened his approach over the years nor evolved a general method specifically relevant to our times.

by seeking out groups of men and women whose own history can illuminate important characteristics of our era. The focus is therefore upon themes, forms, and images that are in significant ways shared, rather than upon the life of a single person as such. I retain a psychoanalytically derived emphasis upon what goes on inside people, upon interviews which encourage the widest range of associations, and also upon the reporting of dreams. But all this is done in a manner departing greatly from ordinary psychiatric protocol, through something close to a free dialogue emerging from the specific situation in which interviewer and interviewee find themselves. The relationship we develop is neither that of doctor and patient nor of ordinary friends, though at moments it can seem to resemble either. It is more one of shared exploration— mostly of the world of my "research subject," but including a great deal of give-and-take, and more than a little discussion of my own attitudes and interests. The method is therefore partly empirical (in its continuing stress upon specific data derived from interviews); partly phenomenological or, as I prefer, formative (in its stress upon forms and images that are simultaneously individual and collective); and partly speculative (in its use of these and other observations to posit relationships between man and his history, or to suggest concepts which eliminate the artificial separation of the two).

These two post-Freudian approaches—the study of the great man and of shared themes—live side by side within the emerging psychohistorical project. My own commitment to the second comes through in virtually all of the essays in this volume, as well as in my first two books: *Thought Reform and the Psychology of Totalism*, which deals with themes extending from Chinese efforts at "reeducation" (or "brainwashing"); and *Death in Life*, which treats the wider ramifications of themes encountered in the survivors of Hiroshima. But in a more recent book, *Revolutionary Immortality*, I have combined the two approaches. I focused upon certain psychological tendencies of Mao Tse-tung as a great revolutionary leader, but only in terms of their specific bearing upon prominent themes of the Chinese Cultural Revolution. When the book appeared, neither I nor anyone else had specifically delineated the two approaches, so perhaps I cannot blame the occasional confusion among reviewers; more surprising perhaps was the extent to which they and other readers responded sympathetically, and themselves entered imaginatively into the psychohistorical vision. My over-all feeling is that there are many more possibilities for combining these and related approaches, most of them still unrealized.

To further their realization through explorations in concept and method, Erik Erikson and I, in 1965, formed a small working group on psychohistorical problems,* in which Kenneth Keniston, Bruce Mazlish, and Philip Rieff have also been particularly active. For three summers now, ten or twelve of us have met for a period of five to seven days, and have known that special exhilaration of those who come together in free and disciplined imagination on behalf of an emerging intellectual project of high challenge and enormous possibility. There are reasons for questioning such exhilaration. But I think it is fair to say that the group has nurtured ideas, books, and controversies of some interest, and should continue to do so.

The geographical setting for more than half of these essays is East Asia—mainly Japan, though also Vietnam (I have not included work on China which both pre- and postdates most of the volume). A student of mine recently took me to task concerning the Asian emphasis. He claimed that it was "too easy" to find psychohistorical principles when working in alien cultures, since at every turn these offer the Western observer contrasts with his own experience. Finding analogous principles in the United States, he insisted, would be much harder. He was right, of course, and similar points have been made before. But I did have an answer for him.

* Group for the Study of Psychohistorical Process, sponsored from 1965–1968 by the American Academy of Arts and Sciences.

My work in Japan does not aim at the exotic. Rather I see that country as unique in its historical combinations—the first non-Western culture to take the plunge into not only the advanced industrial but the postmodern realm, while at the same time retaining (and strikingly so) a variety of premodern psychological and social forms. Japan to me is not a "strange place way out there," but a society that is both culturally distinctive (in ways very different from our own) and deeply involved in the messy panorama of world history.

More than that, I see Japanese society as presenting a very special opportunity for the study of contemporary man—because of the historical combinations just mentioned, and because of Japan's special experience in World War II, including her exposure to nuclear weapons. What I am suggesting is that Japanese, and especially young Japanese, give particularly intense expression to universal psychological struggles. That is why many of the patterns I observed in Japanese youth during the early 1960s have emerged six or seven years later in youth throughout the world. And the general principles I elaborate about contemporary or protean man first took shape in my mind during my work with Japanese youth.

The other side of the dialectic is the specificity of the Japanese immersion. To investigate the most universal of problems, the psychological effects of the atomic bomb, one had to go to Hiroshima. And to understand what happened there, one had to be constantly aware of the twists and turns of Japanese culture and history. Since first being sent to Japan in 1952 by the U.S. Air Force, I have found myself engrossed in that country's postwar psychological and historical convolutions. This has entailed learning a certain amount of the spoken language, and a bit of more or less formal East Asian area study during the late 1950s at Harvard, where I was also involved in psychiatric research and teaching. But a very great deal of my knowledge of Japan has come through collegial friendships with a number of gifted Japanese intellectuals, notably L. Takeo Doi (a psychoanalytic psychiatrist), Masao Maruyama (a political theorist), Jun Eto (a literary critic), Masakazu Yamazaki (a playwright and critic), and Kenzaboro Oë (a novelist); and with a number of talented American and English Japanologists (including Howard Hibbett, Ivan Morris, Donald Keene, Ronald Dore, John Hall, Herbert Passin, Marius Jansen, Albert Craig, and Edwin O. Reischauer).

Apart from questions of specificity and generality, I have tried, throughout my Japanese exposure, to be true to two principles. One of these is openness to information and impressions from all directions, including (perhaps I should say, especially) those having little to do with formal scholarly investigation and arising from odd encounters or day-to-day pleasures and displeasures associated with living there. (For me the former have predominated, but never to the extent of the euphoria I have observed in a few American friends, a euphoria often followed by disillusionment.) The other principle is that of a disciplined effort to keep constantly in mind what I consider (and make clear in several of the essays) the three general dimensions of shared psychological behavior anywhere— *universality* (in a psychological and biological sense), *cultural emphasis or style*, and *contemporary (and modern) historical influences*. My work on contemporary China, in 1954–1955, thrust me into these general dimensions by forcing me to consider all of them in relationship to every individual observation I could make concerning the thought reform process I was then studying. That work also gave me further background for questions of what is generally East Asian, as opposed to specifically Chinese or Japanese. To grasp what I now call the New History of either country (as that term is defined in the last essay), one must bring to individual-psychological studies a knowledge of old cultures and modern dilemmas.

I would not want to give the impression that any of these intellectual or geographical influences developed in an exact or systematic sequence. In mentioning them, I am in fact retrospectively structuring a mental mosaic which, in actuality, evolved by means of unnameable (or at least, untraceable) forms of ambiguity, confusion, and re-creation. But in looking back, I do think I can sense something of an internal ordering process that has been at work. And that process has in turn depended upon my struggle to see, hear, feel, and grasp what I could of two East Asian cultures through images they presented to me, and through the kind of sensibilities that the scientific investigator no less than the novelist must call upon to give form to such images.

But because I am an American psychiatrist and investigator, these sensibilities have been largely shaped by specific encounters with Western thought. Freudian and neo-Freudian currents merged in the atmospheres to which I was exposed during my psychiatric training and early research affiliations, creating an intellectual imprint I experienced as both profound and in certain ways unsatisfactory. I would say the same of a personal psychoanalysis I had as part of Freudian psychoanalytic training. I elected to cut this training short because I felt that the complete program was not only of questionable value for the work I wished to do, but was in fact antithetical to the kind of innovative relationship to the psychoanalytic tradition I wished to evolve. I found organized psychoanalysis to be so bound up with its dogma and hierarchy that it tended to obscure, rather than illuminate, the real intellectual power of its own heritage. Indeed, for the last two decades or so, those at the center of the psychoanalytic movement, while achieving various kinds of consolidation, have produced little in the way of germinal thought. The more original work has come largely from people either entirely outside of its organizational structure, or else technically still within the movement but as spiritual exiles.

This situation will not prevail forever. Mixed developments are taking place within psychoanalysis: tendencies toward liberalization along with occasional "backlash"; strong inclinations on the part of individual practitioners to eschew the total psychoanalytic existence in favor of

various blendings of analytic practice, face-to-face psycho-
therapy, group or community work, and university teaching; indications of diminishing interest in psychoanalysis
on the part of two very important groups—gifted young
psychiatrists who are less likely now than a decade ago to
embark upon its prolonged training procedure, and the
intellectual young in general who no longer find in it invigorating ideas; and a general uneasiness within psychoanalysis itself, reflecting its anomalous combination of
continuing academic and intellectual influence within
American psychiatry, along with a loss of confidence in
its revolutionary ferment or even its relevance for great
social issues and new discoveries.

Psychoanalysis could undergo a renaissance. Or it
could virtually disappear, to be replaced by newer (and
older) intellectual visions and organizational programs.
Much depends upon the power of alternative psychological
and psychiatric movements, as well as upon developments at its periphery (such as psychohistory and small-
group programs on the one hand, and chemical-biological
advances on the other); and upon the extent to which psychoanalysis can continue to relate itself to these as well
as to more general historical trends.

Speaking again more personally, I did not, when first
reading Freud at about the age of nineteen or twenty, experience the sense of revelation described by earlier generations of intellectual voyagers and disciples. For by then
(the mid-1940s) one had already heard something of what
he had to say. While carried along by the power and
elegance of his thought, I also became quickly if dimly
aware of a self-enclosed tortuosity only partly attribut-
able to the Brill translations one then read. Since that
time, I have been convinced that the serious student of
Freud has no choice but to apply a historical perspective—
one which could compare the problems Freud confronted
and the intellectual tools available to him with those of our
own moment. This perspective can deepen one's sense
of Freud's achievement, while minimizing tendencies toward ultimately demeaning worship. Too few have seri-

ously applied it. In my case it was only after embarking upon studies of "ideological totalism" and "the immortalization of words" elsewhere that I came to have some grasp of the source and nature of the theological atmosphere which still, in many places, surrounds Freud and his ideas, whether the man and his words are viewed as godlike or diabolical. To reevaluate—and rediscover—Freudianism and Freud via Chinese thought reform and Mao Tse-tung respectively may sound a bit strange, but that is the way it has been for me.

Well before my work on China, I had been inclined to look beyond Freudian purities toward the work not only of Fromm and Kardiner but also of Franz Alexander and Harry Stack Sullivan. Sullivan is perhaps the most original of American-born psychoanalysts, and I find myself returning frequently to his focus on what goes on between people, especially in connection with my efforts to describe the nature of the psychohistorical research interview. Somewhere along the way I discovered Otto Rank, one of the most gifted and undoubtedly the most neglected of the early Freudian circle, and found his idiosyncratic approach to history of particular value for my work on death symbolism and symbolic immortality (as I suggest in Chapter 6, and discuss more fully in a forthcoming volume, *The Broken Connection*). Thus, over the course of time Freud came to loom for me as a man who had lived the life of the intellectual hero, as a man whose accomplishments, courage, and blind spots were all of noble dimensions.

This view of Freud, along with a sense of the much less heroic limitations of the best of the post-Freudian writers, left me (in a phrase once used by Alfred Kazin on the subject) living intellectually from hand to mouth, until I came under the influence of Erik Erikson. I had read and admired Erikson in the past, but what was for me a major intellectual turn dates back to a kind of "eureka experience" I had one evening in early 1956 when reading his newly published essay, "The Problem of Ego Identity." Much has happened to the world and to identity theory since then—and there may be something absurd about describing a eureka experience in relationship to an essay with so formidable a title. But at the time I was struggling with a vast body of material accumulated in Hong Kong during eighteen months of investigation of Chinese thought reform, and Erikson's concept of identity provided me with a conceptual key to the shifts in self and belief which the Chinese were seeking to bring about. I arranged, through friends, to meet him, and showed him some of my early papers on the research. Erikson was struck not only by the relevance of identity theory for thought reform, but by the psychological connections between this Chinese process and various experiences of the young Martin Luther in which he himself was then intellectually immersed. This was for me the beginning of an extraordinary friendship and a profound education.

All of the essays included in this volume bear in some way the imprint of Erikson. But as I have evolved my own thematic and formative approach, I have begun to find myself, intellectually speaking, increasingly on my own. The pattern is evident in the sequence of concerns of these essays—from Japanese youth, to Hiroshima, to general principles of death imagery and symbolic immortality, to the concept of protean man, and finally to the New History. The sequence could suggest a return to a hand-to-mouth intellectual existence. If so, I would say that when one ventures on to this kind of terrain, one has no choice but to forage for oneself.

In a different way, David Riesman has also had very great influence upon my work. During our marathon conversations—whether in Cambridge, Tokyo, Kyoto, or New Haven—I have learned much about many things, especially about ways in which men and societies act upon one another. No one understands the complexities of these interactions better than he, and no one I know is as articulate and generous in sharing knowledge and in furthering one's own developing ideas. During recent years, at Yale and elsewhere, I have been involved in every variety of mutual enterprise with Kenneth Keniston—including a continuing dialogue about matters psychological and generational—and have felt constantly enriched by his rare personal and intellectual qualities. Leslie Farber has for some time been popping in and out of my life, always with a valuable message about the psychiatric imagination, which is to say, about imagination itself. Exchanges and shared experiences with many other friends and col- leagues—psychiatrists, social scientists, historians, novel- ists, literary critics, and painters—have also been very important to me.

Despite their disparate backgrounds, most of these peo- ple share certain qualities of mind. They tend to live with their attention divided between a particular scholarly- artistic discipline on the one hand (though their responsi- bility to its tradition often takes the form of opposition and innovation), and the larger ethical-intellectual world of continuing confrontation with issues of social good and dignified human survival on the other. This has been my own attempted way, and although it presents its diffi- culties and is hardly conducive to tranquillity, I know of no other worthy of being called a life of the mind. One comes to discover, moreover, that there is unity in the division, that such things as ethical and political commit- ments are necessary rather than antithetical to scholarly work. Nowhere is this more true than in the study of psychohistory.

The interests I have described require certain rhythms, or patterns of movement and stillness. Mine have included intermittent but extensive forays into East Asia—twenty months discovering Japan and Korea in the guise of an Air Force psychiatrist, eighteen months in Hong Kong in- vestigating Chinese thought reform, two years in Tokyo and Kyoto studying Japanese youth, and six additional months in Hiroshima investigating the psychological effects of the atomic bomb. I have also made briefer visits to Japan, Hong Kong, and Vietnam in pursuit of these or related questions; and have spent a bit of time in Europe —notably five months in London—where I have been able to have useful exchanges with like- (and not-so-like-) minded representatives of other cultural traditions. These

forays have alternated with blocks of time spent at home
—which for me means the Eastern Seaboard of the United
States, more specifically certain pockets of New York
City, New Haven, Cambridge, and Cape Cod.

The intellectual similarities of these pockets can be confirmed by the people they attract (mostly the same people), but the places themselves differ greatly. In one part
of my mind I still feel (on the basis of a childhood spent
prowling through Brooklyn and Manhattan) that anywhere in the world other than New York is no more than
an interlude, a vacation, or an exile from "reality." Another side of me, though, makes the opposite judgment:
New York, in its display of contemporary existence, both
in essence and caricature (one leads quickly to the other)
is the epitome of *un*reality. What seems beyond dispute is
that New York is of enormous importance to my imagination, and so I continue to return to it for a week here, a
year there, and the hundreds of weekends without which
life would not seem possible. In New York one laughs and
hates more than one does anywhere else. There is no resolution of my attraction-repulsion toward the city, toward
its endlessly intriguing forward movement on the one
hand, and a surly superficiality, a capacity to destroy or
devour almost anything, on the other. Neither in Paris nor
London nor Tokyo have I encountered anything that
equals New York's combination of violence and affirmation.

Certainly not in either Cambridge or New Haven. But
these two places, by comparison, offer better opportunities for those rewarding moments of sitting down with oneself, another person, or a group of people and pursuing
ideas freely and seriously. The claim that such things are
no longer done at universities is, in my own experience,
simply not true. The two places are hardly the same—
Cambridge's size and resources make it a unique intellectual town with Boston attached; New Haven, in itself dis-
turbingly unsatisfying, offers its special combination of
Yale and New York. For me these university environments
evoke images which are in every sense mixed—of quietude

and abrasiveness, of the plodding sterility of departmental happenings and moments of intellectual excitement (whether during tutorials with students or evening meetings of loosely organized groups of colleagues), of warming responses of students to ideas and their formation (often during seminars or courses they themselves initiate), and of burdensome demands from every direction.

I do not think it inconsistent to place the highest value upon the university and its relationship to the Great Chain of Cultural Being, and at the same time share the conviction, now widespread among students and faculty alike, that universities are in ethical trouble, and require thoughtfully radical kinds of renewal. Or to phrase the matter differently, that the world needs more than ever universities that are capable of the intellectual and moral effort required to confront its staggering dilemmas. The moments when the university seems almost to approach that ideal make all too clear the reasons for dissatisfaction with things as they are the rest of the time.

The last of the places I mentioned, Cape Cod—more specifically, Wellfleet, Massachusetts—is, in the present vernacular, something else. I find it a bit hard to put into words the sense of communion, with both the elements and my fellow men, that I experience there. Much of it, of course, has to do with those incomparable dunes and that magnificent ocean. And of equal importance is the rhythm of days and nights—the unparalleled purity of work and play devoid of interruptions, irrelevancies, and "necessities." People tend to refer to such things as "an escape" or "an escape from modern life." But is it really that? Or is it, as I prefer to believe, an expression of postmodern possibility all too rarely realizable?

My usual sequence has been a total plunge into interviews and other forms of active investigation while in the East Asian environment; then a gathering in of family, data, and acquisitions of various kinds for the "exile's return." In truth, for all of my wandering I lack the temperament of the genuine exile. I seem to require, especially for my writing, that strange familiarity of "home." There one can absorb and sort out, teach and test, and then put to paper the by now familiar strangeness of faraway investigations.

All this is much more harassed than it may sound. Just the mechanical arrangements of travel and housing and provision for children (from diapers to schools and everything in between) can at times become so exhausting as to blur in one's mind the original intellectual purposes of the journey. The whole enterprise depends upon having the kind of wife who can more or less keep things going, address herself both to family and intellectual concerns, and (in the case of my own) apply her creative imagination to the whole adventure in a way that reveals much that would otherwise remain hidden. I confess that there have been moments—perhaps after the fourth or fifth round-the-world journey—when I have said to myself: Enough of this! Time to take more seriously Chuang Tzu's pithy advice expressed in the form of a sage's answer to a disciple who asked permission "to go wandering around the world": "Let it be! The world is right here." But things have gone much too far for that. There is no returning to the life of a proper psychiatrist. I do think it likely, though, that I shall be spending proportionately more time in my own country. Travel fatigue may be a factor, but there is also an element of what a sister profession calls, "the anthropologist coming home"—in this case, the historically-minded psychiatrist returning to the movement of his own, and his blessed-benighted country's, history.

I am aware that my work has been made possible, in fact largely created, by a special constellation of forces from within and without, not all of which I am able to identify. I have in mind such things as the contemporary historical velocity I mentioned earlier, to which I would add the fact of being an *American* investigator during the last half of the twentieth century, which gives one access not only to the money necessary for international research but also to certain kinds of despair-tinged insight emerging from America's extraordinary influence upon the world. Being a Jew is very much a part of the constellation, and has a great deal to do with my concerns with dislocations and survivals, and with man in history in general. My writing about Hiroshima is affected, and I hope informed, by my relationship as a Jew to the Nazi persecutions—and my comparison of the two holocausts° becomes an imperative personal task as well as a logical intellectual one.

My politics and world-view have mattered a great deal, as have the family and intellectual environments which did so much to shape them. My continuously Left position has undoubtedly had its share of inconsistencies, and has certainly undergone a number of changes. But I have been generally sympathetic to radical-liberal, radical, and non-totalitarian socialist positions; and specifically preoccupied with issues of peace and nuclear danger. My bitter sense of opposition to the grotesque American adventure in Vietnam has roots in a longstanding condemnation of America's antirevolutionary interventions in various parts of the world, though my sympathy for political and social revolution in those areas and elsewhere has been tempered by distrust of totalistic dogma wherever it occurs. I find myself more sympathetic than many of my contemporaries on the Left to the cultural and political explorations of the young. When I raise questions about difficulties and dangers in these explorations, I do so as a friendly critic, and in the belief that we all do best by being true to our own experience, even as we recognize the limitations of that experience for coping with forces that are both revolutionary and unprecedented (as argued in Chapters 15 and 16).

Psychohistorians can, of course, be of many different political persuasions, but I think that extremities of contemporary history tend to imbue in us as a group (or else attract people already possessing) concerns about radically new social forms necessary both to understand and alter man's history, and indeed to maintain it. Here I value the rather complicated gropings I went through in seeking

° In Chapter 8, to some extent in Chapter 6, and in more detail in *Death in Life.*

my own voice—as opposed to straight steps up an academic ladder. A background of unorthodox search may not be a prerequisite for this kind of work, but it can contribute to curiosity about certain fundamental, and therefore insoluble, human problems—as opposed to near-total preoccupation with immediate (and much more soluble) questions of standing within an institutional hierarchy.

Publishing a group of essays impresses upon one in a very special way a sense of the limitations of time—something close to what Thomas Mann speaks of as the "artist's fear of not having done, of not having finished before the works ran down." My mixed feelings about some of these writings will be evident from the comments preceding them. And I am aware of the problems created by my own intellectual movement over the decade or so the essays span. What sustains me is a belief that, in this day of extraordinarily rapid obsolescence, their preoccupations might continue to have meaning for a number of people. I look upon them as stones along a very uneven path, a path which has a definite direction but no clear destination.

# I

---

# EMERGENT YOUTH: THE JAPANESE EXAMPLE

---

# YOUTH AND HISTORY:
## Individual Change
## in Postwar Japan

## 1

*The combination here of broad, even cosmic sweep (as suggested by the title) and specific empirical focus (upon interview findings) is one I have continued to make use of in later work. Its pitfalls are undeniable, and it requires intellectual discipline beyond that of available theory. But there were two "situational" influences which had considerable bearing upon what resulted: a slipped disc, and a literary invitation.*

*The slipped disc kept me on my back during most of August, 1961, the position (I hesitate to say "place") from which I wrote the essay. The geographical place was a mountain town north of Tokyo named Karuizawa, whose main virtue (recognized for some time by Western missionaries, Japanese intellectuals, and more recently by Tokyo businessmen) is the relief it provides, for purposes of work or play, from the sweltering Japanese summer. Looking upward and outward from my futon (Japanese sleeping mats, which are ideal for slipped discs) I was, I now realize, especially apt to "see a world in a grain of sand"—or, in a more appropriate version of Blake's metaphor that recently emerged in the mainland Chinese press, "see a world in a grain of rice." The literary invitation came from Steven Graubard, editor of* Daedalus, *and concerned a Japan-focused article for an issue on youth. I had completed more than a year of research and was ready to put down some of my impressions, and in the process clarify for myself where my work was taking me. Hence the statement of man-in-history credo in the first sentence. The remainder of the essay illustrates and conceptualizes that credo.*

*Two innovations in method are worth mentioning. The first of these might be called the "historical dream"—a dream whose narrative and associations reveal ties between intrapsychic and collective experience, between mind and history. Recalling Freud's famous characterization of the dream as "the royal road to the unconscious," I believe we should also see it as at least a royal road to man's historical self. Erik Erikson's work has here too been of enormous importance, particularly his reinterpretation of Freud's famous "Irma dream," the purpose of which Erikson saw as enabling the dreamer to discover psychoanalysis.[1]\** What now seems to be much needed is a careful exploration of dreams and associations in connection with active, ongoing, individual historical involvements. *I plan to attempt just that with a large number of such dreams I have since collected from young Japanese. Indeed, I now find myself impatient with the essay's cursory approach to the dream-history constellation.*

*The second innovation concerns the relating of individual life fragments to specific historical currents. The formidable series of shifts in identification and belief depicted here for one young Japanese later became an important model for my concept of protean man (I described the same series in the original essay bearing that title). Moreover, follow-up interviews in 1967 with this group of "former youths," after an interval of five (in some cases six) years, taught me a great deal about protean man's post-university patterns. Though I had assumed from the begin-*

\* Numbered Notes are listed at the back of the book (pp. 377–394).

ning of my work with them that Japanese youth could teach me much about young people the world over, the widespread youth rebellions of 1968 confirmed this assumption much more emphatically than I would have dared predict.

An extremely important theme in this regard is that of the discovery of self. Young Japanese focus upon differentiating the self from engulfing traditional groups, while young Americans, in possession of a differentiated but chaotic self, look to the creation of new groups to which they can be anchored—but in both cases there is a simultaneous quest for meaningful self-process and community. Similarly, the issues I discuss under "logic and beauty" have come to the fore internationally in the preoccupations of the young with aesthetic and broadly experiential aspects of living (as I emphasize in the last two chapters). And the general theme of historical (or psychohistorical) dislocation, which even in this essay I suggest to be universal, has also become more manifest everywhere.

To be sure, things have greatly changed in Japan during the seven years since I wrote the paper. On my recent revisit I found these same young people to be affected not only by their advancing age and new relationship to society, but by such things as Japanese affluence and the reassertion (however ambivalent) of national pride and international standing. Many of them were inwardly torn over attractions to social rewards and condemnation of the structures and practices making possible those rewards. Here too they resembled young Americans. But unlike young Americans, they were preoccupied with their cultural and racial heritage—with various aspects of their "Japaneseness"—to such an extent that I wondered whether, in this essay, I had overemphasized the psychological importance of postwar Western influence.

I am still not sure, and I think we need at least a few more decades to be able even to begin to sort these matters out. The relationship between traditional cultural forms on the one hand, and modern or Western ones on the other, has always been much more complicated than *most descriptions would have us believe. Only recently have historians begun to appreciate the extent to which the Japanese have re-created and rendered their own that which they originally absorbed from the outside. And during the postwar period, especially the last decade or so, the process has been both intensified and complicated by various kinds of internationalization of culture, and by the expanding radius of shared history. If anything, the essay's emphasis upon new combinations of self-process could have been even greater. And I could have said much more about this kind of absorption and re-creation as individually experienced history.*

*But then, the world does not reveal itself fully in either a grain of sand or rice, and lying on one's back may limit one's vision.*

\*       \*       \*

Youth confronts us with the simple truth, too often ignored by psychologists and historians alike, that every individual life is bound up with the whole of human history. Whether or not young people talk about their historical involvements—Americans usually do not, while Japanese tend to dwell upon them—these involvements are inevitably intense. For those in their late teens and early twenties find themselves entering, sometimes with the explosive enthusiasm of the new arrival, into the realm of historical ideas. And they bring to this realm their special urge toward development and change.

In Japan, the rather sudden emergence of outspoken "youth attitudes" has led to facile generalizations about the nature of young people's contemporary historical experience. There is first the claim (perhaps most popular in the West) that nothing is really changing, that although things may look different on the surface, deep down everything (and everyone) in the "unchanging East" is, and will continue to be, just as it (and they) always have been. And there is the opposite assertion (a favorite of Japanese mass media) that young people have changed absolutely, and beyond recognition, so that they no longer have any relationship to their country's past. To avoid these polarities, I have found it useful to think in terms of the interplay between inertia and flux in cultures and individual people as well as in inorganic matter. For in Japan one discovers that inertia (maintained by traditional psychological patterns) and flux (stimulated by pressures toward change) can both be extremely strong—that individual change is at the same time perpetual and perpetually resisted.

In my work with Japanese students†—done mostly through intensive interviews—I have tried to focus on ways in which they experience and express the wider historical change taking place within their society. I have looked for consistent psychological patterns among them and have then tried to understand these patterns as both old and new, both specific and universal. That is, each is related to the psychological and social currents of Japanese cultural tradition; to psychobiological tendencies common to all mankind; and to forces of historical change, particularly modern and contemporary, in Japan and throughout the world. (I shall refer in this article mainly to young men, since they are most directly involved in the historical issues under consideration. The discussion applies to young women too, but the special features of their changing situation require their own full treatment.)

It is impossible, of course, to make an exact determination of just how much the cultural, universal, or historical factor is at play. But I have found it necessary to take all three into account in order to gain perspective on any immediate observation. This form of perspective seems particularly relevant for Japanese youth, but it is perhaps no less relevant for any other age or cultural group. I have also stressed the *direction of change*, on the assumption that the psychological experiments of outstanding young people can to some extent anticipate future directions in which their culture at large will move.

### HISTORICAL DISLOCATION

The most fundamental of these patterns is the absence in contemporary Japanese youth of vital and nourishing ties to their own heritage—*a break in their sense of con-*

† This study of Japanese youth was supported by the Foundations' Fund for Research in Psychiatry. The research subjects interviewed were largely an elite group, attending leading universities and women's colleges in Tokyo and Kyoto, and in many cases possessing outstanding abilities as students and student leaders. I am grateful to Dr. L. Takeo Doi, with whom I have consulted regularly during the work; and to Mr. Hiroshi Makino, Miss Kyoko Komatsu, and Miss Yaeko Sato for their general research assistance, including interpreting and translation.

*nection.* It is not that Japanese youth have been unaffected by the cultural elements which had formerly served to integrate (at least ideally) Japanese existence—by the Japanese style of harmony and obligation within the group life of family, locality, and nation; and by the special Japanese stress upon aesthetics and the liberating effect of beauty. Indeed, such elements are all too present in the mental life of young Japanese. But they are now felt to be irrelevant, inadequate to the perceived demands of the modern world. Rather than being a source of pride or strength, they often lead to embarrassment and even debilitation.

This lack of a sense of connection extends to their view of the contemporary society which they are preparing to enter. The word "feudalistic" (*hōkenteki*) comes readily to their lips, not only in reference to rural Japan but to "Japanese" forms of human relationship in general; and "monopoly capitalism" (*dokusen shihonshugi*) is the derogatory phrase for the modern—one might almost say postmodern—society that dominates the large cities. Underneath this semi-automatic Marxist terminology is the profound conviction of the young that they can connect nowhere, at least not in a manner they can be inwardly proud of. "Society" is thus envisaged as a gigantic, closed sorting apparatus, within which one must be pressed mechanically into a slot, painfully constrained by old patterns, suffocated by new ones.*

Yet the matter is not quite so simple. What is so readily condemned cannot be so summarily dismissed. By turning to two individual examples, we can begin to recognize the inner paradox and ambivalence of this historical dislocation.

A student leader (whom we shall call Sato) in his early twenties described to me the following dream: "A student [political] demonstration is taking place. A long line of

---

* This in many ways resembles the "apparently closed room" which Paul Goodman describes as confronting American youth.[2] But rather than the "rat race" which American youth encounter, Japanese youth are more concerned with their society's stress upon one's place or slot, which, once assigned, is (at least, occupationally) difficult to change.

students moves rapidly along . . . then at the end of the line there seems to be a festival float (*dashi*) which other students are pulling." Sato laughed uncomfortably as he told his dream, because he could begin to perceive (as he explained later) that it seemed to suggest a relationship between student political demonstrations and traditional shrine festivals. This embarrassed him because such political demonstrations and the student movement which sponsored them (the *Zengakuren*, or All Japan Federation of Student Self-Governing Societies) had been for the past few years the central and most sacred part of his life, in fact the only part that held meaning for him; while a shrine festival, symbolized by the large float, seemed to him something quite frivolous, or worse. He was particularly struck, and dismayed, by the fact that it was *students* who were pulling the float.

In his associations to the dream, he recalled the shrine festivals he had witnessed in the provincial city where he had attended high school; these he remembered as dreary, unanimated, motivated only by commercial considerations, and ultimately degenerate, stimulating in him feelings like those he sometimes experiences when face to face with very old people—a combination of revulsion, sympathy, and a sense of contamination. But he contrasted these negative impressions of relatively recent shrine festivals with the romantic and beautiful atmosphere of great shrine festivals in the distant past, as described in many court novels he had read. And he also thought of smaller festivals held at harvest time in the rural area of central Japan where he was born and had spent his early childhood. He spoke vividly of the sense of total relaxation that came over the entire village, of the bright decorations and gay atmosphere around the shrine, of the exciting horse races made up of local entrants, of big feasts with relatives, of masked dances (*kagura*) giving their renditions of the most ancient of recorded Japanese tales (from the *Kojiki*), of fascinating plays performed sometimes by traveling troupes (*ichiza*) and at times by young people from the village. Sato emphasized that in his dream he was a bystander, standing apart from both the political demonstration and the festival-like activities. This he associated with his recent displacement from a position of leadership within the student movement (because of a factional struggle) and with his feeling that he had failed to live up to his obligations to colleagues and followers in the movement. One meaning he gave to the dream was his belief that the student movement, now in the hands of leaders whom he did not fully respect, might become weak and ineffectual, nothing more than a "festival."

But the dream suggested that Sato was a "bystander" in a more fundamental sense, that he was alienated from those very elements of his personal and cultural past which were at the core of his character structure. These same elements—still the formative essence of his developing self, or self-process—had not only lost their vitality but had become symbols of decay. The dream was partly a longing for childhood innocence and happiness, but it was also an effort at integration. Thus in his nostalgic associations Sato commented that if he really did ever see students pulling a *dashi* in that manner at the end of one of their demonstrations, "I would feel that the world was stabilized," by which he meant in a personal sense that if he could harmoniously blend the old things he carried within himself with the new things to which he aspired, *he* would be stabilized. Like so many young people in Japan, Sato outwardly condemns many of the symbols of his own cultural heritage, yet inwardly seeks to recover and restore those symbols so that they might once more be "beautiful" and psychologically functional.

Another frequent individual pattern demonstrating the break in the sense of connection is one of exaggerated experimentation, of exposing oneself or being exposed to an extraordinary variety of cultural and ideological influences, each of which engages the young person sufficiently to affect his developing self-process, but never with enough profundity to afford him a consistent source of personal meaning or creative expression. Consider the confusing array of identity fragments (as numbered below) experienced—all before the age of twenty-five—by one rather sophisticated Tokyo-born young man whom we shall call Kondo.

As the youngest son in a professional family, he was brought up to be (1) a proper middle-class Japanese boy. But when he was evacuated to the country from the age of eight to eleven during and after the war, his contacts with farmers' and fishermen's sons created in him (2) a lasting attraction to the life and the tastes of the "common man." He was at that time (3) a fiery young patriot who was convinced of the sacredness of Japan's cause, revered her fighting men (especially his oldest brother, a naval pilot saved from a *Kamikaze* death only by the war's end), accepted without question the historical myth of the Emperor's divine descent, and "hated the Americans." Japan's surrender came as a great shock and left him (4) temporarily confused in his beliefs, but toward the first American soldier he met he felt curiosity rather than hostility. He soon became (5) an eager young exponent of democracy, caught up in the "democracy boom" which then swept Japan (especially its classrooms) and which seemed to most youngsters to promise "freedom" and moral certainty. At the same time, Kondo also became (6) a devotee of traditional Japanese arts—skilful at singing and reciting old Chinese poems (*shigin*), passionately fond of old novels, and knowledgeable about *kabuki* drama and flower arrangement (*ikebana*).

During junior high school and high school years he was (7) an all-round leader, excellent in his studies, prominent in student self-government and in social and athletic activities. Yet he also became (8) an outspoken critic of society at large (on the basis of Marxist ideas current in Japanese intellectual circles) and of fellow students for their narrow focus on preparation for entrance examinations in order to get into the best universities, then get the best jobs, and then lead stultifying, conventional lives. He was (9) an English-speaking student, having concentrated since childhood on learning English, stimulated by his growing interest in America and by the size, wealth, and seemingly relaxed manner of individual Americans he had met and observed. Therefore, when he found himself unaccountably (10) developing what he called a "kind of neurosis" in which he completely lost interest in everything he was doing, he decided to seek a change in mood (*kibun tenkan*) by applying for admission to a program of one year of study at an American high school.

He then became (11) a convert to many aspects of American life, enthusiastic about the warmth and freedom in human relationships, and so moved by the direction and example of his American "father" (a Protestant minister and courageous defender of civil rights during McCarthyite

controversies) that he made a sudden, emotional decision
to be baptized as a Christian. Having almost "forgotten"
about his real family, he returned to Japan reluctantly, and
there found himself looked upon as (12) something of an
oddity—one friend told him he "smelled like butter" (the
conventional Japanese olfactory impression of Westerners),
and others criticized him for having become fat and somewhat crude and insensitive to others' feelings. Eager to
regain acceptance, he became (13) more aware than ever
of his "Japaneseness"—of the pleasures of drinking tea and
eating rice crackers (*senbei*) while sitting on floor mats
(*tatami*) and sharing with friends a quiet and somewhat
melancholic mood, particularly in regular meetings of a
reading group to which he belonged.

Yet he did not reintegrate himself to Japanese student
life quickly enough to organize himself for the desperate
all-out struggle to pass the entrance examination for Tokyo
University, failing in his first attempt and thereby becoming
a (14) *rōnin* (in feudal days, a *samurai* without a master,
now a student without a university) for one year, before
passing the examination on his second attempt.* Once
admitted to the university, he found little to interest him
and rarely attended classes until—through the influence of
a Marxist professor and bright fellow-students in an economics seminar—he became (15) an enthusiastic *Zengakuren* activist. His embrace of the *Zengakuren* ideal of
"pure communism," to be achieved through world-wide
workers' revolutions, and his participation in student demonstrations and planning sessions gave him a sense of
comradeship and fulfillment beyond any he had previously
known. But when offered a position of leadership during
his third year at the university Kondo decided that his
character was not suited for "the life of a revolutionary"
and that the best path for him was a conventional life of
economic and social success within the existing society.

* Until recently, more than half the students admitted to Tokyo and
Kyoto Universities spent at least one year as a *rōnin*. Because of the
prestige and better job opportunities accorded graduates of these leading universities, students preferred to spend an extra year (or sometimes two or three years) working to gain admission, rather than
attend a different university. But since the time this essay was written,
student rebels have made the examination system a major target, seeing
in it a means of perpetuating elitist trends throughout Japanese society,
and have in many cases physically prevented examinations from taking
place.

He left the *Zengakuren* and drifted into (16) a life of dissipation, devoting his major energies to heavy drinking, marathon mah-jongg games, and affairs with bargirls. But when the time came, he had no difficulty (because of his Tokyo University background and connections, as well as his ability) in gaining employment with one of Japan's mammoth business organizations. His feelings about embarking upon (17) the life of the *sarariman* (salaried man) were complex. He was relieved to give up his dissipation and find a central focus once more, and in fact expressed an extraordinary identification with the firm. He stressed the benefits it bestowed upon the Japanese economy and the Japanese people, and sought in every way to give himself entirely to the group life demanded of him—to wear the proper clothes, behave appropriately toward superiors and colleagues, and effectively flatter customers (allowing them to seem most popular with bargirls and to win at mah-jongg). At the same time, he retained a significant amount of inner despair and self-contempt, the feeling that capitalism was "evil," and that he himself had become a "machine for capitalism." He had fantasies of total escape from the restraints of his new life, including one of murdering a Japanese or American capitalist, stealing a great deal of money, and then spending the rest of his life wandering about Europe and America amusing himself; and he would also, in unguarded moments, go into tirades against the constricted life-pattern of the "typical salaried man" (*sarariman konjo*).

He attempted to resolve these contradictory feelings by making plans to introduce reforms into his firm that would ultimately encourage greater individual initiative, promote efficiency, and allow for more genuine personal relationships; toward this end he began a study of American writings on human relations in industry. At the same time he was constantly preoccupied with promoting his rise within the firm, with becoming in time a section head, a department head, a member of the board of directors, and if possible not only the president of the firm but also one who would be long remembered in its annals and who would come to exert a profound influence upon all Japanese economic life.

To be sure, neither Sato nor Kondo can be said to be "typical" of Japanese intellectual youth; rather, they express in exaggerated form the experimental possibilities to which all Japanese youth are exposed. (Relatively few become *Zengakuren* activists, but all are confronted with the *Zengakuren* moral and ideological claims which dominate the campuses; even fewer get to America, but none is unaffected by postwar American influences.) Even in the majority of youth, who seem to plod unquestioningly through university and occupational careers, there is something of Sato's quest for the past as he works for a revolutionary future, something of Kondo's diffusion, sudden shifts in ideological and group loyalties, and final ambivalent compromise.

What about the family relationships of Japanese youth? Is there a break in connection here as well? I have found that virtually all my research subjects—whether brilliant students, playboys, plodders, or *Zengakuren* leaders—tend to remain very much in the bosom of their families, nourished by the readiness of Japanese parents to cater to their children's wants and encourage dependency—even when such children have reached manhood or womanhood. This continuity in family life seems to be the balancing force that permits Japanese youth to weather their confusing psychological environment as well as they do. But the continuity is only partial. On matters of ideology and general social outlook, most Japanese students feel completely apart from their parents. A typical constellation (actually experienced for a time by Kondo) is the following: the "radical" son remains on intimate (in fact, mutually idealized) terms with his mother; she is sympathetic to his point of view, confident of the "purity" of her son and his fellow students, although understanding little of the intellectual issues involved; his father, with no firm ideological convictions of his own, disapproves, silently, ineffectually, and from a distance, so that father and son are rarely in open combat. The son's emotional state is less one of "rebellion" than of continuous inner search.

What, then, are some of the wider historical factors associated with this break in the sense of connection? We must first look back beyond World War II and the postwar period to the latter half of the nineteenth century, and particularly to the Meiji Restoration of 1868. Before then, Japanese culture, although by no means as even and consistent as sometimes painted, had maintained an effective stress upon lineage, continuity, and on long-standing Japanese and Chinese moral principles—cemented by the extraordinary experience of more than two hundred years of nearly total isolation from the outside world. At the time of the Meiji Restoration, however, the Japanese faced a very real danger, not only of being militarily overwhelmed by the West but also of being ideologically, institutionally, and culturally overwhelmed as well. The early slogans—"Revere the Emperor, Repel the Barbarian" (*Sonnō-jōi*), and "Eastern ethics and Western science" (*Tōyō no dōtoku, Seiyō no gakugei*)[3]—and the ensuring pattern of an uncritical embrace of things Western, alternating with recoil from them in fundamentalist horror, revealed *the continuing effort to reassert Japanese cultural identity within a modern idiom*.

Thus, ever since the time just before the Meiji Restoration, Japanese, and especially educated Japanese, have looked to the West with a uniquely intense ambivalence. They have felt impelled to immerse themselves in Western ideas and styles of life in order to be able to feel themselves the equal of Westerners, and at the same time they have waged a constant struggle against being psychologically inundated by these same Western influences. In the process they have experimented with a greater variety of ideas, of belief-systems, of political, religious, social, and scientific ways of thinking and feeling than perhaps any other people in the world. And they have as individuals learned to move quickly and relatively easily from one of these patterns to another, to compartmentalize their beliefs and identifications and thereby maintain effective psychological function.* (We would expect an American youngster who actively experienced as wide and con-

---

* I do not mean to suggest that this modern historical experience is the only cause of the Japanese tendency to compartmentalize their beliefs and identifications. Moreover, there is a good deal of evidence that the same tendency existed during the seventh, eighth, and ninth centuries in relation to Chinese cultural influences.[4]

flicting an array of personal influences as Kondo to be incapacitated by his identity diffusion.) Japanese youth are still engaged in the psychological-historical struggle carried over from the time of the Meiji Restoration.

The defeat in World War II, therefore, did not create the conflicts I have been describing but rather intensified them. Yet the intensification has been of a very special kind, adding important new dimensions to the postwar situation. Most important here was the humiliation of the defeat itself, because in that defeat Japan experienced not only its first great modern "failure" (after a series of extraordinary successes) but also had its mystical-ideological concept of *kokutai* undermined. *Kokutai*[5] is usually translated as "national polity" or "national essence," but it also conveys the sense of "body" or "substance," and its nature is impossible to define precisely. Included in *kokutai* are the concepts of "national structure," particularly the emperor system; "national basis," the myth of the divine origin of Japan and of its imperial dynasty; and "national character," those special Japanese moral virtues, stemming from both native and Confucian influences, that are considered indispensable for individual behavior and social cohesion (embodied in *Bushidō*, or the Way of the Warrior). Although *kokutai* is a relatively modern concept—manipulated for political purposes during the Meiji era and again in association with pre-World War II militarism—it had profound roots in Japanese cultural experience and embraced something in the cultural identity of all Japanese.

Most young people (with the exception of rightists) no longer take *kokutai* seriously; they dismiss it as the propaganda of militarists, and even find it laughable. Nevertheless, the dishonoring of *kokutai* has created in many Japanese youth a sense of their own past as dishonored, or even of Japaneseness itself as dishonored. The sudden collapse of *kokutai* revealed its tenuousness as an ideological system. But it also created an ideological void and thus encouraged the polarizing tendencies that still haunt Japanese thought—the urge to recover *kokutai* and make things just as they were, and the opposite urge to break away entirely from every remnant of *kokutai* and make all things new.

Nor can intellectual youth feel comforted by Japan's extraordinary postwar industrial development. As the first generation of Asians to grow up in a country which, at least in its urban aspects, resembles the modern industrial West, they are also the first to experience the dehumanizing effects of mass society (though they sometimes attribute these to capitalism alone). Moreover, they link this industrial development to the "old guard" among their politicians and businessmen, from whom they feel themselves (or wish to feel themselves) completely removed. They find insufficient satisfaction in the democratic freedoms they enjoy—they often do not *feel* free —and they condemn themselves for being attracted to the rewards of their own society.

The collapse of *kokutai* also ushered in a new era of increased receptivity to outside ideological currents. But when young intellectuals now look to the West, they find the Western world itself in a state of profound uncertainty and disillusionment in relation to much of its own great tradition of humanism, individualism, Judeo-Christian religion, and private economic enterprise. They see in Communism a powerful, expanding force, with profound intellectual, emotional, and moral attractions (especially in the case of Chinese Communism), but they have been sufficiently sensitive to the organizational cruelties of Communism for much disillusionment to have set in here as well. Still inspiring and untarnished in their eyes is the social revolution occurring throughout most of Africa and Asia (and in other relatively underdeveloped areas, such as Latin America), whose dynamism has great appeal. But the youth are inwardly torn between their "Asian" identification with this movement and their "Western" separation from it—that is, by the experience of Western-inspired "modernization," which (superimposed on their previous geographical and cultural isolation) has set the Japanese apart from the rest of Asia and has enabled them to accomplish many of the things other Asian countries are just now setting out to achieve.

Surely, it is not only in postwar Japan that such a break in the sense of connection has occurred. To what extent can we say that universal factors are at play? Here we must first consider the ever present ideological gap of the generations, found in varying degrees in all cultures and at all periods of history. Thus, Ortega y Gasset claims that "the concept of the generation is the most important one in the whole of history."[6] He points out that the twenty-year-old, the forty-year-old, and the sixty-year-old create three different styles of life which are blended into one historical period, so that "lodged together in a single external and chronological fragment of time are three different and vital times." Ortega y Gasset calls this "history's essential anachronism," an "internal lack of equilibrium," thanks to which "history moves, changes, wheels and flows." In other words, this generational gap is the psychobiological substrate of the historical process, imperfectly blended with it but necessary to it. Moreover, the occurrence of "youth problems" and "youth rebellions" throughout the world suggests that the gap is universally enlarging. The rapid technological and social change affecting all mankind has created a universally shared sense that the past experience of older generations is an increasingly unreliable guide for young people in their efforts to imagine the future. And individual identity diffusion becomes for many young people everywhere a virtual necessity, a form of sensitive (though often costly) experimentation with historical possibilities. In Japanese youth, cultural and historical influences have brought about diffusion and dislocation of unusual magnitude.

### SELFHOOD

One of the ways in which young people attempt to deal with this predicament is by stressing a developing awareness of their own being, by delineating the self. They do this in many different ways. They speak much of individual freedom in relation to family and society, and strongly criticize the negation of the individual person in traditional (and contemporary) Japanese practice. They respond strongly to those elements of Marxist thought which refer to self-realization. And they frequently combine their Marxism with existentialism, for they are drawn to the ideal of personal freedom they find expressed in the writings of Jean-Paul Sartre and in his life as well. They criticize great nations like Russia and America for what they perceive to be a tendency toward mass conformity and a denial of self. And many criticize their own student political movement on the same basis, despite strong sympathy for it otherwise. Still others conduct their self-exploration through an attitude of negation, through the mood of nihilism and passive disintegration that has frequently appeared in Japanese literature and social behavior; students have this kind of attitude in mind in their use of a coined word meaning "feigned evil" (*giaku*).

Also related to this urge to liberate the self is the extremely widespread fascination, even among intellectual youth, with American Western films. Both Sato and Kondo attend them regularly, and have revealed a variety of reasons for their appeal: the exhilarating spectacle of young men and women engaged in purposeful adventure, free from conventional pressures of social obligation (*giri*), and creating a new way of life solely by their own efforts; the sense of geographical openness and of unlimited possibility; the admirable figure of the hero—his simple courage, direct (unambivalent) action, and tight-lipped masculinity; and the excitement and precision of the gunplay. All this, of course, is contrasted with their own situation in present-day Japan. They perceive in Westerns a world of ultimate freedom, in which the self is clearly defined, unrestrained, and noble even in its violence.[*]

But underneath this ideal of selfhood, however strongly maintained, one can frequently detect an even more profound craving for renewed group life, for solidarity, even for the chance to "melt" completely into a small group, a

---

[*] For a more detailed discussion of Japanese youth and Westerns, see Chapter 4.

professional organization, or a mass movement, and even
at the cost of nearly all self-assertion. Those most concerned with selfhood have often told me (as Kondo did)
that their moments of greatest happiness come when they
feel themselves, in a spiritual sense, completely merged
with groups of young comrades. And I have repeatedly
observed their despair and depression when separated
from groups with which they have been profoundly involved, or when unable to establish meaningful group
relationships. For Japanese of all ages, in virtually any
situation, have a powerful urge toward group formation:
when they wish to do something startling (intellectual,
artistic, social, or political), they are likely to go about it
by forming, joining, or activating a group. The extraordinary array of student circles, of cultural, professional,
political, and neighborhood groups—the "horizontal"
groups so prominent at all levels of society—makes Japan
one of the most group-conscious nations in the world.

One feels this tension between the ideal of individualism and the need for the group in the concern of young
people with that much-discussed, elusive, sometimes
near-mystical, but always highly desirable entity known
as *shutaisei*. *Shutaisei* literally means "subjecthood," and
is a modern Japanese word derived from German philosophy, coined by Japanese philosophers to introduce into
Japanese thought the German philosophical ideal of man
as subject rather than object. But the word has had its
vicissitudes: some philosophers who were sympathetic to
the prewar Japanese ideology sought to combine *shutaisei*
with *kokutai* (thereby almost reversing its original meaning); while in the postwar period it has been a central
concept in intra-Marxist debates about man's nature and
responsibility in relation to the historical process. Continuing in this postwar trend, young people use *shutaisei*
to mean two things: first, holding and living by personal
convictions—here *shutaisei* comes close to meaning selfhood; and second, having the capacity to act in a way that
is effective in furthering historical goals, and (at least by
implication) joining forces with like-minded people in
order to do so—here the word means something like social

commitment. The young Japanese themselves tend to be confused by the conflicts which seem to arise from these two aspects of *shutaisei*. Their greatest difficulty is in realizing to their own satisfaction its first element, that of selfhood; and the sense of "smallness" or the "inferiority complex" which they talk so much about seems to reflect the great difficulty the Japanese have in perceiving and believing in a relatively independent self.

Yet the very groups to which youth are drawn may themselves become arenas for the struggle for selfhood. In this group life there is always a delicate balance between competition (often fierce, though usually suppressed), mutual support and encouragement, and (perhaps most important) constant comparison with other members as a means of self-definition. Moreover, their struggle for selfhood in combination with their historical dislocation has resulted in a burst of literary and artistic creativity among them; such creative accomplishments rarely resolve their dilemmas, but they are energetic efforts to come to grips with them.

Traditional Japanese patterns of group and individual behavior throw a good deal of light upon the present situation. For, in Japan, the stress upon the group as the "cellular unit"[7] of society and the negation of consciousness of self has been carried to an unparalleled extreme. The relatively closed ("vertical") groups constituting traditional society (family, locality, clan, and nation) became the source of all authority in Japanese life. (An outspoken critic of *Tokugawa* society characterized its group hierarchy as "tens of millions of people enclosed in tens of millions of boxes separated by millions of walls."[8]) More than this, these groups have often become something close to objects of worship, resulting in a characteristic Japanese pattern which we may term *deification of the human matrix.*[9] In a culture with a notable absence of universal principles, men have found their sacred cause in defending the integrity of their particular human matrix.

This pattern finds its central symbolization in the idea

of the divinity of the Imperial Family, the Imperial Family having been considered since ancient times the "living totality of the nation." It found later expression in the *samurai*'s absolute submission and loyalty to his feudal overlord, which in turn supplied a psychological model for the modern practice of national Emperor worship. Therefore, it was not simply the experience of *Tokugawa* isolation which brought about the cliquish intensity of Japanese group life, as is often asserted; rather it was the earlier tendency to regard the Japanese human matrix as sacred which created (and then was reinforced by) *Tokugawa* isolation. The Japanese have long had an unconscious tendency to equate separation from the human matrix (or exile) with death—expressed linguistically in the common Chinese character used in the Japanese words *bōmei suru* (to be exiled, literally, to lose life), and *nakunaru* (to die).

All this has resulted in a language and a thought pattern in which "there is . . . no full awareness of the individual, or of an independent performer of actions . . . no inclination to attribute actions to a specific performer."[10] It is the combination of historical inability to delineate boundaries of the self with the modern urge to do so that creates the inner conflicts I have described.

This historical tendency has its counterparts—indeed, they are partly its results—in child-rearing practices and in resulting individual psychological patterns. Japanese children in relation to their parents (and especially to their mothers) are expected to show the desire to *amaeru*. *Amaeru* has no single English equivalent. It means to depend upon, expect, presume upon, even solicit, another's love. According to Dr. L. Takeo Doi, this pattern of *amaeru*—or *amae*, the noun form (both words are derived from *amai*, meaning sweet)—is basic to individual Japanese psychology and is carried over into adult life and into all human relationships. Doi argues further that the unsatisfied urge to *amaeru* is the underlying dynamic of neurosis in Japan.[11] We can also say that the *amaeru* pattern is the child's introduction to Japanese group life; brought up to depend totally on his mother (and to a lesser extent his father and older brothers and sisters within the family group), he unconsciously seeks similar opportunities later on in relation to others who are important to his welfare. The lesson he learns is: you must depend on others, and they must take care of you. It is difficult for him to feel independent, or even to separate his own sense of self from those who care for him or have cared for him in the past. The spirit of *amaeru* still dominates child-rearing practices; and the desire expressed by many young Japanese (especially women) to bring up their own children "differently," more "as individuals," is a form of recognizing that this spirit conflicts with aspirations to selfhood.

The question arises whether there is in the Japanese historical and cultural tradition a tendency opposite to those we have mentioned, one stressing greater independence, more self-expression, and less submission to group authority. Many Japanese feel that such a native tendency did exist before it was submerged by the repressive atmosphere of Confucian orthodoxy, and they point to such early Japanese writings as the *Manyoshu* (a collection of verse recorded during the seventh and eighth centuries) as depicting considerable spontaneity of emotion and independence of spirit. This is a question I will not attempt to take up; but I believe one can say that, despite this early ethos of spontaneity, there remains a rather weak tradition for the ideal of individuation which young people now embrace.

For the concepts of selfhood and of commitment (which implies selfhood), of *shutaisei*, stem almost entirely from Western tradition: from classical Greece of the fourth century B.C., from Judeo-Christian monotheism, from the Renaissance and the Reformation, and from the later philosophical schools which grew out of these traditions. Vital to these Western traditions has been a spirit of universalism—concepts of the universal God, the universal Idea, and the universal State—with which the individual self could come into nourishing symbolic contact and thereby free itself from the influence of more immediate and particularistic human groups. This kind of stress upon individuation has been limited primarily to a very small part of the world, mostly Western Europe and those areas populated by Western Europeans. Non-Western cultures have been profoundly stirred by it, but have invariably found it necessary to make a compromise with it, to adopt a form of *self-expression via the group*. The alternative is a retreat from selfhood into a modern form of collectivism that makes emotional contact with earlier group traditions.

It is perhaps unnecessary to add that the process of individuation has hardly run smoothly and is far from "complete" in those Western cultures where it evolved. Moreover, the exciting appeal of selfhood has created, first in the West and then in those countries influenced by the West, what we might term a myth of absolute individualism, the fantasy of the self existing in total independence from all groups. This, of course, ignores the psychological interdependence between individuation and community.

The dual aspects of *shutaisei* reflect an awareness in young Japanese of the need for both. But they cannot achieve either aspect of *shutaisei* without modifying their overwhelming need for immediate group acceptance, since this can stifle not only selfhood but true social commitment as well. Their inner question is not so much, "Who am I?" (the problem of identity) as, "Can I perceive my own person as existing with a measure of independence from others?" (the problem of selfhood).*

## LOGIC AND BEAUTY

Young Japanese repeatedly assert their desire to be logical, objective, scientific, to be in every way tough-minded. They stress their urge to *warikiru*—a verb which means "to divide" but which now conveys the sense of

---

* This idea of "Self" is closely related to that of Susanne Langer, who states, "The conception of 'self' . . . may possibly depend on this process of symbolically epitomizing our feelings";[12] and also that of Robert E. Nixon: "Self is the person's symbol for his own organism."[13]

cutting through a problem, giving a clear-cut and logical explanation. They are quick to criticize one another's attitudes as *amai* ("sweet"), meaning wishful, rather than realistic (*genjitsuteki*) in one's expectations; or as *kannenteki*, meaning prone to philosophical idealism, overtheoretical, and also unrealistic. A still stronger condemnation is *nansensu* (nonsense) which has been used particularly widely within the student movement to dismiss dissenting opinions and convey the sense that such opinions are a logical impossibility.

These "undesirable" (and "illogical") tendencies are in turn related to one's background and probable future: those judged guilty of them are likely also to be called *botchan*, meaning "little man" or "sonny," and suggesting the softness and self-indulgence created by favored middle-class circumstances; *puchi-buru*, the Japanization of petty bourgeois, which conveys utter contempt in its very sound; or *sarariman* (salaried man), the *bête noire* of Japanese youth in the wider social sense, signifying the selfless, mindless, amoral, modern Japanese automaton, whose thought and life are utterly devoid of "logic" (and which, it must be added, most young Japanese expect to become).

Yet accompanying this strongly held ideal of logic is an inherent predilection for nonrational, aesthetic responses, and this predilection becomes increasingly evident the better one gets to know a young person. Dedicated political activists have told me that they were inspired to join the revolutionary movement through the examples of the heroes of novels by Gorky, Rolland, and Malraux. One *Zengakuren* leader, a central figure in the mass political demonstrations of 1960, told me he had been "profoundly moved" (*sugoku kangeki shita*) by the "absolute sincerity" (*shinjō o tsukusu*) of the revolutionaries in Gorky's novel *The Mother*, by their capacity to hate their exploiters and at the same time to love one another, and that he later found his fellow *Zengakuren* activists to be in the same way inwardly "beautiful" (*utsukushii*). Such sentiments were also prominent in Sato and Kondo.

This emphasis upon the sincere (*seijitsu*) and the pure

(*junsui*) applies not only to politics but to all experience. And among the majority of students (those who are politically moderate or apolitical) there is often a guilty sense of their being unable to match the "purity" and "sincerity" of *Zengakuren* leaders, despite their feeling otherwise critical of their behavior. Many speak of their desire to live seriously and honestly; the word they use is *shinken*, whose literal meaning is "true sword," and which suggests the kind of inner intensity one might find in art or religion or in any dedicated life.

When talking freely, they make extensive use of the rich Japanese vocabulary of aesthetic and emotional experience—*kimochi* (feel), *kibun* (mood), *kanji* (feeling), *kankaku* (sense), *kanjo* (emotion or passion), *kan* (intuitive sense), *funiki* (atmosphere), etc.; and *akarui* (bright) or *kurai* (dark), to convey their impression of almost any event or person. They have an unusually strong aesthetic response to the totality of a situation, and both their immediate and enduring judgments depend greatly on the extent to which purity and beauty are perceived. I believe that one of the reasons for the attraction of Marxism as an over-all doctrinal system is its capacity to evoke this sense of aesthetic totality, of the universal "fit" and feeling of truth. At the same time, Marxism readily lends itself to the equally necessary stress upon "scientific logic" and tough-minded analysis.

The reliance upon aesthetic emotions extends into personal relations, too, in which one finds that these students combine a considerable amount of distrust and criticism (especially toward their elders) with a profound romanticism, a strong tendency to idealize human emotions. Their "wet" (in the slang of postwar youth) quality is especially evident when falling in love: the young man, perhaps after speaking a few words to a young woman in a casual, more or less public situation, or perhaps after simply catching a glimpse of her, sends an impassioned letter declaring his love and accepting the responsibility (meaning his readiness to consider marriage) for having done so; and in the relationship which follows, the letters exchanged (almost entirely devoted to descriptions of feeling and mood) often seem to be of greater importance than the rare meetings for talks in coffee houses. To be sure, there are more "modern" ("dry") relationships also, but it is surprising how frequently one still encounters this older "Japanese" form of love affair among students.*

The efforts to resolve this tension between aesthetic emotion and logic sometimes result in rather problematical attitudes toward ideas in general. At one extreme is the desperate urge to cast off the alien "logic"—the distrust of all ideas, theory, or even talk, and the stress on the pure and spontaneous (aesthetically perfect) act. This pattern is most intense in political rightists, who are rare among intellectual youth, and in certain postwar literary movements whose leaders have emerged as university students, expressing disdain for the intellect in favor of a cult of the senses.

The opposite tendency, and the more frequent one, is to elevate logical and scientific ideas to the status of absolute, concrete entities, which then take on aesthetically satisfying properties and become incontestable—a form of scientism. But one must add that many show great sensitivity in groping toward a balance between their logical and aesthetic inclinations, allowing themselves an increasing capacity for precision and logic while neither disdaining the nonrational nor worshipping a pseudo-scientific form of rationalism.

These conflicts become more understandable when we consider that Japanese youth are heirs to a tradition utterly unique among high cultures in its extraordinary emphasis upon aesthetic experience and the neglect of logical principles. The aesthetic emphasis includes not only a remarkable body of art and literature but also a

---

* In looking toward marriage, most students express a strong preference for "love marriages" rather than the more traditional "arranged marriages." But despite this general trend, a considerable number, when the time comes, resort to the older pattern of family arrangements.

consistent concern with sensitivity to all varieties of beauty and every nuance of human emotion. Such aesthetic sensibility can even become the criterion for human goodness, as suggested by Motoori Norinaga, a leading figure in the eighteenth-century Shinto revival, when commenting (approvingly) upon the morality of *The Tale of Genji* (the great court novel of the early eleventh century):[14]

> Generally speaking, those who know the meaning of the sorrow of human existence, i.e., those who are in sympathy and in harmony with human sentiments, are regarded as good: and those who are not aware of the poignancy of human existence, i.e., those who are not in sympathy and not in harmony with human sentiments, are regarded as bad.

There is a corresponding stress, found in almost every Japanese form of spiritual-physical discipline (Zen, *jūdō*, *kendō*, *karate*), on achieving emotional harmony, purity, and simplicity: a form of aesthetic perfection in which conflict (ambivalence) is eliminated. But among the "impurities" and "complexities" got rid of are ideas and rational principles. Again, Motoori Norinaga:[15]

> In ancient times in our land, even the "Way" was not talked about at all and we had only ways directly leading to things themselves, while in foreign countries it is the custom to entertain and to talk about many different doctrines, about principles of things, this "Way" or that "Way." The Emperor's land in ancient times had not such theories or doctrines whatever, but we enjoyed peace and order then, and the descendants of the Sun Goddess have consecutively succeeded to the throne.

Averse to detailed general principles, the Japanese have tended to turn to their opposite, to brief, concrete, emotionally evocative symbols, as in the short verse forms of tanka and haiku. In the political-ideological sphere, however, this propensity for evocative word-symbols, for what one Japanese philosopher has called the "amuletic" use of words,[16] has had more serious consequences. Words like *kokutai, nipponteki* (Japanese) and *Kōdō* (Imperial Way) seem to have given their users a magical sense of perfection; and this same tendency has made Japanese particularly susceptible to slogans associated with military expansionism. These amuletic words and slogans, within the framework of *kokutai*, offer a sense of aesthetic totality, of both moral righteousness and group invulnerability. And the Japanese language itself reflects the tendencies we have mentioned in its unusual capacity for describing beauty and capturing emotional nuance and in its contrasting limitations in dealing with precise ideas—such that it "has a structure unfit for expressing logical conceptions."[17]

When Japanese students condemn the "irrationalism" of their tradition, they are repeating the attitudes of generations before them, going back to the middle of the nineteenth century; and even today intellectuals of all ages feel themselves to be (rightly or wrongly) an island of logic amid a sea of emotionalism. Their stress on logic represents a cultural countertrend, a rebound reaction against a tradition which has not only neglected scientific and rational thought but also has often condemned it. Such a cultural sequence can readily lead to a form of worship for the thing that has been historically denied, and this makes it difficult for many young Japanese to retain full access to the aesthetic sensitivities still at the core of their self-process.

Turning to the universal aspect of the question, we find that the Japanese have been unique only in the *degree* of their stress upon aesthetics and neglect of logic. Their style of symbol-formation (following the terminology of Susanne Langer)[18] has stressed "non-discursive" elements which rely upon a "total," or essentially emotional and aesthetic, form of reference, in contrast to the relatively great stress in the West on "discursive" (or logical) symbolic forms. But advanced logical skills are a relatively late accomplishment, in a historical as well as an individual-psychological sense, and are always superimposed upon an earlier, nonrational, mental structure. Moreover, the high development of logical thought has created in modern Western man an artificial separation of mind into logical and nonlogical categories. The glorification of the former and the derogation of the latter has left men dissatisfied with the myths and symbols they used to find enriching, although it hardly seems to have eliminated their irrationality. It can be said that this separation of mind has been the price Western man has had to pay for his modern achievements, including that of selfhood.

Japanese intellectuals, especially young ones, are now seeking similar achievements and paying a similar price. Yet Western man has had some second thoughts about the matter, not only in spiritual quests but also in the realization that original discoveries in such logical disciplines as mathematics and the physical sciences depend importantly on aesthetic and other nonrational experience. In the same light, one suspects that the recent emergence of gifted Japanese mathematicians and scientists reflects not only the rapid development of logical thought in post-Meiji Japan but also the capacity of outstanding Japanese to bring to bear upon their intellectual work elements of their exceptionally rich aesthetic tradition.

### DIRECTIONS AND PRINCIPLES

It is clear by now that the psychological directions in which young people in Japan are moving (and in which Japan itself is perhaps moving) are spasmodic, conflicting, and paradoxical. Yet we can discern reasonably definite patterns and crucial pitfalls.

There is first the conscious ideal, the symbolic direction which a large portion of young people chart out for their own character structure. They wish to be, and are to some extent becoming: "new," progressive, innovative, and antitraditional; active, individually independent and socially committed (possessors of *shutaisei*); logical, realistic, tough-minded, and scientific. Summing up the spirit of this ideal path, we may call it "active-Western-masculine."

In opposition to this direction is their negative image,* the things they wish to avoid becoming, but which deep in their mental life (because of their individual and cultural experience) in many important ways, they *are*. They do not want to be: "old," unprogressive, acquiescent, traditionalistic; passive, wholly dependent upon others and socially uncommitted (lacking *shutaisei*); irrational; unrealistic, wishful and unscientific. This path we may term (according to the way they perceive it) "passive-Japanese-feminine."

The inner struggle between these two sets of elements is continuous. The actual psychological task—and one which Japanese have been performing since the seventh century[20]—is that of making use of "old" tendencies when creating new patterns, always careful that the new patterns do not do violence to what is emotionally most important in the old tendencies. Thus young Japanese are seeking to recover their own past even as they move away from it; to maintain their sense of group intimacy, even as they achieve greater individuation; to live by their aesthetic sensitivities, even as they attain greater logical precision. In outstanding youth, much of this process is conscious and self-evaluative, while in the majority it is largely unconscious. In all, the distinction between what is "ideal" and what is "negative" becomes less absolute as it is found necessary to make use of both sets of elements. And even the most mentally adventurous can at most achieve only a slight modification of the psychological patterns which form the core of their developing self-process. But that is achieving a great deal.

The two great problems young people face are, on the one hand, totalism (or psychological extremism),[21] and on the other, a complete surrender of ideals, or what might be called "moral backsliding." They themselves articulate the second problem clearly, the first more vaguely.

* This "negative image" is closely related to Erik H. Erikson's concept of "negative identity," except that it is not, as in the case of the latter, something that youth have been warned not to become, but rather a part of their culture within themselves which they condemn. The general point of view in this article is influenced by Erikson's psychological approach to historical events, especially *Young Man Luther*.[19]

Totalism may take (and has taken) two forms. There is the *totalism of the new*, in which young people carry the elements of the "active-Western-masculine" ideal to the point of creating a closed ideological system (usually derived from Marxism) in which there are combined elements of extreme idealism, scientism, a moral imperative for bold (sometimes violent) action, and a degree of martyrdom. Such totalism has been prominent in the student movement, although actively espoused by only a small minority; and even among this minority, many later struggle against their totalism by questioning the "openness" of the ideology and the nature of their own involvement in it.

The *totalism of the old* disdains the symbols of logic, science, and *shutaisei*, in favor of a traditionalistic reversion to *kokutai*; violent homicidal assaults are made by young rightist fanatics in order to "protect" and "restore" the sacred Japanese identity. Among university students, one encounters, rather than the overt expression of this form of totalism, a certain amount of covert identification with it on the basis of the rightists' youthfulness, sincerity of feeling, and purity of motive.

We have already mentioned some of the elements in Japanese culture which lend themselves to totalism— patterns of absolute self-negation and exaggerated dependency in relation to a deified human matrix. But there are also important cultural elements which resist totalism: a long-standing tolerance toward diverse influences from the outside; a distrust for things which are immoderate or forced (*muri*); a general acceptance of bodily functions and an attraction to the sensual pleasures of this "floating world" (*ukiyo*); and the more recent disillusionment with chauvinistic nationalism and an attraction toward (if only partial comprehension of) moderate democratic patterns. Moreover, what G. B. Sansom refers to as the great sensitivity of the Japanese to the surfaces of existence tends to give a hysterical rather than a profound or totalistic quality to Japanese expressions of extremism.

The second great problem, that of "moral backsliding,"

involves giving up one's ideals in order to make one's peace with organized society (as we saw in the case of Kondo), and reflects a longstanding Japanese tendency known as *tenkō*. *Tenkō* means conversion, a form of about-face, and usually suggests surrendering one's integrity in order to merge with a greater power. In this sense, every youth is expected to have, and every youth expects to have, an experience of *tenkō* on graduating from his university and "entering society," and this is sometimes compared with the *tenkō* of intellectuals who gave up Marxist and democratic ideals during the 1930s to embrace some version of *kokutai*. Thus *tenkō* is basic to Japanese psychology: it reflects patterns of aesthetic ro-manticism, obscurantism, and often shallow experimentation with ideals prior to *tenkō* itself; and it also reflects the ultimate need felt by most Japanese to submit and become part of existing authority, to gain a safe place in a human matrix, rather than risk standing alone. Young Japanese go back on their ideals because their society virtually forces them to; but their own emotional inclinations contribute to this "self-betrayal."

Yet much of what I have described may be understood as youth's efforts to resist *tenkō* and to acquire a new form of integrity. Without and within, their struggle is no easy one. But they bring to it a special intensity that has long characterized their culture.

It is their intensity which helps one, when working with Japanese youth, to think more vividly about general principles. And from this study I believe it is possible to attempt a few general formulations on the relationship between youth and history.

Historical change is not in its most elemental sense brought about by "technology" or "science"; it is human in origin, a product of creative and destructive expressions of the human organism. We have said that the gap between the generations supplies a basic psychological substrate for historical change. But there would be no generational gap—that is, every son would think, feel and do as his father did—were it not for another psychological tendency: the inherent urge toward exploration and change, which is part of the growth process and exists side by side with the more conservative human tendency to hold on to old emotional patterns and adapt to things as they are. The urge toward change becomes closely linked with man's efforts to master his physical environment; it is the source of the ideas, discoveries, and technologies, which in themselves exert so great an effect in reshaping man's experiential world that their own human origins are obscured and often forgotten. The more rapid the over-all process, the greater the generational gap—or, one might say, the shorter the time required for a "new generation" (a youth group with new attitudes) to appear.

Young people in their late teens and early twenties are central to this process, not because they make great historical decisions or discover great truths, but because they feel most intensely the generational gap and the inner urge toward change. At an age when self must be created or defined and identity discovered, their strong response to ideals and ideologies produces pressures toward change—sometimes constant, sometimes explosive—in all societies. (I suspect that even in "primitive" or in "static" societies, careful historical study would reveal evidence of the generational gap and the inherent urge toward change, however these may have been suppressed by techniques of "initiation" into existing patterns of adult life.) In our present era social change has been so rapid and the effects of the "second scientific revolution" so momentous that we are in the midst of universal historical dislocation. Consequently, youth experiences traditional symbols painfully; and the family representative of traditional authority, the father, tends to "disappear." Youth bands together, partly in an effort to set its own standards, partly to experience collectively ideologies that promise to bring about further change felt to be imperative, and partly in the (less conscious) effort to recover something from its own past that might lead to greater stability.

Historical change in all cultures, except those which

are the vanguard of such change (now those of America and Russia), depends very greatly on outside influences, particularly on influences coming from the vanguard cultures. Gifted young people are extremely sensitive to these outside influences but are also ambivalent to them. They are attracted to their liberating elements and at the same time are fearful of having their own cultural identity overwhelmed; and their ambivalence can lead to sudden shifts from near-total embrace to near-phobic avoidance. Moreover, outward acceptance can be a means of maintaining a deeper resistance. Yet even when this is the case, these outside influences do bring about gradual changes in individual psychology. Such changes become significant when core elements of self-process within a particular culture are permitted expression in the new combination taking place.

Finally, youth's intensity in relation to the historical process gives it a particularly strong potential for totalism. This potential is most likely to be realized when young people feel hopelessly dislocated in the face of rapid and undigested historical change, and when they are convinced that their society will afford them no recognition without moral backsliding. But the capacity of young people for self-examination within a social and historical framework—sometimes exasperating in its seeming narcissism—can be an effective source of resistance to such totalism. It can also open up new possibilities in the desperate universal task of coming to grips with the ever accelerating, ever more threatening movement of history.

# IMAGES OF TIME

## 2

*Giving a central psychological focus to perceptions of time turned out to be a more controversial approach than this essay's matter-of-fact tone might suggest. For such a focus turns away from the conventional emphases of depth psychology (instinctual drives, parental influences, attitudes toward authority, interpersonal relationships, etc.). I propose instead a new set of categories or modes (those of restoration, transformation, and accommodation) which depict the individual's stance toward the movement of history, toward historical time. Precisely this psychohistorical heresy led to a troubled rejoinder by one colleague (which I discuss further in Chapter 14), and I have no doubt that it has produced confusion and disagreement in others.*

*Nonetheless, there is a definite psychoanalytic spirit behind my stress upon the contradictions between conscious and unconscious imagery—the hidden nostalgia of the future-minded transformationist, and the past-oriented restorationist's secret attraction to what is most scientifically up to date. Again I make use of the historical dream, this time in relationship to the over-all effort* to rescue one's collective past, whether as buffer to or catalyst for historical change.

The essay probably suffers from being overly schematic; the images and associations quoted are vivid enough, but much of the richness of experience is sacrificed to the austerity of psychohistorical categories. I considered the sacrifice justified by the potential importance of the categories for delimiting something fundamental in the man-history relationship. Were I to write this essay now, I would stress the relationship of these three modes to the principles of death imagery and symbolic immortality which I discuss in Chapter 6. For I believe that a much more extensive inquiry into images of time could reveal a very great deal about relationships to life and death, to stability and change, and to the pressures of the historical process itself. (I take a few small steps in that direction in The Broken Connection.)

Convinced as I am of the significance of time imagery for psychohistorical studies, and even for more usual forms of individual-centered psychological work, I am aware that there has emerged as yet no widespread tendency among psychologists or psychiatrists toward making use of such imagery. They have shown interest in the ideas I express in this essay, as have a number of historians (who, of course, have used similar terms to describe shared attitudes toward time and change). But I have the sense that, generally speaking, man has avoided systematic investigation of his feelings about time—an avoidance which could well be related to the equation, consciously or unconsciously, of time and death ("time running out"). The same principle could also be at play in the general difficulties all of us share in probing the individual relationship to history itself.

❈          ❈          ❈

Man not only lives within history; he is changed by it, and he causes it to change. This interplay between individual lives and wider historical forces is many-sided, erratic, seemingly contradictory, charged as it is by capricious human emotions. Yet there are common patterns —shared images and styles of imagery—which men call forth in their efforts to deal with the threat and promise of a changing outer and inner world. These patterns can sometimes be seen most clearly in cultures outside of one's own, and I have found them to be extremely vivid in present-day Japan.

Through intensive series of interviews with more than fifty young men and women between the ages of eighteen and twenty-five, I was able to observe, for periods of from several months to two years, intellectual and emotional fluctuations in a group particularly sensitive to historical change. Their sensitivity derived first, from their age group, since as young adults they were at a stage of life characterized by an urge to experiment with the ideologies and technologies which motor historical change; second, from their selection, as they were mostly undergraduates at leading universities in Tokyo and Kyoto, outstanding in their intellectual, organizational, or creative abilities; and third, from their modern heritage—since recent generations of Japanese students and intellectuals have been unique in the impressive combination of eagerness, quick mastery, and inner resistance, with which they have embraced outside influences, not only during the years following World War II but from the time of the Meiji Restoration more than a hundred years ago.

I have already described° in Japanese youth a *sense of*

° See Chapter 1.

*historical dislocation* accompanying the rapid social change their country has experienced: the feeling that traditional ideologies, styles of group and family life, and patterns of communication are irrelevant and inadequate for contemporary life, a tendency which I have also called a *break in the sense of connection.* I suggested that this break is only partial, and that lingering influences of the past have a way of making themselves felt persistently within the individual character structure, creating a series of psychological conflicts which in turn add both pain and zest to their lives. Now I wish to carry this analysis further by delineating three more or less specific patterns of imagery\* characteristic for Japanese youth in their efforts to break out of their historical dislocation and reestablish a sense of connection with viable ideas and human groups. This imagery includes emotionally charged convictions about one's relationship to his world (ideology) as well as a sense of personal development within the psychological idiom of these convictions (self-process). I shall focus upon the relationship of this imagery to the individual's *sense of time*: that is, his means of symbolizing past, present, and future, both in his conscious beliefs and in that part of his emotional life which is inaccessible to, and often in direct conflict with, conscious beliefs.

## MODE OF TRANSFORMATION

The first of these three patterns may be called the *mode of transformation*, by which I mean a vision of remaking social and individual existence into something that is fundamentally, if not totally, new. This pattern is best represented by the political revolutionary; but it also includes diverse groups of youth and intellectuals who insist upon a radical political and cultural criticism of Japanese society.

---

\* These patterns of imagery are, of course, by no means absolute or exclusive. They can and do overlap, and appear in various combinations. They may thus be regarded as "ideal types."

Among those I interviewed, the youth who falls into this category tends to hold complex but readily identifiable imagery concerning the element of time in the historical process. His quest for human betterment and self-realization attaches itself strongly to a sense of the future. For he sees in the future man's only hope for overcoming the sordid and demeaning elements of existence which he associates with the present and the recent past. Perhaps the most forceful expression of this transformationist image of the future can be found in the ideology of the student movement, particularly the "mainstream" of the *Zengakuren*: a vision of pure Communism which would transcend and eliminate the evils of both the "monopoly capitalism" held to characterize Japanese and Western society, and the "stagnant bureaucratism" seen to dominate most of the Communist nations.

A student leader vividly described these sentiments to me, referring to the goals he and his followers were seeking to achieve by means of their militant behavior during the mass demonstrations of 1960 (including the violence which took place within the Diet grounds):

> We are seeking something new through our own efforts. . . . Our ideal, according to what we have learned from Marx, is that all human beings are equal . . . and that all are entitled to full realization of their capacities. Our ideal is like that of the Renaissance in which human beings reach the highest possible development. . . . Yet what we do does not simply come from an ideal, but rather is for the purpose of changing the present society . . . and to do this we must somehow destroy its foundation. This is our task now, and the society which will be created in the future—well, I do not think that we ourselves will be able to see it in its magnificence. . . .

In this imagery the future has a near-absolute purity. And in sharp contrast to this purity is the decided impurity of the present. The young transformationist, acutely sensitive to inauthenticity and corruption of any kind, finds much in the contemporary Japanese social scene that grates upon these sensitivities. Combinations of power, wealth, and easy sensuality can trigger a strong reaction in a youth struggling to integrate his austere ideology, his quest for authenticity, and his own compelling sexual urges. And he may also, with the special intensity Japanese have derived from their recent history, deplore another impurity in the world around him—the threat of war—and seek out, however theoretically, a universal symbol of peace.

The transformationist applies similar judgments of impurity to his own individual life, especially to his vision of his own future. The ambivalent symbol here is that of the *sarariman* (salaried man) whom we have seen to be the Japanese version of the American Organization Man, the personification of impure self-betrayal, of rote, purposeless subservience both to his immediate superiors and to the over-all social and economic system; but who is also by no means without attraction, partly because of these very qualities, and partly because of the security, status and even power the *sarariman* may achieve.

The transformationist sees these impurities of the present as having strong roots in the "feudalism" of the past. Under attack here is the complex pattern of human relationships originating in ancient Japanese rural life, and still of great importance for contemporary social behavior and individual psychology. Known as *giri-ninjō*, it involves an interplay of obligation and dependency,* in which, beginning with family relationships but extending into all human contacts, there is an unspoken understanding that one will be loved, nourished, or at least taken care of—if one "plays the game." But the young transformationist expresses disdain for the rules of the game, for the endless rituals of reciprocity, and looks upon *giri-ninjō* as a form of hypocrisy and betrayal of self.

Many have described to me highly unpleasant—even

* Ruth Benedict tended to stress the element of obligation in *giri-ninjō*; while L. Takeo Doi has stressed the underlying element of dependency which he feels was neglected by Benedict in her general approach to Japanese culture.[1]

suffocating—sensations they experience at the very mention of the words *giri* or *ninjō*. Some simply attempt to ignore these concepts, dismissing them as anachronistic holdovers which have no call upon them; others make them the focus of elaborate ideological condemnation. And this ideological attack may extend to every perceived manifestation of *giri* and *ninjō*, including its appearance in relationships between parent and child, teacher and pupil, superior and subordinate, and political boss and local electorate. For transformationists, these traditional rhythms of obligation and dependency—and especially their often-distorted contemporary remnants—become rhythms of master and slave, which must be abolished if society and the individual are to be liberated. They nonetheless, as Japanese, retain these emotions to a significant degree within themselves, as evidenced by the complex *giri-ninjō* relationships (although they may be called something else) within transformationist political and cultural groups. If, however, these tendencies are recognized, they in turn may be condemned as undesirable remnants of the past. For the past remains the ultimate source of evil, the transformationist's ultimate negative symbol.

Yet I gained the strong impression that these same transformationist youth, more than any other group among those I interviewed, had a profound underlying nostalgia for old cultural symbols. In their more relaxed moments, and in their dreams and associations—frequently coming in direct relationship to discussions of ideology—they would repeatedly describe to me sentiments like these:

> There is a big stream in our village—it is really a river where you swim and fish for *ayu* (sweetfish). . . . People in our village have a very strong attachment to that river, though it is not especially beautiful. . . . I have memories of its current dashing against the rocks, and it gives me the feeling of a true river—not like those rivers we so often see with strongly artificial beauty. . . . In the old days the water was very abundant . . . and there was a castle of a

feudal lord. . . . On the site of the ruins of his castle, there are two hills of similar height, and the river flows just between them. In the old days the river was wide and there was a suspension bridge over it . . . and when the water level rose boats would often appear. But now we can no longer see such a scene . . . and the water has greatly decreased. . . .

This is a student leader, not only expressing nostalgic childhood memories, but also speaking symbolically of the beauty, authenticity, and lushness of the past, in contrast to the "dried up" world of the present. And he goes on to reinforce these sentiments in his contrast between new ways of celebrating Christmas (a Western import which has become something of a pagan festival in postwar Japan) and old ways of celebrating the Japanese New Year:

Of course I celebrate Christmas but I don't necessarily find it pleasant. It is just an excuse to go out and drink *sake*— and during the Christmas season you pay a thousand yen for the same cup of coffee that usually costs you a hundred yen. . . . Christmas doesn't matter much to me. . . . But the last night of the year, when people eat what we call *toshikoshi soba* [New Year's noodles], some of the real feelings of the old days comes out. . . . I used to go to the shrine on that night together with my family, with a solemn feeling. . . . There would be a priest, and it would be very quiet around the shrine grounds. Then at the time of the night when the moon hovered above us, when the frost made the ground transparent, the priest would offer us sacred wine (*omiki*). I would clap my hands and, standing in the dark in dim candlelight, I would ring the bell and throw offerings. . . . Only after finishing all of this could I feel relieved and go to bed. . . . These mystical feelings I had during my childhood I no longer feel toward the New Year, but when I look at my mother and father I have the impression that they feel them still. . . .

Here we get a sense of an Ultimate Past in which childhood memory blends with the earliest and most fundamental religious ritual of rebirth from the Japanese cultural past. All is in perfect spiritual and aesthetic harmony. The strength of emotional content gives us the sense that this Past (both individual and cultural) predates, and is symbolically more powerful than, the negatively tinged past we have previously heard about. It has some of the same awesome—one might say "oceanic"*—feeling which transformationist youth also express toward the future, and my impression is that it comes from the same psychological stuff. That is, the transformationist youth embraces a vision of the future intimately related to, if not indeed a part of, his longing for a return to an imagined golden age of the past. Or to put it another way, the transformationist's longing for a golden age of the past—a longing intensified during periods of inner dislocation caused by rapid historical change—supplies a basic stimulus for his future-oriented utopian quest.

## MODE OF RESTORATION

When we turn to the second of these individual patterns in historical change, the *mode of restoration*, we encounter what appears to be the very opposite situation. The restorationist youth repeatedly expresses a strong urge to return to the past, to draw upon great and ennobling symbols of the Japanese heritage as a source of sustenance for the present and of direction for the future. Falling into this catagory are the so-called rightist youth I have mentioned, including at their most extreme those willing to assassinate (and die) for their beliefs, as well as many others less fanatical in their actions but sharing the same passionate vision of restoring a past of divine brilliance.

A twenty-one-year-old leader of a religious youth group with strong rightist tendencies (among the rela-

---

* Sigmund Freud quoted Romain Rolland as looking upon religion as "a feeling which he woud like to call a sensation of 'eternity,' a feeling as of something limitless, unbounded—as it were, 'oceanic.' . . ."[2] The feeling need not, of course, be limited to specifically religious experience, and its emphasis upon the loss of time boundaries is especially relevant to us here.

tively few intellectual youth sharing this vision) told me how, during a visit he made to a sacred shrine area said to be the place where Japan's first Emperor assumed the throne in 660 B.C., "I felt the Emperor Jimmu alive inside myself . . . and the blood of Japanese history running through my veins." And this same young man goes on to describe the absolute purity of the Japanese past, as embodied in the ostensibly unbroken line of Emperors following upon the heavenly origins of this founder:

> The great periods in Japanese history have always been those when the Emperor governed the country himself . . . the time of Prince Shotoku . . . then later on with the Emperor Meiji. . . . We cannot say that the blood of Emperors has never been mixed with *that* of others . . . but the descent from heaven of the Imperial Family of Japan is the fundamental spiritual idea of our nation . . . so that our *kokutai* (national polity or essence) must always have the Emperor at its center. . . . Since the nation of Japan was descended from gods, we call ourselves the nation of truth (*shinri kokka*). . . . I can say that in our history no Emperor has ever governed wrongly, or ever will in the future. . . . It is sometimes said that Kojiki and the Nihonshoki [the two earliest, and partly mythological, historical chronicles] do not describe actual history. But even if they are not historical truth, what is important is that they were written by Japanese. The thoughts of the writers are Japanese. . . . They contain the Japanese spirit. . . .

This East Asian form of fundamentalist imagery characteristically stresses a *sense of organic connection* with the past. The Japanese version expressed here focuses upon a mystical racial identity so pervasive that individuals are perceived as being more or less fused with one another in the pure (unadulterated) racial essence.

Concerning the present, the imagery of the restorationist youth in many ways resembles that of the transformationist. He too sees impurity, corruption, and inauthenticity everywhere around him. But he differs in his vision of the source of these contemporary impurities. Rather than attributing them to the past, he sees them as the

result of evil new influences from the outside which con-
taminate the older Japanese essence. The young rightist
we have already quoted, for instance, condemned the
American Occupation for "weakening the Japanese nation" by destroying its family system, for causing the
perfect harmony of *giri-ninjō* to break down. And he
criticized the over-all "materialism" of Western patterns
of thought brought to bear upon Japan during its recent
history, including the stress upon equality, socialism,
self-realization, and scientific analysis. Indeed, he felt
that he himself had been contaminated by these ideas,
that his persistent tendency to raise questions about historical and archaeological evidence for the existence of
early Japanese Emperors was an unfortunate legacy of
his own postwar exposure to Western ways of thinking,
and that literal scientific findings in these matters were
of much less importance than truths derived from the Japanese emphasis upon intuition and spirit. For him, as for
Asian restorationists in general, it was less a matter of
science versus faith than of science versus feeling.

The young Japanese restorationist's view of the future
is compounded of anxiety and a strange form of utopi-
anism. His anxiety is related to the general forces of
change he sees around him, and aggravated by his inner
awareness that these "impurities"—molded as they are to
the whole apparatus of contemporary society—are becoming increasingly ineradicable. He frequently looks
upon transformationist groups (radical youth and intellectuals) as threatening embodiments of evil, and vents
his anxious hostility upon them. But as a fundamentalist
he derives his vision of the future of Japan—and in this
case of all mankind—from the words and prophecies of the
sacred chronicles of the past, as again expressed by the
same young rightist:

> In the Kojiki there is a prophecy of a time of purification
> (*misogi*) for removing the filth from all of us. This is the
> time we are in now, a period of struggle, of pain before the
> birth of something new—just like that of a mother before
> delivering her child. . . . We have to undergo this birth

pain, which is the coming of the Third World War. . . .
Then, after that, there can be a world state, having the
whole world as one family with the Emperor of Japan at its
center. . . . Just as Christ claimed to be the King of Kings,
we think of the Emperor as the King of Kings. . . . Of
course we must try to avoid World War III . . . and to
defend Japan's *kokutai* is to contribute to world peace,
because the defense of our *kokutai* means the love of mankind. . . . But if World War III comes, Japan's Imperial
House will in some way survive . . . by some power of
God . . . just as the Imperial House survived after the last
war, although Japan was defeated and many royal families
in other countries were abolished . . . because truth and
righteousness endure always. . . . This is the meaning of our
Movement for the enlightenment of mankind, for we believe that world peace can only come when the Emperor is
in the center of the world. . . .

Yet even in the expression of these extreme sentiments,
or perhaps particularly in such expression, the restorationist's attitude toward new historical elements is by
no means as simple as it might appear. One finds that
underneath his antagonism toward "new" Western principles of social equality, selfhood, and science lies considerable fascination and even attraction. We have seen
our young rightist make use of Christian analogies to his
ideological claims, and concern himself with the problem
of scientific versus mythological historical claims. More
significant was his tendency, during discussions with
me, to bring up frequently the names of Marx, Einstein,
and Freud. Marx he mostly condemned, but he expressed
a certain amount of agreement with Marxian economics,
and he and his rightist teachers spoke of their anticipated
world federation as a form of "Emperor-system socialism."
Einstein he approvingly quoted as having favored a
world federation (this much was true) with the Japanese Emperor at its center (this was a good deal less true,
and apparently stemmed from a false quotation circulated
among rightists). And Freud he sought to embrace as a
"scientific investigator of the human spirit." He in fact organized a "Spritual Science Study Group" for the purpose

of strengthening the students' spiritual lives and opposing *Zengakuren* (that is, transformationist) influence; the group was to take up the writings of Freud as its first topic of study, but as it turned out (much to my disappointment) these were postponed in favor of a reconsideration of Japan's *kokutai*.

The point here is that, however the restorationist seeks refuge in his mystical sense of connection with an undifferentiated past, he at the same time feels himself confronted by the powerful Western cultural and technological tradition which asserts itself so forcefully throughout the world. This tradition is symbolized for him by the frightening and alluring image of Science, which he perceives to be the West's most fundamental cultural intrusion—on the one hand a formidable threat to the whole structure of his thought and identity, on the other a beckoning source of unlimited power.

The restorationist thus calls forth his imagery of the past as a means of not only combating threatening new influences, but also of coming to terms with these influences—and, however tortuously and ambivalently, of absorbing them and being changed by them. I believe that Japanese history bears out this interpretation. At times of historical dislocation due to strong cultural influences from the outside, there has been a powerfully recurrent theme of restoration of old Imperial power and virtue, and this restoration has itself been a means of bringing about revolutionary changes in both Japan's national experience and the inner lives of individual Japanese: notably during the period of the Meiji Restoration of 1868,* but also at the time of the introduction of Bud-

---

* Historians have made analogous observations in relation to the Meiji Restoration. Thus Albert M. Craig concludes his book, *Chōshū in the Meiji Restoration*, with the observation: "It was because Japan possessed such [traditional] characteristics when first confronted by the West that it was able so early to achieve a part of the transformation which is the goal of other nations in Asia today. In Japan . . . it is in a large measure to the strength and not to the weaknesses of the traditional society that we must turn to comprehend its modern history." Marius B. Jansen comes to similar conclusions in his *Sakamoto Ryōma and the Meiji Restoration*.[3]

dhism and Chinese learning in the seventh century. Restorationism (like transformationism) always carries within it the seeds of totalism—of an all-or-none psychological plunge into a pseudo-religious ideology.[4] Restorationist movements can, and at various junctures of Japanese history have, become belligerently fanatical—most recently in Japan's prewar and wartime militarism, and in certain postwar demands for a "Showa Restoration" (meaning the reassertion of the Imperial mystique through the person of the present Showa Emperor) much like that expressed by the young rightist we have quoted. But beyond these extreme examples, restorationism must be seen as a general psychological tendency inherent in the historical process. For it is his ambivalent attraction to the symbols of historical change which drives the restorationist back into the past, and this very backward plunge facilitates his partial absorption of these new elements by enabling him to meet them on what is, so to speak, his own psychological ground. He too ends up promoting historical change.

MODE OF ACCOMMODATION

The last of these patterns, that of cultural and psychological *accommodation*, is by far the most common of the three. More than the other two, it has set the tone of historical change in postwar Japan, though at moments of crisis it has been temporarily superseded by each of them. Accommodation is a wide category of compromise. It includes muted elements of transformation and restoration, and is the category encompassing all those who do not fit into either of these two modes. In relationship to the symbols of time, it tends toward an inner *modus vivendi* for blending imagery of past, present, and future. Rather than the zealous focus upon either past or future which we have so far encountered, the young Japanese accommodationist places greatest relative stress upon time imagery closest to his own life—upon the present, the immediate future, and perhaps the recent past.

Like all Japanese youth, he is thrust into a social environment dazzling in its side-by-side diversity of cultural elements: ideological admixtures of Communism, socialism, liberal democracy, existentialism, nihilism, and many versions of Emperor-centered traditionalism; religious influences related to Buddhism, Christianity, Shintoism, and the spate of new religions which combine elements of all of these in highly idiosyncratic ways; recreational disciplines of baseball, sumō (traditional wrestling), golf, karate, tennis, flower arrangement, secular Zen, noh and kabuki drama, games of bridge, go, mah-jongg, and the incomparable pachinko.* Surely there is no other culture in which a young person finds the need to accommodate such an imposing variety of influences. But while the transformationist or restorationist can protect himself from this onslaught with a structured ideological image through which all in turn can be ordered, the accommodationist must face it more or less nakedly. And his psychological equipment for doing so is faulty, since he has been molded by a culture laying heavy stress upon the achievement of inner harmony through following closely prescribed emotional paths within a carefully regulated group structure. No wonder, then, that he places great stress upon ideas of self-realization and personal autonomy as well as group commitment—precisely the things so difficult for him to achieve.

Concerning the past, the accommodationist's imagery lacks the intensity of the transformationist's or restorationist's, but it can be nonetheless painful. He does not escape a sense of historical dislocation, and the feeling that Japan's recent past (and, to some extent, distant past as

---

* Pachinko is a uniquely Japanese creation, a postwar slot-machine game which is a good deal more than a slot-machine game. It involves shooting metal balls in circular trajectories, so that they land, or do not land, in small round holes. It is utterly simple and repetitious. Played in large, crowded pachinko parlors, against a background of loud music and the constant clang of the metal balls, it has a strange fascination—to the point of addiction—for its enormous numbers of devotees. It has been called everything from a contemporary expression of Buddhist mysticism to a sign of Japan's postwar moral deterioration, though more often the latter. It is, in the very least, an interesting invention of a culture in transition.

well) has been dishonored. He feels this way both because of concrete embarrassment at Japan's disastrous military adventures (and the Japanese emotions that went into these adventures), and because this sense of a dishonored past is likely to be present, particularly among the young, in any culture which has been overwhelmed, psychologically or militarily (or, as in Japan's case, both) by outside influences and is undergoing rapid change.

Similarly, his approach to the future includes a concerted effort to make his own way in society and at the same time maintain a sense of moral and psychological integrity, rather than envisage a radical transformation of that society or a radical restoration of the past.

We can appreciate the conflicts involved in this process of psychological and cultural accommodation by turning to an individual example—in this case a very brief dream, and the associations to that dream, of a brilliant student of American history who also happened to be devoted to the traditional art of *karate*, but had temporarily withdrawn from the *karate* group of his university, ostensibly because of the pressure of his academic work:

> I was studying *karate* with a certain teacher who is the head of one of the schools of *karate*, and is also a rightist boss. . . . I asked another student there, "Why does the *karate* spirit become associated with ultranationalism? Why are we asked to demonstrate *karate* in front of a shrine?" I said that *karate* should not be like this. Then the master said, "What was it that this youngster was trying to say?" . . . I didn't talk back to him then, but returned to my place and decided to practice more and become more skillful . . . so that I could defeat that master, a master such as that. . . .

The student's sequence of associations to the dream reveals the uncomfortable symbolism represented by *karate*, and particularly by the *karate* master:

> Since I quit *karate*, it seems that there are *karate* problems even in my dreams. . . . My real master, fortunately, is a very understanding person of a high intellectual level, suitable, I believe, for our university. . . . And the master

who appeared in the dream has no connection with me in actuality. . . . Recently I came across a book with a very silly article about a man who practiced *karate* during the Meiji era, telling about all sorts of silly things such as spying for rightists and bragging about eating snakes. . . . I was surprised that this kind of book is still sold in the postwar period. . . . Somehow, there seems to be the tendency in Japanese society that once the heat around our throats is gone, we forget about that heat. . . . I feel that studious people should express themselves about these problems. . . . We should continue to recognize Japanese culture, not just forget about it and praise only American culture and Americans. . . . But we should not become intoxicated in doing this and decide that fine things are to be found only in Japanese culture, and that Japanese culture must be separated from all others. . . . There are people who do *karate* or *jūdō* or the like without considering these spiritual disciplines. . . . They are only interested in breaking roof tiles [which one does with the side of one's hand in *karate* practice]. We, as young people, should be progressive and create our own society. . . . But too often we indulge ourselves in mood . . . especially a mood of helplessness. . . . Hope is not easily realized in any society . . . and this society is unsteady. . . . But desperation should not be the way of youth. . . .

We may look upon this dream as the student's embarrassed confrontation with undesirable elements in traditional Japanese culture, symbolized here by *karate*. He cannot yet defeat or even talk back to his "bad master," this tainted element of his personal and historical past. But he dedicates himself to an effort to improve his skills—skills related to the various forms of cultural and psychological accommodation he tells us about—so that he might eventually defeat the "bad master" and thus, so to speak, *purify and rescue his own past.* He is troubled, however, by a suggestion of despair, by the fear that this rescue by purification might not after all be possible, that he might not be able to reintegrate the past into his own present and future life experience.*

---

* This dream could, of course, be interpreted in other ways. One could, in a more conventional fashion, look upon the "bad master" as repre-

Thus the psychological tasks of the cultural accommodationist can be overwhelmingly difficult. During periods of great historical dislocation, he may readily find that the cultural symbols around him communicate everything and nothing; he may encounter an unending series of messages, none of which conveys adequate meaning or leads to the kind of imagery which would enable him to re-establish a meaningful sense of connection with his symbolic world. His ever present prospect, as we observed in the case of the young *karate* practitioner, is that of despair—despair which may take the form of nihilism, of experimental plunges into various cults of feeling and sensation; which may lead one to a rote, increasingly constricted journey along the path of social convention; or which may drive one into the more extreme forms of transformationism or restorationism.

But it is also a despair from which one can awaken with much benefit. There is nothing more stimulating to individual and cultural creativity than this struggle for accommodation in the face of profound historical dislocation. Most young Japanese resolve the struggle with at least a measure of success, and in the process of doing so gradually shape new cultural forms—artistic, ideational, or institutional. For in the struggle itself, in the effort to make disparate cultural elements into a meaningful psychological whole, lies the accommodationist's special motor of historical change.

### PATTERNS OF IMAGERY: GENERAL PRINCIPLES

What further conclusions are we to draw concerning these elusive individual patterns in historical change?

First, they are wed to one another in paradox. Those who focus their imagery most strongly upon the symbolism of the future are, to a significant degree, driven toward change by their less apparent nostalgia for the past. Those who feel compelled to reach back into the past for the

---

senting parental authority; and such a symbol of parental authority can then also be equated with the authority of the cultural past. I shall pursue these symbolic relationships in later publications, but here wish to stress (however one-sidedly) the historical elements of the dream.

symbols with which to fight off historical change end up by using the same symbols as a means of enhancing such change. And those who are thrown into despair by their seeming inability to integrate symbols of past, present, and future, may emerge from it by "rescuing" their past and creating new cultural forms, so that the despair itself becomes a vehicle of historical change.

Such paradox exists because it is native to the individual psychological equipment. And in this cursory exploration, we have been observing the fundamentally paradoxical operation of the individual emotional life in the area of historically significant ideas and imagery. I have approached this difficult area by stressing patterns and themes—concepts which unify the individual relationship to historical forces—since I believe this the best way to attempt to extend the insights of depth psychology into a wider historical frame. And if this analysis is to be carried further, indeed to its logical conclusion, it leads us to the ultimate historical experience of death itself. The varying efforts men make to master historical time—to integrate in immediate experience both remote past and distant future—derive ultimately from the ceaseless human effort to transcend death. This effort, carried over from formal religion, perhaps underlies all historical change, and, in a sense, history itself.

Second, these patterns of imagery are, to a surprising degree, interchangeable; young people in particular can readily switch from one to the other. Thus, one of the transformationist youth I quoted had made a sudden shift from a more or less restorationist position; and the restorationist student with the extreme Emperor-system ideology had been converted to this pattern from a near-Communist transformationist stance. I have, moreover, frequently encountered conversions from a transformationist position (and occasionally from a restorationist one) to a pattern of accommodation, particularly at the time of graduation from the university, when most young people feel compelled to find a way of life within the existing social framework.

These shifts in imagery—whether polar and dramatic

or gradual and invisible—defy easy psychological evaluation. They can often combine the most radical change in world-view, group affiliation, and style of psychological functioning on the one hand, with relatively unchanged underlying character structure on the other. I would suggest that this seeming contradiction is explained by the existence of an emotional substrate and a set of symbols common to all three patterns of imagery, which can be shaped or reshaped into any of the three distinctively different forms we have observed. A significant element in this substrate was expressed (particularly vividly by transformationists and restorationists) in what I have referred to as the quest for an Ultimate Past and Ultimate Future. The "ultimate" element sought here is that of ultimate unity—a state of existence in which men and ideas are so harmoniously blended that conflict and strife cease. The individual model for this unity is the original psychobiological unity of the mother-child relationship, prior to the child's sense of differentiation into a separate individual. The cultural model (clearly evident in Japanese thought and in most non-Western tradition, but also in early Western cultural history) is the stress upon a near-mystical social and racial harmony, a harmony felt to transcend historical time. This emotional-symbolic substrate (or at least the portion of it we have been discussing) tends to take on a maternal coloring which communicates a sense of the perpetuation of life itself, to the point, as already suggested, of transcending the always threatening fact of biological death.

It is precisely this commonly held and enduring emotional-symbolic substrate—so enduring that we may well look upon it as a major psychobiological universal underlying all historical change—that makes possible the dramatic shifts from one mode to another. But we must still account for the choice of imagery, whether in conversions or in the establishment of the modes themselves. Here I would stress the interplay of three general factors: historical influences of the kind I have presented in this paper, which not only supply imagery to the individual

but create within him, and within his culture, varying degrees of readiness for that imagery; institutions and organizations, particularly those of youth, which mediate
the imagery and supply the group identities necessary
for its expression; and variations in individual-psychological background experience, which (although neglected in
this paper in favor of other emphases) significantly influence the choice of imagery from among available alternatives, and the manner in which the chosen imagery is
held and expressed.

Thus, for young Japanese, transformationist ideology is
encouraged by a combination of its general strength, particularly in the non-Western world, and by the existence
of historical dislocation; restorationism has been largely
dishonored but still holds considerable underlying emotional appeal; a vision of ultimate unity (transformationist or restorationist) is encouraged by an extraordinary
cultural emphasis upon the undifferentiated intimacy of
the mother-child relationship; but accommodation is demanded by an advanced industrial society, encouraged
by economic rewards, and reinforced by a longstanding utilitarianism within Japanese character structure.

No matter what the combination, historical change cannot be generated without making use of the individual
and cultural past. But in this view of history as "a forward-
moving *recherche du temps perdu*,"[5] I do not speak
either of "regression" or even of "repetition-compulsion"
in the classical psychoanalytic sense (though the latter
is closer to what I mean). I refer to the continuous process of fusion of symbols and reshaping of imagery, to the
symbolic constellation that comes to exist, in restless
equilibrium, within individual minds as a fluctuating
self-process; and which may, in significant degree, become the shared symbols of large groups of people to the
extent of dominating an entire era.[6]

Finally, a beginning knowledge of these patterns of
imagery may shed some light on forces now evolving in
various parts of the world, particularly in the underdeveloped areas of Africa and Asia, but also in the industrial-

ized West, including our own country (here too Japan is a particularly valuable laboratory, because it has one historical foot in the underdeveloped Afro-Asian world and another in the "developed" West). These patterns of imagery may appear more or less spontaneously, as in Japan (the three modes described), in France (the transformationism of intellectuals and the restorationism of *colons*), and the United States (the accommodationism of most segments of the population and the restorationism of the Radical Right). They may be manipulated by mass media, as, for instance in the Middle East (a mixture of transformationist and restorationist imagery). Or they may be stimulated through an organized national program of "re-education" or "thought reform" as in Communist China (mostly transformationist, but with restorationist flashes).[7] In the latter case, and in fact in most manipulated efforts, transformationist images are stressed, since these forms of imagery stimulate passions most useful—perhaps indispensable—for bringing about social change.[*]

The dilemma presented here is that these same passionate modes necessary to historical change are most prone to excess, or to totalism. But whatever their dangers, transformationism and restorationism, no less than accommodationism, are inevitable elements in the historical process, because they reflect fundamental individual psychological tendencies. The great historical problems then—from the standpoint of this psychological perspective—are to attenuate, or at least make creative use of, the despair of accommodationism, and at the same time moderate the despair-relieving excesses of transformationism and restorationism. While one can hardly approach these problems with optimism, much hope lies in the constant reshaping of imagery of which men are capable.

---

[*] If we turn to more primitive cultures, we can see even more vividly the intimate interplay of the three modes in bringing about historical change—the combination of extremist "cargo cults" (consisting of both transformationist and restorationist elements) with more or less rationalized (accommodationist) techniques for modernization.[8]

For just as the full range of human emotional potential seems to be necessary for the assimilation of historical change, so might this richness and diversity lead to new combinations of thought and feeling, and to new possibilities for applying change to man's benefit rather than to his destruction.

# YOUNG
# DEMONSTRATORS

## 3

*Everyone in Tokyo during the spring of 1960 had to have some kind of response to the extraordinary mass demonstrations which took place then. Mine is described here. The essay originated in a series of letters I wrote to David Riesman in the midst of the events described and shortly afterward. Rather than a report of planned research, it is an interpretive account of a highly unscheduled national upheaval in which the people I had come to study—educated youth—happened to be in the vanguard.*

*I had just begun interviews with university students, and a few of the young men I was interviewing were right up front in the demonstrations. During that strange month (mid-May to mid-June) I went to some effort to arrange or attend meetings and social gatherings with Japanese and American acquaintances—the former mostly from university faculties in Tokyo, the latter including academics and writers as well as businessmen and Embassy people—at which the confrontations of the street were often given "instant replay" in the living room. So this essay, unlike the others, describes a "historical event" in process. Its combination of brief composite sketches of participants and equally brief conceptual comments may well do injustice to both description and interpretation. But it does at least attempt to respond flexibly to a sudden unfolding of developments within, but hardly confined to, the general arena I had chosen for investigation.*

*There were certain currents I probably did not adequately convey—the really extraordinary excitement that swept the entire country, the intensity and specificity of the anger directed at then Prime Minister Kishi, the terror that gripped many Americans living in Japan as they felt a reasonably familiar and comfortable environment collapsing beneath them and becoming alien and even dangerous.*

*Indeed, while virtually all observers (myself included) commented upon the volatility of the Japanese—their quick intellectual and emotional turnabouts—not much has been said about the equally impressive volatility of resident Americans. I have vivid memories of a few Embassy officials going about in a state of angry agitation, bristling at suggestions (made by people like me) that there were compelling psychological and historical reasons for the way young Japanese were behaving, preferring to view the whole panorama as nothing but Communist mischief; and then, just a week or two later, of these same people demonstrating a sudden capacity for contemplation and intelligent interest in precisely the psychological and historical factors at play. There were at least three reasons for their impressive turnabout: the demonstrations had subsided, and it had become clear that Japanese and Americans would be able to resume workable relationships of some sort; Edwin Reischauer had written his highly influential* Foreign Affairs *article, "The Broken Dialogue," which brought needed historical imagination to the episode and to Japanese-American conflicts in general; and word had become fairly definite that Reischauer was about to be appointed the new American Ambassador in Tokyo. I am not suggesting that Americans were being hypocritical (any more than the Japanese were) but rather that all people, especially during a crisis of this kind, are profoundly affected by the shifting currents prevailing within their functional groups. And the kind of psychological style emerging virtually everywhere (as I describe in Chapter 15 in my essay on protean man) is likely to make such volatility increasingly commonplace.*

*Two scenes from the demonstrations themselves stick in my mind. The first was an encounter with a very short and very young-looking university student, who emerged from a crowd of thousands of young demonstrators not far from the Diet grounds to talk to my wife and me. Like many others we had spoken to, he wanted to tell us that his friends had nothing against Americans (and, of course, to practice his English a little). But he had the further idea of taking us to meet the leader of his group who would, he assured us, authoritatively confirm what he had told us. So this incredibly slight youngster marched boldly forward, waving his arms and clearing a path through massive tangles of demonstrators for an all too prominent American more than a foot taller, eighty pounds heavier, and fifteen years older than he, and for an American woman of more modest proportions but not without her own blonde prominence. Other demonstrators looked at us with curiosity, amusement, and incredulousness; and my own uneasy feeling, so far as I can recall it, was mostly one of extreme embarrassment and a sense of absurdity. We never did get to that leader—things were much too chaotic. But we had taken our guide's name and address before being separated from him, and he soon became a regular visitor to my study as a participant in my research—the only one in fact recruited in that fashion. The bond between us over the years became all the more intense for this bit of shared history we had known.*

*The other scene also took place at night near the Diet grounds, this time on a particularly clear and balmy evening. My wife and I were with a German-born friend who happened to be an authority on East Asia. We stood on the sidelines watching long columns of students march-ing exuberantly past, then shifting into that now cele-*

brated zigzag dance (recently imitated by American demonstrators), their flags (mostly red\*) held aloft—the whole thing looking like the work of an artist whose genre of socialist realism could not contain his highly romantic impulse. As my friend surveyed the scene, his face became gentle and even beatific, as he said softly, "It is simply beautiful." And there was no denying the beauty of the scene—of that revolution that was not a revolution, that revolutionary gesture without revolutionary violence. Yet, investigator that I am, I recall even at that moment being aware of some of the contradictions and problems surrounding the students, of the kind I describe in the essay. And I now look back at the event as something of a lesson concerning the very fine line between constructive radical protest and destructive romantic totalism—an issue I take up in both of my books on China, and again in the last essay of this collection.

If one considers the matter of violence, however, what was remarkable during these demonstrations was not that it occurred on one or two occasions but that there was so little of it. This was partly because of restraint on the part of most groups of demonstrators as well as the police, but also because of the vast element of what might best be called "performance." By that word I mean to suggest a certain disparity between external display and inner conviction—a recognition on the part of even those demonstrators most committed to the idea of revolution that one simply could not find in Japanese society at that time the economic deprivations and ideological and class antagonisms which have historically accompanied violent political overthrow of governments. That is why one may speak of an atmosphere of revolution, of what I refer to in the essay itself as "a revolutionary feeling in the air"—or what I would now call a dramatization of social revolution. Here again there are many parallels to the "theatrical" quality of recent student rebellions in the West—a

---

\* The flags represented factions of the Zengakuren as well as individual universities.

*quality which by no means renders these rebellions inau-
thentic but does have important effect on their course of
development and on the way in which people respond to
them (see the commentary of Chapter 16).*

Since this essay is more specifically topical than the
others, one might expect the psychological patterns described in it to be more evanescent. Yet my impression
from recent observations is that the profiles of the Zengakuren *activist* and the "moderate student" (the "accommodationist" of the previous essay) would still generally
hold for present-day counterparts. Nor could one say
that it would be impossible for similar demonstrations to
occur, say, in 1970, when the problem of renewing the
Security Treaty once more arises—or some time before,
or after, that date.

Certain general trends, evident during my revisit to
Japan in 1967, have become even more striking since then.
Some groups within the Zengakuren *have* become increasingly militant and violent—training themselves for confrontations with the police, and appearing at demonstrations carrying long sticks as weapons and wearing
protective helmets. At the same time they have become
more and more isolated from middle-class society and,
partly because of these tactics, from other Japanese student bodies. Yet the Zengakuren *activists* have shown
themselves still capable of rallying large numbers of less
militant students around certain explosive issues—the
American military presence in Japan and its relationship
to the war in Vietnam and to the use of Japanese ports by
nuclear-powered submarines, and the conflicts within
Japanese universities paralleling those throughout the
world. Concerning the latter, it is significant that Zengakuren *activists* were employing such militant techniques
as the occupation of university buildings and the temporary incarceration of university officials (usually the
president) about ten years before these practices began to have such wide currency among student radicals
elsewhere.

The night before making my final corrections on this

*copy, I watched, from my home in Connecticut, televised film of the recapturing by Japanese police of the last student-occupied building of Tokyo University—a violent, profoundly destructive, mock-military culmination of a year of student agitation stemming from widespread resentment of residual feudalistic educational practices (especially in the medical school), extreme and unyielding stances of two Zengakuren factions (as well as conflicts with other factions and with each other), and the various in-between currents described in this essay. The event seemed to establish, or perhaps re-establish, Japan's claim to the most militant of all youth rebellions, and to the most polarized and troubled of all national university scenes.*

❋          ❋          ❋

Youth rebellions anywhere reflect, and demand, social change. When a society is particularly confusing, and pressures for change particularly strong—as in postwar Japan—young people may surprise everyone, including themselves, with the sudden prominence they can achieve. For men and women between eighteen and twenty-five are both old enough and young enough to embrace ideas of rebellion and change, and to act boldly, even rashly, upon them.

One could not help but be struck by such youthful passions during the 1960 mass political demonstrations in Tokyo, especially if one happened to be in Japan, as I was, for the purpose of studying the psychological patterns of Japanese youth. Japanese university students never looked so stimulated, so alive with purpose, as they did during the five-week period following the parliamentary maneuver in which the Japanese-American Security Treaty Revision was approved just after midnight of May 19. The rank and file of the students, which had previously held itself somewhat apart from the rivalries among extremist leaders of the *Zengakuren*, now put reservations aside and fell in behind them. Students joined the *Zengakuren* hard core's characteristic zigzag snake dance in such numbers, and with such enthusiasm, that this display of youthful abandon became one of the major tourist attractions of the city. To be sure, there was among the moderately inclined majority some disapproval of the tactics of the *Zengakuren* "mainstream" in storming the Diet grounds. (The "mainstream" was the *Zengakuren*'s dominant group, which split off from Communist leadership in 1958, and whose quest for pure Communism and for world revolution caused some to look upon it as "the most radical organization in the world.") There was also disapproval of the equally violent behavior in the Hagerty incident* of the "antimainstream" faction, still Communist-controlled. Nevertheless, *Zengakuren* leaders were suddenly transformed, in the eyes not only of student followers, but of a large segment of Japan's urban population, from wild extremists to heroic and pure defenders of Japanese democracy.

Watching the students (who with the workers made up the majority of the demonstrators) march through the streets, each group identified by its particular flag, shouting in unison *"Kishi taose"* ("Down with Kishi") or *"Ampo hantai"* ("Down with the Security Treaty"), one sometimes got a sense of ugly hostility that could—and occasionally did—erupt into violence; yet more often these demonstrations created a much less ominous impression of comradely *esprit de corps*, of young people exhilarated by their arm-in-arm intimacy, more proud and happy than violent, and eager to explain to Americans they encountered on the streets that they were not against America but against Kishi.

As the students and laborers were joined in the daily demonstrations by large groups of professors, white-collar workers, entertainers and assorted professional people, and as virtually all of the country's newspapers began to clamor for Kishi's resignation, an aura of unreality

* James C. Hagerty, the Presidential Press Secretary, was sent to Japan on June 10 to make final preparations for President Eisenhower's forthcoming visit. But soon after his car (also containing U. S. Ambassador Douglas MacArthur II and Thomas E. Stevens, Presidential Appointment Secretary) left the terminal building, it was surrounded by a surging crowd of anti-mainstream (pro-Communist) *Zengakuren* students and affiliated workers. The demonstrators showered the vehicle with stones, rocked it back and forth, and then detained the three men for more than an hour before they could be rescued by a U. S. Marine Corps helicopter with the aid of Japanese police. The action was in keeping with the anti-mainstream's conviction that U. S. imperialists were forcing the Security Treaty on Japan—as opposed to the mainstream's more focused attack upon the Kishi government. The Hagerty incident, together with extensive additional protest and threatened general violence, led eventually to the cancellation of the Eisenhower visit.[1]

settled over Tokyo. Nobody seemed to understand exactly what was going on, but everyone was quick with his opinions. I had the strange sense that a great flood of irrationality had inundated the city, affecting Japanese and Americans alike, and lending a combination of extraordinary excitement and confusion to the atmosphere.

There was, of course, a kernel of truth in the then official American explanation that all of this had been skillfully engineered by Communist elements. Communists did do a good deal to agitate, organize, and keep things going. Yet this devil theory, this reduction of all the complexities of human behavior to the distorted focus of the Communist-anti-Communist polarity, was, as an explanation of these events, pitifully inadequate and deeply misleading.

The explanations one heard from Japanese intellectuals usually did not satisfy either. The intellectuals were likely simply to focus upon the resentment against Kishi, and to emphasize (like the demonstrators I mentioned) that it was *only* Kishi who was resented, and not America. But after a while one began to suspect that they were protesting too much regarding America, for there *was* considerable resentment of America: resentment derived from such sources as the war and the Occupation, the fear that military entanglements with America would involve them again in war (a fear reinforced by the U-2 incident and the Summit failure), and the conviction that Japanese foreign policy had been oriented too much in the direction of America. It was, however, an ambivalent resentment: there was (and still is) much good will for America even among the intellectuals; this is partly why they went to such great pains to deny their resentment. Moreover, the Japanese frequently seemed to be leaning on a devil theory of their own when they focused virtually all their hostility upon Kishi himself, a man who did not seem to possess sufficient stature to be worthy of such enormous hostility.

One Japanese psychologist offered the opinion that Kishi stood for "the father" against whom so many Japanese were rebelling; a psychiatrist thought that Kishi was the "mother figure" upon whom Japanese are apt to be so dependent and whom they therefore blame for all their misfortunes. There may be some truth in what the psychologist and the psychiatrist said; a national leader can assume these symbolic roles, particularly in moments of crisis. I would prefer, however, to put the matter in a more general historical perspective: I had the impression that Kishi had come to stand for all that the Japanese condemned in their own past. Rather than representing a particular parent figure, he had become *a symbol of the evil past* from which everyone wished to dissociate himself. The psychological struggle was bound to be painful because emotional remnants of this past inevitably must reside within each individual Japanese, even the most outspoken rebel, and these individual emotional remnants are by far the most difficult to sweep away.

The sense of the past as evil can occur in any rapidly changing culture, but in Japan, where reckless militarism only recently made so tragic a caricature of Japanese tradition, it is particularly strong. And one should not lose sight of the fact that Kishi's own past made him a good candidate for this kind of personal symbol: he had been a prominent member of the prewar and wartime Fascist cabinets, and he was considered a war criminal during the immediate postwar period. Kishi, in this symbolic role, became a target for a wide variety of displaced hostilities, and no one could rest until he had resigned.

In this light the claim of Japanese youth and intellectuals that they participated in the demonstrations to preserve democracy, a claim that many Americans found paradoxical, takes on more meaning. For without saying so, they were defining democracy in terms of attitude and even of character, as well as of external forms, and by these standards a man of Kishi's generation and of his particular background hardly could be looked upon as democratic. Therefore in a crisis, especially one in which he made use of the police within the Diet—this for the Japanese a hateful reminder of physical coercion and thought control in the past—almost everyone was quite ready to pounce upon him in the name of democracy. We in America are used to permitting all kinds of maneuvers as long as the forms of democracy are maintained; but the Japanese, as relatively new converts to democracy, often look upon it in more idealized terms.

During one discussion in which I participated, an American, who held a more or less standard American view of the demonstrations, challenged a group of Japanese intellectuals to tell him in what way Kishi had violated the law that night of May 19. The Japanese reviewed Kishi's behavior—his request for a prolongation of the Diet session to allow for additional consideration of the Security Treaty, and then his sudden call one minute later for a quick vote on the measure; they thought this was two-faced behavior, but they could not find any illegality. Finally, one of them said quietly, "It was as if the Japanese people knew *by instinct* that something was wrong in what happened that night." Here was the Eastern reliance on feeling-tone in conflict with Western logic and legalism. The Japanese, when pressed on the point, were willing to recognize the Socialists' undemocratic behavior in trying physically to prevent the speaker from assuming the rostrum, but they were quick to point out that this was not as dangerous to Japan as Kishi's maneuvers since the Socialists were a minority without control of any of the government sources of power. Here was the modern Japanese intellectuals' traditional watchdog opposition to the party in power; their guilty awareness that they had ceased to maintain this stance during the prewar hysteria seemed to make them all the more determined to maintain it now. Moreover, Japanese intellectuals constantly stress the ties between some Liberal Democrats and the ultrarightists (still a force to contend with in Japan), and they also point out that the prewar police state was built up under a façade of parliamentary democracy. Largely because of past abuses, intellectuals, students, and many among the general population have developed an exaggerated sensitivity to government authority, and a general feeling that in any confrontation the police are always in the wrong.

While all of these factors are important, I believe they are part of a greater theme—the broad social revolution that is taking place throughout the non-Western world. Some people observing the scene of the demonstrations in Tokyo commented that it reminded them of pre-revolution Russia, and others said that it looked like Weimar Germany; certainly there was something of a revolutionary feeling in the air, even though there never appeared to be a possibility of a genuine political revolution. I think the crisis was part of the general movement among non-Western countries toward psychological as well as material entry into the modern world, a movement that began during the last half of the nineteenth century (in Japan just before the Meiji Restoration) and that has reached its greatest momentum during the postwar years. At the time of the demonstrations this social revolution had become reinforced by a consuming fear of war and militarism, a powerful urge toward neutralism, a desire for closer contact with other Asian countries along with greater separation from the United States, and an effort to salvage some form of belief and pattern for action from the wreckage of postwar disillusionment.

Youth has been playing the radical role it usually plays in such a social revolution, even as it did to a considerable extent during the early Meiji era. Both the youth movement and the social revolution itself in Japan can go either in a moderate direction or in the direction of totalist extremism. But surely they cannot be wished away, nor can we, nor anyone else, afford to ignore them—yet this is precisely what America seemed at times to be doing.

Having known only the rightist forms of extremism, Japanese intellectuals tend to be insufficiently aware of the dangers that could confront them from the extreme left.° And there is something quite disturbing about the

---

° Japanese intellectuals of the postwar Old Left have since had reason to come to precisely this awareness. A number have been publicly

way Japanese intellectuals, young and old, so often are
dazzled by Marxist-Leninist abstractions. Yet I feel that
the majority of Japanese youth and older intellectuals
are not so different in many of their aspirations from the
majority of youth and intellectuals everywhere; if they
could find a path to peace and disarmament and a pattern of social progress that would enable them to retain
their individual freedom, they could be quite capable of
choosing this "open" direction—despite the lingering
emotional appeal of totalism.

I have suggested a distinction between Japanese students with totalist psychological tendencies and those
with more moderate inclinations. Let me now describe a
composite representative of each of these two groups.

The totalist is best exemplified by a hard-core member
of the mainstream of *Zengakuren*. He (or she) cannot
be recognized at first glance. When you meet him, he is
as friendly and polite as the next fellow; his eyes may
seem to show a special intensity, but so do the eyes of
many Japanese youth, and you wonder whether because
you know what he stands for you are imagining this intensity. He is likely to have come from a middle-class
background, and to have shown some tendency as a
child toward leadership (although not necessarily a particularly strong political interest). His political radicalism
is apt to have taken shape during his first two years at the
University. The strongest influences in shaping it were
probably the dormitory life during his freshman and
sophomore years, and the theoretical Marxism of some
of his favorite professors (although he, of course, reserves
the right to go further than these professors in the radicalism of his thought and action).

---

denounced by student activists, and a few have had personal files and
property destroyed or have even met with physical abuse. Similarly,
there have been certain changes in the political imagery of *Zengakuren*
activists and moderate students from that expressed in the profiles which
follow. Most notable, and perhaps most dangerous, has been the increasingly angry polarization and factionalism among students, leading
to violent conflicts between Right and Left, and between Left and Left.
But these developments can be viewed as intensifications of conflicts
suggested in the original essay.

Marxist ideology nourishes him emotionally, as do the endless meetings, discussions and demonstrations that he attends. He aspires to a pure form of Communism, to a kind of classless society not yet achieved anywhere. He does not consider himself precisely Trotskyite, although he is frequently so called by newspapers and especially by the rival antimainstream group. But he does favor revolution of the workers everywhere to bring about this classless society. He is disdainful of Russia (a "reactionary" example of "state capitalism"), and especially of revisionist policy of peaceful coexistence. China seems to him to be the best and the freest of the Communist countries, but still not communist enough. He can think of no Japanese political party that adequately represents his beliefs: the Liberal Democrats are hopeless; the Communists are controlled by outside forces; the Socialists are too conciliatory. And besides, none of them can really be trusted. Japan needs, he believes, a new party formed from his own organization. Once he begins to describe his political views, you feel the closed-circuit logic taking over. There is no nonsense about his categories. For instance, if you ask him what he thinks Japan would or should do in this or that situation, he is likely to stop you short and explain that one cannot really speak of "Japan," one must speak of the "exploiting classes" (the capitalists and the bourgeoisie) and the "oppressed classes" (the workers).

He extends this approach to the logic of tactics. He will admit disingenuously that he and his comrades had planned to storm the Diet on the night of June 15, even though some of the students' defenders had said earlier that the *Zengakuren* had intended to remain orderly and had resorted to violence only when attacked by rightists. (It was in this foray that the demonstrations claimed their one death, and the girl killed was a member of this same *Zengakuren* mainstream.) He and his comrades, he will explain, wished to hold a meeting of their own inside the Diet, as they had on previous occasions, as a symbolic gesture. He opposes the Security Treaty less for its tie with America or for its military nature than for its "strengthening" of the designs of the "exploiting classes," both within Japan itself and in future imperialistic ventures. He has nothing in particular against America, and he will remind you that it was the antimainstream element of the *Zengakuren* that was responsible for the Hagerty incident.

When you have talked to him for a while you will be struck by certain words, apart from the standard Communist phrases, that he keeps using. He is especially fond of "reality," "scientific," "the facts," "progressive." It seems no accident that these are precisely what semanticists have found to be "god words" of our modern world; they are the expression of a mystical scientism that afflicts us all, and especially of the "sacred science" that is always a prominent characteristic of ideological totalism.

The mood of this *Zengakuren* activist is often extreme and desperate, but sometimes confident and even gay; his ability to pursue actively his sweeping goals gives him a sense of purpose, of group unity and of power. In his special combination of ideology and identity he has found an all-embracing solution to life's problems, a totalist way that allows expression for his profound rebellion, a highly moralistic cause that can absorb both the hostility and the guilt that must accompany such a rebellion; he has found a means of attacking what he most hates in his own past while at the same time feeling himself to be—as part of an organization unique to his country and centered in his country's universities—wholly Japanese. His numbers in Japan are relatively few; but wherever he exists, he leads others.

The more moderate student cannot necessarily be distinguished by dress or facial expression from the *Zengakuren* activist. But as one talks to him the distinctions soon become apparent enough. Just as the *Zengakuren* student is certain about everything (or at least appears to be), so the moderate student is searching, confused and worried. And nowhere is he more searching, confused and worried than in his concern about "democracy." Also from a middle-class background, less likely than his activist *Zengakuren* counterpart to have shown signs of leadership, he belongs more to the rank and file. There are, of course, among his numbers students of outstanding ability, academic and otherwise, but they do not become student leaders, at least not at the present time. Every question raised with the moderate student remains open and remains troublesome. He is worried about Japanese politics, about the "bossism" and old-fashioned machinations of the Liberal Democratic Party. These to his eyes are far from democratic and offer little promise for Japan in the future. But ask him what does offer promise and you are met with a shake of the head; he does not know, and this worries him. He is passionately concerned about peace, and therefore deeply troubled about the Security Pact; he tends to look critically upon it, and either may oppose it outright or favor additional modification, in the direction of shorter tenure and gradual dissolution. He is worried about Japan's relationship with America. He feels that Japan's ruling party has been too tied to America, although he knows that Japan needs America and although he tends to like individual Americans insofar as he knows them.

His attitude toward Communism is especially tortured: he sees in it danger to individual freedom and he would prefer an alternative; but at the same time there is something in its moralistic stance that constantly challenges him. That is, when his friends espouse either standard Communism or the pure Communism of the mainstream *Zengakuren* group, he wonders whether they are being more self-sacrificing, more noble, more dedicated than he. Above all, he wonders whether he is not guilty of trying to "escape from reality." He shares with these friends a good deal of resentment of his country's past, a considerable involvement in the conflict of generations and a hatred for Japan's big capitalists, the resuscitated *zaibatsu*. His political tendencies are in the direction of democratic socialism; he is likely to admire, for instance, the British Labour Party. And his emotional predilections are toward moderation, compromise, conciliation; he is by no means free of totalist yearnings, but he resists these and tries to avoid all extremism. Therefore he frequently criticizes the extremism of both factions of the *Zengakuren*; yet in a crisis, a situation where he strongly opposes official government policy, he is likely to follow one of these factions. For he needs leadership badly and he can find it nowhere else.

He, too, is part of the general Asian social revolution, but he finds no ready outlet for his resentments and his feelings of guilt. In his very efforts to be moderate, to lead a balanced life, to be interested in mild pleasures or intellectual diversions, he may find additional sources of guilt and shame as he again wonders whether he is being less of a man than his activist *Zengakuren* friends. To be sure, there are among his large numbers many who do not worry about such things, who enjoy their drinking, mountain climbing and reading without much thought about either stream of the *Zengakuren* or about politics in general. But even they, at moments of crisis, are apt to become "engaged"; and if they do not, they are ignored and considered of little consequence. Even the most moderate of Japanese students is likely to have a strong aversion to existing authority and to the authority of his recent past. His moderation is distinctly, at least by American standards, left-oriented; his struggles with identity and ideology are active and confusing; he remains open-minded in his ideas, fluid in his sense of self. And he carries within him all of the pain and satisfaction of such open-mindedness and fluidity.

Significant as these differences are, the totalist and the moderate student possess much in common. Both experience conflicts resulting from the psychological and cultural influences that play upon any Japanese youth at this historical juncture.

First, there is the much talked of problem of individualism, related to what I spoke of before as *self-expression via the group*. Observing some activist *Zengakuren* groups in their demonstrations, one is reminded of the writings of Le Bon and Freud on the tendency of people who are ordinarily restrained as individuals to explode collectively in group expressions of primitive hostility and power. Asians are, of course, like everyone else, subject to this tendency, and I have already commented on the particularly strong groupism in Japanese society.

During the demonstrations one rarely met a Japanese, young or old, who expressed a genuinely idiosyncratic point of view, an individually arrived at set of convictions not held by any existing group. There is an added problem created by mass communications, which, I believe, hold a special fascination for Asians, in that they tend to promote a form of "personality cult" in which the individual is lionized in relationship to the group that he is considered to represent. About this problem, as about so many others, I believe that we must learn to think in terms of new combinations taking place.

Another phenomenon that strikes one in Japan (and I think it exists throughout Asia) is the special aura surrounding the idea of youth. To be sure, seniority-dominated social patterns persist, but newspaper commentators take special delight in contrasting tired and aging Japanese politicians with the youthful, energetic John Kennedy (indeed, much of the "Kennedy boom" that swept Japan immediately after his nomination for the Presidency can be specifically attributed to this fascination with his youthfulness). The current youth upsurge is, therefore, a powerful reaction, much like that we witnessed in China during the years between the two World Wars, against the traditional old-age-centered patterns. And in this reversal youth seems to have become the center of romantic admiration. Even the excesses of young people, while not necessarily condoned, are apt to be looked upon sympathetically as expressions of youthful purity and sincerity. Here, too, there are certain echoes of tradition, but there is also a society's unspoken expectation that in a time of rapid change youth will somehow show the way.

There are Japanese historical precedents for the *Zenga-kuren* quest for ideological purity: one is reminded of the overzealous self-flagellation of early Japanese Christians to the point of embarrassing their missionary mentors; of the prewar fanaticism of the "young officer" cliques and of the government-sponsored wartime suicides of the *Kamikaze* pilot. Yet, as I have indicated, this *Zengakuren* activist brings to his emotionalism the rationale of twentieth-century scientism. He believes that his every step is "logical" and "necessary." Has he not become a personal battleground for this struggle between the exaggerated sentimentalism of his tradition and the exaggerated logic of those who would react against this tradition? The two tendencies are, of course, related mysticisms, but at least one Japanese writer, Fumio Masutani, thinks there is no doubt but that the old one always wins out:

> [The Japanese] . . . while able to think and interested in rational thought, have not the courage to carry their reasoning through to the end. They give up mid-way, and take cover under a misty emotionalism. They esteem the logical way of thinking, yet dislike too much of it. Time and again, they stray off the path of reason into a fog of sentimentality where they rejoice, weep, or enjoy the bitterness of sorrow to their heart's content.

Masutani is perhaps a little harsh in his judgment of his own people; in any case, the problem is hardly limited to the Japanese. Moreover, one does find a continuing quest for a balance between reason and sentiment in the moderate group of youth I have described, and in many others in Japan as well. Yet one can say that the Japanese have particular difficulty in achieving such a balance.

Finally, there is the all-pervading Japanese obsession with China. One hears much about the attitude of middle-aged Japanese intellectuals toward China, of their profound guilt over Japan's recent abuse of its great historical mentor, and of the yearning among many of them to resume a stance of discipleship in relation to China. In younger people there is a good deal less of this guilt but an equally strong attraction. A young artist put it this way to me: "China to us is *continental* . . . big, profound, wide. We Japanese live on islands, which makes us feel small and narrow—like a small lake compared to the great wave of an ocean." Most do not express it so lyrically, but a great many hold an equally romanticized image of China. They profess, and sincerely, I believe, to know nothing of the repressive aspects of Chinese thought reform, and see only the hope that China seems to offer for youth. And I have heard young Japanese describe Chinese people in general as more balanced, less emotional, on the whole more admirable in character than themselves. The question is complicated, but the signs are clear that the young people crave more intimacy in the perennial love-hate relationship between Japan and China. A vitally important factor in this craving is their conviction, right or wrong, that Chinese youth possess a *sense of connection* with the leadership of their own society, something for which Japanese youth appear ready to give up a great deal.

Japanese youth resemble their parents more than they realize, but their personal development is also profoundly affected by forces emanating from America, Russia, and China. In fact, the more I study problems of individual character in relation to historical change, the more I am struck by the necessity of avoiding static labels and of seeing even the most basic and longstanding psychological tendencies primarily in relation to the *direction in which they are moving.* In evolving this direction, Japanese youth—like youth everywhere—are finding old emotions, tenacious though they are, to be increasingly unreliable guideposts.

# WHO IS MORE DRY?

## 4

*Despite the playfulness of this essay, there is violence
at issue here too. But it is the kind safely contained within
old legends of samurai and cowboys, lending itself readily
to the blowing and puncturing of romantic bubbles.*

*Modest as the enterprise is, it owes much to a series
of lively conversations with Nathan Glazer, who shared
with me a great deal of his animated encounter with
Japan.*

*I am concerned here with various images of popu-
lar culture—in comparing two films (the Japanese* Seven
Samurai *and the American* Magnificent Seven*), as well
as in more general images of "wetness" and "dryness."
Japanese popular culture has actually been of much
greater importance to me than most of the essays suggest.
Not only did I find its imagery basic to an understanding of what was happening to the young, but I enjoyed the
popular fare, despite its uneven quality—whether watching television, going to restaurants and bars (which in
Japan must be included when one speaks of popular culture), or having a go at that all-pervasive* pachinko.

*But it was cinema that mattered most to me, and this
was the period (early 1960s) in which the Japanese film*

*was at its height. Kurosawa was emerging as one of the world's most gifted directors (The Seven Samurai ranks among his best), and such others as Ozu, Kinoshita, and Imai were also turning out distinguished work. Donald Richie was similarly emerging as the ranking international authority on Japanese films, and he and Mary Richie were writing very illuminatingly about them in the English-language* Japan Times. *My wife's stint as a reviewer for the* Asahi Evening News *also contributed to my education. Since then, the Japanese film has declined considerably, but talented directors still appear, and there is a flourishing subculture of underground cinema more or less on the American model. In general I share the younger generation's fascination with film. I am convinced that its unique combination of photographic actuality and imaginative freedom gives it special force in expressing—and transcending—the confused perceptions and extreme dislocations of our age.*

*Concerning images of the wet and the dry, these could be explored (in a way the essay does not) to reveal pulls and tensions accompanying accelerated historical change anywhere. "Wetness" could be seen to include a whole constellation of familiar and reassuring emotions derived from one's personal and cultural past—"soft" feelings associated with mother and family, with the geographical and psychological simplicities reminiscent of childhood, nostalgic expressions of sadness and gaiety and of aesthetic and sensual pleasure. Wetness, then, epitomizes the earliest sense of connection to the point of merging with one's original sources of nurture—the "potato love" that Saul Bellow speaks of, safe and unchanging, but also (at certain moments) stifling and even suffocating. "Dryness," on the other hand, suggests that which is new and critical in tone; emotions that are "hard" in their rejection of past niceties and indirections, and in their insistence upon selfhood based upon a new aesthetic and a new sensuality, divested of the encumbrances of traditional cultural learning. The dry vision of liberation from the past and of self-discovery risks the loss of the safe haven of wetness—of connection and tender nurturance—even to the point, at its most extreme, of severing the bonds of identification required by all groups in all societies.*

*The psychoanalytic impulse is to reduce the whole matter to questions of regression and of gender. But the first interpretation quickly breaks down, since neither the dry nor the wet modes have a corner on regression or, for that matter, maturity; whatever their nostalgic or anti-nostalgic emphases, neither emotional style is age-specific. The second interpretation, that of male versus female, is both partly true and misleading. Wetness draws upon emotions we often look upon as feminine, because they tend either to be associated with cultural dictates concerning what can be considered feminine, or else with the universal maternal stress upon organic connection. And dryness makes use of emotions we call masculine, because they are associated with social definitions of maleness and with the kind of outward thrust that has universal biological relationship to the male. But wetness and dryness transcend gender in their back-and-forth emotional movements between old reinforcements and new rejections, and in the accompanying struggle to recover, create, and re-create meaningful styles of living. Indeed the two modes become less discrete as conditions of change become more complex (when young Japanese abandon Hemingway for Mailer, does this make them more wet, more dry, or both?). But then, in work of this kind one learns that the explosive combinations of change in our era tend to blur the distinctions we make concerning that change, even as we are making them.*

❋          ❋          ❋

In postwar Japan, especially among young people, it is good to be "dry" (or *durai*), rather than "wet" (or *wetto*). This means—in the original youth language, as expanded by mass media—to be direct, logical, to the point, pragmatic, casual, self-interested, rather than polite, evasive, sentimental, nostalgic, dedicated to romantic causes, or bound by obligation in human relations; to break out of the world of cherry blossoms, haiku, and moon-viewing into a modern era of bright sunlight, jazz, and Hemingway (who may be said to have been the literary god of dryness). Intellectual youth, of course, disdain these oversimplified categories. But they too have made the words *durai* and *wetto* (typical examples of postwar Japanized English) part of their everyday vocabulary, and they find dry objects of admiration in an interesting place: in American films about cowboys and gunmen.

Students of every kind of background and ideological coloring have told me of this fascination for American Westerns. I was therefore in no way surprised when one of them, after seeing *The Magnificent Seven*, held forth enthusiastically for the better part of two hours on the absolute dryness of the film's hero (as portrayed by Yul Brynner)—on his complete freedom from binding human relationships, his utter indifference to ordinary conventions of propriety and responsibility, as well as to danger and risk. Since this American Western had been adapted from the Japanese film *The Seven Samurai*, I thought this an intriguing cultural sequence—from Japanese film to American film to Japanese youth (leaving aside for the moment the influence of American Westerns on the original Kurosawa film). Indeed, the two films (as I discovered when I saw them myself in Tokyo within a few days of each other) reveal much about the two great warrior myths so central to American and Japanese cultural tradition, and therefore much about Americans and Japanese—especially in regard to their common quest for dryness.

One is struck initially by how similar the American free-lance gunmen and the Japanese free-lance *samurai*, or *rōnin*, can be made to seem. But as one gets a deeper sense of the two groups portrayed in the films, one becomes aware of revealing differences.

The identity of the American warrior-heroes lies almost entirely in their weapons. They refer to themselves and to one another not as gunmen, but as Guns. These Guns seem to have once had homes and families, but no more. Each is a lone-wolf, a rugged individualist of the frontier who earns his bread by his skill at "the draw." He has done a good deal of killing, and without qualm, but in most cases only when necessary. He is a mercenary, and his loyalties last only so long as his employer of the moment makes these loyalties financially worthwhile. At least this is the way he presents himself at the beginning of things. He is a product of the great American cowboy myth, a myth which has elements of a group brotherhood but which is in essence a myth of the magnificent self.

The seven magnificent selves of the American film spring from the relatively antisocial fringes of this all-encompassing myth. The individual Gun has not, like some cowboys, had the habit of applying his expertise to the defense of a form of justice prevailing within existing society; he is much more likely to direct it against the social order, virtually all of which he disdains. His constant urge to "move on" is thus both a flight from authority and a quest for uninterrupted adventure. He is not just a Gun, but a Gun-in-Motion. And he is utterly alone. He indeed strikes us as the very model of dryness.

The Japanese warrior-heroes—*samurai* cast adrift from their former lords during the social chaos following the great battle of Sekigahara just prior to the onset of the Tokugawa era during the early part of the seventeenth century—are also mercenaries who care little about risking or taking life. They too are ultramasculine figures whose value to others lies in their skill with their weapons, in their case usually the sword, occasionally the bow and arrow, never the newly introduced and highly unrefined gun (in a final sequence of the film, the sword is in fact made to defeat the gun).

Yet the *rōnin* differs from his American counterpart in one essential element: he retains a profound relationship to his society, however adrift, lawless, or even destructive he may be within that society. His myth is social rather than individual. His very existence as a *samurai* binds him to society through the *samurai* code of honor, no matter how far he may have strayed from living up to it. Indeed, his sense of honor constantly awaits reactivation, and he can achieve this only by finding a new Lord to serve and becoming part of a new social group. Like the cowboy, he plays an important part in the building of a great tradition; but unlike the cowboy, he has a clear historical precedent on which to build. Historically and ideologically, he is "engaged." In comparison with the Gun, the *Samurai* seems to have a suggestion of wetness.

Consequently, the two groups have somewhat different motivations for coming to the aid of the victimized peasant farmers. Neither group is of course given to such extravagantly wet tendencies as sentimentalism or altruism. The men we are introduced to at the beginning of the two films, whatever their pride of marksmanship or sense of honor, are not the type to rally, with banners unfurled, to the defense of the first underdog in sight. In both cases, the leader of the group does develop a certain sympathy for the peasant farmers, the sympathy of a strong man with courage to spare. Yet this sympathy would hardly in itself have been enough to inspire such seemingly hard-hearted men to become involved in a struggle in which the odds were so heavily against them, and in which they had so little to gain.

In the case of the American Guns, there is a prominent

feeling of "Why not, what the hell?" They have nothing better to do, nothing to lose, it is a form of work they know well, and the very outlandishness of the odds against them serves as a challenge. Moreover, it is a challenge in which they can look forward, at least temporarily, to surrendering their noble burden of loneliness by sharing this preposterous adventure and becoming a viable group of working Guns. Money too is important to them, since they constantly inquire about payment to be received. The smallness of this promised payment, twenty dollars, is a kind of recurring joke; but for hungry men— sometimes hunted as well—twenty dollars matters. And one among them dreams, until the moment of his death, of finding buried treasure, which he, as a pure mercenary, considers to be the only possible explanation for the other Guns' having taken the job in the first place.

The *Samurai* too, in their decision to help, have much of the bravado of adventurers. And they are attracted to the possibility of a regular rice ration—though they can expect nothing more, and are above the mention of money. But among their six rank and file, the great urge and attraction is to fall in behind a new leader. Although this leader is, like themselves, no more than a *rōnin*, they make him in effect, their new Lord. They refer to him as "*Sensei*," which means Teacher, Mentor, or Master, and ask to become his "*deshi*," his disciples or students.

But why does the leader himself accept the peasant farmers as *his* "Lord," which is essentially what he does when he agrees to serve them by doing battle with their enemies? I think we must say that he does so out of his *samurai*'s sense of honor and responsibility. His concern for the peasants is concern from above. Their plight involves him because of his prior commitment to the *samurai* code—to its call for courage, honor, discipline, sincerity, and direct action in defense of what is thought to be right. And what the *Sensei* feels, his *deshi* feel too, as mediated through his personal example. All share in the sense of social responsibility (again a bit moist) demanded of them by their now reactivated *samurai* code,

in sharp contrast to the essentially asocial and nonideo-
logical (and therefore utterly dry) motivation of their
cowboy counterparts.

What happens when the two groups of warrior-
heroes meet their great trial, both in the heat of battle
and in their intimate exposure to the lives of the peasant
farmers? Are we able to retain our original impressions
of them? With the American Guns, one has a strong sense
of a constant test of courage. We are, in fact, witness to
almost as many varieties of courage as there are men involved: the cool, unwavering courage of the Leader; the
icy, supercourage of the Slouch—a man who, in his semi-
reclining, hat-over-eyes, eyes-nearly-closed position during
moments of greatest danger, is the ultimate American-
cowboy answer to the fear of being "yellow" (he is
based on a Japanese counterpart, but one nonetheless
immediately recognizes his true mythological origins);
the courage, failed and regained, of the Killer still plagued
with nightmares of death and guilt; the hearty, amiable
courage of the tough-exterior, heart-of-gold Vagrant,
whose attraction for the children of the village leads ultimately to his death; the honest courage of the boyish, brilliantly expert Number-Two Man, who can admit breaking
out into a cold sweat before every battle; and, most symbolic of all, the hard-won courage of the aspiring Gun—
the youngster who lacks the true credentials of the trade,
admires the excellence of his seniors, and finally gains admission to their ranks after a prolonged bout of exaggeratedly proving his manhood.

Yet, if the American Guns reveal imperfect dryness
through their struggle with courage and manhood, they
do so even more in their developing relationship to the
peasant farmers. Here men differ in their attitudes, and
one or two even remain rather aloof; but the clear trend is
toward a remarkable softening of heart, toward a sentimental attachment to those whom they protect—despite
the farmers' being Mexican, and therefore racially different. Indeed, these tough Guns, in their monologues on the
virtues of farmers and farming as contrasted with the

emptiness of their own rootless existence, become almost slobbering converts to home and family. This unconvincing turnabout is surely a glaring dramatic weakness in the film, but it is a very American weakness. What the Guns want after all is not solitude but togetherness, not fighting but tranquillity. They do succeed in finally remembering who they really are and, with a helpful push from the farmers who no longer want them around, take their leave (all except the young novitiate, who, having established his right to be a Gun, can now cease to be one, settle down with the girl from the village, and return to the peasant farmer's life from which he originally came). But now they have become something of fallen idols. Their dryness has proved itself brittle, if not illusory.

In the Japanese film we get (equally characteristically for the culture) a less clear sense of individuals; rather, the group merges into a more or less collective *samurai*. There are, to be sure, Japanese equivalents of many of the American types already mentioned, but we do not get an equivalent sense of seven different men, each proving his courage and manhood. Even the young would-be *Samurai*—the man without proper credentials—seeks to establish himself first through family lineage (in an early scene he presents a false document in order to demonstrate his ostensible *samurai* pedigree), though he too later demonstrates extraordinary skill and daring in battle. What he is seeking to prove is less a matter of simple courage than of (in all its meanings) *class*. The remaining six *rōnin*, born and bred as *samurai*, have no difficulty at any time in demonstrating *their* class. In general, the behavior of the *samurai*, as compared to that of the gunmen, is steadier, more predictable, and less spectacular. They know what to expect, do what has to be done, take the necessary losses (only two of the seven survive), and emerge—inevitably—victorious. There are no surprises.

Can we say the same of their relationship to the peasant farmers? In this relationship lies the key to our question about relative dryness, and in fact the point of the film it-

self. The *Samurai*, like the Guns, come to experience great
intimacy with the peasant farmers they are employed to
protect—a degree of intimacy which, we are led to believe, is quite new to them, especially in relationship to
their social inferiors. Yet they never for a moment
cease to be *Samurai*, nor wish to be anything else. Indeed
it is inconceivable that they and the farmers could remain together. Thus the *Samurai* survivors accept, with
sadness but without bitterness, their no longer being
wanted by the farmers upon successful completion of
their military task. And the leader's final comment upon
observing the return of the village to its normal pattern is
as profound as it is appropriate: "It is not we but the farmers who have won. It is they who always win." The film's
message becomes clear: men are separate, they come together in crisis, they resume their separateness; but beyond this rhythm of separateness and unity are the larger
rhythms of life and death, of earth and man—the harmony of the elements and the continuity of generations.
To understand this message and to live by it—as the *Samurai* do and the Guns do not—is not only superior dryness but truth itself.

Then why, we may well ask, do Japanese youth (and
not only Japanese youth) continue to chase this brittle
will-o'-the-wisp of American cowboy pseudo-dryness,
rather than seek the authentic dryness of their own cultural tradition? One must remind oneself that the *samurai*
myth of a feudal era can no longer speak to their condition. Living in a world in which one can hardly be sure
of the rhythms of earth and man or of the continuity of
generations, their own warrior tradition largely dishonored by their country's disastrous twentieth-century military adventures—we should not be surprised that they
try to discard their old myth and seek to find meaning
in a new one. Nor is it an accident that this new myth holds
out a promise of liberation of the self from all social constraints, in a society in which these very "wet" constraints
become more, rather than less, burdensome as modern—
and postmodern—life takes shape.

But the past is not so easily dismissed. Japanese youth are both experimenting with new psychological themes and reactivating old ones. Surely they will end up neither cowboys nor *samurai*. Perhaps, after all, they are not chasing after anything so much as following the longstanding Japanese pattern of temporarily merging with an outside force as a means of discovering themselves. And in doing this, they may be dryer than they think.

# II

---

# ON
# SURVIVORS

---

# THE HIROSHIMA BOMB $\qquad$ 5

*My first piece of writing on the atomic bomb was in many ways my transition between Hiroshima and home. I wanted to tell something of what I had learned in that city, convey what people actually felt (and still feel), and at the same time suggest a few principles which demand exploration, ethically no less than psychologically. The essay turned out to be the nucleus for* Death in Life: Survivors of Hiroshima, *and I am convinced that the sense of immediacy—of intense actuality—I brought home with me infused the longer study no less than the shorter one.*

*When the essay appeared in* Daedalus,* *it evoked some rather unusual comments and letters from friends, colleagues, and strangers. They told of having been disturbed, in some cases moved, but often relieved to be able to come to grips with what the bomb had actually done to people—relieved, that is, to be able to break out*

---

* It emerged from a talk I gave in 1962 at a meeting of the American Association for the Advancement of Science, on a panel co-sponsored by the American Psychiatric Association, entitled "The Threat of Impending Disaster." And it was subsequently reprinted in a volume with that title, edited by George H. Grosser, Henry Wechsler, and Milton Greenblatt, and published by MIT Press in 1964.

*of the psychic numbing surrounding Hiroshima specifi-
cally, and issues of death and dying generally. Their reactions meant a great deal to me because I had been quite
concerned about a tone and conceptual framework appropriate to the subject. Later I realized what I should have
known from the start: there is no tone, no framework,
adequate to the nuclear weapons experience. Moreover,
tone is so integral a part of the self that one does not so
much decide upon it as feel impelled toward it as the
matrix of one's moral and intellectual formulation.*

*It was inevitable that over the course of the work my
tone would be questioned. On one or two occasions the
scientific nature of my findings was challenged because
of my ethical involvement in the issue. More ironic has
been the occasional attack (likely, alas, to come from a
pacifist) for my insistence upon exploring the complexities of Hiroshima responses instead of simply emitting a
scream of condemnation and pain. Yet without strong
ethical involvement (made explicit in my National Book
Award acceptance statement) one could hardly mobilize the energy and discipline necessary for a study of this
kind. On the other hand the substitution of blind fury for
thought and honesty would have been a form of investigative kitsch, insulting to the humanity of victims and
survivors alike, an abdication of intellectual responsibility
adding nothing to anyone's knowledge or wisdom.*

*Responses of bilingual survivors at Hiroshima Uni-
versity have been particularly gratifying in this respect;
they have not only felt understood but thought the undertaking sufficiently worthy to organize and embark upon
the really formidable task of translating the book into Japanese.*

*This essay is the only brief overview of the atomic bomb
experience I have attempted, and it now seems to me to
raise two issues directly related to the title of the collection. First, it suggests that one can approach the question
of the impact of the atomic bomb in ways other than armchair speculation—that is, by direct investigation of human experiences, and by focus upon psychological themes*

*that link victims to the rest of us. Second, it insists upon the relationship between nuclear weapons and more general conflicts surrounding death, and points to a vicious circle between the two that interferes with our wisdom in coping with either.*

*These issues reached terrifying proportions for me as I worked on the essay in the midst of the Cuban Missile Crisis of 1962. I became convinced more than ever that the Hiroshima experience, in all of its horror and complexity, must be confronted.*

❋          ❋          ❋

Hiroshima commands our attention now, eighteen years after its exposure to the atomic bomb, perhaps even more insistently than when the event actually occurred. We are compelled by the universal threat of nuclear weapons to study the impact of such weapons upon their first human victims, ever mindful of the relevance of this question to our own future and to all of human survival.

Much research has already been done concerning the physical consequences of the Hiroshima and Nagasaki disasters, particularly in relation to their unique feature of delayed radiation effects.* But little attention has been paid to psychological and social elements, though these might well be said to be at present the most vivid legacies of the first atomic bomb.[2]

My own interest in these problems developed during two years of research, conducted in Tokyo and Kyoto from 1960–1962, on the relationship of the individual character and historical change in Japanese youth.[3] I was struck by the significance which the encounter with nuclear weapons had for the Japanese as a whole, even for

---

* Studies of the effects of ionizing radiation were instituted by Japanese medical and civilian teams within days after the bomb was dropped, with Dr. Masao Tsuzuki of Tokyo Imperial University played a leading role.

American medical groups began their work in early September of 1945, and became consolidated in the Joint Commission for the Investigation of the Effects of the Atomic Bomb in Japan. Studies of longer-term effects of radiation have been conducted at the medical departments and research institutes of Hiroshima and Nagasaki Universities. The largest research program on delayed radiation effects is being carried out at the Atomic Bomb Casualty Commission, in both Hiroshima and Nagasaki, an affiliate of the United States National Academy of Sciences—National Research Council, under a grant from the U. S. Atomic Energy Commission, administered with the cooperation of the Japanese National Institute of Health of the Ministry of Health and Welfare.[1]

young Japanese who could hardly remember the event. Also involved in my undertaking a study in Hiroshima was concern with the psychological aspects of war and peace, as well as previous interest in the behavior of individuals and groups under extreme conditions.[4]

I began the work in April of 1962, first through two brief visits to Hiroshima, followed by four and a half months of residence there. My approach was primarily that of individual interviews with two groups of atomic bomb survivors: thirty-three chosen at random from the more than ninety-thousand survivors (or *hibakusha*), listed at the Hiroshima University Research Institute for Nuclear Medicine and Biology; and an additional group of forty-two survivors specially selected because of their prominence in dealing with A-bomb problems or their capacity to articulate their experiences. Included among the latter were physicians, university professors, city officials, politicians, writers and poets, and leaders of survivor organizations and peace movements.

*Hibakusha* (pronounced hi-bak′-sha) is a coined word which is by no means an exact equivalent of "survivor" (or "survivors"), but means, literally, "explosion-affected person" (or persons), and conveys in feeling a little more than merely having encountered the bomb, and a little less than having experienced definite physical injury from it. According to official definition, the category of *hibakusha* includes four groups of people considered to have had possible exposure to significant amounts of radiation: those who at the time of the bomb were within the city limits then defined for Hiroshima, an area extending from the bomb's hypocenter to a distance of 4000, and in some places up to 5000, meters; those who were not in the city at the time, but within fourteen days entered a designated area extending to about 2000 meters from the hypocenter; those who were engaged in some form of aid to, or disposal of, bomb victims at various stations which were set up; and those who were *in utero* and whose mothers fit into any of the first three groups. In addition to these interviews with *hibakusha*, I sought out all those in Hiroshima (mostly Japanese, but also Americans and Europeans) who could tell me anything about the complex array of group emotions and social problems which had arisen in the city over the seventeen years that had elapsed since the disaster.[*][5]

I was aware of the delicacy of my situation as an American psychiatrist conducting this study, and I relied heavily upon the continuous support and assistance of Japanese groups within the Hiroshima community, so that all meetings and interviews were arranged through their introductions. In the case of the randomly selected group, my first contact with each survivor was made through a personal visit to the home, in the company of a Japanese social worker from Hiroshima University. My previous experience in Japan—including the ability to speak a certain amount of Japanese—was helpful in eliciting the many forms of cooperation so crucial for the work. Perhaps of greatest importance was my conveying to both colleagues and research subjects a sense of my personal motivation in undertaking the work, the hope that a systematic study of this kind might clarify important problems often spoken about loosely, and thereby in a small way contribute to the mastery of nuclear weapons and the avoidance of their use.

Interviews generally lasted about two hours; I tried to see each research subject twice, though I saw some three or four times, and others just once. I tape-recorded all sessions with subjects of the randomly selected group, and did so with many of those in the special group as well, always with the subject's consent. Interviews were

[*] For studying physical aspects of delayed radiation effects, such factors as distance from the hypocenter and degree of protection from radiation (by buildings, clothing, etc.) are crucial, and from this standpoint a large number of those designated as *hibakusha* had little or no exposure to significant amounts of radiation. For psychological and social effects, these factors—and particularly that of distance from the hypocenter—are also of great importance, but one cannot make the same relatively sharp correlations regarding what is, or is not, significant exposure. In this paper I shall emphasize general psychological themes which apply, in greater or lesser degree, to virtually all *hibakusha*.

conducted in Japanese,° and a research assistant was always present to interpret. After making an initial appraisal of the problems involved, I decided to focus my questions upon three general dimensions of the problem: first, the recollection of the experience itself and its inner meaning seventeen years later;† second, residual concerns and fears, especially those relating to delayed radiation effects; and third, the survivor's sense of self and society, or of special group identity. Subjects were encouraged to associate freely to these topics and to any feelings or ideas stimulated by them. And in gathering these data, I sought always to evaluate to what degree exposure to the atomic bomb in Hiroshima resembles psychological and social patterns common to all disasters, as described in the general literature on disaster, and in what ways it might be a unique experience. What follows is a composite description of some of the basic trends I have observed.

### THE EXPERIENCE RECALLED

The degree to which one anticipates a disaster has important bearing upon the way in which one responds, and the predominant tone in the descriptions I heard was that of extreme surprise and unpreparedness. Since it was wartime, people did of course expect conventional bombing; there had been regularly occurring air-raid

---

° The one exception was an interview with a European priest who had been in Hiroshima at the time of the bomb, my only non-Japanese research subject.

† It was, of course, inevitable that, after seventeen years, elements of selectivity and distortion would enter into these recollections. What survivors' recollections revealed was not so much a literal rendition of what had occurred as the symbolic significance that the event held for them at the time of the interview. But I was impressed with the vividness of recall, with the willingness of people, once a reasonable degree of rapport had been established, to express themselves quite freely about painful, and often humiliating, details; and with the overall agreement contained in these descriptions, with each other and with various published accounts, concerning what took place generally and how people behaved. It would seem that particularly impressive kinds of human experience (whether during childhood or adulthood) can create a lasting psychic imprint.[6]

warnings because of planes passing over Hiroshima, though only an occasional stray bomb had actually been dropped on the city. American planes did drop leaflets warning Hiroshima inhabitants that their city was going to be demolished and urging them to evacuate from it. But very few people appear to have seen these leaflets, and those who did tended to ignore them as enemy propaganda. Nor did these leaflets make any mention of an atomic bomb or any other special weapon. Many wondered at Hiroshima's relatively untouched state, despite its obviously strategic significance as a major staging area for Japan's military operations in China and Southeast Asia. There was general apprehension, the feeling that there was something dangerous about Hiroshima's strangely intact condition, that the Americans must be preparing something extraordinarily big for the city (though this latter thought could have been partly a retrospective construction). At 8:15 A.M. on August 6, 1945, the moment the bomb fell, most people were in a particularly relaxed state, since, following a brief air-raid warning, the all-clear had just been sounded. People were unprepared, then, because of a false sense of immediate security; because of the psychological sense of invulnerability all people tend to possess, even in the face of danger; and because of the total inability of anyone to anticipate a weapon of such unprecedented dimensions.

It was only those at some distance from the bomb's hypocenter who could clearly distinguish the sequence of the great flash of light in the sky accompanied by the lacerating heat of the fireball, then the sound and force of the blast, and the impressive multicolored "mushroom cloud" rising above the city. Two thousand meters is generally considered to be a critical radius for high mortality (from heat, blast, and radiation), for susceptibility to delayed radiation effects, and for near-total destruction of buildings and other structures. But many were killed outside of this radius, and indeed the number of deaths from the bomb—variously estimated from 63,000 to 240,-

000 or more—is still unknown. Falling in the center of a flat city made up largely of wooden residential and commercial structures, the bomb is reported to have destroyed or so badly damaged, through blast and fire, more than two-thirds of all buildings within 500 meters—an area roughly encompassing the city limits—that all of Hiroshima became immediately involved in the atomic disaster.[7] Those within the 2000-meter radius could not clearly recall their initial perceptions: many simply remember what they thought to be a flash—or else a sudden sensation of heat—followed by an indeterminate period of unconsciousness; others recall only being thrown across a room or knocked down, then finding themselves pinned under debris of buildings.

*The most striking psychological feature of this immediate experience was the sense of a sudden and absolute shift from normal existence to an overwhelming encounter with death.* This is described by a young shopkeeper's assistant, who was thirteen years old at the time the bomb fell, and 1400 meters from the hypocenter:

I was a little ill . . . so I stayed at home that day. . . . There had been an air-raid warning and then an all-clear. I felt relieved and lay down on the bed with my younger brother. . . . Then it happened. It came very suddenly. . . . It felt something like an electric short—a bluish sparkling light. . . . There was a noise, and I felt great heat—even inside of the house. When I came to, I was underneath the destroyed house. . . . I didn't know anything about the atomic bomb so I thought that some bomb had fallen directly upon me . . . and then when I felt that our house had been directly hit, I became furious. . . . There were roof tiles and walls—everything black—entirely covering me. So I screamed for help. . . . And from all around I heard moans and screaming, and then I felt a kind of danger to myself. . . . I thought that I too was going to die in that way. I felt this way at that moment because I was absolutely unable to do anything at all by my own power. . . . I didn't know where I was or what I was under. . . . I couldn't hear voices of my family. I didn't know how I could be rescued. I felt I was going to suffocate and then die, without knowing exactly what had happened to me. This was the kind of expectation I had. . . .

I stress this sudden encounter with death because I believe that it initiates, from this first moment of contact with the atomic bomb, an emotional theme within the victim which remains with him indefinitely: the sense of a more or less permanent encounter with death.

This early impact enveloped the city in an aura of weirdness and unreality, as recalled by an elderly electrician, who at the time of the bomb was in his mid-forties, working at a railroad junction 5000 meters from the hypocenter.

I was setting up a pole . . . near a switch in the railroad tracks. . . . I heard a tremendous noise. There was a flash . . . a kind of flash I had never seen before which I can't describe. . . . My face felt hot and I put my hands over my eyes and rushed under a locomotive that was nearby. I crawled in between the wheels and then there was an enormous boom and the locomotive shook. I was frightened, so I crawled out. . . . I couldn't tell what happened. . . . For about five minutes I saw nobody, and then I saw someone coming out from an air-raid shelter who told me that the youngest one of our workers had been injured by falling piles . . . so I put the injured man on the back of my bicycle and tried to take him to the dispensary. Then I saw that almost all of the people in that area were crowded into the dispensary, and since there was also a hospital nearby, I went there. But that too was already full. . . . So the only thing to do was to go into [the center of] Hiroshima. But I couldn't move my bicycle because of all the people coming out from Hiroshima and blocking the way. . . . I saw that they were all naked and I wondered what was the matter with them. . . . When we spoke to people, they said that they had been hit by something they didn't understand. . . . We were desperately looking for a doctor or a hospital but we couldn't seem to have any success. . . . We walked toward Hiroshima, still carrying our tools. . . . Then in Hiroshima there was no place either—it had become an empty field—so I carried him to a place near our company office where injured people were lying inside, asking for water. But there was no water and there was no way to help them and I myself didn't know what kind of treatment I should give to this man or to the others. I had to let them die right before my eyes. . . . By then we were cut off from escape, because the fire was beginning to spread out and we couldn't move—we were together with the dead people in the building—only we were not really inside of the building because the building itself had been destroyed, so that we were really outdoors, and we spent the night there. . . .

This rote and essentially ineffectual behavior was characteristic of many during the first few hours, in those situations where any attempt at all could be made to maintain a group cooperative effort; people were generally more effective in helping members of their immediate families, or in saving themselves. This same electrician, an unusually conscientious man, kept at his post at the railroad over a period of several weeks, leaving only for brief periods to take care of his family. Again his description of the scene of death and near-death takes on a dreamlike quality:

There were dead bodies everywhere. . . . There was practically no room for me to put my feet on the floor. . . . At that time I couldn't figure out the reason why all these people were suffering, or what illness it was that had struck them down. . . . I was the only person taking care of the place as all of the rest of the people had gone. . . . Other people came in looking for food or to use the toilet. . . . There was no one to sell tickets in the station, nothing . . . and since trains weren't running I didn't have much work to do. . . . There was no light at all and we were just like sleepwalkers. . . .

And a middle-age teacher, who was also on the outskirts of the city about 5000 meters from the hypocenter, describes his awe at the destruction he witnessed:

I climbed Hijiyama Mountain and looked down. I saw that Hiroshima had disappeared. . . . I was shocked by the sight. . . . What I felt then and still feel now I just can't explain with words. Of course I saw many dreadful scenes after that—but that experience, looking down and finding nothing left of Hiroshima—was so shocking that I simply can't express what I felt. I could see Koi [a suburb at the opposite end of the city] and a few buildings standing. . . . But Hiroshima didn't exist—that was mainly what I saw—Hiroshima just didn't exist.

And a young university professor 2500 meters from the hypocenter at the time, sums up these feelings of weird, awesome unreality in a frequently-expressed image of hell:

> Everything I saw made a deep impression—a park nearby covered with dead bodies waiting to be cremated . . . very badly injured people evacuated in my direction. . . . The most impressive thing I saw was some girls, very young girls, not only with their clothes torn off but with their skin peeled off as well. . . . My immediate thought was that this was like the hell I had always read about. . . . I had never seen anything which resembled it before, but I thought that should there be a hell, this was it—the Buddhist hell, where, we were taught, people who could not attain salvation always went. . . . And I imagined that all of these people I was seeing were in the hell I had read about.

But human beings are unable to remain open to emotional experience of this intensity for any length of time, and very quickly—sometimes within minutes—there began to occur what we may term psychic closing-off; that is, people simply ceased to feel.

For instance, a male social worker, then in his twenties and in military service in Hiroshima, was temporarily on leave at his home just outside of the city; he rushed back into the city soon after the bomb fell, in accordance with his military duty, only to find that his unit had been entirely wiped out. A certain amount of military order was quickly re-established, and a policy of immediate mass cremation of dead bodies was instituted in order to prevent widespread disease, and in accordance with Japa-

nese custom. As a noncommissioned officer and one of the
few able-bodied men left, he was put in charge of this
work of disposing of corpses, which he found he could accomplish with little difficulty:

> After a while they became just like objects or goods that
> we handled in a very businesslike way. . . . Of course I
> didn't regard them simply as pieces of wood—they were
> dead bodies—but if we had been sentimental, we couldn't
> have done the work. . . . We had no emotions. . . . Because
> of the succession of experiences I had been through I was
> temporarily without feeling. . . . At times I went about the
> work with great energy, realizing that no one but myself
> could do it.

He contrasted his own feelings with the terror experienced by an outsider just entering the disaster area:

> Everything at that time was part of an extraordinary
> situation. . . . For instance, I remember that on the ninth
> or tenth of August, it was an extremely dark night. . . . I
> saw blue phosphorescent flames rising from the dead bodies
> —and there were plenty of them. These were quite different
> from the orange flames coming from the burning build-
> ings. . . . These blue phosphorescent flames are what we
> Japanese look upon as spirits rising from dead bodies—in
> former days we called them fireballs.*—And yet at that
> time I had no sense of fear, not a bit, but merely thought,
> "those dead bodies are still burning." . . . But to people who
> had just come from the outside, those flames looked very
> strange. . . . One of those nights I met a soldier who had
> just returned to the city, and I walked along with him. . . .
> He noticed these unusual fireballs and asked me what they
> were. I told him that they were the flames coming from
> dead bodies. The soldier suddenly became extremely
> frightened, fell down on the ground, and was unable to
> move. . . . Yet I at that time had a state of mind in which
> I feared nothing. Though if I were to see those flames
> now I might be quite frightened. . . .

---

* These "fireballs" have no relationship to the fireball of the atomic
bomb previously mentioned, and are here being compared with ordinary
fires caused by the bomb.

Relatively few people were involved in the disposal of dead bodies, but virtually all those I interviewed nonetheless experienced a similar form of psychic closing-off in response to what they saw and felt, and particularly in response to their over-all exposure to death. Thus, many told how horrified they were when they first encountered corpses in strange array, or extremely disfigured faces, but how, after a period of time as they saw more and more of these, they felt nothing. Psychic closing-off would last sometimes for a few hours, and sometimes for days or even months and merge into longer-term feelings of depression and despair.

But even the profound and unconscious defensive maneuvers involved in psychic closing-off were ultimately unable to afford full protection to the survivor from the painful sights and stimuli impinging upon him. It was, moreover, a defense not devoid of its own psychological cost. Thus, the same social worker, in a later interview, questioned his own use of the word "businesslike" to describe his attitude toward dead bodies, and emphasized the pity and sympathy he felt while handling the remains of men from his unit and the pains he took to console family members who came for these remains; he even recalled feeling frightened at night when passing the spot where he worked at cremation by day. He was in effect telling me not only that his psychic closing-off was imperfect, but that he was horrified—felt ashamed and guilty—at having behaved in a way which he now thought callous. For he had indulged in activities which were ordinarily, for him, strongly taboo, and had done so with an energy, perhaps even an enthusiasm, which must have mobilized within him primitive emotions of a frightening nature.

The middle-aged teacher who had expressed such awe at the disappearance of Hiroshima reveals the way in which feelings of shame and guilt, and especially shame and guilt toward the dead, interfere with psychic closing-off and painfully assert themselves:

I went to look for my family. Somehow I became a piti-
less person, because if I had pity, I would not have been
able to walk through the city, to walk over those dead
bodies. The most impressive thing was the expression in
people's eyes—bodies badly injured which had turned
black—their eyes looking for someone to come and help
them. They looked at me and knew that I was stronger than
they. . . . I was looking for my family and looking carefully at everyone I met to see if he or she was a family
member—but the eyes—the emptiness—the helpless expression—were something I will never forget. . . . I often
had to go to the same place more than once. I would wish
that the same family would not still be there. . . . I saw
disappointment in their eyes. They looked at me with great
expectation, staring right through me. It was very hard to
be stared at by those eyes. . . .

He felt, in other words, accused by the eyes of the anonymous dead and dying, of wrongdoing and transgression (a sense of guilt) for not helping them, for letting
them die, for "selfishly" remaining alive and strong; and
"exposed" and "seen through" by the same eyes for these
identical failings (a sense of shame).*

There were also many episodes of more focused guilt
toward specific family members whom one was unable to
help, and for whose death one felt responsible. For
instance, the shopkeeper's assistant mentioned earlier was
finally rescued from the debris of his destroyed house by
his mother, but she was too weakened by her own injuries
to be able to walk very far with him. Soon they were surrounded by fire, and he (a boy of thirteen) did not feel
he had the strength to sustain her weight, and became
convinced that they would both die unless he took some
other action. So he put her down and ran for help, but the

---

* In such profound emotional experiences, feelings of shame and guilt
become intermixed and virtually indistinguishable. In cases like this
one, the guilty inner fantasy is likely to be, "I am responsible for
their (his, her) death," or even, "I killed them." The shameful fantasy
is likely to be, "I should have saved them, or at least done more for
them." But these are closely related, and in mentioning either shame
or guilt in the remainder of the paper, I assume that the other is present
as well.[8]

neighbor he summoned could not get through to the woman because of the flames, and the boy learned shortly afterward that his mother died in precisely the place he had left her. His lasting sense of guilt was reflected in his frequent experience, from that time onward, of hearing his mother's voice ringing in his ears calling for help.

A middle-aged businessman related a similarly guilt-stimulating sequence. His work had taken him briefly to the south of Japan and he had returned to Hiroshima during the early morning hours of August 6. Having been up all night, he was not too responsive when his twelve-year-old son came into his room to ask his father to remove a nail from his shoe so that he could put it on and go off to school. The father, wishing to get the job quickly over, placed a piece of leather above the tip of the nail and promised he would take the whole nail out when the boy returned in the afternoon. As in the case of many youngsters who were sent to factories to do "voluntary labor" as a substitute for their schoolwork, the boy's body was never found—and the father, after a desperately fruitless search for his son throughout the city, was left with the lingering self-accusation that the nail he had failed to remove might have impeded the boy's escape from the fire.

Most survivors focus upon one incident, one sight, or one particular *ultimate horror* with which they strongly identify themselves, and which left them with a profound sense of pity, guilt, and shame. Thus, the social worker describes an event which he feels affected him even more than his crematory activities:

> On the evening of August 6th, the city was so hot from the fire that I could not easily enter it, but I finally managed to do so by taking a path along the river. As I walked along the bank near the present Yokogawa Bridge, I saw the bodies of a mother and her child. . . . That is, I thought I saw dead bodies, but the child was still alive—still breathing, though with difficulty. . . . I filled the cover of my lunch box with water and gave it to the child but it was so weak it could not drink. I knew that people were fre-

quently passing that spot . . . and I hoped that one of these people would take the child, as I had to go back to my own unit. Of course I helped many people all through that day . . . but the image of this child stayed on my mind and remains as a strong impression even now. . . . Later when I was again in that same area I hoped that I might be able to find the child . . . and I looked for it among all the dead children collected at a place nearby. . . . Even before the war I had planned to go into social work, but this experience led me to go into my present work with children— as the memory of that mother and child by Yokogawa Bridge has never left me, especially since the child was still alive when I saw it.

These expressions of ultimate horror can be related to direct personal experience of loss (for instance, the businessman who had failed to remove the nail from his son's shoe remained preoccupied with pathetic children staring imploringly at him), as well as to enduring individual emotional themes. Most of them involved women and children, universal symbols of purity and vulnerability, particularly in Japanese culture. And, inevitably, the ultimate horror was directly related to death or dying.

### CONTAMINATION AND DISEASE

Survivors told me of three rumors which circulated widely in Hiroshima just after the bomb. The first was that for a period of seventy-five years Hiroshima would be uninhabitable—no one would be able to live there. This rumor was a direct expression of the *fear of deadly and protracted contamination from a mysterious poison believed to have been emitted by the frightening new weapon.* (As one survivor put it, "The ordinary people spoke of poison; the intellectuals spoke of radiation.")

Even more frequently expressed, and I believe with greater emotion, was a second rumor: trees and grass would never again grow in Hiroshima; from that day on the city would be unable to sustain vegetation of any kind. This seemed to suggest *an ultimate form of desolation even beyond that of human death*: nature was drying up altogether, the ultimate source of life was being extinguished—a form of symbolism particularly powerful in Japanese culture with its focus upon natural aesthetics and its view of nature as both enveloping and energizing all of human life.

The third rumor, less frequently mentioned to me but one which also had wide currency in various versions, was that all those who had been exposed to the bomb in Hiroshima would be dead within three years. This more naked death symbolism was directly related to the appearance of frightening symptoms of toxic radiation effects. For almost immediately after the bomb and during the following days and weeks, people began to experience, and notice in others, symptoms of a strange form of illness: nausea, vomiting, and loss of appetite; diarrhea with large amounts of blood in the stools; fever and weakness; purple spots on various parts of the body from bleeding into the skin (purpura); inflammation and ulceration of the mouth, throat, and gums (oropharyngeal lesions and gingivitis); bleeding from the mouth, gums, nose, throat, rectum, and urinary tract (hemorrhagic manifestations); loss of hair from the scalp and other parts of the body (epilation); extremely low white blood cell counts when these were taken (leucopenia); and in many cases a progressive course until death.* These symptoms and fatalities aroused in the minds of the people of Hiroshima a special terror, *an image of a weapon which not only kills and destroys on a colossal scale but also leaves behind in the bodies of those exposed to it deadly influences which may emerge at any time and strike down their victims.* This image was made particularly vivid by the delayed appearance of these radiation effects, two to four weeks after the bomb fell, sometimes in people who had previously seemed to be in perfect health.

---

* Oughterson and Warren[9] demonstrate statistically the relationship between incidence of radiation effects and distances from the hypocenter—the great majority of cases occurring within the 2000-meter radius—but these scientific distinctions were, of course, completely unknown at the time, and even after becoming known they have not eliminated survivors' fears of later effects.

The shopkeeper's assistant, both of whose parents were killed by the bomb, describes his reactions to the death of two additional close family members from these toxic radiation effects:

My grandmother was taking care of my younger brother on the 14th of August when I left, and when I returned on the 15th, she had many spots all over her body. Two or three days later she died. . . . My younger brother, who . . . was just a [five-month-old] baby, was without breast milk—so we fed him thin rice gruel. . . . But on the 10th of October he suddenly began to look very ill, though I had not then noticed any spots on his body. . . . Then on the next day he began to look a little better, and I thought he was going to survive. I was very pleased, as he was the only family member I had left, and I took him to a doctor—but on the way to the doctor he died. And at that time we found that there were two large spots on his bottom. . . . I heard it said that all these people would die within three years . . . so I thought, "sooner or later I too will die." . . . I felt very weak and very lonely—with no hope at all . . . and since I had seen so many people's eyebrows falling out, their hair falling out, bleeding from their teeth—I found myself always nervously touching my hair like this [he demonstrated by rubbing his head]. . . . I never knew when some sign of the disease would show itself. . . . And living in the countryside then with my relatives, people who came to visit would tell us these things, and then the villagers also talked about them—telling stories of this man or that man who visited us a few days ago, returned to Hiroshima, and died within a week. . . . I couldn't tell whether these stories were true or not, but I believed them then. And I also heard that when the *hibakusha* came to evacuate to the village where I was, they died there one by one. . . . This loneliness, and the fear. . . . The physical fear . . . has been with me always. . . . It is not something temporary, as I still have it now. . . .

Here we find a link between this early sense of ubiquitous death from radiation effects, and later anxieties about death and illness.

In a similar tone, a middle-aged writer describes his daughter's sudden illness and death:

My daughter was working with her classmates at a place a thousand meters from the hypocenter. . . . I was able to meet her the next day at a friend's house. She had no burns and only minor external wounds, so I took her with me to my country house. She was quite all right for a while but on the 4th of September she suddenly became sick. . . . The symptoms of her disease were different from those of a normal disease. . . . She had spots all over her body. . . . Her hair began to fall out. She vomited small clumps of blood many times. Finally she began to bleed all over her mouth. And at times her fever was very high. I felt this was a very strange and horrible disease. . . . We didn't know what it was. I thought it was a kind of epidemic—something like cholera. So I told the rest of my family not to touch her and to disinfect all utensils and everything she used. . . . We were all afraid of it and even the doctor didn't know what it was. . . . After ten days of agony and torture she died on September 14th. . . . I thought it was very cruel that my daughter, who had nothing to do with the war, had to be killed in this way. . . .

Survivors were thus affected not only by the fact of people dying around them but by the way in which they died: a gruesome form of rapid bodily deterioration which seemed unrelated to more usual and "decent" forms of death.

We have seen how these initial physical fears could readily turn into lifetime bodily concerns. And during the years that followed, these fears and concerns became greatly magnified by another development: the growing awareness among the people of Hiroshima that medical studies were demonstrating an abnormally high rate of leukemia among survivors of the atomic bomb. The increased incidence was first noted in 1948, and reached a peak between 1950 and 1952; it has been greatest in those exposed closest to the hypocenter, so that for those within 1000 meters the increase of leukemia has been between ten and fifty times the normal. Since 1952 the rate has diminished, but it is still higher than in nonexposed populations, and fears which have been aroused remain strong. While symptoms of leukemia are not exactly the same as those of acute radiation effects, the two conditions share enough in common—the dreaded "purple spots" and other forms of hemorrhage, laboratory findings of abnormalities of the blood, progressive weakness and fever and (inevitably in leukemia, and often enough in acute irradiation) ultimate death—that these tend to merge, psychologically speaking, into a diffuse fear of bodily annihilation and death.[10]

Moreover, Hiroshima survivors are aware of the general concern and controversy about genetic effects of the atomic bomb, and most express fear about possible harmful effects upon subsequent generations—a very serious emotional concern anywhere, but particularly so in an East Asian culture which stresses family lineage and the continuity of generations as man's central purpose in life and (at least symbolically) his means of achieving immortality. The Hiroshima people know that radiation *can* produce congenital abnormalities (as has been widely demonstrated in laboratory animals); and abnormalities have frequently been reported among the offspring of survivors—sometimes in very lurid journalistic terms, sometimes in more restrained medical reports. Actually, systematic studies of the problem have so far revealed no higher incidence of abnormalities in survivors' offspring than in those of controlled populations, so that scientific findings regarding genetic effects have been essentially negative. However, there has been one uncomfortably positive genetic finding, that of disturbances in sex ratio of offspring: men exposed to a significant degree of radiation tend to have relatively fewer daughters, while exposed women tend to have fewer sons, because, it is believed, of sex-linked lethal mutations involving the X chromosome —a finding whose significance is difficult to evaluate.* Moreover, there are Japanese physicians who believe that there has been an increase in various forms of internal (and therefore invisible) congenital abnormalities in chil-

---

* Later studies failed to confirm this finding, and suggested it to be of dubious significance. But the general scientific question remains unsolved.

dren of survivors, despite the absence so far of convincing scientific evidence.[11]

Another factor here is the definite damage from radiation experienced by children exposed *in utero*, including many stillbirths and abortions as well as a high incidence of microcephaly with and without mental retardation (occurring almost exclusively in pregnancies which had not advanced beyond four months). This is, of course, a direct effect of radiation upon sensitive, rapidly growing fetal tissues, and, scientifically speaking, has nothing to do with genetic problems. But ordinary people often fail to make this distinction; to them the birth of children with abnormally small heads and retarded minds was often looked upon as still another example of the bomb's awesome capacity to inflict a physical curse upon its victims and their offspring.

There are also other areas of concern regarding delayed radiation effects. There has been a definite increase in cataracts and related eye conditions, which was not stressed to me by survivors as so great a source of emotional concern as the other problems mentioned, but has been nonetheless far from negligible. There is accumulating evidence that the incidence of various forms of cancer has increased among survivors. There has also been evidence of impairment in the growth and development of children, though contested by some on the grounds of inadequately accounting for social and economic factors. And there is a large group of divergent conditions—including anemias and liver and blood diseases, endocrine and skin disorders, impairment of central nervous system (particularly midbrain) function, and premature aging—which have been attributed by various investigators to radiation effects, but have not shown increased incidence in large-scale studies involving control populations. Even more difficult to evaluate is a frequently reported borderline condition of general weakness and debilitation also believed—by a very large number of survivors and by some physicians as well—to be caused by delayed radiation effects.

These fears about general health and genetic effects

have inevitably affected marriage arrangements (which are usually made in Japan by families with the help of a go-between), in which survivors are frequently thought to encounter discrimination, particularly when involved in arrangements with families outside of Hiroshima.

A company employee in his thirties, who was 2000 meters from the bomb's hypocenter when it fell, described to me virtually all of these bodily and genetic concerns in a voice that betrayed considerable anxiety:

Even when I have an illness which is not at all serious— as for instance when I had very mild liver trouble—I have fears about its cause. Of course, if it is just an ordinary condition there is nothing to worry about, but if it has a direct connection to radioactivity, then I might not be able to expect to recover. At such times I feel myself very delicate. . . . This happened two or three years ago. I was working very hard and drinking a great deal of *sake* at night in connection with business appointments and I also had to make many strenuous trips. So my condition might have been partly related to my using up so much energy in all of these things. . . . The whole thing is not fully clear to me. . . . But the results of statistical study show that those who were exposed to the bomb are more likely to have illnesses—not only of the liver, but various kinds of new growth, such as cancer or blood diseases. My blood was examined several times but no special changes were discovered. . . . When my marriage arrangements were made, we discussed all these things in a direct fashion. Everyone knows that there are some effects, but in my case it was the eleventh year after the bomb, and I discussed my physical condition during all of that time. From that, and also from the fact that I was exposed to the bomb while inside of a building and taken immediately to the suburbs, and then remained quite a while outside of the city—judging from all of these facts, it was concluded that there was very little to fear concerning my condition. . . . But in general, there is a great concern that people who were exposed to the bomb might become ill five or ten years later or at any time in the future. . . . Also, when my children were born, I found myself worrying about things that ordinary people don't worry about, such as the possibility that they might inherit some terrible disease from me. . . . I heard that the likelihood of our giving birth to deformed children is greater than in the case of ordinary people . . . and at that time my white blood cell count was rather low. . . . I felt fatigue in the summertime and had a blood count done three or four times. . . . I was afraid it could be related to the bomb, and was greatly worried. . . . Then, after the child was born, even though he wasn't a deformed child, I still worried that something might happen to him afterward. . . . With the second child too I was not entirely free of such worries. . . . I am still not sure what might happen and I worry that the effects of radioactivity might be lingering in some way. . . .

Here we see a young man carrying on effectively in his life, essentially healthy, with normal children, and yet continually plagued by underlying anxieties—about his general health, then about marriage arrangements, and then in relationship to the birth of each of his children. Each hurdle is passed, but there is little relief; like many survivors, he experiences an inner sense of being doomed for posterity.

And a young clerk, also exposed about 2000 meters from the hypocenter, but having the additional disadvantage of retaining a keloid scar resulting from facial burns, expresses similar emotions in still stronger fashion:

Frankly speaking even now I have fear. . . . Even today people die in the hospitals from A-bomb disease, and when I hear about this I worry that I too might sooner or later have the same thing happen to me. . . . I have a special feeling that I am different from ordinary people . . . that I have the marks of wounds—as if I were a cripple. . . . I imagine a person who has an arm or a leg missing might feel the same way. . . . It is not a matter of lacking something externally, but rather something like a handicap—something mental which does not show—the feeling that I am mentally different from ordinary people . . . so when I hear about people who die from A-bomb disease or who have operations because of this illness, then I feel that I am the same kind of person as they. . . .

The survivor's identification with the dead and the maimed initiates a vicious circle on the psychosomatic plane of existence: he is likely to associate the mildest everyday injury or sickness with possible radiation effects; and anything he relates to radiation effects becomes associated with death. The process is accentuated by the strong Japanese cultural focus upon bodily symptoms as expressions of anxiety and conflict. Thus the all-encompassing term "A-bomb sickness" or "A-bomb disease" (*genbakushō*) has evolved, referring on the one hand to such fatal conditions as the early acute radiation effects and later cases of leukemia; and on the other hand to the vague borderline area of fatigue, general weakness, sensitivity to hot weather, suspected anemia, susceptibility to colds or stomach trouble, and general nervousness—all of which are frequent complaints of survivors, and which many associate with radiation effects.\* Not only does the expression "A-bomb disease" have wide popular currency, but it has frequently been used by local physicians as a convenient category for a condition otherwise hard to classify, and at the same time as a means of making it possible for the patient to derive certain medical and economic benefits.

These benefits also loom large in the picture.† Doctors and survivors—as well as politicians and city officials— are caught in a conflict between humanitarian provision for medical need, and the dangers (expressed to me particularly by Japanese physicians) of encouraging the development in survivors of hypochondriasis, general weakness, and dependency—or what is sometimes called "A-bomb neurosis." During the years immediately after

---

\* These borderline complaints, as detected by the Cornell Medical Index[12] are consistently more frequent in *hibakusha* than in non-*hibakusha*. The cultural concern with bodily symptoms is no more than an intensifying influence, and generally similar psychosomatic anxieties would undoubtedly be manifest in other cultures under similar conditions.

† The following discussion of the question of medical benefits is based upon regulations published by the Hiroshima City Office[13] as well as upon extensive discussions of the problems involved with officials responsible for administering the law and physicians who deal with its everyday medical and psychological ramifications. My concern here is to point up these problematic areas as reverberations of the atomic bomb experience, rather than to pass judgment on policies or programs.

the war, when medical care was most needed, very little adequate treatment was available, as the national medical law providing for survivors was not enacted until 1957. But since that time, a series of laws and amendments have been passed with increasingly comprehensive medical coverage, particularly for those in the "special survivors" group (those nearest the hypocenter at the time of the bomb and those who have shown evidence of medical conditions considered to be related to A-bomb effects). In the last few years the category of "special survivors" has been steadily enlarged: distance from the hypocenter, as a criterion for eligibility, has been extended from 2000 to 3000 meters; and qualifying illnesses—originally limited to such conditions as leukemia, ophthalmic diseases, and various blood and liver disorders, all of which were considered to be related to radiation effects—have been extended to include illnesses not considered to be necessarily directly caused by radiation but possibly aggravated by the over-all atomic bomb experience, such as cancer, heart disease, endocrine and kidney disorders, arteriosclerosis, hypertension, and others.°

Maximum medical and economic benefits, however, can be obtained only by those "certified" (through a special medical procedure) to have illnesses specifically related to the atomic bomb; but some physicians believe that this "certification"—which can be sometimes given for such minor conditions as ordinary anemia (as well as for more serious illnesses)—tends to stamp one psychologically as a lifetime A-bomb patient. The rationale of these laws is to provide maximum help for survivors and to give them the benefit of the doubt about matters which are not entirely scientifically resolved. But there remains a great deal of controversy over them. In addition to those (not only among doctors, but also among city officials, ordinary people, and even survivors themselves) who feel that the laws foster an exaggerated preoccupation with atomic bomb effects, there are other survivors who criti-

° Additional amendments in 1963 and 1965 further extended the category of the "special *hibakusha*."

cize them as being still insufficiently comprehensive, as having overly complicated categories and sub-categories which in the end deny full care for certain conditions.

My own impression in studying this problem is that since "A-bomb disease" is at this historical juncture as much a spiritual as a physical condition (as our young clerk made so clear)—and one which touches at every point upon the problem of death—it is difficult for any law or medical program to provide a cure.

The general psychological atmosphere in Hiroshima—and particularly that generated by the effects of the mass media—also has great bearing upon these psychosomatic problems. As one would expect, the whole subject of the atomic bomb and its delayed radiation effects has been continuous front-page news—from 1945–1952 within the limits of the restrictions upon publicizing these matters imposed by the American Occupation,† and without such restrictions thereafter. Confronted with a subject so emotionally charged for the people of Hiroshima—its intensity constantly reinforced by world events and particularly by nuclear weapons testing—newspapers in Hiroshima and elsewhere in Japan have dealt with it dramatically, particularly in circulating the concept of "A-bomb disease." Mass media are caught in a moral dilemma in some ways similar to that I have al-

† Censorship on matters relating to the atomic bomb and its various effects was imposed almost immediately by the American Occupation; fears of retaliation were undoubtedly an important factor, though it is likely that over the years other concerns and influences affected this policy. Reviewing Japanese perceptions of the censorship[14] one gains the impression that its implementation was often inconsistent but sufficient to be felt keenly by writers, and even to interfere with adequate dissemination of much needed medical knowledge about the A-bomb; that descriptions of the A-bomb experience—reportorial, literary, and ideological—nonetheless made their appearance during the early postwar years; that restrictions diminished sufficiently during the last two years of the Occupation for writers to deal freely with the subject; but that the full revelation of the horrors associated with the atomic bomb did not occur for the majority of Japanese until the end of the Occupation in 1952 with the circulation of a now famous issue of the Asahi Graphic (a weekly pictorial of Japan's leading newspaper) in which these horrors were vividly depicted.

ready described for physicians, city officials, and survivors themselves: there is on the one hand the urge to give full publicity to the horrors of nuclear weapons through vivid description of effects and suspected effects of atomic bomb radiation—thereby serving warning to the world and also expressing a form of sympathy to survivors through recognition of their plight—and on the other hand the growing awareness that lurid reports of illness and death have a profoundly disturbing effect upon survivors. Responsible media have struggled to reconcile these conflicting moral pressures and achieve balanced treatment of an unprecedentedly difficult problem; others have been guided mainly by commercial considerations. In any case, the people of Hiroshima have been constantly confronted with frightening descriptions of patients dying in the "A-bomb Hospital" (a medical center built specifically for the treatment of conditions related to the bomb) of "A-bomb disease." In the majority of cases the relationship of the fatal condition to delayed radiation effects is equivocal, but this is usually not made clear, nor does it in any way lessen the enormous impact of these reports upon individual survivors.* Also furthering this impact have been the activities of peace movements and various ideological and political groups—ranging from those whose universalistic dedication to peace and opposition to nuclear weapons testing lead them to circulate the effects of the bomb on a humanistic basis, to others who seek narrower political goals from the unique Hiroshima atmosphere.

What I wish to stress is the manner in which these diverse passions—compounded of moral concern, sympa-

---

* Leukemia, despite its disturbing increase in incidence, remains an infrequent cause of death (Hollingsworth, quoting Heyssel, reports that, up to 1960, 122 cases of leukemia had been discovered in Hiroshima residents); and where death is caused by other conditions it is extremely difficult to assess the influence of radiation effects. But the individual survivor will often automatically associate the A-bomb Hospital with radiation effects, and the situation is further complicated by the medical and legal complexities already mentioned, and by the generally sensitive psychological atmosphere of Hiroshima.

thetic identification, various forms of fear, hostility, political conviction, personal ambition, and journalistic sensationalism—interact with the psychosomatic preoccupations of survivors. But I would also emphasize that these passions are by no means simply manufactured ones; they are the inevitable expression of the impact of a disaster of this magnitude upon basic human conflicts and anxieties. And whatever the medical exaggerations, they are built upon an underlying lethal reality of acute and delayed radiation effects, and upon the genuine possibility of still-undiscovered forms of bodily harm.

Yet, in bodily terms or otherwise, human beings vary greatly in their capacity to absorb an experience of this kind. And one's feelings of health or invalidism—as well as one's symbolic attitude toward the bomb—have much to do with individual emotions and life-patterns. This is made clear by a middle-aged female artist who experienced the bomb just 1500 meters from the hypocenter, and during subsequent years suffered continuously from a variety of bodily symptoms of indefinite origin, as well as from general unhappiness in marital and family relationships:

It looks as though marriage and the normal life one leads with marriage is good for the health. . . . Among A-bomb victims, those who are married and well established with their families have fewer complaints. Of course, even those who are settled in their families remember the incident. But on the whole they are much better off and feel better . . . their attitude is "shōganai" [it can't be helped]. "It is useless to look back on old memories," they keep saying. They are simply interested in their immediate problems of marriage and everyday life. They look forward rather than backward. . . . Those without families, on the other hand, keep remembering everything. Clinging to their memories, they keep repeating the experience. . . . They curse the whole world—including what happened in the past and what is happening now. Some of them even say, "I hope that atomic bombs will be dropped again and then the whole world will suffer the same way I am suffering now."

This kind of hostility is likely to occur together with psychosomatic complaints, and particularly in those people who feel that their life has been blighted by the atomic bomb—those who lost close family members or who in one way or another feel themselves unable to recover from the experience. The cosmic nature of the emotion—its curse upon (and in some cases wish for total annihilation of) the whole world—resembles in some ways the retaliatory emotions of hurt children. But it contains additional elements of personal recollection: the experience of "world-destruction" at the time of the bomb. And it is a projection into the future: the even greater world-destruction one can envisage as a consequence of a repetition of the use of nuclear weapons.

### UNWANTED IDENTITY

It is clear by now that exposure to the atomic bomb changed the survivor's status as a human being, in his own eyes as well as in others'. Both through his immediate experience and its consequences over the years, he became a member of a new group; he assumed the identity of the *hibakusha*, of one who has undergone the atomic bomb. When I asked survivors to associate freely to the word *hibakusha*, and to explain their feelings about it, they invariably conveyed to me the sense of having been compelled to take on this special category of existence, by which they felt permanently bound, however they might wish to free themselves from it. The shopkeeper's assistant expresses this in simple terms characteristic for many:

> Well . . . because I am a *hibakusha* . . . how shall I say it—I wish others would not look at me with special eyes . . . perhaps *hibakusha* are mentally—or both physically and mentally—different from others . . . but I myself do not want to be treated in any special way because I am a *hibakusha*. . . .

To be a *hibakusha* thus separates one from the rest of humankind. It means, as expressed by a young female clerical worker left with a keloid from her atomic bomb exposure at 1600 meters, a sense of having been forsaken.

> I don't like people to use that word [*hibakusha*]. . . . Of course there are some who, through being considered *hibakusha*, want to receive special coddling (*amaeru*). . . . But I like to stand up as an individual. When I was younger they used to call us "atomic bomb maidens." . . . More recently they call us *hibakusha*. . . . I don't like this special view of us. . . . Usually, when people refer to young girls, they will say girls or daughters, or some person's daughter . . . but to refer to us as atomic bomb maidens is a way of discrimination. . . . It is a way of abandoning us. . . .

What she is saying, and what many said to me in different ways, is that the experience, with all of its consequences, is so profound that it can virtually become the person; others then see one *only* as a *hibakusha* bearing the taint of death, and therefore, in the deepest sense, they turn away. And even the special attentions—the various forms of emotional succor—which the survivor may be tempted to seek, cannot be satisfying because such succor is ultimately perceived as unauthentic.

A European priest, one of the relatively few non-Japanese *hibakusha*, expresses these sentiments gently but sardonically:

> I always say—if everyone looks at me because I received the Nobel Prize, that's okay, but if my only virtue is that I was a thousand meters from the atomic bomb center and I'm still alive—I don't want to be famous for that.

*Hibakusha* look upon themselves as underprivileged in other ways too. Not only are they literally a minority group (one-fifth of the city's population), but they are generally considered to be at the lower socioeconomic levels of society, and have even at times been compared to the *burakumin*, or outcast group.* For once it was realized

---

* Nakano gives evidence for the lower socioeconomic position of *hibakusha*, and discusses other social and psychological problems they face.[15]

that Hiroshima was not permanently contaminated after all, not only did the survivors attempt to rebuild their homes, but hordes of outsiders—some from overseas areas, some from the industrial Osaka region, some of them black marketeers and members of gangs who saw special opportunity beckoning: all of them both physically and culturally more vigorous than the atomic-bombed, traditionalistic Hiroshima population—poured into the city, and became perhaps the main beneficiaries of the economic boom which later developed. Survivors have encountered discrimination not only in marriage but also in employment, as it was felt that they could not work as hard as ordinary people and tended to need more time off because of illness and fatigue. Of course, survivors nonetheless regularly work and marry; but they often do so with a sense of having, as *hibakusha*, impaired capacity for both. They strongly resent the popular image of the *hibakusha* which accentuates their limitations, but at the same time accept much of it as their own self-image. Thus, concerning occupational competition, older survivors often feel that they have lacked the over-all energy to assimilate their economic, spiritual, and possibly physical blows sufficiently to be the equal of ordinary people; and young survivors, even if they feel themselves to possess normal energy, often fear that being identified by others as a *hibakusha* might similarly interfere with their occupational standing. Concerning marriage, the sense of impairment can include the need to have one's A-bomb experience more or less "cleared" by a go-between (as we have seen); fears about having abnormal children, or sometimes about the ability to have children at all;* and occasionally, in males, diminished sexual potency (thought of as organic but probably psychogenic).

However well or poorly a survivor is functioning in

---

* Survivors often marry one another, and frequently feel that by doing so they are likely to be best understood. But some express a strong preference to marry a non-*hibakusha*, and claim that by marrying one another they increase their possibilities for giving birth to abnormal children; they also here reflect an urge to transcend through marriage, rather than intensify, the *hibakusha* identity.

his life, the word *hibakusha* evokes an image of the dead and the dying. The young clerk, for instance, when he hears the word, thinks either of the experience itself (". . . Although I wasn't myself too badly injured I saw many people who were . . . and I think . . . of the look on their faces . . . camps full of these people, their breasts burned and red. . . .") or, as we have already heard him describe, of the aftereffects: "when I hear about people who die from A-bomb disease or who have operations because of this illness, then I feel that I am the same kind of person as they. . . ."

We are again confronted with the survivor's intimate identification with the dead; we find, in fact, that it tends to pervade the entire *hibakusha* identity. *For survivors seem not only to have experienced the atomic disaster, but to have imbibed it and incorporated it into their beings, including all of its elements of horror, evil, and particularly of death.* They feel compelled virtually to merge with those who died. And they judge, and indeed judge harshly, their own behavior and that of other survivors on the basis of the degree of respect it demonstrates toward the dead. They condemn, for instance, the widespread tendency (which, as Japanese, they are at the same time attracted to) of making the anniversary of the bomb an occasion for a gay festival—because they see this as an insult to the dead. Similarly they are extraordinarily suspicious of all individual and group attempts to take any form of action in relationship to the atomic bomb experience, even when done for the apparent purpose of helping survivors or furthering international peace. And they are, if anything, more critical of a survivor prominent in such programs than they are of "outsiders," constantly accusing such a person of "selling his name," "selling the bomb," or "selling Hiroshima." The causes for their suspiciousness are many, including a pervasive Japanese cultural tendency to be critical of the man who shows unconventional initiative (as expressed in the popular saying "A nail which sticks out will be hammered down"), as well as an awareness of how readily the Hiroshima situation can be "used" by ambitious leaders. But there is an ultimate inner feeling that any such activities and programs are "impure," that they violate the sanctity of the dead. For in relationship to the atomic bomb disaster, it is only the dead who, in the eyes of survivors, remain pure; and any self- or group-assertion can readily be seen as an insult to the dead.*

Finally, this imposed identity of the atomic bomb survivor is greatly affected by his historical perceptions (whether clear or fragmentary) of the original experience, including its bearing upon the present world situation. The dominant emotion here is the sense of having been made into "guinea pigs," not only because of being studied by research groups (particularly American research groups) interested in determining the effects of delayed radiation, but more fundamentally because of having been victimized by the first "experiment" (a word many of them use in referring to the event) with nuclear weapons. They are affected by a realization, articulated in various ways, that they have experienced something ultimate in man-made disasters; and at the same time by the feeling that the world's continuing development and testing of the offending weapons deprives their experience of meaning. Thus, while frequently suspicious of organized campaigns against nuclear testing, they almost invariably experience anxiety and rage when such testing is conducted, recall the horrors they have been through, and express bitter frustration at the world's unwillingness to heed their warnings. And we have seen how this anger can at times be converted into thoughts of cosmic retaliation. There remains, of course, a residuum of hostility toward America and Americans for having dropped the

---

* I have in this section barely suggested the Japanese cultural influences—particularly the tendency toward a sense of continuity with the dead—which affect survivors' reactions. These cultural influences are important. But I believe that the close identification with the dead which I have described, like the psychosomatic patterns discussed in the previous section, should not be thought of as exclusively "Japanese"; rather I would claim that it is also related to the nature of the disaster, although expressed in a particular (Japanese) cultural style.[16]

bomb, but such hostility has been tempered over the years and softened by Japanese cultural restraints—except, as we have also seen, in individuals who experienced personal losses and blows to self-esteem from which they have been unable to recover. More than in relation to the dropping of the bomb itself (which many said they could understand as a product, however horrible, of war), survivors tend to express hostility in response to what they feel to be callousness toward their plight, or toward those who died, and also toward nuclear weapons testing. Thus, in singling out President Truman as an object of hatred, as some do, it is not only for his having ordered that the bomb be used but also for being assertively unapologetic about having done so.°

Survivors tend to be strongly ambivalent about serving as symbols for the rest of the world, and this ambivalence is expressed in Hiroshima's excruciating conflict about whether or not to tear down the so-called "A-Bomb Dome" (or "Peace Dome")—the prominent ruins of a dome-shaped exhibition hall located almost directly at the hypocenter. The dome has so far been permitted to stand as a reminder of the experience, and its picture has been featured in countless books and pamphlets dealing, from every point of view, with the A-bomb problem. Three different sets of attitudes on the question were expressed to me. The first: Let it remain permanently so that people (especially outsiders) will remember what we have been through and take steps to prevent repetitions of such disasters. The second: Tear it down for any of the following reasons: it does no good, as no one pays any attention to it; we should adopt the Buddhist attitude of resignation toward the experience; the dome is inauthentic, does not adequately convey what we really experienced, and is not in fact directly at the hypocenter; it is too painful a reminder for us (hibakusha) to have

° These attitudes are related to Japanese cultural tendencies to stress human considerations, including apologetic sympathy where this is felt indicated, rather than more abstract determinations of right and wrong or matters of individual conscience. But again it is by no means certain that in similar circumstances, even in cultures with a reverse emphasis, similar hostilities might not occur.

to look at every day (perhaps the most strongly felt objection); and, we should look ahead to the future rather than back to the unpleasant past. And the third: Let it neither be permitted to stand indefinitely nor torn down, but instead left as it is until it begins to crumble of its own, and then simply removed—a rather ingenious (and perhaps characteristically Japanese) compromise solution to the dilemma, which the city administration has proposed.* Most survivors simultaneously feel various conflicting elements of the first and second sets of attitudes, and sometimes of all three. The inner conflict is something like this: For the sake of the dead and of our own sense of worth, we must give our experience significance by enabling it to serve wider moral purposes; but to do so—to be living symbols of massive death—is not only unbearably painful but also tends ultimately to be insincere and to insult, rather than comfort, the dead.

## BEYOND HIROSHIMA

We return to the question we raised at the beginning: Does Hiroshima follow the standard patterns delineated for other disasters, or is it—in an experiential sense—a new order of event? We must say first that the usual emotional patterns of disaster[17] are very much present in what I have already described. One can break down the experience into the usual sequence of anticipation, impact, and aftermath; one can recognize such standard individual psychological features as various forms of denial, the "illusion of centrality" (or feeling of each that he was at the very center of the disaster's path),† the apa-

---

* In 1965 a nine-story business building was constructed right next to the dome, greatly obscuring it as a landmark. But the next year the city administration decided to change its policy and maintain the dome permanently. Money has been raised, and the difficult technical task of preservation has been initiated.

† It is to those who were several thousand meters from the hypocenter, including many beyond the outskirts of the city, that the term "illusion of centrality" and its psychological mechanisms (as described in the literature on disaster) apply. Those who were closer, in terms of effects experienced, were sufficiently central to the disaster for the term "illusion" to be inappropriate.

thy of the "disaster syndrome" resulting from the sudden
loss of the sense of safety and even omnipotence with
which we usually conduct our lives, and the conflict between self-preservation and wider human responsibility
which culminates in feelings of guilt and shame; even
some of the later social and psychological conflicts in the
affected population are familiar.* Yet we have also seen
convincing evidence that the Hiroshima experience† no
less in the psychological than in the physical sphere, transcends in many important ways that of the ordinary disaster. I shall try to suggest what I think are some of the

* As in other recent disaster studies[18] I did not (from discussions
with medical, psychiatric, and other authorities) have the impression
of a large increase of severe mental illness, such as psychosis, at the
time of the disaster or immediately afterwards; in view of the limited
available statistical data it would be extremely difficult to study this
problem, and I did not attempt to do so. My findings differ, however,
from those of other disaster studies in the extent of the psychosocial
consequences I encountered which, although emotionally profound, are
not of a variety classifiable as "mental illness." This important difference
stems mainly, I believe, from special features of the atomic bomb
experience, but may also be related to variations in approach and
method.
† I have in this paper dealt only with Hiroshima as it was there that
I conducted the research, although I did have the opportunity to make
briefer observations in Nagasaki as well. In both cities there is a
widely held impression that general reactions to the atomic bomb—
mass media dissemination of its effects, peace movements, and even
fears and concerns of hibakusha—are considerably more intense in
Hiroshima than in Nagasaki. I believe this is true, but only in degree,
and not in the more or less absolute sense in which it is sometimes
depicted. There are a number of factors which have contributed to
this difference in intensity, and to Hiroshima's assuming more of a
symbolic role for both hibakusha and outsiders: Hiroshima was the first
to be struck by the new weapon; the bomb fell in the center of
Hiroshima, a flat city made up almost entirely of flimsy structures, so
that the entire city was virtually devastated, while in Nagasaki the
bomb fell at some distance from the center and destruction was limited
by the hilly terrain so that the greater part of the city (including a
somewhat larger number of concrete structures) was left standing, and
casualties and general effects were not so great despite the fact that the
Nagasaki bomb was of greater explosive power; Nagasaki could therefore more readily resume some of its previous identity as a city—which
included a unique history of having served for several centuries as
Japan's main contact with the Western world—while Hiroshima had
to recreate itself almost entirely, and without the benefit of a com-
parable tradition; and Hiroshima is closer to Tokyo and more sensitive
to intellectual and ideological currents stemming from Japan's dominant
city.

important ways in which this is true. And when these special psychological qualities of the experience of the atomic bomb have been more fully elaborated—beyond the preliminary outlines of this paper—I believe that they will, in turn, shed light on general disaster patterns, and, of greater importance, on human nature and its vicissitudes at our present historical juncture. We may then come to see Hiroshima for what it was and is: both a direct continuation of the long and checkered history of human struggle, and at the same time a plunge into a new and tragic dimension.

The first of these psychological elements is one we have already referred to, the continuous encounter with death. When we consider the sequence of this encounter—its turbulent onset at the moment the bomb fell, its shocking reappearance in association with delayed radiation effects, and its prolonged expression in the group identity of the doomed and near-dead—we are struck by the fact that it is an interminable encounter. There is, psychologically speaking, no end point, no resolution. This continuous and unresolvable encounter with death, then, is a unique feature of the atomic bomb disaster. Its significance for the individual survivor varies greatly, according to such factors as previous character traits, distance from the hypocenter at the time the bomb fell, fatalities in his immediate family, and many other features of his bomb experience and subsequent life pattern. There is little doubt that most survivors lead reasonably effective personal, family, and occupational lives. But each retains, in greater or lesser degree, emotional elements of this special relationship to death.

In the light of the Hiroshima experience we should also consider the possibility that in other disasters or extreme situations there may also be more significant inner encounters with death, immediate or longer-term, than we have heretofore supposed. Psychiatrists and social scientists investigating these matters are hampered by the same factors which interfere with everyone else's approach to the subject: first, by our inability to imagine death, which deprives us, as psychiatrists, of our usual reliance upon empathy and leaves us always at several psychological removes from experiential understanding; and second, by the elaborate circle of denial—the profound inner need of human beings to make believe that they will never die—in which we too are enclosed. But these universal psychological barriers to thought about death become much greater in relation to a nuclear disaster, where the enormity of the scale of killing and the impersonal nature of the technology are still further impediments to comprehension. No wonder, then, that the world resists full knowledge of the Hiroshima and Nagasaki experiences, and expends relatively little energy in comprehending their full significance. And beyond Hiroshima, these same impediments tragically block and distort our perceptions of the general consequences of nuclear weapons. They also raise an important question relevant for the continuous debate about the desirability of preparedness for possible nuclear attacks: If the human imagination is so limited in its capacity to deal with death, and particularly death on a vast scale, can individuals ever be significantly "prepared" for a nuclear disaster?

The Hiroshima experience thus compels us, particularly as psychiatrists, to give more thought to psychic perceptions of death and dying.[19] Here I would particularly stress the psychological importance of identification with the dead—not merely the identification with a particular loved one, as in the case of an ordinary mourning experience, but rather, as we have observed in atomic bomb survivors, a lasting sense of affiliation with death itself. This affiliation creates in turn an enduring element, both within, and standing in judgment of, the self—a process closely related to the experience of shame.[20] Also of great importance is the *style of dying*, real or symbolic, the way in which one anticipates death and the significance with which one can relate oneself to this anticipation. Among those I interviewed in Hiroshima, many found solace in the characteristically Japanese (partially Buddhist) attitude of resignation, but virtually none was able to build a framework of meaning around their overwhelming immersion in death. However philosophically they might accept the horrors of war, they had an underlying sense of having been victimized and experimented upon by a horrible device, all to no avail in a world which has derived no profit from their sufferings.

And this sense of purposeless death suggests the second special feature of the atomic disaster: *a vast breakdown of faith in the larger human matrix supporting each individual life, and therefore a loss of faith (or trust) in the structure of existence.* This is partly due to the original exposure to death and destruction on such an extraordinary scale, an "end-of-the-world" experience resembling the actualization of the wildest psychotic delusion; partly due to the shame and guilt patterns which, initiated during the experience itself, turned into longer-lasting preoccupations with human selfishness (preoccupations expressed to me by a large number of survivors); and partly due to the persisting sense of having encountered an ultimate form of *man-made* destruction. Phrased in another way, the atomic bomb destroyed the complex equilibrium which ordinarily mediates and integrates the great variety of cultural patterns and individual emotions which maintain any society, large or small. One must, of course, take into account here the disruption accompanying the extensive social change which has occurred all over Japan immediately following World War II; and one must also recognize the impressive re-emergence of Hiroshima as an actively functioning city. Nonetheless, this profound loss of confidence in human social ties remains within survivors as a derivative of the atomic bomb experience.

A third psychological feature of particular importance in the Hiroshima disaster is that which I have called *psychic closing-off*. Resembling the psychological defense of denial, and the behavioral state of apathy, psychic closing-off is nonetheless a distinctive pattern of response to overwhelmingly threatening stimuli. Within a matter of moments, as we have seen in the examples cited, a person may not only cease to react to these threatening stimuli but in so doing, equally suddenly, violate the most profound values and taboos of his culture and his personal life. Though a highly adaptive response—and indeed very often a means of emotional self-preservation—it can vary in its proportions to the extent at times of almost resembling a psychotic mechanism. Since psychic closing-off, at least in the form it took in Hiroshima, is specifically related to the problem of death, it raises the question of the degree to which various forms of psychosis might also be responses to the symbolic fear of death or bodily annihilation.

The psychic closing-off created by the Hiroshima disaster is not limited to the victims themselves, but extends to those who, like myself, attempt to study the event. Thus, although I had had previous research experience with people who had been exposed to extreme situations, I found that at the beginning of my work in Hiroshima the completion of each interview would leave me profoundly shocked and emotionally spent. But as the work progressed and I heard more and more of these accounts, their effects upon me greatly lessened. My awareness of my scientific function—my listening carefully for specific kinds of information and constantly formulating categories of response—enhanced the psychic closing-off necessary to me for the task of conducting the research (necessary also for a wide variety of human efforts which deal with problems in which death is a factor). It is this vast ramification of psychic closing-off, rather than the phenomenon itself, that is unique to nuclear disaster, so much so that all who become in any way involved in the problem find themselves facing a near-automatic tendency to seal themselves off from what is most disturbing in the evidence at hand.

Finally, there is the question of *psychological mastery of the nuclear disaster experience*. Central to this problem is the task of dealing with feelings of shame and guilt of the most profound nature: the sense that one has, however unwittingly, participated in this total human break-down in which, in Martin Buber's words, "the human order of being is injured."[*][21] That such feelings of self-condemnation—much like those usually termed "existential guilt"—should be experienced by the *victims* of a nuclear disaster is perhaps the most extreme of its many tragic ironies. Faced with the task of dealing with this form of guilt, with the problem of re-establishing trust in the human order, and with the continuing sense of encounter with death, the survivor of a nuclear disaster needs nothing less than a new identity in order to come to terms with his post-disaster world. And once more extending the principle beyond the victim's experience, it may not be too much to say that those who permit themselves to confront the consequences of such a disaster, past or future, are also significantly changed in the process. Since these consequences now inhabit our world, more effective approaches to the problem of human survival may well depend upon our ability to grasp the nature of the fundamentally new relationship to existence which we all share.

---

[*] Feelings of shame and guilt, at their most profound level—their psychological meeting ground—as I suggest below (following Buber, Lynd, Erikson, and my own previous work) can be overcome only through a change in one's relationship to the world, and can be under certain conditions creatively utilized on behalf of achieving such a change. But my impression regarding the atomic bomb experience was that this constructive utilization was the exception rather than the rule, since there was so much that tended to block it and to cause feelings of shame and guilt to be retained in their negative, unresolved form.

# ON DEATH AND
# DEATH SYMBOLISM

## 6

*Here again I examine the Hiroshima experience, this time with a more interpretive emphasis upon various kinds of death imagery. I develop a concept of symbolic immortality which has since become central to my work. This concept, as applied to the historical process in general and to the impact of nuclear weapons in particular, has become the basis for* The Broken Connection. *It also provided the framework for* Revolutionary Immortality.*

*From the standpoint of psychological theory, one could say that this paper deals with more technical questions than the others. But to speak of death and dying as technical matters is to cease to speak of them at all. What I attempt is a thematic and broadly humanistic approach which retains its connection with the scientific spirit, but through a science of forms rather than one of mechanism.*

*Working with these particular forms—forms concerning death—has had its personal impact. I have found myself "living in death" a good part of the time, much more of the time than I would have wished to during my late thirties and early forties. Such a death-focused imagination has its elements of somberness; one becomes pain-*

*fully sensitized to sadness and loss. But its other side is an
equal sensitivity to absurdity and mockery, to the extremities of humor as well as pain.*

*The study of death symbolism not only involves one in
complex emotional matters but in equally profound intellectual difficulties. Even (perhaps especially) on the
conceptual plane, the problem of death is so formidable
and elusive that significant insights, certainly in the psychological field, have been extremely rare. On the other
hand the whole subject has been, at least until recently,
so neglected by psychiatric and psychological thought
that one begins with minimal dogma. One works, moreover, with the tragic advantage of living in the nuclear
age. Thus, as this essay argues, the Hiroshima experience
can be an occasion for directing our imaginations toward
places they have rarely inhabited—toward (in a much
different spirit from that originally associated with the
phrase) "thinking about the unthinkable."*

*The paradox is an ultimate one: the existence of weap-
ons that can annihilate man and his history could also,
however indirectly, be a stimulus toward a deeper and
more humane grasp of the same. Hiroshima was the
prelude to all this—an expression of technological evil
and madness which could, but will not necessarily, be a
path to wisdom.*

❊          ❊          ❊

The larger a human event, the more its significance eludes us. In the case of Hiroshima's encounter with the atomic bomb—surely a tragic turning point in man's psychological and historical experience—the meaning is perhaps only now, after nineteen years, beginning to reveal itself. Yet the event has much to teach us that is of considerable value in our struggles to cope with a world altered much more than we realize, and made infinitely more threatening by the existence of nuclear weapons. In this chapter I shall describe a portion of a larger study of the psychological effects of the atomic bomb in Hiroshima. I shall focus upon what I believe to be the central psychological issue in both the actual disaster and its wider symbolism—the problem of death and dying. The work represents a continuation of an effort, begun ten years ago, to develop a modified psychoanalytic research approach to broad historical problems.

There are many reasons that the study of death and death symbolism has been relatively neglected in psychiatry and psychoanalysis: Not only does it arouse emotional resistances in the investigator—all too familiar, though extraordinarily persistent nonetheless—but it confronts him with an issue of a magnitude far beyond his empathic and intellectual capacities. Yet, whatever the difficulties, the nuclear age provides both urgent cause and vivid stimulus for new efforts to enhance our understanding of what has always been man's most ineradicable problem. Certainly no study of an event like the Hiroshima disaster can be undertaken without some exploration of that problem.

In the previous essay I described the general psychosocial patterns of the atomic bomb experience and related them to the predominant theme of death. Now I wish to explore more specifically the psychological elements of what I have referred to as the *permanent encounter with death* which the atomic bomb created within those exposed to it. I shall discuss, in sequence, four different stages of experience with death—that is, four aspects of this encounter. Under examination, therefore, will be shared individual responses to an atmosphere permeated by death. Then, in the latter portion of the paper, I shall attempt to suggest a few general principles in the difficult area of the psychology of death and dying, essentially derived from this investigation but by no means limited to the Hiroshima experience.

### IMMERSION IN DEATH

The overwhelming immersion in death directly following the bomb's fall began with the terrible array of dead and near-dead in the midst of which each survivor found himself. Anyone exposed relatively near the center of the city could not escape the sudden sense of ubiquitous death around him—resulting from the blast itself, from radiant heat, and from ionizing radiation. For instance, if the survivor had been within 1000 meters (.6 miles) from the hypocenter, and out of doors (that is, without benefit of shielding from heat or radiation), more than nine-tenths of the people around him were fatalities; and if he had been unshielded at 2000 meters (1.2 miles), more than eight of ten people around him were killed. For those indoors mortality was lower, but even then in order to have even a 50-percent chance of escaping both death and injury, one had to be about 2200 meters (1.3 miles) from the hypocenter.[1]

Among the initial emotions experienced at the time, many stressed (partly, undoubtedly, with retrospective reconstruction, but not without significance in any case) feelings related to death and dying, such as: "My first feeling was, I think I will die"; "I was dying without seeing my parents"; and "This is the end for me."

Beyond this sense of imminent individual death was

the feeling of many that the whole world was dying. A science professor, covered by falling debris, found himself temporarily blinded:

> My body seemed all black, everything seemed dark, dark all over. . . . Then I thought, "The world is ending."

A Protestant minister, himself uninjured, responded to the evidence of mutilation and destruction he saw every where around him when walking through the city:

> The feeling I had was that everyone was dead. The whole city was destroyed. . . . I thought all of my family must be dead—it doesn't matter if I die. . . . I thought this was the end of Hiroshima—of Japan—of humankind.

And a woman writer:

> I just could not understand why our surroundings had changed so greatly in one instant. . . . I thought it might have been something which had nothing to do with the war, the collapse of the earth which it was said would take place at the end of the world, and which I had read about as a child. It was quiet around us. In fact, there was a fearful silence, which made one feel that all people and all trees and vegetation were dead.[2]

This "deathly silence" was consistently reported by survivors. Rather than wild panic, most described a ghastly stillness and a sense (whether or not literally true) of slow motion: Low moans from those incapacitated, the rest fleeing, but usually not rapidly, from the destruction, toward the rivers (whose many branches run throughout the city), toward where they thought their family members might be, or toward where they hoped to find authorities of some sort or medical personnel, or simply toward accumulations of other people, in many cases merely moving along with a growing crowd and with no clear destination. This feeling of *death in life* was described by a store clerk as follows:

The appearance of people was . . . well, they all had skin blackened by burns. . . . They had no hair because their hair was burned, and at a glance you couldn't tell whether you were looking at them from in front or in back. . . . They held their arms bent [forward] like this [and he proceeded to demonstrate their position] . . . and their skin—not only on their hands, but on their faces and bodies too—hung down. . . . If there had been only one or two such people . . . perhaps I would not have had such a strong impression. But wherever I walked I met these people. . . . Many of them died along the road—I can still picture them in my mind—like walking ghosts. . . . They didn't look like people of this world. . . . They had a special way of walking —very slowly. . . . I myself was one of them.

Characteristic here is the other-worldly grotesqueness of the scene, the image of neither-dead-nor-alive human figures with whom the survivor closely identifies himself. Similar emotions were frequently described in the imagery of a Buddhist hell, or expressed even more literally—as one man put it, "I was not really alive."

Examining the further psychological meaning of this early immersion in death, one is struck by the importance of feelings of helplessness and abandonment in the face of threatened annihilation. The fear and anticipation of anni- hilation dominate this phase, though it is not always easy to say exactly what it is that the *hibakusha* fears is about to be annihilated. Here I believe that his over-all organ- ism is included insofar as he is capable of symbolically perceiving it—in other words, he fears annihilation of his own self.[3] But one also must include his sense of relation- ship to the world of people and objects in which he exists: he anticipates the annihilation of both the field or con- text of his existence and his attachment to it—of his "be- ing-in-the-world," as the existentialists would put it,[4] and his "non-human environment," as described in recent psychoanalytic writings.[5] And he fears the annihilation of that special set of feelings and beliefs which both re- late him to others and allow for his sense of being a unique and particular person—in other words, his sense of inner identity.[6] This *anticipation of annihilation—of* self, of being, of identity—was related to overwhelming stimuli from without and within, an ultimate sense of threat that has been referred to by such names as "basic fear" and "the fear of the universe."[7]*

And indeed so overwhelming was this experience that many would have undoubtedly been unable to avoid psychosis were it not for the extremely widespread and effective defense mechanism of psychic closing-off. This defense mechanism was specifically related to the grotesque evidences of death and near-death. People had a clear sense—sometimes within seconds or minutes—of what was happening around them, but their emotional reactions were unconsciously turned off.

A physicist, observing this process in himself, compared it to an overexposed photographic plate. A clerk who witnessed others dying around him at a temporary first-aid area reached a point at which "I just couldn't have any reaction. . . . You might say I became insensitive to human death." And the woman writer quoted before described "a feeling of paralysis that came over my mind."

The unconscious process here is that of closing oneself off from death itself; the controlling inner idea, or fantasy, is, "If I feel nothing, then death is not taking place." Psychic closing-off is thus related to the defense mechanisms of denial and isolation, as well as to the behavioral state of apathy. But it deserves to be distinguished from these in its sudden, global quality, in its throwing out a protective symbolic screen which enables the organism to resist the impact of death—that is, to survive psychologically in the midst of death and dying. It may well represent man's most characteristic response to catastrophe: one which is at times life-enhancing, or even, psychologi-

---

* Erik H. Erikson[8] speaks of "a shudder which comes from the sudden awareness that our nonexistence . . . is entirely possible"; and I found similar responses in many exposed to Chinese thought reform.[9] It seems particularly significant that this anticipation of annihilation can occur under a wide variety of circumstances in which one's sense of relationship to the world is profoundly impaired, whether or not actual death is threatened. It represents a symbolic expectation of death, which is the only kind of anticipation of death possible for humankind.

cally speaking, life-saving; but at other times, particularly when prolonged and no longer appropriate to the threat, not without its own dangers. Certainly the investigator of nuclear disaster finds himself experiencing a measure of such closing-off, as indeed does the reader of an account such as this one.°

I have suggested that psychic closing-off, effective as it is, has its limitations even as a protective reaction. It cannot entirely succeed in neutralizing either the threatening stimuli from without nor those from within—the latter taking the form of self-condemnation, guilt, and shame. For at the very beginning of the atomic bomb experience a need is initiated for justifying one's own survival in the face of others' deaths, a form of guilt which plagues the survivor from then on, and to which I shall return. Here I shall only say *that the quick experience of self-condemnation intensifies the lasting imprint of death created by this early phase of atomic bomb exposure.* Contained within this imprint is something very close to witnessing in actuality that which ordinarily takes place only in psychotic fantasy—namely, an end-of-the-world experience. Normally a projection of inner psychological "death" onto the outside world, the process is here reversed so that an overwhelming external experience of near-absolute destruction becomes internalized and merged with related tendencies of the inner life.† Highly relevant here is what I described before as the ultimate horror—especially one particular form which, more than any other, seemed to epitomize the association of death and guilt. It was the recollection of requests (whether

° The term "psychic closing-off" conveys a threefold process: numbing of affect, symbolic walling-off of the organism, and abrupt disconnection in communication between inner and outer worlds. Elsewhere I refer to more chronic manifestations of the process as "psychic numbing."
† In other words, one may assume that everyone has some tendency toward this form of "psychological death"—toward withdrawal of psychic connection to the world—originating in earliest separation experiences, including that of birth itself; but that the tendency becomes most characteristically predominant in psychosis. Thus, when *hibakusha* underwent their end-of-the-world experience, they had, so to speak, a previous psychic model for it, upon which it could be grafted.[10]

overt or implicit) by the dying which could not be carried out, most specifically their pleas for a few sips of water. Water was withheld not only because of survivors' preoccupation with saving themselves and their own families, but because authorities spread the word that water would have harmful effects upon the severely injured. The request for water by the dying, however, in addition to reflecting their physical state, has special significance in Japanese tradition, as it is related to an ancient belief that water can restore life by bringing back the spirit that has just departed from the body.[11] These pleas were therefore as much psychological expressions of this belief as they were of physical need; indeed, one might say that they were pleas for life itself. The survivor's failure to acquiesce to them, whatever his reasons, could thus come to have the psychological significance for him of refusing the request of another for the privilege of life—while he himself clung so tenaciously to that same privilege.

### INVISIBLE CONTAMINATION

The second encounter with death took the form of *invisible contamination*—the toxic radiation effects which occurred after the bomb fell, sometimes within hours or even minutes, often during the first twenty-four hours, and then for weeks afterward. No one at first had any understanding of the cause of the symptoms, and in the few medical facilities that were still functioning, isolation procedures were instituted in the belief that they were part of some kind of infectious gastrointestinal condition.* Ordinary people also suspected some form of epidemic, possibly in the nature of cholera. But very quickly, partly, by word-of-mouth information and misinformation about the atomic bomb, people began to relate the condition

---

* For a vivid description of these reactions in one of the hospitals that remained functional, see Michihiko Hachiya, *Hiroshima Diary*, admirably edited and translated by Warner Wells; Chapel Hill, Univ. of North Carolina Press, 1955.

to a mysterious "poison" emanating from the weapon itself. Survivors were terrified by its combination of strangeness and deadliness. They were struck particularly by the loss of scalp hair, the purple spots on the skin, and (whether or not always true) by the way in which victims appeared to remain conscious and alert almost to the moment of their death. As a middle-aged electrician relates,

> There was one man who asked me for help and everything he said was clear and normal. . . . But in another three hours or so when I looked at him he was already dead. . . . And even those who looked as though they would be spared were not spared. . . . People seemed to inhale something from the air which we could not see. . . . The way they died was different . . . and strange.

Some were intrigued, and even attracted, by the weirdness of the symptoms—as in the case of a doctor quoted in a later written account:

> I know it is terrible to say this, but those spots were beautiful. They were just like stars—red, green, yellow, and black . . . all over the body, and I was fascinated by them.[12]

But the predominant feeling among survivors was that they themselves were imminently threatened by this same "poison"—as conveyed in such statements as: "Soon we were all worried about our health, about our bodies—whether we would live or die"; "I thought, sooner or later I too will die. . . . I never knew when some sign of the disease would show itself"; and, "We waited for our own deaths."

The three rumors which swept Hiroshima right after the bomb—that all exposed would die, nature itself would dry up, and the city would be totally devitalized—reveal the extremity of the death symbolism of this second stage. Other rumors expressed further ramifications of these emotions: there were rumors that there would be new attacks with "poison gases" or "burning oil"; that

America, having dropped such a terrible "hot bomb," would next drop a "cold bomb" or "ice bomb" which would freeze everything so that everyone would die; and there was even a rumor that America would drop rotten pigs so that, as one man put it, "Everything on the earth would decay and go bad." These additional rumors conveyed the sense that the environment had been so fundamentally disturbed, and the individual sense of security and invulnerability in relationship to life and death so threatened, that further life-annihilating assaults must be anticipated.

The psychological aspects of the second encounter with death may thus be summarized as follows: There was a fear of epidemic contamination to the point of bodily deterioration; a sense of individual powerlessness in the face of an invisible, all-enveloping, and highly mysterious poison (and in regard to this mysteriousness, there has been some evidence of psychological resistance toward finding out the exact nature of radiation effects); the sense, often largely unconscious and indirectly communicated, that this *total contamination*—seemingly limitless in time and space—must have a supernatural, or at least more-than-natural origin, must be something in the nature of a curse upon one's group for some form of wrongdoing that had offended the forces which control life and death. This latter formulation was occasionally made explicit in, for instance, survivors' Buddhistic references to misbehavior in previous incarnations; it was implicit in their repeated expressions of awe, in the elaborate mythology (only a portion of which I have mentioned) they created around the event, and in their various forms of self-condemnation relating to guilt and punishment as well as to shame and humiliation.

•

## "A-BOMB DISEASE"

The third encounter with death occurred with later radiation effects, not months but years after the atomic bomb itself, and may be summed up in the scientifically inaccurate but emotionally charged term, "A-bomb disease." The medical condition which has become the model for "A-bomb disease" is leukemia, based upon the increased incidence of this always fatal malignancy of the blood-forming organs.

Psychologically speaking, leukemia—or the threat of leukemia—became an indefinite extension of the earlier "invisible contamination." And individual cases of leukemia in children have become the later counterpart of the "ultimate horror" of the first moments of the experience, symbolizing once more the bomb's desecration of that which is held to be most pure and vulnerable—the desecration of childhood itself. Indeed, Hiroshima's equivalent of an Anne Frank legend has developed from one such case of leukemia in a 12-year-old girl, Sadako Sasaki, which occurred in 1954; her death resulted in a national campaign for the construction of a monument (which now stands prominently in the center of Hiroshima's Peace Park) to this child and to all other children who have died as a result of the atomic bomb.[13]

And just at the time that the incidence of leukemia was recognized as diminishing and approaching the normal, evidence began mounting that the incidence of various other forms of cancer was increasing among survivors—including carcinoma of the stomach, lung, thyroid, ovary, and uterine cervix. Leukemia is a rare disease (even with its increased incidence, only 122 cases were reported in Hiroshima between 1945 and 1959) but cancer is not; and should the trend continue, as appears likely, the increase in cancer will undoubtedly give further stimulus to various elaborations of death symbolism, just as some of these were beginning to decline. Thus on a chronic level of bodily concern, there is again evoked the feeling that the bomb can do anything, and that anything it does is likely to be fatal.

The exact consequences of radiation effects in many other medical areas remain controversial and are still under active investigation by both American and Japanese groups. My concern here, however, is the association in the minds of survivors of any kind of ailment with atomic bomb effects—whether it be fatigue, mild anemia, fulminating leukemia, or ordinary cardiovascular disease; and whether a scientific relationship to radiation effects seems probable, or possible but inconclusive, or apparently nonexistent. And with the continuous publicizing of "A-bomb disease" by the mass media, the ordinary survivor tends to identify himself directly with those said to be afflicted, and with the process of dying. As one man stated, "When I hear about people who die from A-bomb disease . . . then I feel that I am the same kind of person as they."

The psychosomatic dilemma can also take on complicated ramifications. For instance, some survivors develop vague borderline symptoms, inwardly fear that these might be evidence of fatal "A-bomb disease," but resist seeking medical care because they do not wish to be confronted by this diagnosis. When such a pattern occurs in relationship to physical disease, it is usually referred to as "denial of illness"; but here the "illness" being denied is itself likely to be a symbolic product of psychological currents; and the "denial" is a specific response to the death symbolism associated with these currents. Others become involved in lifelong patterns of "A-bomb neurosis"; they become weak and sometimes bedridden, are constantly preoccupied with their blood counts and bodily symptoms, and precariously maintain an intricate inner balance between the need for their symptoms as an expression of various psychological conflicts and the anxious association of these symptoms with death and dying. At best, survivors find themselves constantly plagued with what may be called a nagging doubt about their freedom from radiation effects, and look upon themselves as people who are particularly vulnerable, who cannot afford to take chances.

Thus, at this third level of encounter with death, the sudden "curse" mentioned before becomes an *enduring taint*—a taint of death which attaches itself not only to one's entire psychobiological organism, but through potential genetic defects to one's posterity as well. Although in most cases survivors have been able to live, work, marry, and beget children in more or less normal fashion, they have the sense of being involved in an *endless chain of potentially lethal impairment*, which, if it does not manifest itself in one year—or in one generation—may well make itself felt in the next. Once more elements of guilt and shame become closely involved with this taint. But the whole constellation of which they are part is perceived not as an epidemic-like experience, but as a permanent and infinitely transmissible form of impaired body substance.

## IDENTIFICATION WITH THE DEAD

The fourth level of encounter is a lifelong identification with death, with dying, and with an anonymous group of "the dead." Indeed, the continuous encounter with death, in the sequence described, has much to do with creating a sense of group identity as *hibakusha*, or survivors. This unwanted, or at best ambivalent, identity is built around the inner taint I have discussed, and symbolized externally by disfigurement—that is, by keloid scars, which, although possessed only by a small minority of survivors, have come to represent the stigmata of atomic bomb exposure.

A central conflict of this *hibakusha* identity is the problem of what I have come to speak of as *survival priority*—the inner question of why one has survived while so many have died, the inevitable self-condemnation in the face of others' deaths. *For the survivor can never, inwardly, simply conclude that it was logical and right for him, and not others, to survive. Rather, I would hold, he is bound by an unconscious perception of organic social balance which makes him feel that his survival was made possible by others' deaths: If they had not died, he would have had to; and if he had not survived, someone else would have.* This kind of guilt, as it relates to survival priority, may well be that most fundamental to human existence. Also contributing greatly to the survivor's sense of guilt are feelings (however dimly recalled) of relief, even joy, that it was the other and not he who died. And his guilt may be accentuated by previous death wishes toward parents who had denied him nurturance he craved, or toward siblings who competed for this nurturance, whether this guilt is directly experienced in relationship to the actual death of these family members, or indirectly through unconsciously relating such wishes to the death of any "other," however anonymous.

In ordinary mourning experiences, and in most ordinary disasters, there is considerable opportunity to resolve this guilt through the classical psychological steps of the mourning process. But with the atomic bomb disaster, my impression was that such resolution has been either minimal or at best incomplete. As in other mourning experiences, survivors have identified themselves with and incorporated the dead (both as specific people and as an anonymous concept). But they have found no adequate ideological interpretation—no spiritual explanation, no "reason" for the disaster—that might release them from this identification, and have instead felt permanently bound by it. They have felt compelled virtually to merge with the dead and to behave, in a great variety of ways, *as if* they too were dead. In judging all behavior by the degree of respect it demonstrates toward the dead, they must condemn any effort which suggests, too much self-assertion or vitality—that is, which suggests life.

The *hibakusha* identity, then, in a significant symbolic sense, becomes an identity of the dead—taking the following inner sequence: I almost died; I should have died; I did die, or at least am not really alive; or if I am alive it is impure for me to be so; and anything I do which affirms life is also impure and an insult to the dead, who alone are pure. Of great importance here, of course, is the Japanese cultural stress upon continuity between the living and the dead; but the identity sequence also has specific relationship to the nature of the disaster itself.*

---

* The point of view I wish to suggest about cultural factors in this response—and in other responses to the disaster—is that they are particular emphases of universal tendencies. Here, for instance, sur-

Yet one must not conclude that all survivors are therefore suicidal. This is by no means the case, and I was in fact struck by the tenacity with which *hibakusha*, at all of the stages mentioned, have held on to life. Indeed, I have come to the conclusion that this identification with death—this whole constellation of inwardly experienced death symbolism—is, paradoxically enough, the survivor's means of maintaining life. In the face of the burden of guilt he carries with him, and particularly the guilt of survival priority, his obeisance before the dead is his best means of justifying and maintaining his own existence. But it remains an existence with a large shadow cast across it, a life which, in a powerful symbolic sense, the survivor does not feel to be his own.°

---

vivors' identification with the dead reflects a strong Japanese cultural tendency related in turn to a long tradition of ancestor worship; but this cultural emphasis should be seen as giving a special kind of intensity to a universal psychological pattern. Thus, "extreme situations" such as the Hiroshima disaster, through further intensifying culturally-stressed behavior patterns, throw particularly vivid light upon universal psychological function.

° This "identity of the dead" strikingly resembles findings that have been reported in survivors of Nazi concentration camps. William G. Niederland[14] describes a "psychological imprint" in concentration camp survivors which includes elements of depressive mood, withdrawal, apathy, outbursts of anger, and self-deprecatory attitudes which, in extreme cases, lead to a "living corpse" appearance; this is in turn attributed to their owing their survival to maintaining an existence of a "walking corpse" while their fellow inmates succumbed. Without attempting a full comparison here, one may say that in Nazi concentration camps, in addition to the more prolonged physical and psychological assault upon identity and character structure, the problem of survival priority was more directly experienced: Each inmate became aware that either he or someone else would be chosen for death, and went to great lengths to maintain his own life at the expense of the known or anonymous "other."[15] In the atomic bomb experience, the problem of survival priority was more symbolically evoked, as I have described, though the end result may be psychologically quite similar. Moreover, two additional factors—the fear of aftereffects (of "A-bomb disease"), and the survivors' tendency to relate their experience to the present world threat of nuclear weapons—have the effect of perpetuating their death symbolism and their sense of permanent encounter with death in a manner not true for concentration camp survivors (although the latter have had their anxieties and concerns over survival priority revived and intensified by such reminders of their experience as outbreaks of anti-

GENERAL PRINCIPLES

Through the experiences of Hiroshima survivors we have been thrust into the more general realm of the interrelationship between the anticipation of death and the conduct of life. It is an interrelationship that has been recognized and commented upon by generations of philosophers, though mentioned with surprising infrequency in psychiatric work. There are many signs that this psychiatric neglect is in the process of being remedied,[16] and indeed the significance of problems in this area so impresses itself upon us in our present age that matters of death and dying could well serve as a nucleus for an entire psychology of life. But I will do no more than state a few principles which I have found to be a useful beginning for comprehending the Hiroshima experience, for relating it to universal human concerns, and for examining some of the impact upon our lives of the existence of nuclear weapons. Attempting even this much is audacious enough to warrant pause and examination of some rather restraining words of Freud, which are made no less profound by the frequency with which they have been quoted in the past:

> It is indeed impossible to imagine our own death; and whenever we attempt to do so we can perceive that we are in fact still present as spectators. Hence the psychoanalytic school could venture on the assertion that at bottom no one believes in his own death, or, to put the same thing in another way, that in the unconscious every one of us is convinced of his own immortality.

These words, which were written in 1915, about six months after the outbreak of World War I,[17] have

---

Semitism anywhere in the world and, more importantly, the Eichmann trial). Despite their importance, these psychological problems of death symbolism have too often been overlooked or minimized by psychiatric examiners and other investigators concerned with later behavior of concentration camp victims, and by those studying other forms of persecution and disaster as well.

found many recent echoes. (Maurice Merleau-Ponty, the distinguished French philosopher, has said, "Neither my birth nor my death can appear to me as *my* experiences. . . . I can only grasp myself as 'already born' and 'still living'—grasping my birth and death only as pre-personal horizons."[18])

Profound as Freud's words are, it is possible that psychological investigations of death have been unduly retarded by them. For they represent the kind of insight which, precisely because of its importance and validity, must be questioned further and even transcended. I believe it is more correct to say that our own death—or at least our own dying—is not entirely unimaginable but can be imagined only with a considerable degree of distance, blurring, and denial; that we are not absolutely convinced of our own immortality, but rather have a need to maintain a *sense of immortality* in the face of inevitable biological death; and that this need represents not only the inability of the individual unconscious to recognize the possibility of its own demise but also a compelling universal urge to maintain an inner sense of continuous symbolic relationship, over time and space, to the various elements of life. Nor is this need to transcend individual biological life *mere* denial (though denial becomes importantly associated with it): rather, it is part of the organism's psychobiological quest for mastery, part of an innate imagery that has apparently been present in man's mind since the earliest periods of his history and prehistory. This point of view is consistent with the approach of Joseph Campbell, the distinguished student of comparative mythology, who has likened such innate imagery or "elementary ideas" to the "innate releasing mechanisms" described by contemporary ethologists. It also bears some resemblance to Otto Rank's stress upon man's longstanding need of "an assurance of eternal survival for his self," and to Rank's further assertion that "man creates culture by changing natural conditions in order to maintain his spiritual self."[19]

The sense of immortality of which I speak may be expressed through any of several modes. First, it may be expressed biologically—or, more correctly, biosocially—by means of family continuity, living on through (but in an emotional sense *with*) one's sons and daughters and their sons and daughters, by imagining (however vaguely and at whatever level of consciousness) an endless chain of biological attachment. This has been the classical expression of the sense of individual immortality in East Asian culture, as particularly emphasized by the traditional Chinese family system, and to a somewhat lesser extent by the Japanese family system as well. But it is of enormous universal importance, perhaps the most universally significant of all modes. This mode of immortality never remains purely biological; rather, it is experienced psychically and symbolically, and in varying degree extends itself into social dimensions, into the sense of surviving through one's tribe, organization, people, nation, or even species. On the whole, this movement from the biological to the social has been erratic and in various ways precarious; but some, like Julian Huxley and Pierre Teilhard de Chardin,[20] see it as taking on increasing significance during the course of human evolution. If this is so, individual man's sense of immortality may increasingly derive from his inner conviction, "I live on through mankind."

Second, a sense of immortality may be achieved through a theologically-based idea of a life after death, not only as a form of "survival" but even as a "release" from profane life burdens into a "higher" form of existence. Some such concept has been present in all of the world's great religions and throughout human mythology. The details of life after death have been vague and logically contradictory in most theologies, since the symbolic psychological theme of transcending death takes precedence over consistency of concrete elaboration. Christianity has perhaps been most explicit in its doctrine of life after death, and most demanding of commitment to this doctrine; but intra-Christian debate over interpretation of doctrine has never ceased, with present thought tending toward a stress upon transcendent symbolism rather than literal belief.

Third, and this is partly an extension of the first two modes, a sense of immortality may be achieved through one's creative works or human influences—one's writings, art, thought, inventions, or lasting products of any kind that have an effect upon other human beings. (In this sense, lasting therapeutic influences upon patients, who in turn transmit them to their posterity, can be a mode of immortality for physicians and psychotherapists.) Certainly this form of immortality has particular importance for intellectuals conscious of participating in the general flow of human creativity, but applies in some measure to all human beings in their unconscious perceptions of the legacy they leave for others.

Fourth, a sense of immortality may be achieved through being survived by nature itself: the perception that natural elements—limitless in space and time—remain. I found this mode of immortality to be particularly vivid among the Japanese, steeped as their culture is in nature symbolism; but various expressions of Western tradition (the romantic movement, for instance) have also placed great emphasis upon it. It is probably safe to say—and comparative mythology again supports this—that there is a universal psychic imagery in which nature represents an "ultimate" aspect of existence.

These psychological modes of immortality are not merely problems one ponders when dying; they are, in fact, constantly (though often indirectly or unconsciously) perceived standards by which people evaluate their lives. They thus make possible an examination of the part played by death and death symbolism during ordinary existence, which is what I mean by the beginnings of a death-oriented psychology of life. I shall for this purpose put forth three propositions, all of them dealing with death as a standard for, or test of, some aspect of life.

(1) Death is anticipated as a *severance of the sense of connection*—or the inner sense of organic relationship to the various elements, and particularly to the people

and groups of people, most necessary to our feelings of continuity and relatedness. Death is therefore a test of this sense of connection in that it threatens us with that which is most intolerable: *total severance*. Indeed, all of the modes of immortality mentioned are symbolic reflections of that part of the human psychic equipment which protects us from such severance and isolation.

Another expression of the threat to the sense of connection represented by death is the profound ambivalence of every culture toward the dead. One embraces the dead, supplicates oneself before them, and creates continuous rituals to perpetuate one's relationship to them, and (as is so vividly apparent in the case of the Hiroshima survivors) to attenuate one's guilt over survival priority. But one also pushes away the dead, considers them tainted and unclean, dangerous and threatening, precisely because they symbolize a break in the sense of connection and threaten to undermine it within the living. These patterns too were strongly present in Hiroshima survivors (and can be found in general Japanese cultural practice), although less consciously acceptable and therefore more indirectly expressed. Indeed, in virtually every culture the failure of the living to enact the rituals necessary to appease the dead is thought to so anger the latter (or their sacred representatives) as to bring about dangerous retribution for this failure to atone for the guilt of survival priority.

(2) Death is a test of the meaning of life, of the symbolic integrity—the cohesion and significance—of the life one has been living. This is a more familiar concept, closely related to ideas that have long been put forth in literature and philosophy, as well as in certain psychoanalytic writings of Freud, Rank, and Jung; and it has a variety of manifestations. One is the utilization of a *way or style of dying* (or of anticipated dying) as an epitome of life's significance. An excellent example of this is the Japanese *samurai* code, in which a heroic form of death in battle on behalf of one's lord (that is, a death embodying courage and loyalty) was the ultimate expression of the meaning of

life.[21] Various cultures and subcultures have similarly set up an ideal style of dying, rarely perfectly realized, but nonetheless a powerful standard for the living. The anticipation of dying nobly, or at least appropriately—of dying for a meaningful purpose—is an expression of those modes of immortality related both to man's works (his lasting influences) and his biosocial continuity. And I believe that much of the passionate attraction man has felt toward death can be understood as reflecting the unspoken sense that only in meaningful death can one simultaneously achieve a sense of immortality and articulate the meaning of life.

Apart from dramatically perfect deaths on the *samurai* model, timing and readiness play an important part. Can one visualize, in association with death, sufficient accomplishment to justify one's life? Or has life become so burdensome and devoid of meaning that death itself (whatever the style of dying) seems more appropriate? The latter was the case with a remarkable group of people undergoing surgery recently described by Avery Weisman and Thomas P. Hackett. These "predilection patients" were neither excessively anxious nor depressed, and yet correctly predicted their own deaths. For them, "death held more appeal . . . than did life because it promised either reunion with lost love, resolution of long conflict, or respite from anguish,"[22] and one is led to conclude that this psychological state interacted with their organic pathology and their reactions to surgical procedures to influence significantly the timing of their deaths. Their surrender to death was apparently related to their sense that they could no longer justify their continuing survival.

A classical literary expression of anticipated death as a test of the integrity of one's entire life (and one which has inspired many commentaries) occurs in Tolstoy's "The Death of Ivan Ilyich."[23] Here the protagonist, in becoming aware of the incurable nature of his illness, reviews his past and is tormented by the thought that "the whole arrangement of his life and of his family, and all his social

and official interests, might all have been false," and that
the only authentic expressions of his life have been "those
scarcely noticeable impulses which he had immediately
suppressed." His lament in the face of approaching death
is that of wasted opportunity ("I have lost all that was
given me and it is impossible to rectify it") and existential
guilt: the awareness of the enormous gap between what
he has been and what he feels he might have been. But
his torment disappears through a sudden spiritual revelation, his own capacity to feel love and pity for his wife
and son. And at this point, for Ivan Ilyich, "death" disappears: "Death is finished . . . it is no more!" "Death" has
meant emptiness, the termination of a life without significance; death is transcended through a revelation which
revivifies Ivan Ilyich's sense of immortality by transport-
ing him, even momentarily, into a realm of what he can
perceive as authentic experience, and one in which he
can feel in contact with eternal human values of pity
and love, whether these are derived from a theologically-
defined supernatural source, or from man's own creative
works and influences.

Highly significant in Ivan Ilyich's search for integrity is
his disgust for the lying and evasiveness of those around
him concerning the true nature of his illness (and concerning everything else), his yearning for an end to "this
falsity around and within him [which] did more than
anything else to poison his last days." But his family
members are incapable of acting otherwise, because their
deception is also self-deception, their own need to deny
death; and because they are immersed in their own guilt
over survival priority in relationship to Ivan Ilyich—guilt
made particularly intense by their hypocrisy, lack of love
for him, and relief that death is claiming him and not
them. Similar emotions are present in his colleagues and
friends immediately after his death: "Each one thought
or felt, 'Well, he's dead but I'm alive!'" The one voice of
integrity around Ivan Ilyich is that of a simple peasant
servant who makes no effort to hide from him the fact
that he is dying but instead helps him understand that

death is, after all, the fate of everyone, that "We shall all of us die. . . ." Here the "survivor" lessens the emotional gap between himself and the dying man by stressing their shared destiny; this in turn enables the dying man to see his experience in relationship to the larger rhythms of life and death, and thereby awakens his biologically linked mode of immortality.\*

Very similar in theme to the death of Ivan Ilyich, and probably influenced by it, is the Japanese film *Ikiru* (To Live), made by the accomplished director Akira Kurosawa. The film is also about a dying man who critically reviews his life—a petty official whose past actions have been characterized by bureaucratic evasion, and who overcomes his self-condemnation by an almost superhuman dedication to a final task, the building of a park for children. He thus achieves his sense of immortality mainly by his "works," by the final monument he leaves behind for others (even though surviving fellow bureaucrats, who had actually tried to block the enterprise, claim complete credit for it). This form of immortality is more consistent with East Asian stress upon the contribution to the social order—and with the Japanese *deification of the human matrix*†[25]—than is the Western mode

---

\* Psychiatrists attending dying patients serve functions similar to that of the peasant servant in *The Death of Ivan Ilyich*. Eissler (see Chapter 5, note 19) speaks of helping the patient during the "terminal pathway" to "accomplish the maximum individualization of which he is capable." And Weisman and Hackett similarly stress psychiatric intervention "to help the dying patient preserve his identity and dignity as a unique individual, despite the disease, or, in some cases, because of it." I would hold that achieving these goals depends also upon restoring the patient's sense of immortality through the various modes which have been discussed. Weisman and Hackett[24] describe a "middle knowledge," or partial awareness which patients have of their impending death, and find that patients' relatives (like those of Ivan Ilyich) and attending physicians, because of their own conflicts over death, often have a greater need to deny this outcome than the patient himself. A situation is thus created in which the patient is reluctant to admit his "middle knowledge" to those around him for fear (and it is by no means an inappropriate fear) that they will turn away from him—so that he feels threatened with total severance.

† There are, of course, East Asian forms of spiritual revelation, particularly in Buddhism, but these are of a somewhat different nature;

of spiritual revelation or faith expressed in the Tolstoy story. Moreover, the sequence of the bureaucrat's behavior on discovering he is dying—first his withdrawal into petulant inactivity and then his extraordinary rush of productive energy—provides evidence of the East Asian tendency to deal with problems of despair over life and death by means of a polarity of purposeless withdrawal or active involvement, rather than by the more characteristically Western pattern of self-lacerating inner struggle against the forces creating despair.[26]* But concerning the problems of death and the sense of immortality, the essential message of *Ikiru* is not different from that of "The Death of Ivan Ilyich."

The foregoing may suggest some of the wider meaning of the concept of the survivor. All of us who continue to live while people anywhere die are survivors, and both the word and the condition suggest a relationship which we all have to the dead. Therefore, the Hiroshima survivors' focus upon the dead as arbiters of good and evil, and invisible assigners of guilt and shame, is by no means as unique as it appears at first glance to be. For we all enter into similar commitments to the dead, whether consciously or unconsciously, whether to specific people who lived in the past or to the anonymous dead; or whether these

---

moreover, as Buddhism has moved eastward from its Indian origins—and particularly in its expressions in Japan—it has lost much of its original concern with spiritual revelation, and with doctrine in general, and these have become in various ways subordinated to the sectarian tendencies of the various human groups involved.

* Again the distinction should be understood as reflecting patterns emerging from varying degrees of psychological emphasis rather than absolute difference. Nonetheless, this East Asian, and perhaps particularly Japanese, pattern of despair has considerable importance for such problems as the emotional context of suicide in Japanese life, and the differences in Japanese and Western attitudes toward psychological constellations which the Westerner speaks of as tragedy. In all of these, I believe, Japanese show less of an inner struggle against the forces of nature or man creating the despair, potential suicide, or tragedy, and instead a greater tendency either to acquiesce to these forces or else to cease life-involving activity altogether. The degree of relevance of Western writings on despair for the Japanese situation can best be appreciated by keeping these distinctions in mind.

commitments relate to theological or quasi-theological ideas about ties to the dead in another form of existence, or to more or less scientific ideas about a heritage we wish to affirm or a model we wish to follow. In fact, in any quest for perfection there is probably a significant identification with the imagined perfection of the dead hero or heroes who lived in the golden age of the past. Most of our history has been made by those now dead, and we cannot avoid calling upon them, at least in various symbolic ways, for standards that give meaning to our lives.

(3) And a last proposition: Death, in the very abruptness of its capacity to terminate life, becomes a test of life's sense of movement, of development and change—of sequence—in the continuous dialectic between fixed identity on the one hand and individuation on the other. To the extent that death is anticipated as absolute termination of life's movement, it calls into question the degree to which one's life contains, or has contained, any such development. Further, I would hold that a sense of movement in the various involvements of life is as fundamental a human need, as basic to the innate psychic pattern, as is the countervailing urge toward stillness, constancy, and reduction of tension which Freud (after Barbara Low) called the "Nirvana principle."[27] Freud referred to the Nirvana principle as "the dominating tendency of mental life" and related it to the "death instinct"; but I would prefer to speak instead of polarizing psychic tendencies toward continuous movement and ultimate stillness, both equally central to psychic function. Given the preoccupation with and ambivalence toward death since mankind's beginnings, Freud's concept of the death instinct may be a much more powerful one than his critics will allow. At the same time, it may yield greater understanding through being related to contemporary thought on symbolic process and inner imagery, rather than to older, more mechanistic views on the nature of instinct.[28]

To express this human necessity for a sense of movement, I find it often useful to speak of "self-process" rather than simply of "self." And I believe that the perpetual quest for a sense of movement has much to do with the appeal of comprehensive ideologies, particularly political and social ones, since these ideologies contain organized imagery of wider historical movement, and of individual participation in constant social flux. Yet ideologies, especially when totalist in character, also hold out an ultimate vision of Utopian perfection in which all movement ceases, because one is, so to speak, *there*. This strong embodiment of both ends of the psychic polarity —of continuous movement as well as perfect stillness— may well be a fundamental source of ideological appeal. For in this polarity, ideologies represent a significant means of transcending linear time, and, at least symbolically, of transcending death itself. In the promise of an interminable relationship to the "Movement," one can enter into both a biosocial mode of immortality and a very special version of immortality through man's works, in this case relating to man's symbolic conquest of time. Nor is it accidental that ideologies appear and gather momentum during periods of cultural breakdown and historical dislocation, when there tends to be a sense of cessation of movement and of prominent death symbolism. For central to the revitalizing mission of ideologies is their acting out, in historical (and psychological) context, the classical mythological theme of death and rebirth.[29]

The psychic response to a threat of death, actual or symbolic, is likely to be either that of stillness and cessation of movement, or else of frenetic, compensatory activity. The former was by far the most prominent in the Hiroshima situation, though the latter was not entirely absent. The psychic closing-off which took place right after the bomb fell was, in an important sense, a cessation of psychic motion—a temporary form of symbolically "dying"—in order to defend against the threat of more lasting psychological "death" (psychosis) posed by the overwhelming evidence of actual physical death. And the same may be said of the later self-imposed restraint in living which characterizes the "identity of the dead," an identity whose very stillness becomes a means of carrying on with life in the face of one's commitment to death and the dead. But there were occasional cases of heightened activity, usually of an unfocused and confused variety, even at the time of the bomb. And later energies in rebuilding the city—the "frontier atmosphere" that predominated during much of the postwar period—may also be seen as a somewhat delayed intensification of movement, though it must be added that much of this energy and movement came from the outside.

Can something more be said about these propositions concerning death, and about the various modes of immortality, as they specifically apply to the nuclear age? I believe that from these perspectives we can see new psychological threats posed by nuclear weapons—right now, to all of us among the living.

Concerning the first proposition, that death is a test of our sense of connection, if we anticipate the possibility of nuclear weapons' being used (as I believe we all do in some measure), we are faced with a prospect of being severed from virtually all of our symbolic paths to immortality. In the postnuclear world, we can imagine no biological or biosocial posterity; there is little or nothing surviving of our works or influences; and theological symbolism of an afterlife may well be insufficiently strong in its hold on the imagination to still inner fears of total severance. Certainly in my Hiroshima work I was struck by the inability of people to find adequate transcendent religious explanation—Buddhist, Shinto, or Christian—for what they and others had experienced. This was partly due to the relatively weak state of such theological symbolism in contemporary Japan, but perhaps most fundamentally due to the magnitude of the disaster itself. And whatever the mixed state of religious symbolism in the rest of the world, there is grave doubt as to whether the promise of some form of life after death can maintain symbolic power in an imagined world in which there are none (or virtually none) among the biologically living. This leaves only the mode of immortality symbolized by nature, which I found to be perhaps the most viable of all among Hiroshima survivors—as expressed in the Japanese (originally Chinese) proverb quoted to me by several of them: "The state may collapse but the mountains and rivers remain." And with all the other modes of immortality so threatened, we may raise the speculative possibility that, independent of any further use of nuclear weapons, one outcome of the nuclear age might be the development of some form of natural theology (or at least of a theology in which nature is prominent) as a means of meeting man's innate need for a sense of immortality.

Concerning the second proposition, relating to the meaning and integrity of life, we find ourselves even more directly threatened by nuclear weapons. As many have already pointed out, nuclear weapons confront us with a kind of death that can have no meaning.[30] There is no such thing as dying heroically, for a great cause, in the service of a belief or a nation—in other words, for a palpable purpose—but rather only the prospect of dying anonymously, emptily, without gain to others. Such feelings were prominent among Hiroshima survivors both at the time of their initial immersion in death and during the months and years following it. They could not view their experience as purposeful, in the sense of teaching the world the necessity for abandoning nuclear weapons, but rather saw themselves as scapegoats for the world's evil, "guinea pigs" in a historical "experiment," or else as victims of a war made infinitely more inhuman by the new weapon. Part of their problem was the difficulty they had in knowing whom or what to hate, since, as one of my colleagues put it, "You can't hate magic." They did find in postwar Japanese pacifism an opportunity for organized rechanneling of resentment into a hatred of war itself; this was of considerable importance, but has by no means resolved the issue. The only consistent "meaning" survivors could find in all of the death and destruction around them was in the application of an everyday expression of East Asian fatalism—*"shikataganai"* ("It can't be helped")—which is a surface reflection of a profoundly important psychological tendency toward accepting whatever destiny one is given. But however great the psychological usefulness of this attitude, one can hardly say that it enabled survivors to achieve full mastery of their experience. And concerning the question of the "appropriateness" of anticipated death, Hiroshima survivors were the very antithesis of the "predilection patients" mentioned before: Rather than being ready for death, they found its intrusion upon life to be unacceptable, even absurd; and when seeming to embrace death, they were really clinging to life.

But considering the destructive power of present nuclear weapons (which is more than a thousandfold that of the Hiroshima bomb), and considering the impossibility of a meaningful nuclear death, is not life itself deprived of much of its meaning? Does not nuclear death threaten the deep significance of all of our lives? Indeed, the attraction some feel toward the use of nuclear weapons might be partly a function of this meaninglessness, so that in a paradoxical way they want to "end it all" (and perhaps realize their own end-of-the-world fantasies) as a means of denying the very emptiness of the nuclear death toward which they press. Here the principle of individual suicide as an attempt to deny the reality of death[31] is carried further to encompass nuclear suicide-murder as an attempt to deny the threat to meaningful human existence posed by these weapons.

And finally, in relationship to the propositon of death as a test of life's sense of movement, I think the matter is more ambiguous, though hardly encouraging. There is a sense in all of us, in greater or lesser degree, that nuclear weapons might terminate all of life's movement. Yet there is also, at least in some, a strange intensity and excitement in relationship to the confrontation with danger which nuclear weapons provide; and this, it might be claimed, contributes to a sense of movement in present-day life.

But this exhilaration—or perhaps pseudo exhilaration—
is less a direct function of the nuclear weapons themselves than of the universal historical dislocation accompanying a wider technological revolution. In other words,
there is in our world an extraordinary combination of potential for continuously enriching movement and development of self-process, side by side with the potential for
sudden and absolute termination. This latter possibility,
which I have called the *potentially terminal revolution*,[32]
has not yet been seriously evaluated in its full psychological consequences; and whatever its apparent stimulus to
a sense of movement, one may well suspect that it also
contributes to a profound listlessness and inertia that lurk
beneath.

I am aware that I have painted something less than
an optimistic picture, both concerning the Hiroshima disaster and our present relationship to the nuclear world. Indeed, it would seem that we are caught in a vicious
psychological and historical circle, in which the existence
of nuclear weapons impairs our relationship to death
and immortality, and this impairment of our symbolic
processes in turn interferes with our ability to deal with
these same nuclear weapons. But one way of breaking out
of such a pattern is by gaining at least a dim understanding of our own involvement in it. And in studying the Hiroshima experience and other extreme situations, I have
found that man's capacity for elaborating and enclosing
himself in this kind of ring of destructiveness is matched
only by his equal capacity for renewal. Surely the mythological theme of death and rebirth takes on particular
pertinence for us now, and every constructive effort we
can make to grasp something more of our relationship to
death becomes, in its own way, a small stimulus to rebirth.

# ATOMIC-BOMBED
CHILDREN

## 7

*Perhaps the most significant thing about this little essay on a rather inconspicuous book of Hiroshima children's compositions was that the editors of* The New York Review of Books, *then a struggling new venture with a vision of becoming a major intellectual forum, saw fit to request it for their first issue. That was in February, 1963, and one can now view this interest as an early manifestation of revived concern with subjects like Hiroshima that has come to characterize the radically (and often bitterly) probing world intellectual-cultural climate of the mid- and late sixties.\**

*About the matter of how the bomb looked to the children of Hiroshima, one can say with considerable truth: pretty much as it did to adults, only more so. This is not because children are psychologically the same as adults, but because the extremity of the experience reduced everyone's response to something akin to childlike awe and terror, and in this sense swept away age-specific psy-*

---

\* This revived concern has not always been specific or articulate. And in Chapter 16 I discuss, as part of a particular kind of generation gap, the relatively indirect and inchoate influence of Hiroshima upon present-day student radicals.

*chological distinctions. By their very intensity and con-
creteness the children lay bare the images of guilt,
abandonment, and world-destruction which they shared
with their elders.*

*Of course, there are differences as well, as I suggest in
Death in Life on the basis of interviews with these "children" who have by now become young adults. The special
psychological malleability of the young gave them a better over-all capacity for recovering and moving on from
the experience. On the other hand, their susceptibility to
the assaults of their environment—particularly an assault of such totality—caused them to retain an especially indelible imprint of their atomic bomb exposure,
most specifically of its component of world-destruction.*

*Even more important for us to understand, however, is
that these "children of the A-bomb" are—psychologically,
technologically, and ethically—the children of our era,
our children, ourselves.*

✳          ✳          ✳

The thing we dread really happened in Hiroshima and Nagasaki. One would think that there would be nothing more important for the world to understand than the full consequences of a nuclear holocaust, even in a "miniature" atomic version. Yet everything seems to work against this understanding.

The world resists full comprehension of an event that can only symbolize massive death and annihilation. Even the spate of best-selling novels dealing with the problem, useful and provocative though they may be, are to a considerable extent science fiction alternatives to such comprehension. Not only does the universal denial of death intervene, but few can imagine an event of dimensions which utterly transcend their minds' experience, particularly the ways in which it devastates actual human lives.

Atomic bomb survivors in Hiroshima, on the other hand, have no such limitation. They can imagine it all too well. But they too have great difficulty in conveying to others the nature of what they have been through. They have in fact become suspicious of all attempts to communicate the experience to others, even those of their fellow survivors. Their suspiciousness, as we know, is based partly upon an awareness of having been deceived by groups which, under the banner of peace, have made use of Hiroshima for specific political purposes or narrow self-interest; partly upon a Japanese cultural tendency to be immediately critical of people who take initiative and stand out from the group; and, perhaps most important, upon the feeling, largely unconscious, of atomic bomb survivors that any vigorous self-assertion is, by definition, "impure"—since the only truly "pure" path would

have been joining the dead, with whom they feel themselves so closely identified.

The problem is particularly acute among Hiroshima
writers. Most of those I have spoken to gave me the sense
of neither being able to deal with the atomic bomb adequately as a literary subject nor to let it alone. No subject
took the author more quickly out of the realm of literature
into that of propaganda, however laudable, and they
were aware of this. No subject was more difficult to scale
down to the dimensions of fictional symbols. Indeed,
the question of how much Hiroshima people themselves
should serve as living symbols is perplexing to them as
individuals and to the city administration as well: to what
extent should one leave the experience behind and permit oneself (and one's city) the luxury of looking ahead to
a brighter future? to what extent is there an obligation to
serve as a constant warning to the world, to remain, in
effect, a perpetual symbol of death? The problem defies
solution. And there is no precedent for how a person, or
a city, victimized by an atomic bomb should behave.

Perhaps we should not be surprised that the children
of Hiroshima, through a remarkable collection of compositions,[1] have been called upon to solve this dilemma. After all, we ourselves have grown used to thrusting our
children into the vanguard of national and international
dilemmas and asking them to do our historical dirty
work—whether enrolling them in schools in which their
race is not welcome, or wheeling them in baby carriages
at the head of Ban-the-Bomb parades. And this may be
only appropriate. Children are a universal symbol of purity and vulnerability, and in a world as impure and lethal
as our own, where else are we to turn for a reminder of
ourselves the way we used to be, before our lives became
contaminated by the barbaric instruments from which
we cannot shake ourselves free?

Children bring to their description of any experience
a special kind of honesty, an honesty which has nothing
to do with moral courage but rather is a function of spontaneous emotional expression, of not yet having learned

the conventional ways of ordering their emotions into culturally acceptable responses. To be sure, the compositions which make up this book, written by children from about the ages of ten to eighteen, six years after their experience (they were therefore roughly four to twelve years old when the bomb fell), and at the request of an older educator, cannot always maintain this level of spontaneity. They do not, for instance, describe the full gamut of jealousies and hostilities of which children are capable and which they no doubt felt in relationship to the atomic bomb experience (for this one should perhaps go to the novelist William Golding). But the children express themselves spontaneously enough, indeed quite chillingly.

They describe the sudden shift from normal existence on a hot August morning (playing, eating breakfast, beginning a class at school) to a weird, highly unreal world dominated by death. An eleven-year-old girl, five years old at the time, tells us what she felt when walking the streets with her parents, shortly after the bomb fell, looking for a missing relative: "The fires were burning. There was a strange smell all over. Blue-green balls of fire were drifting around. I had a terrible lonely feeling that everybody else in the world was dead and only we were still alive." And from an older youngster, a seventeen-year-old boy, we get a more drastically comprehensive description:

> . . . the wretched scenes of that time . . . come floating one after another like phantoms before my eyes. . . . The flames which blaze up here and there from the collapsed houses. . . . The old man, the skin of his face and body peeling off like a potato skin, mumbling prayers while he flees . . . the faces of monsters reflected from the water dyed red with blood. They had clung to the side of the water tank and plunged their heads in to drink and there in that position they had died. From their burned and tattered middy blouses I could tell that they were high school girls, but there was not a hair left on their heads; the broken skin of their burned faces was stained bright red with blood. I could hardly believe that these were human faces. . . .

The message could not be more clear. And the same is true in the simple expression of deprivation of a fifth-grade girl, five years old at the time of the bomb:

> Since my house was . . . close to the place where the bomb fell, my mother was turned into white bones before the family altar. . . . Mother is now living in the temple at Nakajima. On the sixth of every month Grandfather and I go to visit Mother. But no matter how much I try I can't remember how Mother looked. All I can see is the Memorial Panel standing quietly there. . . . I think Mother can see me. Mother must be so pleased to see how big I've grown. . . . When I think that for all those years I haven't been able to talk to Mother, I feel so sad. . . . When I see the mothers of my classmates I suddenly feel so lonely that I want to cry.

But there are other places where one must read between the lines to grasp the psychological meaning of what is said—as in the frequent experience of children making their escape while leaving their parents to die in the flaming debris ("Mother was saying urgently, 'Mother will come after you, Set-chan, so you get away first. Now quickly, quickly'"), undoubtedly resulting in a lacerating sense of guilt because of the child's general tendency to feel itself implicated when parents die (having, during moments of resentment, wished them dead, and making no clear distinction between wish and event), and because in this case the parent's death appears (to the child) to have taken place for the specific purpose of its own survival.

Of the dread evoked by the special new feature of nuclear weapons—their radiation effects, immediate and delayed—we get only fragmentary, though strongly suggestive, indications; "Mother . . . touched poison and died rather a long time later." Or: ". . . still people are dying in a way that reminds us of that day. I can't think that those people who died are different people from us. . . ." And:

> I don't know whether this is the reason but because of the poison that was in her [Mother's] body, three or four

days before she died brown spots about a quarter or a half an inch in diameter appeared all over her body, and she became deaf. . . . Then after about two more days on the 9th of September she became a person of another world. After several more days my younger sister died just the way Mother had. And in the latter part of September my other sister died too.

There are suggestions too in these compositions of the more intangible loss of faith in the general structure of human existence, which we know to be prominent among adult survivors. Children expressed this in relationship to the annihilation of the bulwarks of their world ("But my dad is a strong, splendid person—you can't get him with any old thing like an A-bomb. . . . Because he had a bad dose of poison, he died after all, about noon on the 16th") in addition to the demolition of their homes, indeed of their entire city, and the radical interruption in the rhythms of their lives. They felt it also in their awareness that, outside of immediate family members, people did little to help one another at the moment the bomb fell—partly because they simply were unable to, and partly because of the widespread pattern of psychic closing-off. The children themselves experienced the same defense mechanism, as revealed in one of the most powerful passages in the book, a composition of a girl, eleven years old at the time of the bomb, who became confused and immobilized at hearing her mother's cries from under the debris of their house: "Mother's voice died away. I didn't feel especially sad, and I don't even think that I wanted to get her out. I just stood stupidly there in a daze, looking at the underside of the roof."

This breakdown of faith in the human order is also, in older children, related to the sense of having been victims of a horrible experiment ("Hiroshima was being saved as some kind of testing ground"). It is this latter feeling that gives rise to adult survivors' repeatedly expressed complaint of being made "guinea pigs," often mentioned in relationship to participation in American-sponsored studies of the long-range physical effects of irradiation (and encouraged by groups who wished to embarrass America for political reasons), but ultimately derived, as we know, from their awareness of having been the first people in the world to experience nuclear weapons, and, in that sense, of having been historical guinea pigs. It is significant that the same boy (a ninth-grader) who spoke of Hiroshima as a "testing ground" also said, "I think it would have been a good thing if, in the course of this war, atom bombs had fallen on every country and the people of all those countries had experienced the atom bomb"— an expression of the survivor's bitter frustration in his efforts to convince others to take heed of his experience, but also of retaliatory hostility directed not only at America but toward the world as a whole: for having created the bomb, dropped it, and brought about his personal plight. We have seen this fury to exist among adult survivors, particularly where they felt their entire lives to have been blighted by the bomb, but it tends to be attenuated both by Japanese cultural dampening of hostility and by time itself.

Clearly, the children have much to tell us—even if the book is marred by occasionally awkward translation; by an unfortunate jacket, which follows every cliché of jackets of books about Japan, including not only Japanese characters but even a rising sun; and more important, by the lack of background material, perhaps in the form of an introduction, which might have, at least for American readers, done much to enhance understanding of what the children had to say. But these are small matters. The book is an extraordinary document. However its readers —and nonreaders—mobilize themselves against receiving its full impact, something is bound to get through. And this might be a great help to us.

# JEWS AS SURVIVORS

## 8

*Though Hiroshima is more than enough for one investigator, in the course of my work I came to feel that it had to be understood in some relationship to Nazi genocide. The two very different kinds of brutalization turned out to have much in common, psychologically as well as historically (as I stress in the last section of* Death in Life). *What they share is their relationship to the contemporary technology of murder—a relationship which is well recognized in regard to Hiroshima, but much less so in regard to Nazi genocide. Hence my claim in this review essay of Jean-François Steiner's* Treblinka *that much of the public debate about how Jews behaved under the Nazis is misdirected. The recognition that massive technological murder produces certain kinds of more or less predictable group psychological response may be even more painful (especially for Jews, but for non-Jews too) than the kind of moral judgment on victims' behavior that have been so prominent in that debate. My further contention, here and elsewhere, is that the very dimensions of contemporary technology can influence responses to these holocausts and render them in some way unique.*

*By insisting that the general principle of psychic numb-
ing had greater significance for behavior than did any
specific attribute of Jewishness, I am by no means negat-
ing the importance of the specific cultural evolution of a
particular people. Rather I am questioning the deter-
ministic stress upon a static model of national character
which, without ever fully identifying itself, has come to
dominate most of the polemics on the subject. For these
extreme historical experiences make clear that national
character can be a highly misleading concept unless
understood as itself always historically acted upon. Indeed, for answers to certain questions about behavior, issues of national character may be infinitely less important
than the exact nature of the shared event. And that event
can be understood in neither purely external-environ-
mental nor internal-individual terms, but in the kinds of
imagery it (in its material reality) mobilizes within a
group of people.*

*This imagery ultimately develops into what we have
been referring to as shared psychological themes. And
when imagery and themes observable among European
Jews coincide so strikingly with those found among secular and religious-minded Japanese Buddhists and Shin-
toists, then one must ask questions about exactly what
was similar in the lived (if death-dominated) history of
extermination camp and atomic bomb victimization.\**
*In holocaust, and in contemporary life in general (more
dominated by images of holocaust than we realize),
our ways of feeling and behaving seem to be increasingly
influenced by the impact of a history that all men share
upon a psychological potential inherent to the human
condition.*

---

\* Of course there are significant differences in these two "lived histories," and there are other forms of survival—of the plagues of the
Middle Ages, of natural catastrophes of various kinds, and even of
ordinary deaths of people close to one—in which there emerge psychological themes similar to those of Hiroshima and Treblinka. What
I am suggesting, as I do in *Death in Life*, is that we need to pay
attention to the ways in which mid-twentieth-century technology contributes to and alters the general psychohistorical themes of death and
survival.

*I wrote this review after completing my Hiroshima book, and I had by then learned to pay close attention to the survivor's intense concern with historical record. Relevant to this concern is the distinction (and confusion) between a somewhat solipsistic notion of psychic truth and a more integrated idea of historical actuality. Erikson has suggested that Freud's exclusive stress upon the former (inner symbolism more or less divorced from external events) interfered with the therapy of his famous early patient, Dora, who was seeking, above all, the latter.* Erikson includes under historical actuality the individual's sense of active involvement in specific events: the inner state retains its importance but in connection with, not isolation from, the world in which it operates. In this sense the historical record, whether of events humble or great, has considerable importance for the individual's continuing life process. And that importance is enormously magnified by the survivor's need to formulate and render significant his death immersion (as discussed both in this essay and in Death in Life).*

*Eugene Genovese, from the standpoint of a historian, puts the problem this way: "The revolutionary task of intellectuals is . . . not to invent myths, but to teach each people its particular contradictory truth. . . . Until a people can and will face its own task, it has no future." Nor is the principle entirely new: one thinks particularly of Collingwood's idea that each generation of historians must re-create, inevitably in its own image but ideally with maximum intellectual discipline, man's over-all historical past. All of this confirms the principle, suggested by Freud, that the psychological recovery of the individual and collective past is a fundamental means of defining the present self and of shaping its future destiny. For survivors of Treblinka and Hiroshima this principle is no less true but infinitely more painful in operation.*

*       *       *

* Dora's celebrated case of hysteria established that concept within the psychoanalytic literature, and was one of the great building-blocks of psychoanalysis itself.[1]

Too much discussion of behavior under Nazi persecution has been focused on "Jewish character" and not enough on the more general question of twentieth-century holocaust. Yet concentration camp survivors have much in common with atomic bomb survivors I have worked with in Hiroshima, despite the very great differences in the two experiences. One way to move beyond the confused polemic that has surrounded the still disturbing issue of Jewish response to the Nazi program of extermination is to relate it to the psychology of massive death immersion. Such a perspective helps us to approach Jean-François Steiner's alternatingly brilliant and misleading account of a "model death camp" and of the rising of its inmates in armed rebellion.[2]

In first depicting the Jews' failure to resist being herded off to Treblinka, Steiner emphasizes their historical conditioning through persecution in Lithuania and elsewhere in Eastern Europe ("Suffering was their business"), as well as the deceptiveness of Nazi manipulations ("based on a rather shrewd understanding of the Jewish [speculative] intelligence"). But probably more important than their taking advantage of any specifically Jewish traits was the constant aura of death the Nazis imposed by means of their pre-camp brutalizations. For a central feature of anyone's encounter with death, most characteristically during massive holocaust, is a cessation of feeling, a desensitization or psychic numbing.

We know how Hiroshima survivors recall being fully aware, immediately after the bomb, of the grotesque scene of dead and dying around them, but of very quickly finding themselves feeling no emotion whatsoever—how one woman experienced what she called "a paralysis of the mind." Such psychic numbing includes not only elements of denial ("If I see nothing, then death is not taking place"), but the severance of ordinary human bonds of identification ("I see you dying, but I am not related to you or to your death"). It can be a highly useful defense against death anxiety, the terror of contemplating one's own annihilation; and against death guilt, or self-condemnation for remaining alive while others die. But like all defenses, it can overstep itself and then become in itself a kind of dying; it can produce the "death-like submission" Steiner describes, and thereby facilitate the Nazi program of "death in two stages: you put men to sleep, then you kill the sleepers." Partly aware they were being annihilated and strongly resisting this awareness, Jewish communities would either ignore or treat with great hostility carriers of bad news and would-be resistors. Steiner's picture of the Jewish Councils as aiding the Nazis' deception and organization is close to Hannah Arendt's, but one must also recognize that the Councils were serving as a kind of repository for *all* Jewish numbing—that is, for the idea that submission, hard work, or compliance with some as yet unfathomed system could preserve lives.

Concerning behavior in the camps themselves, Steiner has been unfairly criticized for his unsparing depiction of Jewish participation in the Nazi program of murder, though the same thing has been previously recorded by many camp survivors, much more brutally in fact by Tadeusz Borowski in his *This Way for the Gas, Ladies and Gentlemen*. To some extent the relationship between Nazis and Jews followed conventional patterns of victimizer and victim: the former establishes his sense of omnipotent conquest of death by means of rendering the latter, with whom he can compare himself, ahuman and death-tainted. What was extraordinary was the nature of the Nazis' project—the systematic murder of millions of Jews—*and the extent of psychic numbing this project required of both victim and victimizers*. Steiner is superbly ironic in his evocation of the mentality of the

Nazis and the extremity of the numbing *they* required for their task. In order to circumvent technologically the intolerable guilt of direct killing ("it was not the will of the victims that was an issue, but the human inadequacy of the executioners"), they found it "necessary to invent a killing machine." And we read how gas van gave way to gas chamber as "engineering took over where good will left off. An almost perfect system had been created. A new world was about to be born."

This mentality finds full expression in the grotesque perfectionism of Kurt Franz (Franz Stangl), the head of the Treblinka camp. But in emphasizing Franz's psychological astuteness in manipulating the Jews, Steiner overlooks the extent to which these manipulations might have been necessary to the victimizers for maintaining their numbing. The false train station constructed at Treblinka (synthetic ticket window, painted first- and second-class waiting rooms, clock fixed at 3 P.M.) was something more than merely a means of deceiving Jewish arrivals until the last possible moment: it maintained an "as-if" situation for the SS as well, an image of a peaceful town in an ordinary world of decent men. The Nazis' absolute focus upon technology and technique took on a numbed logic of madness: pride and dedicated efforts to carry out the seemingly impossible task of burning eight hundred thousand bodies within a feasible time schedule, eventually solved by a "specialist" applying the principle of "using the good ones to burn the bad ones"—the good ones being old bodies, fat ones, women, and children, because these are the most inflammable. (One can say that related patterns of numbing, though with greater technological distancing and easier ideological justification, have surrounded the making, testing, and using of nuclear weapons.) Then, in the Nazis' pagan victory celebration (on solving the corpse-burning problem) we encounter momentary evidence of their special aberration, of the madness beneath the numbing. But it is well to keep in mind that the vision of immortalization through killing which they carried to such a macabre extreme—

of murder for a "sacred purpose"—remains an active one in many quarters, and can be found in the conspiratorial images of such groups as the American Radical Right.

Steiner is a little less reliable in his representation of the numbing of Jewish inmates. At times he seems almost to romanticize the psychological process taking place by attributing it to a unique spiritual commitment to survival, and insisting that men raised entirely on Jewish culture are "inaccessible to despair." At other times he is closer to the truth when he tells how the Jewish inmate "ceased to be a man," how "in order to survive . . .[he] drowned his own sensibility." Here too I was reminded of Hiroshima survivors—of one who stayed for some time after the bomb fell in a damaged railroad station filled with dead and dying, and told me "we were just like sleep-walkers," and of Dr. Michihiko Hachiya's classic description of survivors who "walked silently toward . . . the distant hills . . . like automatons . . . the exodus of a people who walked in the realm of dreams." Underlying this generalized atmosphere of numbing encountered in massive holocaust is an imposed image of the "end of the world," together with a lingering sense that the principles governing life and death have been violated once and for all and that one has, even as a victim, participated in this violation.

Jews were psychically driven into one of two directions of numbing: that of the "walking corpse" or *"Muselmänner"* (so named by prisoners under the mistaken notion that absolute submissiveness was characteristic of Moslem psychology), a state so extreme that, as Primo Levi once put it, "One hesitates to call them living: one hesitates to call their death death"; or else a much more integrated state characteristic of privileged Jewish prisoners who (we learn from Steiner) "know nothing [and] act as if death does not exist." In this last pattern numbing is an aid to survival, while in the first its extreme form is a surrender (and prelude) to death. No inmate could avoid elements of one or both of these states, which in fact tended to overlap with each other. Even such things as

gallows humor and eroticism (which had their counterparts in Hiroshima also) could reinforce numbing: the
first by assuming what Steiner calls "professional attitudes" of corpse-carriers as a means of warding off the
realization of what one was actually doing ("Hey,
Moshe! don't eat so much. . . . Think of us who'll have to
carry you!"); and the second resembling the orgies taking place at the time of the plagues of the Middle Ages
and denying the pervasiveness of death by means of a
pseudo-affirmation of life.

What eventually emerged was a form of *collaborative
numbing*, which was perhaps the unique psychological
feature of the concentration camp experience. It was
maintained through a tenuous but functional equilibrium
in the victimizer-victim relationship. This equilibrium
required sufficient brutalization to keep the Jews in a
numbed, nonresistive state and at the same time to permit
victimizers their sense of omnipotence, but it had to stop
short of either producing too many *Muselmänner* (which
at first actually occurred and greatly interfered with
getting the work done) or interfering with guards' own
numbing by making them aware of the consequences of
their actions. The key to collaborative numbing was a
gruesome work ethic, the psychological significance of
which has not been adequately appreciated. In addition
to their own conscientiousness in carrying out their project, victimizers succeeded in conveying to victims the literal message that "work equaled life." The gas chamber
became "the factory" and everything was organized along
assembly-line principles. Precisely this numbing focus
upon "work" obscures the issue of "works." Never has the
distinction been more critical.

Contributing to collaborative numbing was a series of
everyday "games" ending in death and humiliation for
Jews, a rather dramatic festival of arts and sports staged
by Franz with performing musical, literary, and boxing
talents drawn from among the prisoners, and a strange but
significant pattern of "socializing" between victimizers
and victims which began to take place toward the end.

Steiner tells us that the two groups were a bit stiff with each other until "the ice was broken," and ironically points up the absurd collaboration involved throughout: "This did not prevent the SS from killing the Jews during the day, but the prospect of having to part company soon mellowed them a little. They had been together for such a long time, they had so many memories in common; and this camp was a kind of joint production." The "as if" situation, then, was a collaborative phenomenon of denial and numbing (" 'The gas chambers? What gas chambers? The smell? What smell?' "); even concerning the approaching end of Treblinka itself "everyone . . . pretended not to know it." What this meant for Jewish prisoners in general was that "all of their activities . . . contributed to the same end: the death of their people."

But not quite. Despite everything, the Jews rebelled, and Steiner's central purpose in writing the book is to tell the story of their rebellion. Since all action depends upon images, rebels of any kind must have the capacity to imagine the overturning of their immediate world. Jews were for the most part denied this capacity by the numbing imposed upon them—hence the wisdom of the statement attributed to a physician-prisoner, when discussing the possibilities of fellow inmates joining in a rebellion: "First they will have to come to terms with death." What he meant was the necessity not only of taking risks but of confronting the true nature of the environment. In this sense there may be truth in Steiner's claim that suicides among those facing almost certain death represented a "first affirmation of freedom" in that prisoners were assuming a certain amount of autonomy and "had ceased to be perfect slaves"—though we also wonder to what extent this is a Camus-like reconstruction of what must have been a dismal and dispiriting scene.

In explaining the extraordinary transformation of numbed prisoners into organized rebels, Steiner emphasizes one overriding principle: that of "bearing witness," of sending "a message to the future." As one dying prisoner puts it, "What we need is a . . . victory of the dead

. . . a victory and witnesses to tell about it." The rhetorical tone with which he has prisoners express this principle has led some reviewers to reject it, and to emphasize more conventional explanations for rebellion—feelings of hatred and revenge. But what Steiner is getting at, correctly I believe, is the sense of special mission characteristic of survivors (or those who must survive by proxy), the need to render significant the deaths they have seen. Bearing witness has been of great importance for concentration camp and atomic bomb survivors in carrying out what is for many a permanent task, the inner formulation of their experiences in a way that restores balance to death and life. In Hiroshima this mission became quickly tied in with the elimination of nuclear weapons and the quest for world peace. With concentration camp survivors it has been actively associated with the establishment of a Jewish State in Israel, images of which, Steiner tells us, existed during incarceration and served as inspiration for rebellion. In this way the formulations of survivors become related to the reassertion of what Steiner calls the "immortal community," but he is wrong in his implication that this is a specifically Jewish need or accomplishment. Rather, the quest for such symbolic immortality, for living on through the larger groups and images to which one is attached, is part of a compelling universal urge, and in fact man's only way of coping with the fact of death.

For Treblinka inmates the idea of carrying out such a mission through rebellion was strongly reinforced by news of the Warsaw Ghetto uprising, as well as by witnessing the unusually vicious treatment given its participants when they arrived at the camp. But the leaders of the uprising, one suspects, tended to be less susceptible to numbing than did most—whether because they had experienced less brutalization, or because they were the kinds of Jews whose assertiveness had led them to reject the submissive stance of ghetto life and make their way in the larger world.

The final stimulus to rebellion in Treblinka was, of course, the mounting evidence that the camp and all of

its inmates were headed for extinction. One may therefore say that the anticipation of individual death merged
with the fear of collective disappearance; the rebellion became a means, as Steiner suggests, of transcending an
ultimate sense of nothingness.

Steiner's problem with the book resembles that of the
prisoners themselves: the nature of *his* historical record.
Certainly his relationship to Treblinka—his father died
there—is a valid reason for undertaking a work of this
kind. Nor can his impulse to vindicate his father's memory
serve as an adequate reason for dismissing the product as
a mere act of filial piety. But the form he has chosen gets
the book into deep trouble. It is a kind of "nonfiction
novel," which aims at both documentary accuracy (based
upon study of written records and interviews of survivors
of the Treblinka rebellion) and the novelist's imaginative
freedom (in tone, general details, and especially in conversational dialogue). And to these contradictory pulls is
added a somewhat histrionic romanticization of Jews and
Jewishness which both oversimplifies the issues surrounding the rebellion and renders the conversations of its plot-
ters stiff and unreal.

About midway through the book one begins to lose faith
in the narrative, both in the historian's accuracy of docu-
mentation and the novelist's psychic truth—while at
the same time retaining admiration for Steiner's frequently
impressive insights. It is with considerable relief that
one encounters such a statement as "The oral tradition of
Treblinka has not preserved what Berliner did that morning"—because then one at least knows where one stands.
But the relief is accompanied by the distressing uncertainty about whether that same oral (or written) tradition
had actually preserved all the other details put forth.
And when, toward the end of the book, a long passage is
quoted from written testimony describing a key moment
in the rebellion, one reads it with both fascination and
reassurance, so much so that one is a bit reluctant to return to the author's less authoritative voice.

The blurring of assumptions contained in the "nonfiction novel" is undoubtedly part of the general ambiguity surrounding contemporary standards of reality. But Steiner also struggles with the more specific problem of re-creating twentieth-century holocaust. Japanese attempting to produce what is called "A-bomb literature," like their Western counterparts who write of the concentration camp experience, find their creative powers blunted by the unmanageable dimensions of technological violence, the absurd or disconnected deaths, and by a particularly intense form of creative guilt. For whether or not the writer (or artist in general) is actually a survivor of one of the two holocausts, he experiences a survivor-like sense of being bound to the dead. Haunted by what he perceives as their judgments, he is likely to impose upon himself an impossible standard of literal re-creation of "how things were," a kind of sacred historical truth, which leads him to what might be called the documentary fallacy; or else a need to glorify the dead and deny them the dignity of their limitations.

Steiner is prevented from fully transcending these difficulties by certain assumptions he makes and by the form he has chosen. As a second-hand documentary his account cannot have the immediacy of Yoko Ota's and Dr. Hachiya's memoirs of the atomic bomb, or the early concentration camp writings of David Rousset, Primo Levi, Elie Wiesel, or Bruno Bettelheim; and he makes no attempt to apply the quality of documentary imagination which Alain Resnais did in a different medium in *Night and Fog*. Nor does he embark on the kind of literary experiment which might be equal to the subject novelistically, as, for instance, in Piotr Rawicz's *Blood from the Sky*, Jorge Semprun's *The Long Voyage*, or André Schwarz-Bart's *The Last of the Just.** 

Yet Steiner does succeed in doing something that no one else writing about concentration camps has up to now been able to do. By telling the story of one of them, he

° I discuss problems of creative response, as well as most of the writers and artists listed here, in *Death in Life* (especially in Chapters 10 and 11).

powerfully and simultaneously evokes two seemingly in-
compatible actualities: the combined Nazi and Jewish
numbing associated with mass murder, and the remarkable accomplishment of a few hundred prisoners in breaking out of that numbing to rebel and produce a handful
of survivors to tell the tale. His own mission of re-establishing Jewish courage has undoubtedly led him to exaggerate the importance of the rebellion in relationship to the
more fundamental question of the Nazi extermination
project; and one would have wished for the disciplined
integrity of form which this kind of extreme event demands of historian and novelist alike. But the rebellion
the book depicts has considerable significance, and not
only for Jews, because it raises questions about human
possibilities that must be taken into account as we continue to examine man's ways of coping with the unlimited
dimensions of twentieth-century killing.

# III

DECEPTIONS
OF
WAR
AND
PEACE

# AMERICA IN VIETNAM—
# THE COUNTERFEIT
# FRIEND

## 9

*I wrote this essay immediately after returning to America (in August, 1967) from a week in Vietnam, and the sense of outrage I experienced during every moment in that country had in no way abated. It has not abated yet.*

*I had not especially wanted to go to Vietnam. I would have preferred to return to the United States directly from Tokyo (where I had been conducting follow-up interviews with former students) or from Hong Kong (where I had been looking into the Great Proletarian Cultural Revolution). But I felt I simply could not, in good conscience, not go there. I was, after all, in that part of the world, and I knew how important it was for critics of the war to acquire additional first-hand information, especially as gathered by someone with a certain amount of knowledge of East Asia. My wife, who had been to Vietnam as a correspondent years before, encouraged the side of me that knew I had to go. She went with me, of course, contributed greatly to my understanding of things, and later recorded her own impressions.[1]*

*We both found Vietnam uniquely disturbing. Over the previous fifteen years we had been in almost every kind of*

*Asian environment, but we had never before been witness
to an American presence so self-deluded (the article's
original title was "The Circle of Deception") and morally
compromised. (Had we witnessed the last mainland
days of Nationalist China, we might have found that atmosphere similar; even on Taiwan it has some resemblance.)*

*Relationships between Vietnamese and Americans were
(are) mutually resentful and mutually corrupting. And the
sense of entrapment and despair of articulate Vietnamese
was matched by the fortress mentality (without even the
possibility of an effective fortress) of Americans. The latter felt virtually everyone around them to be either an
enemy, a potential enemy, or at least an unreliable friend.
(The depth of these feelings in American soldiers was later
conveyed to me very vividly by Dr. Gary Tischler, who
spent a year in Vietnam as an Army psychiatrist, during
a seminar he gave on his observations there.) Yet whatever one's feelings about the American military-adminis-
trative presence in Vietnam, every non-Vietnamese in the
South, however brief or long his stay, becomes profoundly
dependent upon it—for everyday needs of various kinds,
for proper legal status, for the all-important function of
transportation, and indeed for remaining safe and alive
(as much as one can depend upon anyone in Vietnam for
that).*

*I myself was appalled by what my "protectors"—my
countrymen—were doing to that nation. The anxious discomfort I experienced was compounded of horror at just
this, as well as at the possibility of an even larger war
(with North Vietnam or China); of a sense of guilt toward
not only the Vietnamese but also in a way toward the
American authorities because of so strongly resenting their
actions while having to be so dependent upon them; and
of a certain amount of simple fear, which I probably shared
with every Westerner (and most Vietnamese) in South
Vietnam. My resentment was never much below the surface, but was usually (not always) at least partially suppressed—whether because of the dependency upon*

*Americans, the need to gain information from them, or the realization that there was no point to directing rage at them as individuals.*

That week was as condensed as it was informative. Wishing to learn as much as I could in a short period of time, I decided to stay in Saigon and do what I knew best how to do, talk to people. (My wife, in contrast, spent most of the time traveling about the country, visiting hospitals and investigating the problem of civilian casualties.) It turned out that educated Vietnamese were both easy to meet (via introductions by certain trusted Americans and then by one another) and eager to express themselves—not too many Americans had been interested in listening to them, and the climate of repression was such that they found it highly inadvisable to air their views publicly. Over breakfasts, lunches, dinners, drinks, or during mid-morning or mid-afternoon visits to universities, homes, hospitals, or offices of one kind or another, I found myself immersed in animated conversation (mostly in English, but with occasional reversions to French), now with a young political scientist or writer, now with a neurologist or medical administrator, now with an intellectual politician or a not so intellectual one. The Americans I spoke to (mostly civilians working in various official administrative capacities) tended to be only slightly more guarded; some were interesting men with whom I might have felt much in common were it not for the barrier created by their mission. In the course of all this, often over late drinks, I discussed my impressions with a few American journalists. They included R. W. Apple, Jr., of The New York Times, *who was himself on the verge of producing some of the most thoroughgoing and effective reports on the inconsistencies of the American presence in Vietnam;* Richard Harwood of The Washington Post, *by his confession a hawk-turned-dove, unique in his concern about Vietnamese opinion, especially that of intellectuals;* and William Touhy of The Los Angeles Times, *immensely knowledgeable, wavering in his overall judgment of the situation but full of uniquely reveal-*

ing (in my opinion, damning) anecdotes about American self-deception. Their journalistic skepticism—at its best, a form of suppressed idealism—was of enormous help to me, not only in providing concrete evidence disproving official American claims but in forcing me to defend and deepen the fundamental criticism of American imagery and behavior I was struggling to evolve.

The few rewarding experiences in Vietnam had to do with moments of mutual understanding about dreadful events, whether with Americans or Vietnamese. There was the continual sensual pleasure afforded by the extraordinary beauty of so many Vietnamese women, perhaps especially highlighted by the crumbling context in which they were observed. And with Vietnamese in general there were a number of poignant surprises.

I recall particularly one rather remarkable dinner party given for me by a Vietnamese colleague. The entire atmosphere—food, language, and conversational style— was French-bourgeois. (A typical subject was a comparison of current favorites among Paris comedians, about whom I had to admit my ignorance; and when I tried to tell them instead something about Lenny Bruce and the serious trends in American humor he exemplified, I had the impression my remarks might have been considered a little out of place.) After dinner the group assembled in a modest but comfortable living room, and when someone handed the host a violin, I envisioned the situation deteriorating further into a polite little musicale.

But the violinist in question performed differently than I had expected. Revealing himself to be a composer, he first plucked out a little love song he had written in his youth, and then a lively march, of which he said rather impishly, "They still play this one quite a bit in Hanoi. If you listen to the radio, you can hear it." Only later, when talking to me alone, did he explain what he had meant. He had written the march during his student days in Hanoi, shortly after joining the Communist movement; had spent two years in the jungle with the Viet Minh doing medical work, numbering among his patients such dignitaries as General Giap; and had left the movement not because of any basic disagreement with its program but because of a sense that, coming as he did from a well-to-do family closely associated with the French, he could never be fully trusted. Now highly critical of the American presence in Vietnam (along lines I discuss in the paper) and yet having special reason to fear a Communist victory, he was one of many I met who had no clear avenue of hope.

All this left me with exactly the kind of burden I had anticipated in my initial reluctance to go to Vietnam. Proceeding from Saigon to Cape Cod (with just an overnight stop in Tokyo to pick up our children and to say a few good-byes), we experienced a strange nightmare-to-paradise transition which brought relief but not joy. Indeed the transition could not be inwardly accomplished —and I felt I had no right to return to more contemplative professional pursuits (even if they themselves were hardly of the most joyous nature)—until I had succeeded in making some kind of statement about what I had seen. Not only did I believe I could contribute usefully to the debate on Vietnam, but, as I now realize, I had a survivor-like sense that the only way to absorb such an "extreme experience" was to give it form and significance for myself and for others.

Though the form I have chosen is clearly polemical, I would also claim for it some of the intellectual discipline mentioned earlier as necessary for a psychohistorical approach. I have made clear that I do not advocate the substitution of emotion for reasoned argument, but this does not mean that there is no place for a scholar's indignation. Indeed, our country's behavior on too many occasions, and in relationship to too many problems, has been such that we are all rendered collaborators in evil unless we find ways of blending anger with reason in protest and renewal.

\*            \*            \*

It is becoming more and more apparent that the American presence in Vietnam is enclosed in a circle of deception. Distorted perceptions, false interpretations, and misguided actions have been reinforcing one another in a self-defeating process. During a recent revisit to South Vietnam, I had a chance to talk at some length with various articulate Vietnamese and Americans. Their conflicts revealed to me some of the psychological and historical dilemmas underlying our ever deteriorating military and political involvement. The Tet offensive of early 1968 suddenly exposed this deception—reaching into every aspect of American activities in Vietnam—for all who had eyes to see.*

I

Beginning with the military situation itself, one could not help but note an element of George Orwell's "Newspeak" in official American versions: "progress" means disintegration, and "victory" stalemate. American correspondents told me how they would over the course of a year accompany American troops three or four times through the same woods or highlands, each time be informed of the impressive number of Viet Cong killed, only

---

* Our relationship to Vietnam has, of course, been altered by the initiation of peace negotiations in Paris in May, 1968—and it is quite possible that before long there will be further modifications in the war itself, or even a cease-fire. But as of mid-1969, I would say that virtually everything described in the essay still prevails. (It is important to keep in mind that the peace negotiations themselves could not begin until America agreed to stop bombing North Vietnam.) So I have refrained from updating the essay, and have left intact my original impressions and interpretations.

to end up finding things back the way they were with nothing really settled, nothing held, nothing secure. Indeed, the word "stalemate," so repugnant to our President and Secretary of State, if anything gives us the benefit of the doubt. It is difficult to estimate how much Americans promulgating this Newspeak believe in it, but any circle of deception involves a considerable amount of self-deception.

Everybody seems to agree that a major cause for these difficulties is the fact that the Vietnamese Army won't fight. When one inquires why they won't fight, Americans have a quick answer: "Lack of leadership." This explanation is put forth as though one were discussing a large machine in which a few key gears (leaders) were missing, with the implications that if *we* (Americans) could only "instill leadership" in *them* (Vietnamese), they would then fight and all would be well. This *mechanistic fallacy* pervades much of American thinking about Vietnam in general, and is a means of dismissing the more fundamental human dimensions of the problem (the National Liberation Front and the North do not seem to "lack leadership"). Americans are reluctant to look beyond the immediate "operation" into the chasm, preferring to reinforce at every point the circle of deception.

The truth is that South Vietnam is a society so dislocated and fragmented that no amount of American technology or technique, military or rehabilitative, can put it together again. The dislocation goes back at least two centuries, and includes pre-colonial, colonial, and post-colonial social conflicts, as well as certain "post modern" confusions now found in all societies. The present war accelerates processes of breakdown at every level, especially in its annihilation of village life, the main source of social stability in Vietnam. And what is too often overlooked is the extension of these disintegrative tendencies into the realm of idea systems and images. There has been a breakdown not only of social institutions but of the shared symbols necessary to ordered existence—symbols defining rhythms of life and death, group loyalties, and the nature of reality. This "desymbolization" reaches deeply into the individual mental life and undermines collective efforts of all kinds, including that of fighting a war. Whatever success Communism has had as a cohesive social force in the North or the South has resulted from its capacity to provide meaningful new images and symbols, or to revitalize old ones.

While all South Vietnamese are involved in this process of desymbolization, you begin to appreciate its national consequences when you observe some of the convolutions in the lives and thoughts of would-be leaders.

One former high-ranking diplomat I spoke to had a background of diverse intellectual and political allegiances (he had lived in China, Japan, and the United States); of long and close association with Diem; and of continuing leadership in a prominent religious sect (which itself combined mystical, clan-territorial, and political elements). He could speak from experience when he described to me the last thirty years of Vietnamese history as "nothing but explosions." But he went on to characterize all existing political systems—"so-called American democracy," European parliamentary methods, and the various kinds of communism and socialism—as inadequate for Vietnamese needs: "We have to find our own way." He added somewhat vaguely, "These days all ideologies are a little outmoded." I was left with the impression of a man both knowledgeable and confused, in whom the pulls of old Vietnamese and contemporary international images had resulted in a facile end-of-ideology perspective which covered over a more fundamental absence of any viable ideas at all.

Another prominent public figure, after a strikingly uninhibited account of pervasive governmental corruption, including manipulation of the then impending elections, considered the elections nonetheless hopeful because "people are learning to play the game of the constitution." Again I had the sense of a post-modern distrust of all thought systems—of the whole thing being a "game" or "scenario" (perhaps a "bag") which had to be played out but was not to be taken seriously—in a man who, like his country, could construct little that was cohesive out of damaged old goods and tarnished new ones. (He did not remain hopeful when the elections were over: he condemned them as fraudulent.)

The American response to Vietnamese dislocation and emptiness is more and bigger war. And this, of course, means more deception, more claims that things are getting better and that progress is being made.

I found myself reminded of two rather terrifying psychological analogies. First, the tendency of people committed to certain beliefs, when circumstances have proven their beliefs to be wrong, to refuse to surrender them but instead embrace them with renewed intensity while rationalizing their error. The second, based upon my own work relating to death imagery, is that men are most apt to kill or wish to kill when they feel themselves symbolically dying—that is, overcome by images of stasis, meaninglessness, and separation from the larger currents of human life.

## II

To pursue an understanding of the circle of deception is to examine more closely the nature of the American presence in Vietnam. One is immediately confronted with the theme of the impotence of American power—of the Blind Giant. This is not to say that American men and machines count for naught, but rather that America-in-Vietnam, despite its vast technological and bureaucratic dimensions (one must go to Vietnam to grasp these), is incapable, *in this situation*, of doing what it says it is doing or wants to do (defend the South against Communism, help strengthen democracy, defeat the NLF and the North or weaken them sufficiently to cause them to seek peace). Here the circle of deception works something like this: The giant has been called forth, fully equipped; one cannot admit that he is helpless. But the giant *is* helpless, not because he lacks strength or even intelligence, but because, in a psychological and historical sense, his vision is profoundly impaired. Unable to "see" the actual dimensions of the environment in which he finds himself, he resorts to blind technological saturation of it with his destructive fire-power; unable to see the enemy, he shoots blindly at elusive figures who might just as well be his wards or allies.

Yet in another sense the giant seems all-powerful. There is often the feeling in South Vietnam that if America does not take care of things, nothing gets done—as well as a tendency among a dislocated people, new to Western technology, to lean on America more and more to do everything. What is beginning to become clear, however, is that Vietnamese immobilization is not relieved but increased by the giant's presence. This is so because of an unhealthy relationship between Vietnamese and Americans around psychological themes of power and dependency—or what I call a *situation of counterfeit nurturance*. Colonialism is a classical example of such a situation, but one finds the pattern also existing in association with American aid to underdeveloped countries, in Negro-white relationships within the United States, and in virtually all programs of social welfare attempted anywhere. It can develop around any one-sided relationship, and consists of feelings of special need on the part of the weak, together with strong resentment of help offered because the help is perceived as a confirmation of weakness. The key problem is the absence of a sense of autonomy—indeed, the perpetuation of a situation which makes autonomy impossible.

I constantly came upon precisely this combination of dependency and antagonism in South Vietnamese feelings toward Americans. The sense of help received as counterfeit was enhanced by the fact that the help was directly accompanied by broadening areas of destruction. Moreover, Vietnamese hold the most extreme images of Americans. They see them sometimes as an omnipotent force, a hidden manipulative hand behind everything, and at other times as ineffectual innocents repeatedly duped by a tough enemy. In a situation of counterfeit nurturance, a balanced view of Americans becomes impossible; and many aspects of the American presence perpetuate this psychological imbalance.

The majority of Americans are new to the country and relate to it mainly on the basis of the present war. One may say that for them there are "two Vietnams" in a sense different from that usually meant by the term, one of fighting and killing (the predominant American contingent concerned in one way or another with military operations), and the other with healing and rebuilding. This "second Vietnam" is made up of such people as physicians, agriculturalists, and providers of various forms of social and economic relief—of every variety of the Humane American. But however valuable and even heroic the contributions of the humane American may be, his efforts tend to be tainted by his ultimate involvement with the first group—either because he is officially sponsored, because he must depend upon the American military (dispensers of transportation and much else in South Vietnam) to sustain himself, or simply because he is American (though a few in private medical and welfare groups struggle valiantly to avoid military or political taint, and their non-American counterparts can of course stand apart from it). In these and other ways services offered by the humane American are likely to become enmeshed in conflicts surrounding suspicion of counterfeit nurturance. Their healing efforts are in fact associated with a strange twentieth-century moral inconsistency: on the one hand, the assumption (though belated and in response to outside pressure) of considerable medical and social responsibility for injured and dislocated civilians; on the other, the willingness to sacrifice these same civilians, and indeed entire villages, to the goals of war.

There are also many individual examples of what might be called the Poignant American, who becomes increasingly aware of the larger contradiction surrounding his energetic and often compassionate reconstructive or therapeutic work. He is an entrapped idealist, and the agent of his entrapment is the official bureaucracy he serves and the mission it assigns him. He tries to cope with his situation through a form of "bureaucratic ideal-ism," but this is likely to be heavily flawed by some ver-sion of the mechanistic fallacy mentioned before. One able young foreign service officer working in "pacifica-tion" thus said to me: "If I had three or four hundred good dedicated men, I could get the job done." When I asked him whether he meant Americans or Vietnamese, his answer—"Of course, if they could be Vietnamese that would be fine"—made it clear that he had Americans in mind. Although well informed about the historical com-plexities responsible for the absence in such a program of "three or four hundred good dedicated" Vietnamese, he chose to brush these complexities aside in favor of a char-acteristically American vision of the most efficient way to "get the job done." In the fashion of most Americans, he attributed the continuing success of the Viet Cong (de-spite severe stresses) to their "organization"—and sought to equal that organization as a way of defeating it. But in Vietnam this kind of efficiency becomes inefficiency, es-pecially when attempted by an alien force—a blind giant —whose vast resources can find no point of local integra-tion, and whose actions, even on behalf of reconstruction, must be perceived as externally imposed.

These realities were impressed upon me even more forcefully by another poignant American doing similar work. Unusually well trained (he spoke both French and Vietnamese) and well regarded, his administrative posi-tion had been preceded by extensive work in the field. Af-ter outlining to me the steps in the program he and his team sought to carry out—establishment of security, eval-uation of social and economic needs, institution of neces-sary changes—he admitted that the major impediment to the whole thing was the simple fact that security was at best tenuous because "the Vietnamese won't fight." He went on to describe how he and his group would seek out a village head and coax his participation while instructing him on necessary procedures, then rush off to the provincial office to smooth the way for the expected application, and then struggle with various forms of bureaucratic resistance (not to mention the resistance of villagers afraid of retaliation from the Viet Cong). He defined his own role in all this as a "catalyst." But it was clear that under such conditions an American is less a catalyst than a desperate energizer—one who initiates and oversees (rather than merely enhances) a reaction that is not primarily a Vietnamese one, and, for that matter, is not really taking place.

There are many varieties of the Numbed American—intellectually aware of death and suffering but emotionally desensitized to them. Such "psychic numbing" is a useful defense in various encounters with death, but also permits man's most extreme violations of his fellows. One of its forms is a preoccupation with "professional" concerns. Emphasized to me repeatedly was the widespread awareness among Americans of the importance for professional advancement of a stint in Vietnam—whether for journalists ("the place where the story is"), foreign service officers, or career military men (it was said that a record of some form of command in Vietnam would in the future be a prerequisite for highest military appointments). And in all three groups a large percentage of men conducted themselves as "professionals" in the sense of knowing their work and performing well in adversity. In Vietnam, ordinary professional numbing perpetuates the circle of deception by enabling each to think only of "doing his job"; only occasionally does one encounter men who both "do their jobs" and transcend them —doctors who combine their healing with outspoken moral revulsion toward killing, journalists who by telling the truth lay bare the circle of deception.

I heard much of another kind of numbed American —officials who, when asked about the killing of civilians would answer, "The numbers have been exaggerated, and anyhow civilians always get hurt in war"; and about the jailing of intellectuals: "We haven't heard about that —after all we can't keep up with everything that goes on

—and besides, we are guests in this country." This last form of numbing emerges directly from the contradiction surrounding American influence in Vietnam, as well as from the deception that we are there merely to help a worthy government in its uphill fight to create a free society.

Still other forms of numbing derive from American frustration at Vietnamese immobilization, as the case of a provincial USAID (United States Agency for International Development) representative who spoke of the dreadful predicament of "unofficial refugees" who camp along the roads in order to avoid the gunfire in the villages —and a minute or two later, when discussing a campaign to collect blood for needed transfusions, declared angrily: "No American should give a single pint of blood to the Vietnamese until they learn to do things for themselves." GIs, facing similar frustrations, sometimes with life-and-death consequences, in a strange country that seems to offer them so little and demand so much, often characterized Vietnamese as "dirty," "cowardly," "not willing to do a damn thing for themselves," and "not worth fighting for." I heard extreme attitudes emerging from combinations of numbing and rage: "We should use every single weapon we have—including nuclear weapons. We used the atomic bomb in Hiroshima, didn't we?" Nor need one dwell on the brutalization of combatants, or on patterns of "military necessity" prominent on both sides: American firing at "anything that moves," and Viet Cong killings of those thought to collaborate with Americans or simply to possess needed equipment.

The psychological purpose of numbing is the warding off of anxiety about death, and of guilt toward the dead and dying. In the case of Americans, both in Vietnam and at home, it prevents awareness of what is happening to combatants on all sides as well as to noncombatants, but is easier to call forth in relationship to an alien nonwhite people than to our own dead.

The closest to the Quiet American among those I encountered were, alas, the resident social scientists. One

I talked with, a man with a considerable academic repu-
tation who had been supervising a series of studies under
government contract, exuded an unnerving enthusiasm
—about the country ("a fascinating place") and his research (also "fascinating" and "rewarding"). There was
an aura of unreality about this scholar's exuberance in
the midst of disintegration as he discussed problems of
South Vietnamese and NLF "attitudes," and then the
measuring of responses of villagers to the presence of television sets provided by the Americans for experimental
purposes. When I originally read the Graham Greene
novel, I thought its portrait of the quiet American in Vietnam a bit overdrawn. But I think I now understand a little
more about what Greene was trying to convey: a form
of misplaced decency, an altruistic commitment at once
naïve and arrogant in its ideological presuppositions,
ending up in the most disastrous actions. Certainly the social scientist in Vietnam has been much less destructive
than many of his fellow countrymen, but he has a special
relationship to one aspect of the circle of deception implicit in Greene's concept—the fiction that a mixture of
expert technical knowledge and dedicated anti-Commu-
nism would enable Americans to show the way toward
a "solution" of the Vietnamese problem.

Finally, there was the Tired American, emotionally
drained by weeks, months, years of experiencing a deteriorating situation and explaining, to others and to
himself, its positive possibilities. One should never under-
estimate the psychological work necessary to maintain
illusion against continually impinging actuality. A number of Americans I met fell into this category, but it was
perhaps best exemplified by a high-ranking official spokesman. He responded to my initial expression of doubts
about our position in Vietnam with skillful open-mindedness: "One *should* have doubts. Nothing is clear-cut."
But a distorted version of events quickly emerged: "We
have always been in favor of negotiations, but no one
answers the phone." And he buttressed his interpretations
with a series of "scholarly" half-truths, including an in-

genious justification of the American presence in the form
of a discovery by an American psychologist that Vietnamese "have a strong need for a father figure"—a vulgar-
ism impressive in its psychological, historical, and moral
reach.

Even more revealing was his consistent technique of
affirmation by negation. On the subject of economic suffering of Vietnamese with fixed salaries because of spiral-
ing prices caused by American spending: "There has as
yet been no *runaway* inflation." About the poor performance of Vietnamese troops and their tendency to desert:
"There has been no defection of whole *battalions*." And
about the burgeoning resentment of Americans: "There
have been no all-out anti-American *riots*." Here the circle of deception operated on the assumption that, since
one could imagine (anticipate?) much worse developments, things must be quite good now. About the use of
American influence to curb flagrant violations in election
procedures, he wavered between decorous restraint—
"It's their country"—and sly admission that "we do, of
course, talk to people." The fatigue and despair in his
voice became all the more understandable when I later
learned that he had been among the minority of top-
ranking Americans in Saigon favoring stronger support
of civilian government, since he was now in the position of
daily defending the course he opposed. One must keep in
mind that there are doves and hawks of sorts among resident American officials—and that, as one knowledgeable
journalist put it to me, "Everyone but the generals wants
out." But the tired American must remain, and justify being, "in."

### III

Unknown to most Americans, there are large numbers
of Vietnamese who refuse to enter the circle of deception,
who are painfully aware of the negative consequences of
the situation of counterfeit nurturance. Political leaders,
university professors, and writers and editors conveyed to

me in our talks various messages of extreme dissatisfaction.

One predominant message was: *You are curing us to death.* A prominent political candidate, who is also a physician and therefore given to medical metaphors, referred to America as an "iron lung" now being used to help "the patient" (Vietnam) to "breathe." Then he added, with considerable emotion: "But this iron lung should be for the purpose of the patient learning how to breathe by himself and becoming healthier—not to take over his breathing for him." A newspaper editor wrote in a similar metaphor: "The injection of a right dose—in the right place—will cure; but an overdose—injected in the wrong place—will kill." He went on to refer to American assistance in an even more telling idiom: "A moderate drink . . . once in a while will improve health and morale. But too many drinks too often will poison the blood, and eventually destroy the brain and the liver. Barrels of it will drown the drinker." Here the message is: *Your "help" is poisoning (drowning) us.*

He went on to specify that "excessive and prolonged aid" would further an already harmful tendency in South Vietnam for the city to be alienated from the countryside, and make them both "dependent on the donor country" in a way that would "sap . . . physical as well as moral strength, and render [South Vietnam] powerless in the face of a threat to its social body from the inside . . . [and would be one of] the worst gifts ever made to this country, for it would mean eventual destruction . . . of its capacity to think, plan and execute, and its will to work and struggle, that is to live." Here we encounter what is perceived as the most extreme form of counterfeit nurturance: help meant to be lifegiving becomes deadly; in political terms, assistance meant to thwart Communism speeds up its victory.

In his talk with me he emphasized not only that South Vietnam was being overwhelmed, psychologically as well as economically, by the various facets of the American presence, but lashed out at what he saw as the hypocriti-

cal nature of the American effort: "We know you are
not fighting for Vietnam but against China. If you want
to fight China, why not go there, to her borders, and
fight?" As a Southerner, he was especially bitter about the
destruction of the country ("Everyone talks about bombing the North, but what about the bombing of the
South?"), and in his writings referred to the "preposterous situation" in which Americans supply not only the
military force to impose an unpopular government upon
a rural population but "even . . . carry out psychological
warfare and civic action to win the population over to the
government side." And in our talk he also brought forth
what is for an Asian intellectual the most extreme kind of
condemnation, referring to his country as "like a colony
but worse."

Essentially the same message was conveyed to me by
a university professor in the midst of a quiet discussion
over apéritifs, when he suddenly launched into an angry
monologue about the blind giant in intellectual spheres.
He compared the modest office of his university president with the suite maintained on the floor below by the
resident American "advisor," complained of American dic-
tation of educational policies in ignorance of Vietnamese
needs and desires, and concluded bitterly: "Americans always think their ways, their ideas, their teaching, their
food, their way of life are the best." Like the other two
Vietnamese quoted above, he was by no means free of
need for the Americans, but found himself humiliated,
and at times paralyzed, by the form the American presence has taken.

We see, then, that the message *You are curing us
death* readily extends itself into *Give us back our country!*
Such was vividly the case with a young writer who had
spent several years at an American university and now belonged to a loosely organized oppositional group of intellectuals—highly nationalistic and vaguely socialist,
with contempt for their government and respect for the
NLF ("We are against their terror but we understand
them, and consider many of them patriots"). He spoke to

me at length about America's takeover of South Vietnam, summing up his bitterness in the phrase "This is not our country." Throughout our talk he struggled with feelings of humiliation, and with the quest for renewed individual and national pride. He expressed contempt for Vietnamese who had in the past become French citizens; asserted "I am Vietnamese and shall be Vietnamese until I die!"; and summed up his convictions about his country's situation as follows: "I don't care so much whether it is Communist, anti-Communist, nationalist, or imperialist [then, more slowly and pointedly] *as long as it is Vietnamese!*"

He resented Americans' collusion in the fraudulent situation he saw confronting Vietnamese intellectuals: "A friend of mine tried to publish an academic study of Marxism, but it was disapproved by the censor, so he wrote another book entitled *Sexual Response*, which was easily approved." He illustrated the helplessness of the blind giant in Vietnam by suddenly asking me the question, "Can you sleep at night?" I thought at first that he was raising a problem of American conscience, but he was referring to the noise of artillery fire one hears in Saigon every evening; his point was that it was occurring on the very outskirts of the city. Yet with it all he in no sense gave up on America. He recalled with great affection the warm and stimulating student community he had known there, in contrast to the "other America" of generals and bureaucrats he found in Vietnam. He seemed to be asking for a reassertion of the libertarian spirit he had associated with America in the past. He went so far as to suggest that, since "the problem is not the North but the Chinese" (a point of view of many Vietnamese nationalists), even if the North were to take over the country, "it might want an American base in Vietnam." However one might question the accuracy of this assumption of joint interest in preventing Chinese incursion, it would seem to contain a lingering wish to remain allied to America in the struggle for national independence.

But to conclude that men with this kind of intellectual and emotional tie to the West can be counted upon to support Western—or in this case American—political policies is to enter further into the circle of deception. Indeed, for almost a century Asian intellectuals have been emerging from their Western experiences as revolutionaries combating Western domination. If one looks to such examples as Chou En-lai, Krishna Menon, or Ho Chi Minh, one suspects that much of the hostility ultimately felt toward the West has to do with precisely the kind of ambivalence we observed in this young writer. The strong initial attraction, followed as it is by profound personal and political disillusionment, becomes viewed as an evil seduction which must be violently resisted in the name of individual and national integrity. And there are many "Wests" to draw upon for ideological commitments. The connection with the West is never entirely broken, but it is used mainly as a means of self-discovery.

Other frequent messages Vietnamese conveyed to me about Americans were variations of: *We feel that we need you but. . . .* A woman of about thirty, the daughter of a plantation owner from the North who had lived in Paris for some time, was appalled at the generally corrupt and "Americanized" atmosphere she observed upon her return to Saigon. She spoke even more bitterly about the effects of American-induced inflation upon Vietnamese civil servants and soldiers, going so far as to claim that many incidents of stealing and killing attributed to the Viet Cong were actually the work of destitute members of the South Vietnamese Army—virtually attributing these crimes to American influence. Her proposed solution to these problems was a Vietnamese version of the circle of deception: a strongman to run the government who would put to death a few of those indulging in graft to set examples for the others; and more American soldiers "to fight the Communists." But she seemed extremely uneasy about reports of hesitation on the part of Americans, and repeatedly asked me to tell her "what Americans think about the war." This kind of anxiety in Vietnamese seemed to stem from doubts not only about American staying power, but about the validity (in the face of the deep deterioration they know to exist in their country) of the demands they were making of Americans. And such uneasiness and guilt are always likely to increase resentment.

The combination of demand and resentment could take various symbolic forms. On a visit we made to a Saigon hospital my wife distributed little dolls to war-injured children. She had given away almost all of them when one of the parents rushed up to her, holding the head of a doll in one hand and the rest of it in the other to demonstrate that the doll had broken in half—all the while smiling with discomfort in the East Asian fashion, and making clear that she expected the broken doll to be replaced (which it was). The incident seemed to suggest several dimensions of the situation of counterfeit nurturance: the help needed and demanded is endless; the American giver will be resented for the imperfections of his gifts; and (somewhat more abstractly) Americans are expected to put severed things and people together—because they possess such great power, and because they are largely responsible for severing them in the first place.

I encountered another symbolic expression of this demand-resentment constellation in the delusion of a young female dancer hospitalized at a psychiatric center in Saigon. She had lived for some time in London, and had returned to her country because of developing symptoms of mental illness. But she was convinced that "the Americans" had abducted her in London and carried her forcibly back to Saigon, and now wondered what I could suggest to make her better. Again, Americans are seen as all-powerful—the ultimate source of both benevolence and suffering. The pattern is of course by no means unique to Vietnam: General MacArthur frequently appeared in the delusions of Japanese mental patients during the early postwar years, in this and other ways replacing the Emperor. But it is illustrative of the American-Vietnamese relationship.

The prevailing atmosphere one senses among intellectuals is that of despair and helplessness, or *immobilisme*. Similarly, the people in general seem to react neither with enthusiasm nor opposition but rather with passive resistance: general resistance to government programs; peasants' resistance to taxes; young men's (especially students') resistance to the Army; and, of course, the Army's resistance to fighting. The general mixture of lassitude, cynicism, and aggressive self-seeking pervading Saigon is reminiscent of accounts of the atmosphere in large cities in China just before the Communist takeover (remnants of which one could observe in Taiwan shortly afterward), suggesting that there is a certain style of American interplay with Asian corruption, of joint participation in the fiction that a highly unpopular and ineffectual government is a dynamic and virtuous force around which free men must rally. In truth, the most efficient and wholehearted American-Vietnamese collaboration I encountered in Saigon was a bar-whorehouse featuring beautiful Vietnamese girls and elite (mainly Embassy) American clientele—with no complaints about Vietnamese "organization" or "leadership."

### IV

If Vietnamese themselves reject the circle of deception, are there any authentic ideas and images to which they are capable of responding? I had the clear impression that there were three, none of them new to the world but all extremely important in this specific setting: images of nation, social transformation, and peace. To grasp their importance, one must remember that the human mind lives on images, absorbing and re-creating them as a basis for all understanding and action. The problem in Vietnam is less a matter of "getting the bugs out of the machine," as the fallacy of mechanism would have it, than of evolving shared world-pictures which inspire and cohere. I would suggest that the unpalatable truth concerning the American presence in Vietnam is that it radically undermines each of the three significant images I have mentioned.

We have already observed the force of the *image of na-*

*tion*; it has been rendered especially compelling by the very precariousness of Vietnam's historical status as a nation, by old national struggles as well as recent dismemberment. To be considered a nationalist is to wear a badge of honor, and much of the admiration in the South for Ho Chi Minh has to do with his capacity to make psychological contact with all Vietnamese through this shared image (enhanced by his creating a form of "national Communism" with its considerable independence from larger Communist nations). Similarly, Vietnamese who feel threatened by the Viet Cong are nonetheless willing to speak sympathetically of "nationalists" among them.

Many stressed to me the South's need for a leader who could, like Ho, reanimate the national image—always making clear that men who have fought on the side of the French during the struggle for independence, as did most of the present military junta, would be immediately disqualified. One young political scientist with experience in government expressed to me the opinion that Vietnamese have been searching in the wrong places for models of leadership and economic development, and advocated someone on the order of Ayub Khan of Pakistan. Most looked toward eventual reunification of their country, though differing on how that could or should be achieved. Virtually all stressed that the American presence painfully violates the image of nation, and that this violation had direct operational significance: guerrillas with minimal military equipment can harass and outmaneuver the blind giant because he is widely identified as an alien threat to their nation.

We have of course by now become familiar with the excesses that can surround the image of nation, with aggressive national*ism*, but this should not cause us to lose sight of the profoundly integrative force exerted by a shared sense of geographical-racial-cultural destiny. The root of the word nation is the same as that of "origin" or "birth," and in our desperate need to extend the concept outward from its beginnings in clan and tribe to include all of mankind, we may too readily forget that men still require it for their sense of immortalized human continuity.

Clearly the idea of nation is not something that one people can provide for another, least of all Americans in Asia. The refrain I heard from Vietnamese again and again was that "America must take a risk" and support the kind of leaders who were sufficiently independent of her to make it likely that they would question her policies. Both sides are thus presented with an excruciating paradox which the elections have by no means resolved: the American need to support opponents of American power; and the Vietnamese need to call upon American power to help them overcome it. This is part of what the editor quoted earlier meant by the "preposterous situation"—a situation which will find no solution that does not include a reassertion of Vietnamese autonomy.

The significance of the second general image, that of *social transformation*, is attested to by the recent use of the term "Revolutionary Development" for the American-South Vietnamese village pacification program. The military regime's miserable record on all aspects of social transformation, especially the fundamental issue of land reform, renders this terminology sadly ironic. I was told by a leading legislator who studies the problem how landlords would return right behind government soldiers when territory was retaken from the Viet Cong. But a vision of major social reform remains fundamental to reversing the symbolic social death of South Vietnam and bringing about a collective sense of rebirth.

While a number of the people I spoke to condemned the Communists for their "betrayal of the revolution," there was little doubt that *some* form of revolution had to take place. Thus the same editor called for "a new army and a new civil service . . . [which] would have to be built up *in the field* [italics his] away from the capital and cities, around a nucleus of revolutionary men . . . living simply among the peasants." The idea sounds familiar; its proponent readily admits that it has much in common with the successful approach of the Viet Cong. The American claim to have favored such transformation is very much part of the circle of deception. For while it is true that we have applied pressure upon a reluctant government in the direction of reform, our relationship to that government (not to mention the nature of that government itself) makes impossible the actual accomplishment of transformation from within. A related deception is the dismissal, as irrelevant or disruptive, of those groups which have most strongly articulated the widespread urge toward transformation—militant Buddhists, students, and younger intellectuals. They will surely be heard from in the future.

An even more extreme deception has surrounded the American underestimation of the significance for Vietnamese of the *image of peace*. The perception of South Vietnamese as determined to continue their military struggle should have been shattered, once and for all, by the results of the recent elections. Despite the ruling generals' questionable manipulations, they drew fewer votes than the combination of three candidates who had declared themselves for peace; and the most outspoken "peace candidate" surprised everyone by coming in second. From all that I heard when I was in Vietnam, I would tend to agree with the opinion expressed by journalists that the dove symbol used by the peace candidate on the ballot had much to do with his impressive showing. For anyone who has talked to Vietnamese during the past few months could readily sense something close to a ground swell of peace sentiment. What more than a dove could appeal to an electorate that is largely illiterate but by no means indifferent to the sufferings of war and the attractions of peace? The image of peace includes relief from a long and terrible cycle of death anxiety and death guilt, and—whatever the qualifications put forth about the kind of peace there would be—an opportunity to reverse the increasingly intolerable pattern of disintegration.

I had an encounter with a "former peace candidate" which, I believe, illustrates some of the complicated dimensions of the peace image. He was an economist who, though still in his late thirties, had been finance minister in three cabinets—and *his* campaign emblem was a bomb crossed out by two diagonal lines drawn over it. Since peace talk had in the recent past been associated by the military regime with such dangerous tendencies as "neutralism" and Communism, this kind of campaign by so prominent a person was creating quite a stir. At the time Americans were divided about him—on occasion one would hear him spoken of as "unrealistic" or "put up to it by someone," and at other times he would be praised for his accomplishments as finance minister and described as "one of the best minds in South Vietnam." No one was too surprised when, on the day before I went to see him, he was publicly denounced by the police as having "Communist affiliations," leaving his future as a campaigner and indeed as a free man in doubt.

He told me that he welcomed talking to me as he too wished to stress a psychological perspective. And he immediately handed me a brief essay (translated from the original French) in which he somewhat abstractly discussed the motivations of the Vietnamese as people caught up in revolution, in opposition to revolution, and now in "the powerful psychological motivation" surrounding "the desire for peace." He insisted that the elections should give the people a chance to express this desire, stressing to me his sense of the urgency of proper timing—since in the past there did not exist the necessary combination of war exhaustion and political climate for peace, and in the future there might be little left of the country to salvage. He spoke of a "war mechanism"—a self-perpetuating system—with no possibility of anyone winning but all continuing to fight "because they don't know anything else to do" (I was later reminded of this when I read Kenneth Galbraith's contention that "War turns reason into stereotype" and freezes participants in original error). He felt that the mechanism could be interrupted only by installing a government

committed to peace through negotiations, that such a
commitment would cut down the effectiveness of the
Viet Cong who thrive on an atmosphere of war and
chaos, and that it would evoke a strong general response
in the Vietnamese people which would in turn impel
the NLF and the North to join the South in negotiations.
He thought that all of this would take time, and that
American troops would remain in Vietnam during protracted negotiations, but that once the general undertaking had been initiated it would succeed in bringing
peace to the country.

One could raise various issues concerning his program, but what struck me about it was the serious effort
not only to rally the country round the image of peace
but to evolve a workable theory of peace as well. He
told me that the government was spreading false stories
about him in order to prevent him from running in the
election, and when I asked him why they were so determined to do so he answered, "Because the idea of peace
is extremely popular." It would seem that he was right on
both counts: he was officially eliminated as a candidate
a short time later, and the elections proved that peace
was indeed a popular idea.

But images are not eliminated as easily as candidates.
Once safely established in their campaigns, a number of
others (especially the peace candidate who did so well)
actively committed themselves to negotiations and the
search for peace, and even the military rulers themselves
were forced to make very uncharacteristic obeisance in
the same direction. Many elements seem to be converging
—the influence of the "former peace candidate," an increasing American realization that there is no feasible
course other than negotiations, strong pressure from the
rest of the world—but underneath everything is the extreme power of the image of peace and its ultimate capacity to break through the circle of deception.

Ever since World War II, Vietnam has been living out
in the most extreme way the painful problems besetting

the world at large. Thinking back to my first visit to Saigon thirteen years ago, I recall mainly scenes of ordinarily well-intentioned men—Vietnamese, French, American—arguing passionately, sometimes intelligently, always endlessly, about what should be done, behaving as men do when confronted by a terrible problem which, however approached, will not go away. What I have tried to suggest here is that the problem is being confounded rather than solved by the American presence—because that presence works against Vietnam's only viable psychological and historical possibilities. Is it not time for the giant to begin to see? Can he not recognize, and then step out of, the circle of deception?

# REASON,
# REARMAMENT,
# AND PEACE

## 10

*Also on the subject of war, this essay is much more muted
in tone than the previous one, for at least two reasons.
The war in question is not one actually in progress; and I
speak as an outsider—a semipolite foreign observer—
commenting from Japan upon a Japanese problem
(though, as the title suggests, it is really a universal problem in vivid Japanese contours). Japanese intellectuals
commenting on the same subject tend to sound more
the way I do on Vietnam. Still another reason might be
the six-year span between the two essays—the world of
1961 (when this one was written) seemed, at least in its
East Asian aspects, a little less menacing than that of
1967. Even so, I need do no more than reread a few paragraphs of this piece to rediscover the indignation that
lay behind it.*

*The editor of* Asian Survey *requested the article because he seemed to want to right his balance sheet after
having just published an essay by a Japanese military
spokesman advocating rearmament. I was chosen not
only because of my relationship to Japan and my concerns
about war and peace but because of my adversary's use
(I would claim, abuse) of the all too convenient polarity
of rationality versus irrationality. As I see it, Mr. Atsushi*

*Oi (the military spokesman in question) is guilty of a form of psychologism immediately recognizable to anyone familiar with psychoanalytic approaches to society and history—the use of a psychological language to obscure implicit political and moral judgments.*

*Also involved are dangerous fallacies surrounding the ubiquitous principle of "military realism"—and the relationship of that principle to what Philip Green has aptly termed "deadly logic."[1] Green's strictures concerning "the pseudo-science of strategic analysis" apply here, as they do also to the kind of mechanistic fallacy I spoke of in the last essay. Green has brilliantly undermined the "realistic" position of many nuclear strategists and uncovered the falseness of their claim to ethical neutrality as well as to rationality. Had I had the benefit of reading his work before writing the essay, my discussion of even the specifically psychological issues surrounding military realism, which I now consider quite deficient, could have been deepened. Were I to write it now, I would also discuss these issues in relationship to symbolic aberrations in our thought induced by the weapons themselves, as suggested in "On Death and Death Symbolism" and carried further in* The Broken Connection. *Perhaps the only thing this essay succeeds at all in doing is in suggesting a few psychological fallacies underlying a certain kind of lethal conventional wisdom.*

*Unhappily, Japanese thinking since 1961, at least in official places, has moved more in Oi's direction than in mine or Green's. Rearmament has been stepped up and there has been increasing talk of Japan's acquisition of nuclear weapons, the latter partly stimulated by Chinese nuclear developments. Nonetheless, the issues I discuss concerning Japan's peace symbol remain excruciatingly alive. Images of Hiroshima and Nagasaki may be fading somewhat, but they are not easily obliterated. They continue, in fact, to affect a great deal of what happens in Japan, and to render that country both unique and quintessential in the universal struggle to reclaim—and enlarge—Reason.*

No problem tortures the world more than that of evolving a "rational" approach to peace, and no country has been more tortured by this problem than Japan. So complex is the problem, so unpredictable its elements, and so grave its consequences, that the most intelligent and well-intentioned men anywhere are likely to find themselves in violent disagreement over means of solution. It is therefore well to be humble (though not timid) in approaching the problem, and to recognize the inherently tragic dimensions involved. In this spirit I wish to mention a few psychological and semantic considerations, partly stimulated by, and largely opposing, views expressed by Mr. Atsushi Oi.[2]

Mr. Oi's major thesis is that opposition to rearmament in Japan is based upon "sentimentalism," and that "rational rearmament" in association with American military alliance is the best means of maintaining peace. Therefore, he argues, America must correct misunderstandings among Japanese regarding its basic objectives, and Japanese "should have confidence in the strength and judgment of the United States." I believe that Mr. Oi serves us well by raising the large question of the relationship between reason, rearmament, and peace, but less well in his facile answers to it.

To be sure, anyone who has observed the Japanese scene has been struck by the sentimentalism and emotionalism of many peace demonstrations, and of other aspects of the Japanese peace movement. At the same time, one can say the same of many of the voices clamoring for rearmament. In truth, one must conclude that both groups are subject to long-standing tendencies within Japanese character to lean heavily upon emotional and aesthetic sensibilities at the expense of what we usually term logic—though one must also add that there are many within both groups who reflect the modern Japanese struggle against these tendencies in favor of a more balanced, and therefore more rational, thought pattern. The point at issue is whether or not opposition to rearmament within Japan—on the basis of its motivation and its relevance to actual events—can, in itself, be judged to be irrational and unreasonable.

We may define reason as the capacity to learn by experience, to relate relevant events in formulating general principles, and to make use of acquired knowledge for constructive and life-enhancing purposes. By these criteria it is reasonable to favor any group program which will prevent war, unreasonable to support (or fail to oppose) measures which make war more likely to occur. The question then becomes one of whether or not Japanese rearmament is more likely to prevent, and to bring on, war; and since no one can give an absolute answer to this question, Japanese must rely upon their own experience and upon knowledge available to them.

On the basis of this experience and knowledge, can we say that Japanese are being unreasonable when they oppose rearmament on such grounds (listed by Mr. Oi on the basis of public opinion surveys) as: fear of war, economic hardship, fear of militarism, the constitutional prohibition, and the futility of armaments? Surely there is sufficient cause in recent Japanese experience—and in knowledge of other historical experience—to have a reasonable fear of rearmament and its relationship to militarism, war, and to economic hardship; and equally reasonable cause to look upon armaments as futile for Japan in the present world situation, and to wish to live by the letter and spirit of the famous antiwar clause in Article Nine of the Japanese Constitution. Nor can we use as evidence of the irrationality of attitudes against disarmament (as Mr. Oi seems to) the findings that rearmament is favored more by men than by women, more by older than younger persons, and more by businessmen and self-employed individuals than intellectuals and company employees. I am afraid that it has never been established, in Japan or elsewhere, that men are less sentimental than women, that older people are more logical than younger ones, or that businessmen or self-employed individuals are more rational than intellectuals.

I would suggest that underneath Japanese fear of rearmament lies the fear of personal annihilation. This fear contains profoundly nonrational elements; and it can emerge in anyone in situations of danger (or even in situations free of external danger); but in the world's present plight it is, unfortunately, no longer an unreasonable fear. And I am afraid that the concerns and fears expressed by Japanese in relationship to rearmament can be neither stilled nor rendered irrational by Mr. Oi's discussions of constitutional interpretation, economic solvency, controls over militarism, or even faith in America and courage in resisting the Soviet Union.

This last element—the faith and courage asked by Mr. Oi—also demands further scrutiny. For it seems to me that he is asking Japanese to give up their fears, doubts, and questions and to put complete trust in America's strength and purity of motive, just as they were asked to put similar trust in their Emperor—or in those who claimed to represent his wishes—not too long ago. Such a request (and the accompanying exhortation to boldly resist the Soviet Union) plays upon long standing Japanese sensitivities to relationships of power, and willingness for dedication to noble causes; but it ignores the modern struggle, dating from the Meiji era but reaching its peak in the postwar period, for a greater critical faculty in individual weighing of issues, and for emergence from traditional power relationships within Japanese society. It also fails to take "reasonable" account of Japanese awareness of a geographical proximity to Russia and China and the powerful (however ambivalent) ties which Japanese feel toward other parts of Asia (particularly China) and to the non-Western world—on the basis of race and culture, and of the profound historical experience (shared by all countries outside of the Western orbit) of having been technologically and intellectually overwhelmed by the West.

But let us return for a moment to the question of the special Japanese attitude toward peace itself. Perhaps more than in any other country in the world, peace became, in postwar Japan, a rallying symbol—an absolute moral imperative. People had suffered greatly, and to little avail; theirs was the disillusion born of false expectations and disastrous repercussions. For the overwhelming majority of the Japanese population, much that had seemed honorable, or at least permissible, now became acutely dishonored: Japan's allegedly sacred historical mission, the Rightist leaders whose militaristic policies in support of this mission had contributed so much to the disaster, and most dishonored of all—the phenomenon of war itself. Peace came to symbolize avoidance of annihilation and a new way for the future. It became a symbol for life rather than death or half-life.

This symbolic power of the idea of peace has managed to survive the moral complexities of the postwar period. Though sometimes temporarily dormant, it has repeatedly reasserted itself with great strength, as one could observe during the mass demonstrations of 1960.

Yet in recent years one has also been able to observe apparently opposite tendencies, a pattern which at times seems even to suggest a nostalgia for war. I have in mind here the great response to war films, the return to popularity of old military songs, and the new fascination with books and magazines describing war and with accounts and charts of great battles. This pattern is sometimes related to an even more general "Revival Boom" (*Ribaibaru Bumu*) and has affected highly diverse elements of the Japanese population—from old-timers in their sixties and seventies who can look back to the "good old days" of the Meiji era, to high school and junior high school students who have known only postwar life. Moreover, there is no doubt that groups advocating peace and opposing rearmament have at times assumed a militancy inconsistent with an atmosphere of peace, and have on some occasions revealed themselves to be more concerned with supporting the political claims of China or the Soviet Union, or the ideological claims of Marxism-Leninism, than with peace itself.

These apparent contradictions in Japanese attitudes toward peace (and toward rearmament) cannot, however, be comprehended merely by cynically dismissing them as "insincere" or "sentimental." We must here keep in mind that every individual Japanese carries within himself—as part of the human psychological condition— a blend of love, creativity, aggressiveness, hate, and destructiveness. All five of these emotions, at varying times and at varying degrees, become attached to the over-all human urges toward self-preservation, sexual expression, and the continuity of generations. The last three of these five emotions (aggressiveness, hate and destructiveness) most readily become associated with the symbolism of war and armaments, though the first two (love and creativity) may as well; similarly, the first two most readily become attached to the symbolism of peace, though—as we have seen—so may the last three. All we can say in this regard, then, is that Japanese are neither more nor less noble in their emotions than anyone else, but that, more than most others, they have managed to maintain a peace symbolism which, whatever its limitations, is able to appeal to some of the more constructive human tendencies.

Moreover, the nostalgia of which I have spoken, when examined more closely, seems to be more a nostalgia for order and sense of purpose, even for past glory, than for war itself. Yet the fact is that Japan's past glory has been intimately associated with military prowess: since the Meiji era, with matching the military strength of Western countries; before that with attaining the individual and cultural martial skills associated with Japan's central myth of the warrior-hero, as elaborated in the celebrated code of *Bushidō*. To maintain the symbolism of peace, therefore, has been a considerable accomplishment, an example of a cultural countertrend in which available emotional combinations have had to be altered or even reversed.

But such achievement is never without its emotional cost. We can see evidence of the strains in Japanese society to which this maintenance of peace symbolism contributes: in the Revival Boom and in the militant behavior already referred to, in the painful discussions of the *degree* of possible rearmament (which, one must add, is by no means an irrelevant consideration)—and, most of all, in the violence and belligerence of Rightist extremists, now in themselves a fringe group, but nonetheless commanding what many Japanese consider to be a dangerous combination of influence and potential sympathy among powerful groups within existing society, including government and military leaders. The maintenance of peace symbolism at the expense of military outlets may also contribute to everyday hostilities in Japanese group life and to the competitive strains which exist throughout the society, though these problems of course originate from other sources.

Peace symbolism, then, is more complex than meets the eye. But is it "unreasonable" or "irrational"? I think not. Like all symbols evolved in man's perpetual mental activity of symbol-formation, this one has both rational and nonrational elements. When we test it by our three criteria of reasonableness, we find it will satisfy at least two of them: it is based upon Japanese people's capacity to learn by experience, and it is constructive and life-enhancing. It has a more equivocal relationship, however, to the third criterion, in that Japanese have had difficulty in drawing upon the relevant factors around it (relevant for Japan and for the rest of the world) that would enable them to relate it to more general principles. Japanese use of the peace symbol could therefore become more rational by applying it to wider considerations, by relating Japan's hard-won wisdom more effectively to the present world situation, by contributing to a universalistic theory of peace, and by taking desperately needed initiative in bringing about international nuclear disarmament as a means of lessening the present danger of destroying all human life.

I have taken exception to Mr. Oi's approach because

I believe it to be an expression of a general tendency, in political and military thinking throughout the world, to distort the fundamental concept of reason. Surely Japan, on the basis of its special experience with war and peace, would better serve as a vantage-point for developing within us all the realization that reason lies only in finding the broadest basis for solving the universal dilemma of how best to preserve and enhance the human species.

# WHAT AILS MAN?

## 11

*The question itself is grandiose. I raise it not for the purpose of making a medical diagnosis of the disease of my species but to counter precisely that tendency. What I attack particularly is an attempt by Arthur Koestler to explain man's age-old political, ideological, and theological disturbances—and particularly his persistence in warmaking—by means of an organic theory of neurophysiological deficit.*

*I realize now that Koestler's view is part of a recent revival of nineteenth-century-style organic-instinctual theories of violence. It is as if the threat of annihilation, and the terror man feels in the face of that threat, cause him to turn away from his mind, his institutions, his history—to turn away from himself—and find a grand explanation in some form of impulse or deficiency propelling him toward destruction. Could this not be still another example of the mechanistic fallacy?*

*The model used is generally the pre-human animal— whether defending its territory or requiring expression for an "aggressive instinct," which, like steam under pressure, must be given an "outlet," lest it burst out in the wrong place at the wrong time and do damage. Thus*

*Konrad Lorenz[1] ends up advocating bigger and better Olympic games, and Anthony Storr[2] heaps praise upon democracy as "a practical system for controlling and making use of competitive aggression." Both authors combine ethological observations with classical psychoanalytic theory in ways that shut out the area of human experience in which, in my view, the greatest problems lie—that of man's collective symbolic life. The ethological observations are not in themselves wrong; they have in fact been an exciting new source of knowledge, and Lorenz is one of the most gifted of the ethological school. The difficulty emerges in what I would consider a misguidedly literal application of these findings to man which divests ethological principles of their subtlety (a more sensitive use of them could lead one to exactly opposite conclusions). The mechanistic fallacy, then, has to do with a denial of man's fundamental need to render into viable psychic forms (that is, recreate or symbolize) all that he experiences. Once this formative process is properly understood, older closed-system views of man no longer satisfy.\**

*Koestler's book is the most extreme of the group, and in some ways represents an even more malignant intellectual position than my review suggests. Under a neurophysiological and evolutionary shield, it really suggests a contemporary form of predestination, to be countered by a new alchemy. There are, to be sure, profound dilemmas surrounding man's evolutionary and neurophysiological heritage. And these do affect his symbolic life and his relationship to technological destruction, as writers like*

---

\* One could use such terms as "animalistic fallacy," "instinctual fallacy," and "evolutionary fallacy" for the phenomena I am describing here. These fallacies are embedded in various forms of scientific and intellectual tradition, as opposed to the technicism I spoke of earlier in connection with the American approach in Vietnam. The latter is more the kind of machine-modeled outlook on political and military problems so vividly described by Jacques Ellul (in *The Technological Society*[3]), and so eloquently denounced by Noam Chomsky (in *American Power and the New Mandarins*[4]). But I include both groups of phenomena under the mechanistic fallacy because they share a denial of man's formative and symbolic processes and assume instead a mechanical form of determinism.

René Dubos and Albert Szent-Györgyi, among others, have pointed out. Paradoxically, portions of Koestler's discussions of psychological and evolutionary theory demonstrate precisely the kind of breadth the subject calls for, only to be abruptly cut off in favor of a flattened, absolute "diagnosis."

Such diagnosis and therapy, in fact, constitute a new totalism of evolutionary deficit and biochemical resolution. Rather than the deification of History found in classical revolutionary forms of totalism, we now have the elimination of same. Historical man and psychological man give way—first to wounded neurophysiological man, and then triumphant chemical man. In the process there is little room for exploring man's true possibilities for coming to sufficient terms with himself, and his environment, to survive.

\*        \*        \*

It is easy these days—this century—to defend the idea that something ails man. His extraordinary impulse to make war upon his own species in the name of his sanctified idols has reached grotesque proportions. Nor does he seem to be improving.

To the contrary, consider an up-to-the-minute example of something approaching collective madness. The most powerful nation in the world intervenes in a civil war (following upon an anticolonial one) in a small faraway country, and saturates that country with its destructive fire-power and indiscriminate killing; is profoundly resented by virtually all factions there as well as by the rest of the world, and finds itself stymied both politically and militarily. It stations five thousand men at a small outpost in an exposed valley surrounded by hostile forces of many times that number and insists (against prevailing objective military judgment) that the outpost can be defended; and to buttress that assumption, considers escalating the war still further, and even the use of tactical versions of man's ultimate weapons, though such measures could well result in a general holocaust in which most or all of mankind would be annihilated. Yes, something ails man, but what is it?

In search of an answer Arthur Koestler[5] posts "some built-in error or deficiency," or, more vividly, "a screw loose in the human mind." He takes us on a long journey through psychology and evolution to conclude: man's difficulty is his proneness to delusion; he suffers from "an endemic form of paranoia" which dominates his entire history and which is "built into the wiring circuits of the human brain."

This is so, Koestler goes on to tell us, because *Homo sa-*

*piens* is a "biological freak, the result of some remarkable mistake in the evolutionary process." The mistake resulted from the speed with which the hominid brain evolved (the whole thing took only half a million years), or from what is known as "explosive evolution." Koestler follows the neurophysiologist Paul MacLean in stressing the "unseemly haste" with which the specifically human areas of the brain were superimposed upon the phylogenetically older structures, resulting in "insufficient coordination" between older (emotional) and newer (intellectual) functions.

Koestler cites MacLean's theory of the "three brains" coexisting within the human skull: the oldest being basically reptilian, the next inherited from the lower mammals, and the third peculiarly human. The difficulty according to this theory is that each functions more or less autonomously. This means that man, in effect, sees the world through two television screens: one old and wired into brain areas responsible for "animal" feelings and functions, such as sex, hunger, fear and aggression; the other new and connected with brain areas attuned to the more "human" achievement of reason. The more crude screen —"the crocodile and horse we carry in our skulls"—insists upon supplying its own picture, upon "making up its own mind," and thereby undermines the more elevated images of the other screen. The result is a form of "schizophysiology," an antagonistic split in function which is "built into our species." It is always the crude (animal) screen, detached from and inadequately coordinated with the nobler (human) one, which leads man to delusion and mass murder.

The thesis has an everything-falling-into-place aura, as it accounts for things that do *not* fall into place; it may therefore appeal to those who still believe, or wish to believe, that all truths, scientific or otherwise, are simple ones. But as an explanation for "modern man's predicament" and his "urge to self-destruction," I find this arbitrary dichotomy of the bad old brain and the good new one a misrepresentation of the way man's brain and mind work, and a neurological retreat from his psychology and history.

The shortcomings of the theory become painfully clear when it is applied to man's most difficult dilemmas. For instance, concerning man's uniqueness in knowing that he must die, Koestler claims that "the discovery [of death] originates in the new brain, the refusal [to accept death] in the old." This all-important refusal is responsible for the witches, ghosts, ancestral spirits and gods which inhabit the human mind, and also for "comforting promises of eternal survival." And the cause of it all, Koestler believes, is "instinct," which "takes existence implicitly for granted, and defends it against threats in anger and fear, but it cannot conceive of its change into nonexistence." Yet one could just as well argue the other way around. The human infant possesses an innate (or "instinctual") sense of connection and a tendency known as "attachment behavior" toward other human beings. This innate tendency finds later expression in various relationships of blood, sexual love, and friendship, as well as in more symbolic ties to various social groups and to past and future generations.

Maintaining this "instinctual" sense of connection greatly enhances man's always limited capacity to accept his own death, because he "survives himself" through his attachments. On the other hand, man's "acquired" and ostensibly higher achievement of reason can greatly contribute to his *refusal* to accept death. For man's increasing knowledge of natural and human phenomena has been accompanied by a trend toward individuation, and this in turn has weakened his sense of connection and presented him with the unacceptable prospect of death as total extinction.

The point is that our present understanding of man no longer permits us to posit a simple dichotomy of "instinct" (and "faith") versus "reason"; and the error is compounded by extending the dichotomy into such discrete anatomical and physiological assumptions about the brain. The dichotomy can be transcended by the kind of unitary approach which many writers have recently emphasized (including Lancelot Law Whyte, whom Koestler quotes in other contexts). One must then consider the symbols and forms man requires in order to make sense of his world and act upon it—and the way in which these combine various elements of emotion (or "faith") and reason (or "logic"). As Susanne Langer has emphasized, man's life-long mental task is one of continuous "transformation" of the "data" reaching him from within and without. And this "symbol-making function is one of man's primary activities, like eating, looking, or moving about . . . the fundamental process of his mind."[6]

From this standpoint man's quest for "eternal survival" can be seen as symbolically realized by artistic and other cultural "works" he transmits to future generations, as well as by his simple biological continuity in families and nations. The quest is most likely to take dangerous forms during periods of historical upheaval when this symbolic continuity is impaired. At such times members of one group may feel compelled to reaffirm this immortality by murdering members of another.

Indeed the example of "collective madness" I mentioned before—the American stand at Khe Sanh—is, among other things, a product of distorted symbolization. Adrift in a revolutionary period of rapid historical change and threatened nuclear apocalypse, we find old symbols (of family, religion, or "American individualism") increasingly irrelevant, and authentic new ones extremely difficult to acquire.

Terrified by an image of the "death" of our culture (of "the American way of life"), we grasp at false symbols. Khe Sanh thus becomes "a symbol of American determination to defend democracy" against "Communist expansion," even though the militaristic regime we defend has no popular support, and our adversary fights on his own soil and, quite understandably, sees us as the outside invader. The source of such tragedy and evil is not "the crocodile and horse we carry in our skulls"; rather it is the way in which this kind of distorted symbolism allies itself with the psychological potential for aggression, and above all with our murderous technology.

Throughout his elaborate re-examination of psychological theory, Koestler nowhere mentions recent work most relevant to man's predicament—that dealing with his present symbolic struggles, and with the general interplay of mind and history. Nor does Koestler stop to examine the possible limitations of MacLean's "three brains" theory, at least for the purposes he assigns it; or to consider alternative neurophysiological views. José Delgado, for instance, holds that there is nothing intrinsically wrong with the anatomy and physiology of our brain, and that our problem lies in the cultural and educational patterns to which the brain is submitted. There are flashes of brilliance in Koestler's ambitious explorations, especially in his general ordering of evolution and in his compelling description of some of the radical new features of the post-Hiroshima world. But the book's erratic combination of unfocused and overfocused argument eventually renders it tedious.

Its ending is worse than that—an anticlimactic suggestion of a biochemical cure for man's deficiencies, so cursorily and simplistically stated as to make one wonder whether the author really believes in it. The issue he raises, that of chemical interference with man's genetic processes, is one which must be seriously confronted—but not by embracing it uncritically as a medical cure for the whole of human history. Earlier in the book Koestler angrily denounces remnants of the nineteenth-century mechanistic fallacies for their tendency to eliminate man, only to end up with a "chemistic" fallacy of his own which is more characteristic of the twentieth century. But man remains our problem, whatever we put into him, and however shaky his future as a species.

# IV

## ON CONTEMPORARY MAN AND WOMAN

# WOMAN AS KNOWER

## 12

*I have a special fondness for this essay—not just because of its subject matter, but because it evolved unexpectedly and gave me a chance to experiment a bit with certain facets of the psychohistorical approach.*

*Let me say first that I claim no special knowledge of women. When invited to serve as a kind of free-lance commentator (as opposed to paper-presenter) at a conference (at the American Academy of Arts and Sciences) devoted to the subject of women, I raised a few general issues—and the upshot was that I was asked to edit the volume produced from that conference.[1] With a minimum of encouragement I added an essay of my own. At the time I must have needed a bit of relief from my Hiroshima work. And the essay on women taking shape within me seemed to travel well enough to permit me to prepare a sizeable portion of it during a Christmas vacation in New York. It turned out to be a first attempt to combine observations on Japan, China, and America into a single theoretical statement—in this and other ways a prelude to the essay on protean man. Written specifically for that volume, it is the only essay in the collection that has never appeared in a magazine or journal. But I was pleased to learn that*

for a time it achieved a kind of underground popularity
at one or two girl's colleges.

All the more so because it now seems to me to demand
quite a bit of the reader, perhaps more than any of the
other papers collected here. For it stresses complexity,
the nuance of contending forces—a stress which seemed
necessary for introducing a series of ideal forms (woman
as nurturer, temptress, and knower) that are neither individual-psychological nor historical per se, but include both
dimensions in relationship to change.

Much simpler is the following dialogue, which consti-
tuted the bulk of a very short Introduction I wrote for
The Woman in America:

INERTIA      No matter what people say these days, I
   still think there is much to the idea of "eternal
   woman." I agree with the man who said some time
   ago: "It is a great consolation to reflect that, among
   all the bewildering changes to which the world is
   subject, the character of woman cannot be altered."

FLUX      False consolation, my dear Inertia. Women
   are, in fact, changing much more rapidly than our
   ideas about them. The question is whether we can at
   least make an effort to catch up by casting off precisely the shibboleths you express.

INERTIA      Well, the principle that "anatomy is destiny" was good enough for both Napoleon and Freud.
   They held to the idea of the biological basis of
   woman's nature. It seems to me that we should hold
   to it too.

FLUX      I couldn't disagree with you more. There is,
   in fact, no such thing as woman's nature. Woman,
   like man, is a product of human history.

INERTIA      Come now, Flux. You can't mean that.
   Take the American woman, for example. Whatever
   her special history, she is, deep down, like all other
   women—concerned with love, marriage, family, and
   so on.

FLUX        *Wrong again. She seems to me to be different from other women in every way. And, in case you haven't heard, she is interested in quite a few things besides love, marriage, and family.*

INERTIA        *Well, let's look at the matter another way. Women in America have been given extraordinary opportunities to express themselves—whether in work or in social or family life. But has this made them any happier or given them real fulfillment?*

FLUX        *Frankly, I don't think that American society has been as generous to its women as people think it has. Women are still discriminated against in most professions, and there are so many ways in which our institutions place great limitation upon their freedom. America has a long way to go before it can claim to have created large numbers of truly emancipated women.*

INERTIA        *I doubt whether any society ever "creates" its women, but let that pass. Consider for a moment the intellectual woman in America. Now she has certainly involved herself in a lot of areas that we used to think were limited to men. But I get the impression that these involvements have only caused her confusion and a feeling of being pulled in all directions.*

FLUX        *Well, give her time. Offered the chance, there's no telling what kind of things she might be capable of doing. She may, in fact, turn into a totally new kind of woman.*

INERTIA        *I'll tell you what your trouble is, Flux. You are too restless. And that is exactly the trouble with those American women you have been talking about. If they would just settle down and be women, everyone would be better off.*

FLUX        *Inertia, my friend, no one settles down any more. These days it just isn't done. The only way for American women to be women is to go on changing indefinitely. . . .*

*The point of the dialogue was that precisely the simplicity of these two extreme positions—the "biological destiny" and "androgynous" schools—are inadequate and distorting. The biological-destiny school, at least in pure form, has little currency at present—except perhaps with small groups of restorationists, whether political (romantic reactionaries) or psychological (ultra-orthodox Freudians). But the androgynous school is having something of a revival: it has been a periodic psychological accompaniment of—one could say exaggerated psychological rationale for—what are otherwise very laudable feminist political and social programs. The androgynous theme has also been invoked for today's young—either as a condemnation of them, or by way of welcoming them into the fold. But I think this misunderstands what the young are up to, and applies a convenient biological (or antibiological) category which shuts out, rather than illuminates, the exploratory sexual and psychological innovations taking place. These innovations seem to me to be part of the general quest (discussed in the last two chapters) for extending the field of psychological possibilities; and the alleged male-female sameness is more apparent than psychologically or sexually real.*

*I would not now retract my suggestion that woman as knower could greatly contribute to human survival through her special potential for psychohistorical innovation, but I do think I would place greater stress upon the obstacles involved. For the forms of psychic breakthrough required are barely imaginable at present; and in seeking them, women are of course subject to the symbolic impairments discussed throughout this volume. But when weighing these various possibilities, one should keep in mind the intensity of need for what women might create, as well as the speed with which psychological forms and human actions can shift from one manifestation to another.*

❊          ❊          ❊

Is it not time for us to turn from the question (and expression of weary male chauvinism) "What does a woman want?" to the more pertinent inquiry "What does a woman know?" My assumption, of course, is that women do know something *as women*, not entirely different from what men know but in a different way. In speaking of woman as knower, I refer to her potential for possessing insight or wisdom. My emphasis is upon experiential patterns of cognition and feeling, particularly in relationship to changing social forces.

I shall shift back and forth between specific observations and highly speculative suggestions which emerge from a generally psychoanalytic orientation but move in directions quite outside prevailing psychoanalytic theory. I follow the perspective outlined in earlier work, within which every psychological pattern is seen as part of a trinity, including universal psychobiological tendencies (in this article, those notably strong in women, but by no means entirely absent in men), currents given special stress within a particular cultural tradition, and modern (especially contemporary) historical influences. By referring frequently to Japanese (and occasionally to Chinese) women, as well as to American women, I shall try to explore patterns common to all women. This requires consideration of enduring tendencies as well as of those in flux, since only in this interplay can we glean what is most true of our subject and most pertinent for us to understand.

I

There is some usefulness in distinguishing three general aspects of womanhood, and in doing so in a culture that has institutionalized their discreteness. For in Japan women have long been divided, at least to a very considerable extent, into those who primarily nurture, those who provide sensual pleasure, and those who convey social wisdom.

The nurturers, of course, have been the culture's wives and mothers, the great majority of its women. And there has been no society anywhere in which the nurturing function has received greater emphasis. Indeed, there is evidence that, over the centuries, Japan has evolved a mother-child pattern unique in its stress upon symbolic oneness—upon a shared image of inseparability that continues to dominate much of Japanese psychological life and to serve as a model for relationships quite beyond those between parent and child. We may thus, in relationship to Japan, speak of a *cult of nurturance* based upon a kind of utopian imagery held by both nurturer and nurtured: through their earliest exchange of gestures and other emotional messages, they come to agree upon a standard of more or less absolute care and dependency which has no clear point of termination. A woman's life-tasks come to center on nurturing, particularly in relationship to her children, but also to her husband, and, in fact, to almost every task she performs. Japanese culture has thus made a way of life out of this aspect of essentially feminine potential.

In Japan, as throughout East Asia and much of the non-Western world, marriage is essentially a vehicle for the procreation and nurturing of children, rather than in itself a "holy bond" as in the Christian West. Marriage has been one thing, and sexual pleasure—either of love or simple lust—quite another. This separation necessitated the existence of woman as temptress in a form quite distinct from woman as nurturer. The woman dedicated to sensuality has had her special social identity, within a large category of amusement professions—prostitutes, geisha, entertainers, servants at inns and restaurants, and recently bargirls—or what has become known as the *mizu shōbai* or "water world," so named because of the amorphous

ebb and flow of life within it. We shall not concern ourselves here with the elaborate rules governing the sexual
availability of women in the "water world": these relate
to the specific profession and position within it, as well
as to the status and wealth of patrons and to elements
of mutual attraction and taste—but it is probably safe
to say that few if any women in the "water world" are
entirely unavailable, given a sufficiently favorable commercial or personal situation. For the seductive pleasures
of atmosphere, artistic performance, conversation, or
personal service, as well as sexuality per se, have been the
*raison d'être* of the woman living and working in the "water world," and of the "water world" itself. While such
women have undoubtedly varied in their own capacity
for sexual pleasure, it has been they, rather than conventional wives and mothers, who have been the traditional
female participants in romantic love and lustful encounter; and it is significant that, at least according to literary
legend, a frequent combination for a geisha was to become the long-term mistress of a man of wealth and high
social standing for the sake of her personal security and
prestige within her profession, and at the same time engage
in briefer, clandestine affairs with actors, reputed to be
skilled in the arts of love, for the sake of personal romance
and sensual pleasure.

Literary legend thus suggests that the "water world,"
to which actors of course belong, alone possessed the key
to erotic mysteries. Given this general cultural imagery,
and the absence of ideologies which denigrate the experience of pleasure in the sexual act or of pleasure in general (Japanese ideologies tend rather to place restrictions
on appropriateness of time, place, and partner, and upon
the proper balance of sensual activity and the more oblig-
atory aspects of life), it is probably fair to say that the
temptress in Japanese society has preempted much of the
sexual pleasure available to women in that society.* Such

---

* I assume here that the psychology of the divergent group of women
who entered—or, in most cases, were sold into—the Japanese "water
world" cannot be directly equated with that of contemporary Western

institutionalizing of woman as temptress, not only in Japan but in traditional cultures throughout the world, may be seen as the social formulation of a universal psychological pattern: namely, the unspoken assumption that a psychic emanation from woman's being sets in motion the sexual act, that the woman, in sexuality, is acted upon, literally entered into—which makes her by no means necessarily "passive," but rather, in a fundamental psychobiological sense, the source and the ground of heterosexual encounter.

Woman as knower has been best exemplified in Japan by creative women, particularly women writers, beginning with Murasaki Shikibu, author of *The Tale of Genji,* not only one of the first novels ever written (early eleventh century) but one of the greatest as well. Nor was Lady Murasaki the only prominent female knower of her era. As Ivan Morris points out, "During the period of about 100 years that spans the world of *The Tale of Genji,* almost every noteworthy author who wrote in Japanese was a woman."[2] Morris goes on to note the uniqueness of such female literary dominance in any culture at any time, as well as the paradox "that it should occur in a part of the world where women have traditionally been condemned to a position of irremediable inferiority." But Heian women, particularly court ladies like Lady Murasaki, had considerably more freedom than did women in subsequent periods of Japanese history;* moreover, as we shall soon see, the "irremediable inferiority" of Japanese women, even under conditions of their greatest social suppression, has by no means been what it has appeared to be.

---

prostitutes; and the psychological studies which have demonstrated various kinds of sexual aberration in the latter do not necessarily apply to the former.

* Morris points out that "it is not only since the Second World War that the position of Japanese women has become better than that of their ancestors a thousand years ago." And indeed, these feminine "ancestors" of the Heian period—or at least those elevated few who were part of Court life—were notable not only for their literary interests but for their erotic ones as well. Their tendency to combine feminine functions at so advanced a level anticipates the modern con-

In this literary emergence of women during the Heian period, there is one factor of particular psychological significance. Men who had literary aspirations persisted in the use of the Chinese language, then considered elegant, dignified, and prestigious—"the language of scholars, priests, and officials, occupying a role analogous to that of Latin in the West." But women, unburdened by psychological pressures of the sociopolitical hierarchy, "were free to make the fullest possible use of the *kana* phonetic script, which allowed them to record the native Japanese language, the language that was actually spoken, in a direct, simple fashion that was impossible either in pure Chinese or in the hybrid Sino-Japanese known as *kambun*." So sharp was this differentiation that the term used for the native syllabary (*onnade*) literally means "woman's hand," while that used for Chinese ideographs (*otokomoji*) means "men's letters." It is true that men were much more likely to have the educational opportunities to learn the Chinese language, but it is also probable that women turned naturally to the vernacular in order to describe the kinds of things they were most interested in. For women writers presented

a one-sided picture, concentrated almost exclusively on the social and cultural aspects of life. From reading works like the *Tale of Genji*, *Gossamer Diary*, and the *Pillow Book* [all classics by women of that era] we should hardly guess that the men described were often leading figures in the government of the day and that they spent at least as much of their time in political intrigues as in those of an erotic nature. Still less should we imagine that many of them, especially members of the northern branch of the Fujiwara family, were hard-working officials, seriously devoted to their public duties. . . .

---

dition, as I shall attempt to demonstrate. Women of their literary attainment and individuated life patterns do not seem to have again made their appearance in Japanese life until well after the Meiji Restoration of 1868. For this long period of feminine decline, in China as well as in Japan, many historians blame the suppressive influence of Neo-Confucian doctrine in both countries.

Similarly Arthur Waley, referring to the same era, speaks of the "extraordinary vagueness of women concerning purely male activities." Women writers, in other words, in direct contrast to their male counterparts, dealt with immediate, personal, mostly sensual experience; with feelings, longings, aesthetic responses, and personal encounters. They concerned themselves with what might be termed *informal knowledge* rather than with the more structured, theoretical, and formal knowledge of men. And in this and other respects, woman as knower in Heian Japan was not a unique entity, but merely more advanced than her counterparts in other cultures.

These three categories—nurturer, temptress, and knower—are clearly aspects of a psychic unity. Every woman, tenth-century Japanese or twentieth-century American, is in some measure all three. But what, we must then ask, is their unifying aspect? Are they merely, as some might claim, expressions of male fantasy—in the way that Freud described the need of many men to envision women as either asexual mothers or debased—and debasing—seductresses,[3] that is, as "madonna" or "whore"? There can be no doubt that elements of male fantasy—and, for that matter, female fantasy as well—enter into the formation of cultural institutions delineating the three types of women, but it would be misleading to attribute the categories to such fantasy alone. Rather we are confronted with three aspects of woman's psychic potential to which the institutions of every society have given expression during the course of cultural evolution. And the unifying element in all three categories—the focus from which woman's psychological life emanates—is *close identification with organic life and its perpetuation.*

This identification with organic life is most obvious in woman as nurturer, since this function stems directly from her role in procreation and is psychologically inseparable from it. But the identification holds in the other two categories as well. Woman as temptress, in a fundamental sense, creates conditions which favor procreation. And even where she contributes to the cultivation of sexual pleasure per se rather than to a procreative outcome, such cultivation may be part of a psychosocial balance between pleasure and procreation that enhances both. Moreover, in Japanese culture we are particularly struck by the way in which a nurturing aura dominates even seductive behavior. The present-day temptress, whether geisha or bargirl (and presumably prostitute, though prostitutes are now officially outlawed), approaches the male in a manner that is at the same time sexually provocative and maternal, seeming to combine encouragement of his manhood with an assumption of his childlike helplessness. It is, in fact, specifically this combination of attitudes that constitutes the much appreciated Japanese style of feminine service. Woman as knower similarly allies herself to organic life by drawing upon her functions as nurturer and temptress, which become not only starting points for her knowledge but the source of specific qualities in her style of knowing. This prominent psychological tone of nurturance throughout all female function is made unusually explicit in Japanese culture and demonstrates that the most complex attainments of women are likely to be colored and enriched by it.

## II

During periods of rapid historical change, the social structuring of these three feminine identities becomes unstable and confused, and women most sensitive to such change experience considerable psychological discomfort. Again the tendency is dramatically visible in Japan. The patterns found there have been bound up with social, economic, and sexual exploitation of women; and modern, mainly Western, ideologies of self-realization for men and women (beginning in the late nineteenth century and achieving particular force during the recent postwar era) have brought them under sharp attack. The resulting institutional breakdowns or, more frequently, partial breakdowns, have created a special form of conflict. We usually think of modernization, or of patterns of postmodern development, as requiring a high degree of specialization; but in the case of contemporary trends of individuation in women, the reverse is true. Each woman tends to become a "generalist"—to become, in a new way, nurturer *and* temptress *and* knower.

In work with young Japanese women, most of them in their early twenties, from middle-class backgrounds, and at the time of our interviews in a transitional state between completing their university work and moving out into "the world," I discovered how difficult this contemporary task can be. For many in this group, conflicts are made vividly manifest by the opportunity and threat of marriage, and in relationship to the already classic, modern Japanese ambivalence in the choice between the "arranged marriage" (*miai kekkon*) and the "love marriage" (*ren'ai kekkon*), and the often ingenious compromises which the culture has evolved—as four very brief examples suggest.

One girl spent much of our interview time, over a period of many months, castigating the institution of the arranged marriage, articulately exploring its derivation from feudalistic patterns of feminine inferiority, and affirming the importance of the love marriage as an expression of the individuality of the two people concerned. But just before her graduation she suddenly agreed to a marital arrangement initiated by the two families, in which there was only a single more or less formal meeting, in a group situation, with her prospective husband. She expressed the vague hope that she would be able to salvage some of her original personal and intellectual ideals by becoming a working wife.

Another girl wavered in her actions concerning marriage, backing out of one parentally engineered arrangement at the last moment through a show of tears, after having seemed, in her ambivalent silence, to have acquiesced to it. Meanwhile she continued an affectionate but rather theoretical relationship with a reticent male fellow student whose ambivalence and search matched her own. In the process, her scholarly interests in contemporary literature waned. She complained of feeling purposeless, as if "floating," but she persisted, though with limited enthusiasm, in her efforts to find a teaching position that would give expression to this intellectual interest.

A third student became involved in an affair with a married writer whose unstable emotional pattern included feelings of guilty obligation toward his wife and concern for his infant child. When the student herself became pregnant, she suddenly shifted her full commitment toward *her* (unborn) child and refused to have an abortion performed (a legal medical procedure in Japan), despite urgent advice from many sides that she do so. After several conferences among the various parties involved over a considerable period of time, during which the student herself experienced feelings of unreality and depression and had occasional thoughts of suicide, a solution seemed to be in the offing: the wife kept her child (something of a concession in Japan, where, until recently, children of broken marriages were generally given to the husband or his family); and the student, encouraged by her lover's hesitant steps toward committing himself to her in eventual marriage, began to make plans not only for having her baby but for returning to her university and continuing studies that would prepare her for professional work with children.

A fourth girl identified closely with the writings and the life-pattern of Simone de Beauvoir and rebelled vigorously against her comfortably conventional middle-class background. She succeeded in gaining admission to a leading national university (something of an accomplishment for a girl, but often looked upon as an equivocal one, since those who did so were labeled "unfeminine"), where she went through relatively familiar patterns of enthusiastic embrace of, then disillusionment with, Marxist ideology and action programs; she also embarked upon a love affair with a brilliant fellow student who shared many of her intellectual and literary interests, and to whom she eventually became engaged. But with the approach of her graduation and wedding date, she felt increasingly moody and pessimistic, seemed at times depressed, and complained of feeling unreal. Although she still considered herself to be in love with her fiancé, she had strong doubts about her capacity to tolerate life in the provincial area to which he had been temporarily assigned, and about their longer-range ability to achieve happiness and fulfillment with each other.

I have of course omitted the complex individual-psycho-logical factors which contributed to these outcomes, or temporary outcomes. My only purpose here is to suggest the difficulties faced by young women at the forefront of their culture's historical development in coming to terms with changing combinations of imagery and self-imagery concerning what a woman might or should be. As they perceive ever enlarging and confusing possibilities (not only from reading Simone de Beauvoir, but from the various communication media, and from the examples of prominent women within Japanese culture), such young women quickly form partial identifications with these new patterns, and evolve new criteria of judgment according to which they find themselves wanting. They are likely to internalize ideal visions which require that they themselves not only become feminine "generalists," but that they do so in "expert" fashion. They expect themselves to become not only a mother but a "modern mother" conversant with the latest approaches to child-rearing; not merely a sexual partner, but one capable of giving and receiving pleasure according to the latest ideas of how such pleasure is defined; not only an intellectual but a holder of ideas of depth and relevance equal to those held by men. No wonder, then, that these young women frequently falter, make sudden retreats into earlier cultural patterns they have seemingly abandoned but which actually still hold great emotional force, make blind forays of a self-destructive nature, achieve "victories" in which the accomplishment is so fraught with ambivalence and guilt as to be almost incapacitating. No wonder, also, that, whether retreating, advancing, or making intricate compromises, such women experience feelings of transience and unreality which epitomize their sense of historical dislocation, their inability either to live by the old imagery or master the new. Much of their discomfort may be thought of as the adult psychohistorical counterpart of the phenomenon of "separation anxiety"; for the imagery of helplessness and abandonment experienced by the very young child when separated from its mother can be unconsciously revived with every subsequent act of individuation.

Contributing to this separation anxiety is acute sensitivity to stringent criteria for what constitutes femininity. The dreaded accusation of being "unfeminine" becomes an all-too-easy epithet which may reflect both male anxiety concerning woman's increasing explorations and female anxiety lest these explorations result in disqualification from participation as women in the various male-female rhythms which each culture establishes and defines, as well as universal anxiety that woman's quest for knowledge might impair her sensual and nurturing capacities. A vicious circle then develops: these very anxieties, together with persisting rigidities of definition (for instance, Japanese feminine requirements of reserve, acquiescence, and a semblance of ignorance), make it almost inevitable that women who break out of these limitations do so by way of identification with their fathers and brothers, competition with men, and the acquisition of "masculine" traits—which in turn stimulate the anxieties, and so on. Only gradually, after many generations, are such definitions enlarged and women given more leeway for imagery concerning their own femininity. But the dilemma persists in all cultures, ever fed by new anxieties of both men and women.

### III

Conflicts, however, beget possibilities. I have suggested that much of woman's psychic potential stems from her close identification with organic life and its perpetuation; from this potential she derives a special capacity to mediate between biology and history. Such mediation becomes particularly necessary under present conditions of unprecedented historical velocity. For with so much of psychic imagery confused and in flux, biologically rooted modes of knowing could have a uniquely steadying influence. Mediating between biology and history, of course, is by no means solely a female function; and exploring it in women may well shed light upon man's related, though not identical, psychic possibilities.

Woman's organically rooted traditional function as informal knower can be distinguished from man's traditional explorations of ideas and symbols on abstract planes far removed from organic function.[4] Yet her knowledge has been "informal" only in the sense that it has been relegated to a kind of social underground, as if such knowledge were not quite proper or acceptable, unworthy of having its forms recognized. But recent developments in many fields of thought have created radical shifts in standards of intellectual acceptability, and have, in fact, placed special value on those very modes of knowing which had been previously part of the feminine informal underground. Michael Polanyi, for instance, traces the evolution of—and sees as crucial to man's future—a form of "personal knowledge" characterized by "the personal participation of the knower in the knowledge he believes himself to possess," and which "transcends the disjunction between subjective and objective."[5] The concept which Polanyi evokes here might also be termed *organic knowledge*; it requires rigorous cognitive standards but at the same time takes account of the self-process of the knower. It parallels the recent emphasis of depth psychology, social science, biology, and even physics, upon the significance of the contribution of the "observer" or knower to the outcome and formulation of his scientific work. The prevailing male domination of these sciences (with the possible exception of depth psychology) makes clear that women have no monopoly on "personal" or organic knowing; and it is difficult to gauge the extent to which women may have indirectly played a part in bringing about the present emphasis upon this form of knowing. What we can say is that given women's special aptitude in this direction—along with the instability of cultural contexts and criteria for knowledge in general— we may well expect a series of extraordinary developments in modes of knowing in which feminine influence becomes increasingly significant, though in ways we can as yet only dimly perceive.

Also operating here is what I would call a general shift in the psychology of knowing, affecting men and women alike: a change in the way ideas are held, which depends in turn upon a new form of self-process. In more than a decade of work with Chinese and Japanese young adults, I have found them, and many of their elders as well, to be capable of surprisingly rapid shifts in ideas, imagery, and ideology, even when these have been related to the most central issues of individual and group existence, and often without undergoing the painful sequence of resistance, internal conflict, and dramatic "conversion" which we traditionally tend to associate with such shifts. East Asian cultural patterns play a part here: rather than the Western focus upon the fateful encounter between self and idea, they have stressed group hegemony at the expense of either self or idea. But this cultural principle does not, in itself, suffice as a causative explanation. For one can observe a similar tendency in young people, and in some older ones too, in America and elsewhere. There would appear to be a convergence between premodern, non-Western patterns and postmodern tendencies, a much more frequent convergence than is generally realized. In any case, this *mutability of ideation and imagery* is a function of a contemporary style of self-process that has emerged from the breakdown of stable sources of identification (which in the past made shifts in ideation a more serious internal matter), and from the unprecedented flux in new objects of identification, ideational and technological, to which everyone is exposed.

We may thus speak of a *protean style of self-process*, characterized by an interminable series of experiments and explorations, which we shall examine more closely in Chapter 15. What I wish to suggest here is that feminine knowing may make specific contributions to this style.

For lurking beneath the protean style of self-process—perhaps primarily reactions to it—are a pair of related myths, essentially male in their theoretical absoluteness: the myth of the magnificently independent and wholly unfettered self; and the polar myth of the totally obliterated self, whether obliterated in the service of an all-embracing social movement or of an equally imprisoning "spontaneity."[6] Elements of both myths are everywhere operative, in music and painting as well as in philosophy and politics. Both can tend toward that combination of psychic and ideational excess, or ideological totalism, which we have come to associate with severe historical dislocation; but both are also capable of serving as evocative, if unattainable, ideals for creative Protean exploration. And it is just possible that woman's way of knowing can help guard against the former danger and enhance the latter possibility; that her form of organic knowledge may humanize these harshly abstract polarities. A gifted young American novelist suggests, through one of his female characters, the kind of feminine knowing I have in mind; he has her speak as the wife of an artist, but in a way that applies for women in general:

> We women are only human . . . and . . . no matter how we feel we can touch . . . on their masculine power, we still remain rooted in life, at a much more primitive, invariable, more logical level . . . and we are never capable of a total sacrifice of ourselves to their ends. . . . We must go along, *but we must not leave the ground.*[7]

Important here is the refusal of self-surrender and the reassertion of the organic foundation of feminine knowing. Identification and empathy are distinguished from total merging, to create the psychic basis of what Camus has called "thought which recognizes limits."

To suggest an even more speculative possibility, woman's innate dependence upon biological rhythms—particularly the several rhythms central to her nurturing capacities—may provide her with psychobiological sensitivities useful for grasping the more irregular historical rhythms which confront us. This potential insight into the rhythmic is of course difficult to assess; and I in no way wish to suggest that magic combinations of numbers derived from physiology can be applied to social process. But neither should we assume that woman's accustomed psychobiological rhythmicity has no relevance or potential value for comprehending events in the cultural sphere.

Whether or not we are justified in such speculation, it is possible to identify more specific features of woman's relationship to historical change. Here one often encounters the assumption that "women are more conservative than men," that during periods of change women tend to cling to old forms of custom and belief that men are more willing to relinquish. There is some truth in this assumption; the organic aspect of feminine knowing can lead women to distrust and resist technological and ideological innovation that seems to threaten the structure of long-standing, biologically based social patterns. But woman's attachment to the old and familiar has been both exaggerated and oversimplified. For there are significant ways in which her organic conservatism, epitomized in her nurturing, and specifically maternal, function, becomes a crucial vehicle of social change. The set of feelings and images she transmits to the infant constitute an individual basis for cultural continuity and a psychic imprint of the perpetuation of life itself, surely a genuinely conservative function. But during periods of great historical pressure toward change, precisely this imagery makes possible the individual participation in change by providing a source of constancy—what in Chapter 2 I spoke of as an "emotional-symbolic substrate"—with which subsequent imagery of change can interact without threatening the basic integration of the self. And even when this substrate becomes a psychic basis for nostalgic, or restorationist, longings for the individual or cultural "golden age" of harmony and unity, the dynamic interplay of past- and future-oriented imagery becomes a propulsive force toward change.[8]

We recall this change-enhancing potential in the parental relationships of militant Japanese students: their intense relationships with their mothers, in contrast to their distance from their quietly disapproving fathers. While usually claiming little knowledge of the ideological issues involved, they simply expressed the conviction that their sons' goals and motives, and those of their fellow students, must be "pure" and worthy, and raised objections mainly because of fears that their sons might meet with physical harm in clashes with the police which sometimes occurred. The emotional support received from their mothers could thus often confirm the students' own sense of the nobility of their group's vision. Here the emotional-symbolic substrate transmitted in the mother-son relationship served not only as a source of constancy for these students, but also provided, in its original stress upon "purity," an ethical model for the son in his ideological aspirations and for the mother in her support for these aspirations. Her support in turn tended to reinforce his innovative identity and "confirm" him in his change-promoting activity. In these ways the mothers' nurturing function provided something very close to a psychic mandate for change.

But there were also pitfalls. There was an emotional price paid for this maternal support in the form of life-long patterns of marked dependency—not only that traditionally transmitted in mother-son relationships, but magnified by the special nurturing these mothers had been called upon to provide under changing social conditions. This dependency was evident in the students' exaggerated group needs in relationship to the *Zengakuren* itself, and to the decision many of them subsequently made to put their radical pasts behind them in favor of a career in one of Japan's large, paternalistic industrial organizations. Thus in a sense the mother-son alliance played a part in subverting the very autonomy sought in the change-promoting involvements that it supported. Maternal support also did much to ease the "moral backsliding" (or what the Japanese call *tenkō*) inherent in this switch to the "enemy camp," and to minimize, though by no means eliminate, feelings of self-betrayal and permit these young men to function successfully in their new occupational (and in a different way still change-promoting) identities. These psychological pitfalls therefore do not negate the woman's influence in promoting social change; they merely suggest its complexity.

## IV

Hidden feminine influences operate in historical change in America no less than in East Asia. Depth-psychological work with American students, notably that of Kenneth Keniston,[9] suggests the importance of the mother-son relationship for creating and sustaining innovative potential among young Americans; Keniston's group was both intellectually outstanding and psychohistorically alienated, and probably reflects generalized American patterns writ large.

But there are also important differences in the way in which women affect social change in America and in East Asia, differences growing out of very divergent histories. Important here is the fact that America has not only lacked a feudal social structure but has grown out of a series of specific breakdowns of feudal structures in other cultures, or else out of the piecemeal sequestering of deviant individuals and groups from every variety of larger social unit. The resulting strain upon Americans' sense of the past—our polar tendencies to deny on the one hand that any past has existed or is needed, and on the other hand to expand in idealized, sometimes desperate, terms the past we possess—can hardly be argued. Nonetheless, compared to the radical upheavals that have taken place in modern Asia, America has emerged out of relatively mild social and psychological dislocations. We have, moreover, at least until recently, evolved a cultural style for the channeling, even taming, of ever-present social change. Since the rapid development of movements for feminine self-expression, including ideologies of feminism, may be looked upon at least in part as phenomena of release accompanying social breakdown and historical change, we are not surprised that American versions of these, however lurid they may have appeared to many, have also been relatively mild. And the American struggle for women's rights has been tempered by a frontier tradition—and later, in a different way, a tradition for acculturating immigrants—which either contained imagery of equality consistent with the expression of such rights or at least did not serve as a nucleus for absolute opposition to them.

The "release phenomenon" of which I speak—the sudden emergence in often exaggerated form of psychological tendencies previously suppressed by social custom—has been much more dramatic in China and Japan. One can, for example, contrast the classical stance of the Chinese woman, her bound feet literally restricting her motion and symbolically restricting her "life space," with the recent displays of assertion and unwavering ideological aggressiveness by female cadres in Communist China. This does not mean that the women of China have been suddenly transformed from weakness to strength. Rather, it suggests that an important group of them have undergone a shift in the areas within which they can operate as knowers, from family to society, along with a similar redirection of intellectual and emotional expression. Such release and redirection often tends toward excess, as was made clear to me not only in the behavior of female cadres, but in the examples I encountered of extraordinarily domineering and shrewish behavior in Chinese women who were still operating primarily within their families at a time when the society surrounding these families was literally falling apart. Indeed, it may well be that "the shrew," whenever she appears in significant numbers, whether in China or Elizabethan England, is a specific product of social breakdown and of such a release phenomenon.

By these standards, American shifts in the life space permissible to women have been minor ones, taking place within a more established ideological tradition of feminine self-realization. Educated East Asian women are well aware that their historical experience with such ideologies is brief indeed, and that their serious confrontation with them is still in its infancy. Leaving aside the psychological complexities and mixed benefits of this confrontation, my point here is that American women, and in different ways European and Russian women, are in a real historical sense a vanguard group. Indeed, although

American and East Asian women tend to have complicated feelings about one another—or about themselves in
relationship to each other—they seem to agree upon the
observation that East Asian women have only begun to experiment with matters that their Western counterparts
have been struggling with for centuries. (No doubt the
time will come when East Asian women will feel the need
to rediscover some of their own cultural values here as in
other areas, but that is another matter.)

As a vanguard group, American women are capable of
institutional inventions that are bound to be of interest to
the rest of the world. One of these inventions, made, of
course, in collaboration with men, is the new marriage
pattern described by Edna Rostow,[10] in which mutuality of
care and individual realization, as well as intellectual and
emotional sharing, have been achieved, or at least sought
after, to an unprecedented degree. But it inevitably follows that American women must also be in the vanguard
of despair—despair related to the gap between the nobility of this kind of vision, whether in marriage or other aspects of life, and the more ambiguous, disappointing, often
painful actualities. Yet large groups of women throughout
the world seem determined to have an opportunity to experience this vanguard despair.

One sometimes has the impression that such feminine
despair increases directly in proportion to the development of feminine capacities. There are additional reasons
for this, one of which is suggested by the simple, somewhat accusatory claim, made about thirty years ago by a
prominent American journalist, that "modern women
are . . . unhappy and . . . unconsciously hate men . . . because they have gotten better and men have gotten
worse."[11] Rather than simply dismissing this statement by
Dorothy Thompson as that of an aggressively competitive woman, or as merely an expression of "penis envy," we
do better (whatever her psychological makeup) to see in
it the possible suggestion of a general principle: Both men
and women experience considerable psychological conflict in relation to rapid historical change, but the conflict

in women is more likely to carry at least the seed of personal liberation, while in men the greater commitment to the ideological superstructure which is undergoing deterioration is likely to imbue the conflict with profound psychological threat. This principle is, of course, bound to have a great number of exceptions, depending upon the nature of the change and the context in which it takes place. But I have found it to apply in a variety of situations under differing conditions, and I believe it to be generally consistent with the psychohistorical factors we have so far discussed. If the principle is true, and there will be additional evidence for it in what follows, historical change creates a disparity in psychological balance between the sexes in which feminine achievement becomes something of a pyrrhic victory, accompanied as it is by impaired capacity of both men and women to relate to one another. Yet precisely this combination of disappointment in male partners and expanding criteria for self-realization gives women particular capacity for new kinds of accomplishment, for the development of new forms of knowing. Men may then feel themselves doubly threatened: not only dislocated and possibly emasculated, but also "seen through" in their weaknesses more clearly than ever before by women whom they can no longer dominate and to whom they feel distinctly inferior. At this juncture, their latent psychic tendency to view all women as dangerous devourers is likely to be activated, whether or not these devourers are felt to be allied with an imprisoning society, as Diana Trilling suggests is the case in contemporary American masculine literary fantasy.[12] This particular aspect of historical dislocation, however uncomfortable, seems to be the source of a great variety of literary and depth-psychological discoveries by both men and women.

We would seem now, willy-nilly, to have entered into the arena of the "battle of the sexes," an arena which the historically minded psychiatrist should neither flee from nor accept on its own terms. Substituting the metaphor of the dance for that of the arena, we may say that in all cultures there is a complex rhythmic patterning of emotions between men and women, in the continuous effort at definition and reassertion of what is to be considered properly "masculine" and "feminine." Within the dance one inevitably encounters a discrepancy between public and private gestures, between outer appearance and inner actuality. For the Japanese woman, for instance, the definition of femininity has traditionally contained requirements of charm and service; definitions of femininity have been less precise for the American woman, but, at least when compared to the Japanese, she has been permitted much greater public assertion. I have, in fact, repeatedly noted the fascination and horror with which Japanese men and women alike have observed the American woman's public self-assertions, and particularly her readiness to contest male authority. But when we look at the more hidden aspects of the dance within the two cultures, a very different image presents itself. It turns out that the Japanese woman has an actual authority in human relationships within the family, often over her husband as well as her children, in many ways far greater than that of her American counterpart. Within this realm her service to others—her nurturing function—is her means of rule; her influence is all-pervasive as she doles out both financial (she tends to be in control of the purse strings and to receive her husband's paycheck in toto, from which she grants him his allowance) and emotional succor to those around her. And when Americans have become sufficiently intimate with Japanese life to observe these patterns, it has been their turn to look on with horror and fascination at the Japanese woman's way of treating her husband in public as uncontested lord and master, and in private as another child in need of maternal care.

But what of the *direction* of the movements of the dance within the two cultures? In Japan, there is a saying that during the postwar period "women and nylon stockings have grown stronger." The first part of the claim is untestable. But whatever the fits and starts and mutual ambivalence (and we have seen that women can be very ambivalent about becoming "stronger"), there has been a clear if grudging tendency toward the loosening of existing definitions of femininity. This tendency shows itself in beginning opportunities for women to work in areas previously confined to men, and to participate in various intellectual activities without totally destroying their capacity to be considered, and to consider themselves, feminine. We have already witnessed the difficulties of achieving even this much; and there have inevitably been enormous strains, residual forms of discrimination (not only financial, but more subtle patterns which include relegating women employees to serving tea and in various ways waiting on men), and even "restorationist" demands that all of society return to an idyllic past that never was, in which women were totally subservient to men and all lived in perfect harmony. But these resistances do not alter the basic direction of the dance.

For the American woman, the direction, as might be expected, is considerably less specific. For she lacks both the exaggerated restrictions of traditional definitions of femininity (although restrictions have of course been present) or actual models to follow (such as her Japanese counterpart has in identifying with American or generally Western patterns). Still subject to psychological and financial discrimination in her efforts to broaden her knowing, her social gains offset by her culture's traditional stress upon something resembling a male-female "alliance for progress" (that is, for visible, often technological, accomplishment), rather than upon celebration of the genuinely sensual and spiritual possibilities of male-female interplay, it is no wonder that she often seems brittle beneath her attainments, uncertain of her femininity, and equally uncertain of what would improve her situation. Yet out of this very ambiguity of direction, new generations of American women are engaging in a variety of experiments, sexual and otherwise, which would seem to offer as much promise for creative innovation as they do cause for concern.

The strains that accompany changing definitions of

femininity can cause women to retreat into highly damaging distortions of their nurturing function. What we Americans so possessively refer to as "Momism" is by no means confined to American culture, but is rather a compensatory plunge, taken by dislocated women of any culture, into a more or less *totalistic nurturing ethos*: into a despairing effort to achieve self-esteem and power through a mother-child relationship which goes even beyond that of a cult of nurturance in the direction of total maternal control over the child, achieved by the alternate promise of total sustenance and threat of abandonment, neither of which is carried out.

Such totalistic nurturing imagery can, moreover, lead to malignant consequences, whether or not these take the form of mental illness per se.\* Children so brought up may not only go through life unconsciously seeking new combinations of total dependency and total submission, but, equally important, inevitably experience a sense of profound disillusionment at the failure to achieve what they seek, the disillusionment itself a repetition of the original mother-child pattern. They may come to distrust all relationships as falling short of what is craved, and develop a sense of what Japanese intellectuals have termed (referring to themselves and their fellow countrymen) "victim-consciousness"—which, in psychological terms, really means a gnawing sense of resentment over unfulfilled, and unfulfillable, dependency. Those so affected can become suspicious to the point of paranoia, and particularly *suspicious of counterfeit nurturance*: that is, exaggeratedly on guard lest the help or sustenance they seek be predicated upon their being considered weak and

---

\* Such totalistic nurturing imagery also bears considerable relationship to the kind of mother-child relationship which is thought to contribute to the development of schizophrenia. Recent work on schizophrenia emphasizes the entire family constellation rather than the mother-child relationship alone; but if an actual increase in the incidence of schizophrenia has been occurring during the past few decades in America and elsewhere, a debated issue, it is quite possible that the patterns of historical dislocation and attendant disturbances in mother-child relationships we have been discussing might be a factor in this increase.

inferior—precisely the way they feel about themselves. Such patterns of suspicion of counterfeit nurturance can operate within any group of people who feel themselves unusually dependent and helpless in relationship to stronger groups—whether arising from actual victimization of any kind, such as racial prejudice, or even from the circumstances of international politics, particularly those involving programs of economic or other aid. I do not wish to suggest that totalistic nurturing imagery (or "Momism") in itself causes these momentous problems, but rather that it becomes part of an active constellation of psychological and historical elements for which there is no clear starting point; it is both a product of, and a further stimulus to, the essential historical dislocation.

I have confined myself to Japanese examples because I have had specific opportunity to observe them, but my impression is that people in non-Western cultures are more generally prone to patterns of totalistic nurturing imagery and suspicion of counterfeit nurturance than are Americans. There are several reasons for this: non-Western cultures have traditionally emphasized the unity of the mother-child relationship to a greater extent than in the West, to a point sometimes approaching totalism; these same cultures have undergone much greater modern and contemporary historical upheavals; and, equally important, the nations formed from non-Western cultures find themselves in the position of requiring various forms of help or sustenance from Western countries.* Yet American culture may, in a special way, have a particular sensitivity to "Momism" precisely because it has long emphasized an opposite myth of absolute "individualism"—that of the child's eventual capacity to achieve total independence from its parents (and from everyone else)—and this

---

* The great exception in American life is, of course, Negro culture, in which suspicion of counterfeit nurturance as well as patterns of maternal domination are strong. Especially crucial here is the long victimization of the American Negro in American life and his continuing position of inferiority and dependency, though the other features I mentioned in relationship to non-Western cultures also play a part.

sensitivity makes us the first to seek out "Momism" in our midst.

The alternative to these dislocations and explosions of mistrust lies in various kinds of social inventiveness. New psychological discoveries concerning the interplay of the sexes and the special potential of each sex are as necessary as are political and economic advances. All three may, in fact, be inseparable; women might, for instance, be able to make use of their characteristic focus upon immediate human relationships to evolve modes of knowing that could "soften" prevailing political and economic approaches, and bring enriching elements of sensuality and nurturance back into knowledge itself. But a conspiratorial theory which sees the difficulty as the imposition of feminine standards by women's magazines or psychoanalysts is not adequate for grasping the dilemma.° The actual problem is a more difficult one: How can women make their way in a technologically dominated, in this sense "man-made," world and claim their full share of the contemporary historical adventure while remaining true to their psychological nature as women?

v

There is an additional expression of feminine knowing that could have enormous significance in our present historical situation, pertaining to ways of symbolizing death and immortality in relationship to the needs of life. It stems from the general human need for a sense of connection, for meaningful ties to people, ideas, and symbols, derived from the past and projecting into the future. This sense of connection is initiated through innate patterns

---

° A recent, forceful presentation of what comes close to this conspiratorial point of view is that of Betty Friedan, in *The Feminine Mystique*.[13] While I am sympathetic to Mrs. Friedan's concern with enlarging prevailing imagery about what constitutes femininity, and would agree that women's magazines and psychoanalysts have at times promulgated overly narrow definitions of femininity, I would insist upon the importance of broader psychohistorical currents rather than the groups she singles out for attack.

of the human infant toward what John Bowlby has called "attachment behavior."[14] Bowlby has identified five "component instinctual responses" (sucking, clinging, following, crying, and smiling), inborn impulses in the infant which both promote, and are further stimulated by, maternal care, and which therefore have "survival value" to the child and "underlie the child's tie to his mother," his earliest and most fundamental human bond.

I would make the further claim that the sense of connection so initiated extends not only into adult life but beyond it. That is, for a sense of connection to be experienced during adult life, one requires a form of imagery, conscious or unconscious, which is felt to perpetuate that connection after one's death. This inner imagery constitutes what I have referred to as a *sense of immortality*,[15] and may be expressed in the biological, theological, and interpersonal or creative spheres, or through identification with nature itself. I have also suggested that the existence of nuclear weapons has, in itself and independently of any use of these weapons, posed a significant, though usually unrecognized, psychological threat in the form of interference with this symbolic need: that in the post-nuclear world we can imagine no biological or biosocial posterity, little or nothing surviving of our works or influences; theological symbolism of an afterlife becomes threatened or blurred, leaving only nature itself as a potentially important but ambiguous means of perpetuating a sense of individual connection and maintaining a sense of immortality.*

I believe that this fundamental threat to human connection must inevitably affect attachment behavior in a more general sense. Our imagery of connection does not necessarily distinguish between present and future attachments, and if one is threatened, so is the other. It may not be too much to say that the combination of unprecedented historical velocity (which in itself presents a severe threat

---

* There is still another mode, that of "experiential transcendence," a feeling state so intense that time and death seem to disappear. (See Chapters 15 and 16.)

to connection and attachment) and the existence of nuclear weapons create a revolutionary degree of potential suspiciousness of all human connection. There results not only the sensitivity to counterfeit nurturance I have already mentioned, but also a variety of psychosocial patterns both destructive and potentially creative: these include such things as severe youth rebellions, widespread lassitude and rote behavior, engagement in various forms of pseudo-attachment characterized by the appearance of a meaningful bond without its emotional content, every form of plunge into social movements that promise new solidarity, followed by rapid disillusionment with these movements and with the possibility of achieving solidarity or connection. These reactions to impaired connection represent another form of separation anxiety, which, according to Bowlby, is a "primary anxiety . . . not reducible to other terms." Therefore, to say that we are faced by psychohistorical threats to our sense of connection of a revolutionary intensity is also to say that we are faced with unprecedented eruptions of anxiety of the most elemental nature.

These are root problems of the human situation, and can hardly be solved by any individual or group, or by members of either sex alone. But it would seem that women have a special relationship to them that we may do well to explore, and to a degree quite beyond the fragmentary suggestions presented here, a relationship based upon her nurturing function and upon her particular capacity to bridge biology and history. If, as I am suggesting, an impaired sense of immortality, severed symbolic connection, and intensified separation anxiety are all of a psychohistorical piece, they create a self-reinforcing cycle which threatens not only general psychic balance but the continuity of the human species. Insofar as women can contribute to counter-tendencies which interrupt this cycle in favor of constructive and even extraordinary possibilities equally open to the human future, her capacity as knower meets its ultimate test. We might of course say that she makes just this kind of contribution through each child she helps to instill, during its earliest years, with a reasonable balance of connection and autonomy, in the face of pressures that make even this modest contribution ever more difficult. But I am suggesting something more: that, given the precarious nature of our psychic and physical existence, we have no choice but to return to organic principles even as we extend our cognitive and emotional discoveries; and that woman as knower, closest to these principles, can—like the goddess Demeter, who taught mankind to raise itself "above the life of beasts" and became the "giver of immortality"[16]—bring her wisdom to bear where it is most needed.

# PSYCHOANALYSIS
# AND HISTORY

## 13

*I made this review of a diverse collection of essays into a kind of position paper on the psychohistorical project. I think it was a fair picture of how the matter then stood in 1965. Much has happened since, but the essay still has something to say about the forces operating against the coming together of psychonanalysis and history.*

*At the time I wrote it, a few of us were attempting to come to grips with some of these obstacles through the formation of the psychohistorical group mentioned earlier. We still meet regularly, but have been reticent to publish anything as a group. For this some have criticized us, but I think the reticence well founded. Were I to write this review now, I would emphasize still more the pitfalls of bringing together psychology and history: the difficulties, especially during the present era, of finding interpretive categories which themselves have the right balance of stability and malleability.*

*For the symbolic and intellectual confusion of our period is bound to affect the work of the psychohistorian, whether or not he makes that confusion his subject of study. Even retrospective interpretations of history must be made through contemporary eyes, which cannot (and should not try to) screen out the dilemmas always within immediate view.*

*I would therefore say even more loudly now than I did in the essay itself: our historical and psychoanalytic traditions are in themselves woefully inadequate to the tasks of psychohistory. We need new concepts, new modes of observation, new relationships to what we are observing. Like everyone else these days, we need a new language and even a new life-style in order to connect with, no less interpret, the world we inhabit.*

❊          ❊          ❊

"We are caught in the teeth of history." So James Baldwin recently characterized the distorted relationships now prevailing between whites and Negroes in the United States. What Baldwin meant was that, without some grasp of the debilitating historical interplay between the two groups, there would be little possibility for improving these relationships. For in dealing with human crises, we, to a significant extent, *are* our history. But the present rate of technological and social change adds a note of paradox. Our history may indeed be largely what we are, but a good deal of the time it appears to be less than useless for providing guidelines for meeting the revolutionary situations we constantly face. In this sense the devouring "teeth" of history are not so much its distortions as its irrelevance.

What has psychoanalysis to do with this paradox? Everything, one would think, since, in its central principles, psychoanalysis is one of the most historical of sciences. Baldwin's words might, in fact, have come straight out of Freud. For psychoanalysis stands fast on the principles of historical causation—so much so that Erik Erikson has cautioned against its "originitis," its tendency to see man as *nothing but* the historical origins of his individual conflicts, whether these conflicts are rooted in environmental trauma or biological instinct. As Bruce Mazlish points out in his illuminating introduction to the volume of essays he has edited:[1] "Historians study man's collective past: psychoanalysts study his individual past. Surely, one would have thought that a mental bridge could be built to connect the two investigations." Mazlish also recognizes that no such bridge has as yet been built, and goes on to deplore the neglect ("nay, the deliberate ignoring") by historians of relevant works in psychoanalysis. Yet one could, with equal justice, rebuke most psychoanalysts for similarly neglecting history—that is, for failing to see individual man in relationship to his wider collective experience. The "mental bridge" which seems so logical a connection turns out instead to be something of a Bridge of Sighs.

Mazlish has made a useful distinction between two categories of application of psychoanalysis to history: the "fundamental historical explanation . . . of the origin of human society," which he calls "Freud's philosophy of history"; and psychoanalytic approaches to "more limited problems of historical explanation," which he refers to as "the application of psychoanalysis to history." But the first of these categories, with its stress on archaic origins, is more in the nature of psychobiological evolution, that is, prehistory. And the second category all too frequently reduces itself to classical analysis of individual psychopathology seeming to take place more or less outside "history." We may thus say (by carrying the argument further than Mazlish does) that much psychoanalytic work that specifically addresses itself toward gaining an understanding of history ends up either ignoring or eliminating the very object of its study. Add to this the barriers to a psychological approach inherent in the academic historical tradition, and it is no wonder that "psychoanalytic history, except for the work of a few hardy pioneers, can hardly be said as yet to exist."

Philip Rieff, in his essay on "The Meaning of History and Religion in Freud's Thought"—the most penetrating individual paper in the collection—relates this problem to what he calls Freud's "model of time." As Rieff points out, Freud saw the "*remoteness* of time" as the "really decisive factor" in the experience of the unconscious, so that "a certain event, or events, necessarily in remote rather than near history—indeed, at the beginning—becomes determinative of all that must follow." "Reducing change to constancy, Freud collapses history into nature, religion and politics into psychology." The difficulty of Freud's method is precisely that of "originitis": the exaggeratedly causal focus through which, as Rieff puts it, "history is predestination." Here are the beginnings of the dictum from which efforts to combine psychoanalysis and history have since suffered, the insistence that there is nothing new under the psychohistorical sun.

Yet the sensitive reader of *Moses and Monotheism*, a book which contains the most characteristic expression of Freud's historical method, is given one particular insight so powerful that it literally launched the fields of psychoanalytic history and historical psychology. I refer to the idea of the psychological past as the motor of history, of the sense of history as (in the phrase of Norman O. Brown quoted earlier) "a forward-moving *recherche du temps perdu*." Anyone who has attempted to investigate historical process through the psychological study of individuals can attest to the basic truth of this principle. Indeed, the central problem of the enterprise under discussion is precisely that of formulating more exactly the ways in which individual and collective pasts come together to create this psychohistorical motor.

The essays by A. L. Kroeber and Salo W. Baron—the first a retrospective appraisal of *Totem and Taboo*, and the second a book review of *Moses and Monotheism* at the time it appeared—do little to further our grasp of the problem. While they are interesting reflections of distinguished thinkers' understandable struggles with these two elusive, often brilliantly wrong-headed Freudian classics, I would question whether they retain sufficient importance to justify their inclusion in the volume.

In the case of Hans Meyerhoff's well-known essay on "Freud and the Ambiguity of Culture," there is no doubt that we encounter a formidable statement on Freud. But for all of its erudition and forceful argument, it is marred by its fundamentalist tone. Meyerhoff, here as elsewhere, lashes out at neo-Freudians and "revisionists" who have departed from the word, and enjoins all to return to the literal wisdom of that which has been bequeathed. One cannot quarrel with much of what he says about the power of Freud's ambiguity and the weakness of neo-Freudian writings. He is willing, moreover, to be almost as severe with contemporary Freudians. But I think he is wrong in his unqualified distinction between the intellectual sins of the neo-Freudians and the absolute intellectual virtue of Freud himself. It was not just the former who took the "utopian leaps" Meyerhoff so deplores; Freud surely took them also, and his greatness may well have depended upon them. Nor is either camp free of the charge of having "provided religious inspiration"; Freud's writings have provided just that for large numbers of people, however skeptical he himself was about the nature of such inspiration. To be sure, no neo-Freudian, or for that matter Freudian, has been able to equal Freud's genius. But we should by now be beyond the stage of Freudian-neo-Freudian name-calling. Indeed, for many of us in psychoanalytic psychiatry who are struggling with unsolved issues, these epithets seem to be lingering echoes of old calls to battle to which we can no longer respond. Surely we do greater justice to Freud's revolutionary thought by reappraising it critically, and seeking to grasp the spirit that made it revolutionary, rather than by looking upon it as fixed and final. And in the tenuous field of historical psychology, we particularly delude ourselves if we look upon any thought—even Freud's—as adequate to our need. In this light, I would have expected Mazlish to include some representation in the volume of Erich Fromm, Abram Kardiner, and Otto Rank—all "deviants," the first two contemporary and the third a psychoanalytic pioneer, who have had important things to say about psychoanalysis and history.

Geza Roheim's essay on "The Evolution of Culture" demonstrates the pitfalls of a literal approach to Freud's work, most specifically those of describing society in terms of individual stages of libidinal development. Much of Roheim's thesis has been undermined by recent anthropological studies, particularly his somewhat idealized version of precivilized man. Yet his work has considerable value; and in his concept of the "group ideal," as well as in his concentration upon social aspects of myth and ritual, we find important early psychoanalytic efforts to apply depth-psychological concepts to units beyond the individual.

Turning to Mazlish's second category, that of more limited and clearly "historical" areas, it is difficult to tell whether or not "The Next Assignment," William Langer's eloquent plea to his fellow historians to apply themselves to creating a discipline of psychological history, has been adequately heeded. The combination of the work depicted in this section—of the Georges on Wilson (although this book was written before Langer's original essay) and Renzo Sereno on Machiavelli—as well as other recent writings by such historians as Stuart Hughes, Norman Cohn, and Stanley Elkins suggests that there is something indeed in the air. These historical writings vary greatly in their approach, but the essays by Sereno and Brodie, the latter on the Georges' book, deal essentially with the individual psychopathological model mentioned previously; and this model in turn is represented in classical form by Flugel's essay on Henry VIII.

Flugel's tracing of unconscious motives in Henry's sexual life to "the primitive Oedipus complex" does, in its elaboration, enhance our understanding of this important historical figure (although alternative interpretations and emphases are possible). But it suffers from an exaggerated sense of purity of focus in which psychoanalyst and subject seem to be, as it were, uncontaminated by the wider historical process. The crucial interplay between individual and collective pasts—or, more broadly, between individual psychology and general historical pattern—is not given expression. To be sure, professional historians, even when following an individual psychopathological model, are not likely to fall into this ahistorical fallacy; and the work of Sereno and the Georges shows a good deal more sensitivity to the psychohistorical interplay under consideration. Nonetheless, if such a model becomes the dominant one, psychoanalysts and historians alike will find themselves limiting the possibilities of their approach; and not only will our understanding of wider historical currents be impaired, but so will our grasp of the psychology of the individual historical subject.

What all this seems to suggest is that we cannot solve our problems simply by bringing together the traditions of psychoanalysis and history. Quite the contrary, for there is much evidence to suggest that, in a number of important ways, these traditions work against each other. Much of the intellectual impulse of psychoanalysis has been toward extracting man's psychobiological self *from* the historical process, to be seen independently of it; and much of the intellectual impulse of history (as a discipline) has been toward depicting an amalgam of man's sequential group behavior, viewed independently of his individual psychology. Thus we may say—and I exaggerate only slightly—that psychoanalysis seeks to eliminate history; and history seeks to eliminate psychological man. It is in fact quite possible that many psychoanalysts and historians enter their professions with precisely these unconscious motivations—a situation perhaps encouraged by the medical domination of psychoanalysis, and by certain ideological traditions of the historical establishment. If these assumptions are correct—and whether or not they are, we must, above all, be both historical and psychological about ourselves—the much-commented-upon resistance of historians to psychological matters, as well as the ultimately ahistorical nature of much psychoanalytic work, would both become more understandable. And while we would still wish to decry these tendencies on both sides, we might, from the impasse itself, evolve a much more wise and profound psychohistory.

There are in fact signs that just this is beginning to happen; I refer most specifically to the work of Erik Erikson, as dealt with by Lucian Pye and Donald Meyer in the last two essays of the book. These papers provide valuable elucidation of the relevance of Erikson's ideas for history and political science, though one cannot help wishing that one of Erikson's own essays had been included. In any case, what is unique to Erikson's approach (particularly in *Young Man Luther*) is his ability to maintain an individually oriented depth-psychological perspective while simultaneously immersing himself and his subject in the ideological currents of the period under study. This is still psychobiography, but the psychopathological model has given way to a model of man in history. The new model moreover, is specifically sensitive to what may be termed the psychohistorical breakthrough—to that coming together of individual and history which produces a new dimension of psychic experience. To be sure, there is much that is still problematic in the approach, and the model is more readily built upon by a man of Erikson's extraordinary sensitivities than by most others who attempt to employ it. Moreover, the identity theory which Erikson puts forth as his conceptual core has its own elusiveness, and its broad emotional resonance leads many to use it promiscuously. Yet the approach and the theory are already producing impressive results: from within history and literature as well as from psychiatry and psychoanalysis, and most of all from Erikson's own continuing work.

Erikson sees himself as still working within the framework of Freudian psychoanalysis, and places his identity theory within the recently emphasized realm of "ego psychology." But his depiction of Luther's—and man's—inner struggles for new psychohistorical synthesis strains at the very limits of ego psychology; the latter, in fact, becomes transformed into something it had not been before. And whatever we are ultimately to call the development Erikson represents, we are seeing now only its beginning stages. But the combination of intellectual excitement and social relevance it seems to contain suggests that a means of bringing psychoanalysis and history together in a way that does justice to the richness of human experience is at last taking shape.

Let me mention a few of the characteristics which I believe that this psychohistorical development will come to embody, many of them either already present in Erikson's writings or at least consistent in spirit with these writings. It will retain a "model of time," but will expand this model into new concepts that combine, and give more subtle expression to, man's individual and collective feelings toward his past and his future. It will evolve a genuinely dialectical position concerning the interplay of man's psychobiological nature on the one hand, and his historical experience on the other—avoiding the historicism of Marx (the claim that man is *nothing but* his history) and the psychologism of early psychoanalysis (the claim that history is *nothing but* the re-enactment of man's psychobiological evolution). It will retain Freud's principle of the past as motor for historical change, while at the same time taking account of *that which is new in the patterns which emerge* from the three-way interplay of man's psychobiological nature, his cultural past, and the existing historical currents acting upon him. It will similarly stress the dialectic between the reality of external events and man's unique need to perceive these events only through some form of symbolic re-creation. In this way it will maintain the psychoanalytic emphasis upon symbolic behavior, but broaden its areas of symbolism beyond those of classical psychoanalytic theory, taking seriously the work of such philosophers as Ernst Cassirer and Susanne Langer. It will stress man's innate need for exploration and change as a fundamental element in the creation of his history, as well as the countervailing tendency toward stability and stillness expressed in Freud's "Nirvana principle."

In all these ways, the new historical psychology and psychological history—they may finally come to be brothers—can gradually free themselves from two intellectual polarities which have all too frequently dominated both historical and psychological work: first, the lingering Newtonian legacy of the closed, mechanistic world of absolute cause-and-effect relationships; and second, the intellectually nihilistic rejection of all general principles or causative elements. It will instead evolve a stress upon patterns and constellations whose cause-and-effect relationships are the intricate transactions of elements always in process.

Standing back for a moment from this psychohistorical utopia, I do not believe it is an impossible one to approach. I would in fact suggest that the direction of contemporary scientific thought, as well as the nature of current human struggles, demands nothing less. Mazlish's sympathetic evocation of the possibilities before us brings it one step closer. But it might have been well for him to emphasize more than he did the inevitability of profound changes taking place in both psychoanalysis and history as they come together. To return for the last time to that much-abused metaphor, the work of contruction on the "mental bridge" must come from both banks of the stream. And wherever the individual worker originates, he has no choice, if he is to work creatively, but to cross over to the other side. Nor will he be the same when he returns.

# COMMENTS ON METHOD

## 14

*There is always something jarring about old polemical exchanges and this one is no exception ("But I confess that his claim . . ." "But I thought it quite clear . . ." "While I would agree with Professor Wyatt that . . ." etc.)—perhaps because of the unnatural combination of concepts and muted personal-professional attack and counterattack. My justification for including this particular rejoinder to Frederick Wyatt's criticism of my essay on time imagery (Chapter 2) lies in Wyatt's having pressed me into a rather concrete statement on method—on my own specific relationship to psychoanalytic and other traditions, and on the pitfalls of pristine thought categories. One is inevitably a bit unfair when paraphrasing an adversary, but my purpose here is not to reconstruct the debate as such.[1] What can be said here is that Wyatt disapproved of my eschewing the classical approach to the "psychodynamics of [individual] development," and made it clear that he thought it necessary, when approaching history, to be either psychological or sociological.*

*The trouble of course is that insistence upon this kind of intellectual pigeonholing leads to conceptual steril-*

ity. It allows no place for precisely the integrative ideas
that might take us a bit beyond the unsatisfactory state of
things, and instead leaves us just where we were, or worse.
"Individual psychodynamics," as I attempt to show in the
essay, can often obscure rather than illuminate the extra-
individual dimension; while shared imagery of certain
kinds, including that surrounding the idea of time, can
provide "a point of intersection" for the individual's
struggles with ideologies and social institutions as these
pertain to his continuity with personal and cultural past.
Keniston, in his contribution, buttressed my position
(though recognizing the value of the issues raised by
Wyatt) by stressing the principle of multiple causation behind my concepts of time imagery, and saw them as "in-
terestingly related to other important concepts . . . and . . .
likely to prove a fruitful typology for characterizing historical change, and eventually accounting for it." He spoke
of the danger of "over-personalization" in the "case-
historical" approach of individual psychodynamics. (Apart
from the fact that he essentially agrees with me, I find
Keniston's commentary especially valuable because of his
discussion of just what makes a psychological concept
useful.)

Speaking generally, I would now take a still more radical position. I would claim that all of the disciplines considered most relevant to the study of psychohistory—
psychiatry, psychoanalysis, psychology, sociology, and history—by the very structure of their traditional ideas,
turn out to be antagonistic to the undertaking. The insistence upon "individual psychodynamics"—or in the same
vein, upon "a genuinely sociological perspective," "a clinical [psychiatric] focus," or "proper history"—is an insistence upon staving off the psychohistorical integration. I
do not advocate immediate dissolution of all of these intellectual disciplines and professional guilds (though I
would not deny a fleeting impulse now and then along
those lines). For the psychohistorical project requires the
kind of intellectual immersion and inquiry into methods
which these disciplines provide. I shudder at the thought

*of totally circumventing traditional modes of knowledge, and at the idea of creating instant psychohistorians. What we really need are new and much more imaginative intellectual "disciplines"—combinations of knowledge and approach that permit both depth of immersion and free-flowing boundaries, and encourage within a single mind a dialectic of versatility and specialization appropriate to our time.*

*About the exchange in question, there is a bit of an epilogue to report. Not long after our controversy I invited Wyatt (who has written brilliantly on the nature of the historical past) to join our psychohistorical study group, and he and I have since become friends. If the truth be told, I think we probably still disagree on most of the issues raised in our exchange. One of the things the experience taught me is the difficulty within American intellectual life of combining a friendly personal relationship with significant intellectual disagreement. To be sure, there are certain kinds of disagreements so fundamental that attempts to bridge them can only be destructive and irritating all around. But the requirement, however unspoken, that a friend be in complete intellectual accord is in itself anti-intellectual in the extreme—a form of basic disrespect for ideas as such, an assumption that these can be subsumed to a comfortable collectivity of "nice guys."*

❋        ❋        ❋

The attempt to apply psychological methods to the study of history leads one immediately to ask: What psychology? And what history? Whoever makes the effort to bring to bear one of these disciplines upon the other quickly discovers that the union, however desirable, is not an easy one. Nor should one expect it to be. As we have seen, the problem is not so much that of combining established bodies of knowledge in their present form as it is creating a new approach to knowledge which is continuous with, though significantly different from, the two parent sources —in other words, the problem of historical innovation.

During the early struggles to create this new approach, dialogue is likely to be difficult; concepts taken directly from either field usually prove themselves inadequate, while new concepts that attempt to span both fields are suspect in their absence of definite moorings. It is something like the dialogue between Alice and the Caterpillar:

> "I can't explain *myself*, I'm afraid, sir," said Alice, "because I am not myself, you see."
> "I don't see," said the Caterpillar.

Professor Wyatt, in his comments on my paper "Individual Patterns in Historical Change," has raised fundamental issues which will certainly not be settled by this exchange, particularly that of "the place of psychological concepts in explaining historical change." But I confess that his claim that the modalities I suggested were "but an extrapolation of the psychodynamics of development" reminded me all too much of the above dialogue. For in this claim— and in what I would hold to be a similarly erroneous claim that the typology is "based on the model of an individual coping mechanism"—he establishes, all too conveniently I am afraid, a closed line of argument which runs something like this: The modalities are nothing but outgrowths of individual psychodynamics; individual psychodynamics cannot explain historical change; therefore, these modalities "will not easily give us cues" concerning the forces of historical change. But I had thought it quite clear that these modalities were something other than simply extrapolated individual psychic mechanisms. While I would agree with Professor Wyatt that psychological concepts of a purely individual nature are inadequate for comprehending historical change, I would insist that psychosocial or psychohistorical concepts—related both to individual depth-psychological experience and to wider group tendencies—are essential to such comprehension. And although it is dubious that they or any other concepts will, in a complete sense, "explain" historical change, they might very well be one of the better avenues of approach for understanding the complex constellation of forces that operate in historical change.

In speaking of modes of imagery, I was seeking a level of discourse that draws upon three contemporary interpretations of human experience: the classic psychoanalytic concept of the image or "imago"; the more recent use by social scientists (notably Kenneth Boulding) of the concept of the image as a unifying idea which spans biology, psychology, and sociology; and the current philosophical stress upon man's basic need to symbolize, particularly Susanne Langer's recent emphasis upon the symbol as a means of formulation. The tradition from which I work remains essentially psychoanalytic, but modified in a way that can connect with the wider historical realm. Thus, rather than utilize classical concepts of the *imago* as parental images preserved indefinitely in the unconscious, I have found it more useful, for this purpose, to describe a later form of imagery experienced by large numbers of individuals as their means of symbolically combining inner emotional experience with various prevailing ideological currents. The three modes of imagery

I put forth are, in other words, *shared psychohistorical themes*. Although not the same as the patterns of shared identity described by Erik Erikson, they owe much to his pioneering efforts to bring psychoanalysis into history; and they provide what Erikson has described as a sense of psychohistorical actuality. That is, through this shared imagery, young Japanese can experience a sense of psychological immediacy and relevance which they strongly seek. These patterns of imagery are not exclusively derived from either internal psychological processes or social currents of thought; rather, they bring together, and symbolically re-create, the two.

The paper stresses the overriding significance of the past, individual and collective, for the accomplishment of historical change; and this stress, it seems to me, is the great Freudian contribution to historical psychology. Professor Wyatt is therefore right when he points out that both the restorationist and the transformationist, in my terminology, are concerned with the past, and differ only in their schemes for mastering it. But I believe that he and I differ greatly in what we mean by mastering one's past. I would emphasize here the importance of thinking in terms of motion and flow. Thus, when the restorationist youth I describe bring forth visions of restoring an idealized collective past, at the same time they relate this past to the most powerful symbols of contemporary life, and in this way they create the psychological ground on which they can participate in historical change. They would have felt considerably less need for this idealized vision were it not for the powerful threat and attraction which these contemporary forces exert upon them. Without this psychological pressure—and without the more general sense of what I have called historical dislocation—they could more comfortably relate themselves to existing traditions which, during periods of less rapid social change, modify themselves at a relatively slow rate over the course of time.

To be sure, as Professor Wyatt suggests, the restorationist is likely to have difficulty dealing with unconscious hatred of authority, and his participation in restorationist imagery does help him to accept a pattern of dependency he might otherwise find intolerable. But these individual psychodynamics do not, in themselves, create the phenomenon of restorationism (which would be more or less the case if the latter were merely an "individual coping mechanism"). Rather, they are part of a larger constellation and a constantly active process: the authority conflicts themselves are likely to be activated by widespread historical dislocation and identity confusion; the combination of historical dislocation and intensified authority conflicts increases the general need for clarifying (and often polarized) imagery; and the imagery in turn partly resolves and partly intensifies both authority conflicts and the sense of historical dislocation. Individual psychodynamics are just one element in the constellation, and not necessarily the decisive one: the same underlying psychodynamic pattern can, so to speak, find a home in any of the three modes of imagery, as was forcefully demonstrated to me in the tendency of many young people to shift from one to the other. Indeed, a crucial factor in such a shift was often exposure to a particular kind of youth group dominating a specific university setting, and this institutional factor is in turn dependent upon all of the other elements mentioned. Thus we grasp nothing of the nature of this imagery if we do not see its *extra-individual* —its social and historical—connections. And returning to the question of mastery, the imagery can, of course, help one to adapt or to cope with one's present environment; but it also does something more: it provides a *formulation* of the social boundaries of one's individual existence, a formulation which has to be based upon experience— and therefore upon individual and collective pasts—but which also projects itself, as an active process, into an imagined future.

Regarding applicability to historical situations, I believe that the concept of restorationism can shed some light not only on Japan's Meiji Restoration (perhaps the classical historical example of heroic cultural revitalization, the accomplishments and psychological costs of which are still being felt today), but also on such extremist and explosively violent developments as Japan's post-Meiji Rightist movements, and the Nazi movement in Germany. Indeed, the present existence of important restorationist trends in the United States—and I mean not only the Radical Right, but the Black Muslims within the Negro movement as well—suggests that its stimulus is not so much the existence of a centuries-old cultural past as a sense of having been precipitously expelled from any past.

Professor Wyatt is, then, correct in stating—as I did myself in the original article—that these phenomena are in no way peculiar to Japan. Japan simply provides a fruitful laboratory for the study of restorationism in particular, because of the great influence of this mode of imagery upon its entire history; and of historical change in general, because of the intensity of its recent cultural dislocations (along with the impressiveness of many of its continuities). The modes described are not peculiar to youth either; but young adults can render such imagery with particular vividness, because it becomes their vehicle for making sense of their entry, so to speak, into history— their means of articulating ideas and emotions, previously latent or less structured, which can relate them to the general process of human experience. But I differ strongly with Professor Wyatt in his assumption that these phenomena are not peculiar to historical change. Comparative research of the kind he suggests could be illuminating here. Yet I would claim right now that these patterns exist only insofar as historical change takes place, and are both a stimulus and a manifestation of that change. The fact that they can be shown to have always existed means that historical change has similarly always been taking place. But their increasing intensity in the contemporary world, particularly in those cultures under greatest pressure toward change (as in Africa, for example, in the various forms of restorationism related to the mystique of *Négritude*, side by side with transformationist tendencies) parallels the general acceleration of the rate of historical change.

Concerning the difficult question of the relationship between individual and historical pasts, Professor Wyatt's request for more data from life histories and interviews is certainly justified. These data will be forthcoming, and the article itself was meant to be no more than suggestive of crude beginnings. But here again it will not do to bring forth the call to arms of classical psychodynamic formulations to explain the psychosocial modes I have suggested. Professor Wyatt may be correct in saying that the transformationist "has reason to be afraid of his past: or he would not repudiate it with so much fervor," and that he reacts strongly against the oppressive authority of his childhood and the "secret pull of dependency in himself that would bring him back under that authority again." But once more we may say that this psychodynamic pattern is just one element in a constellation, and that fear of one's past can by no means be viewed as a specific cause of transformationism. The psychodynamic pattern of one's individual past must come together with larger influences of the Japanese ancient and recent cultural pasts to produce the styles of imagery depicted. The potential for a young man to find his parental authority oppressive has always been present in Japan (as suggested in the popular saying "There are four things to fear: earthquake, thunder, fire, and father"); but the kinds of ideology that could combine with such individual emotions to create the specific forms of transformationist imagery I described became available to Japanese only through the influence of various Western idea-systems around the time of the Meiji Restoration and afterward, then later through the diverse exposures of the postwar period. Moreover, without these ideological influences, young Japanese might not have felt their parental authority to be oppressive—it might well have seemed to be simply part of the natural order of things—and their unconscious antagonism to parental authority might have been either converted into zealous defense of that same authority, or else more effectively repressed.

For the basic patterns of individual psychodynamics

within a particular culture—that is, the psychic mechanisms derived from the individual past—change very slowly over centuries; institutional patterns change a little more readily, though still not easily; ideological influences can change a good deal more rapidly. The typology I propose is meant to suggest a point of intersection of these elements of varying stability—and therefore of portions of individual and collective pasts as well. One of the reasons that more precise formulation of these intersecting levels of experience is so difficult is that the resulting imagery—that is, the point of intersection—is itself constantly changing, now drawing more upon one element, now another. Nonetheless, more precise approaches, particularly to the intersection of individual and collective pasts, are necessary and possible. The three modes I have suggested are by no means the only possible ones; other typologies will supplement or replace them. But this kind of approach at least affords a means of bringing a psychological perspective to general historical data—and general historical data are a great deal more than just individual psychopathology.

For instance, we can now see how the most intense kinds of coming together of the elements just mentioned in more or less perfect "fit," particularly for transformationists and restorationists, can produce a sense of psychohistorical actuality so strong that it resembles Freud's "oceanic feeling." And this in turn helps us understand the historical dangers that confront us: for the most vivid sense of actuality is likely to coincide with the most extreme forms of individual relationship to ideology, in other words with ideological totalism. Putting the matter another way, the total surrender of the self to an all-embracing ideological crusade characterized by imagery of uncompromising dogma and violence, may create (at least temporarily, and that may do damage enough) the most vivid sense of unity between individual and collective pasts.

Finally, I wish to return to the basic question Professor Wyatt raises about the relevance of psychological concepts for comprehending historical change. Given the frequently disastrous psychoanalytic forays into history, I admire his sense of restraint. For the misapplication of psychoanalytic concepts leads readily to a one-sided focus upon individual psychopathology, or to so thoroughgoing a reductionism that the data of history more or less disappear. But Professor Wyatt goes further than mere restraint: he makes a more or less absolute distinction between "essentially psychological concepts," which he thinks of "little help when we want to understand change in societies," and "concepts derived from sociological . . . models," which he feels "will do better." This distinction may be useful for the purpose of delineating academic disciplines in university departments, but adhering to it strictly in our quest for comprehension of historical change would very soon lead to an intellectual dead end. For it is precisely the in-between area—the realm in which man's inner life makes contact with his history—that we need to know more about if we are to grasp something of what is happening to us in the midst of the human experiment, and indeed begin to exert a measure of desperately needed mastery over our own history.

The intellectual task then, as I see it, is the difficult one of formulating concepts which draw deeply from, and yet bridge, the traditions of our psychological, social science, and historical disciplines, and at the same time transcend the strict limitations of any one of them. For history is no more "a kind of random sociology" than it is, say, a psychological progression from the oral to the anal to the genital stages of human development. It is—or at least can be viewed as—a series of shared psychosocial experiences, reactive and creative, constantly carried forward on the momentum of what has taken place in the individual and collective pasts. The fields of psychoanalytic psychology and psychiatry can and should have a great deal to say about the historical process, but only if they themselves evolve sufficiently to take their place alongside of the more illuminating developments of contemporary thought. They will have to surrender old notions of absolute cause-and-effect in favor of more subtle formulations,

consistent with current scientific developments, of inter-
acting patterns and constellations always in flux. Historians have a lot to contribute to these formulations: they
can help create a new dialogue, moving beyond that of
intramural debate among psychologists and psychiatrists.
For the very nature of the problem demands that we all
share in the universally increasing historical consciousness, and consciousness of self in history, so characteristic
of our time.

# PROTEAN MAN

## 15

*This essay arouses people. I can remember one occasion at the University of Sussex (one of England's liveliest centers of higher education) when a few among the senior faculty could scarcely wait for me to finish my discussion of protean man before expressing their disapproval. What I talked about, they insisted, did not exist, was nothing new, and was the kind of thing that contributed to the downfall of Western civilization. Younger faculty and students, in contrast, responded to the talk with intellectual and personal resonance. And in America, where the pattern I describe has been more prominent and closer to general conscious recognition, most reactions have been of the kind any writer or teacher appreciates—combinations of enthusiasm, confirmatory associations, and thoughtful criticisms—though there has also been, here and there, a bit of headshaking incredulity and passionate disagreement.*

*Why the intensity? I think it has to do with my positing a change in psychological style, which some perceive as a profound threat to the way in which they have viewed their own relationship to the world, and others as a liberat-*

*ing formulation of what they had surreptitiously sensed to be taking place within themselves. In addititon, the essay touches directly upon highly charged quests for both a sense of immediacy and a grasp of what is about to happen to people—concerns about "where it's at" and "where it's headed." Finally, I have made a rather forthright but preliminary statement on a phenomenon that really requires much more detailed treatment—that requires additional distinctions, and discussions of conceptual byways—affording readers and listeners little opportunity to clarify, and in a sense calm, their enthusiasms or objections. Yet all in all I must admit that I find the contours of protean man to have become, if anything, more vivid during the four or five years since I first began to talk and write about them.*

*My claim is that certain contemporary historical trends, acting upon universal psychological potential (within many divergent cultures), have become sufficiently powerful and novel to create a new kind of man. The claim and the man are elaborated in the essay, but three important questions about the over-all concept are worth considering a bit further. First, is protean man—with his continuous psychic movement, his shifts in identity and belief —always a young man? Second, is he really new man —or is he merely a resurrection of a type familiar from many periods of the past? Third, what if anything in him, midst his fluidity, remains stable?*

*To which I would answer, very briefly, as follows.*

*The fluctuating pattern I describe is indeed most prominent in the young (late teens and early twenties), but for the rest of us to assume that we are totally immune to it would seem to me a great mistake. My contention, in other words, is that protean man inhabits us all. And although men somewhat like him have probably existed in earlier historical periods which were, like our own, notably "out of joint," the extremity of recent historical developments has rendered him a much more discrete and widespread entity. Concerning his stability, it is true that much within him must remain constant in order to make possible his psychological flux. I would include here certain enduring elements in the mother-child relationship (such as the "emotional-symbolic substrate" referred to in Chapter 2), various consistencies in style (including elements of mockery and the sense of absurdity, approaches to individual and group relationships, and a generally aesthetic emphasis), as well as the stabilizing aspect of anticipation and experience of change itself. The whole stability-change issue badly needs careful psychological reevaluation, especially in regard to the kinds of significant change that can take place within a person while much else remains constant.*

*In a brilliant review of Jung's posthumous autobiography (Memories, Dreams, Reflections) which appeared in The New Yorker a few years ago, Lewis Mumford discussed the life patterns of both Freud and Jung from this standpoint. According to Mumford, it was the very stability of the two men—as heads of families and as responsible physicians—that permitted them their extraordinary flights of psychological imagination. Yet, although they are hardly figures of the remote past, I would insist that their world be distinguished from our own. For them "society" (the anchoring psychological force of institutions and symbols) was "there" in a way it is not for us. Hence, when Mumford goes on to warn today's young that some such stability is necessary for genuine innovation, he is both correct and too simple in his analogy. For under historical pressure, stability itself can undergo change, in the sense that men create styles of inner constancy which no longer follow previous models.*

*My assumption in writing the essay is that we have lacked a model of man adequate to what is now happening to him. But I would see two immediate antecedents to protean man: David Riesman's concept of other-directedness, which suggested a great deal about the evolving responsiveness to environmental influence in post-modern society; and Erik Erikson's work on identity, with its evocation of twentieth-century struggles for self-definition. Neither the concept of other-directedness nor that of identity, however, is exactly applicable to protean man —because his quest for new forms is not so much an expression of sensitivity to his environment as it is a means of innovation and re-creation, and because what is revolutionary in him is precisely his break with the idea of identity as we have known it.*

*The liberties the essay takes in its sequence of illustrations—its easy movement from general conceptual statement, to research findings, to psychotherapeutic interviews, to observations on literature, art, and film—have led some to find it lacking in proper social science methodology. But I would see this approach as appropriate to the phenomenon I describe. Freedom of method (not "methodology," which suggests to me a pseudo-scientific limitation of freedom) can be fully consistent with intellectual discipline—if one identifies the kinds of assumptions one is making, as well as the nature of one's evidence. I would hope that the essay can be accepted as a reasonably well-argued statement—something less than final "proof," but more than idle speculation.*

*I came to the idea of protean man before reading Marshall McLuhan, and well before McLuhan's extraordinary rise to fame. But aspects of it have much in common with his work—especially my stress upon the importance of the "flooding of imagery" accompanying the communications revolution. What I have tried to do, in contrast to McLuhan, is to view such questions from the standpoint of man's inner symbolic life. This in turn requires an exploration of the kinds of dislocation that make man psychologically ready for, and influence his response to, the flooding of imagery to which he is exposed. To put the matter another way, I believe that "the medium is the message" only to the extent that one considers that medium in its entirety—as a convoluted arena of man's inner and outer environments and their respective histories, an arena which far transcends his electrical extensions of himself. Similarly, the images which constitute the "message" are shaped not only by the media themselves but by the symbolic homelessness and hunger of media operators and their audience.*

*Protean man continues to inhabit every facet of my work. Even* Revolutionary Immortality *concludes with a view of China's Cultural Revolution (of 1960–1968) as, among other things, a last stand against an already evolving Chinese version of protean man. The concept of "counterfeit nurturance," which I see as so relevant to protean man, arose originally from my study of Hiroshima survivors; and this essay's stress upon absurdity and mockery has close bearing upon my forthcoming study of death symbolism. I continue to have the image of protean man very much in mind in evaluating data on Japanese youth, and even more so (as the next chapter makes clear) in my observations on youth rebellions in this country and throughout the world.*

*I have sometimes been told that I am unduly optimistic about protean man—that I do not sufficiently emphasize the potential harm in such developments as hippie-style withdrawal and drug use, and in New Left intransigence, anti-intellectualism, and totalism. One or two friends have especially objected to the suggestion at the end of the essay that protean man might be the instrument of our survival. I would say that I do not consider this last speculation a wildly optimistic one. More generally, I find myself, here as elsewhere, simultaneously impressed by man's incessant destructiveness (and self-destructiveness) and equally incessant capacity for renewal. Demonstrating both tendencies as he does, protean man may be very old-fashioned after all. I would not see him as possessing either magic strength or unique virtue. But I do ask that we cease looking upon our contemporary innovations as nothing but pathology or alienation, and that we take a look at what there is in us, at this stage of things, that helps to keep life going.*

\*          \*          \*

I should like to examine a set of psychological patterns characteristic of contemporary life, which are creating a new kind of man—a "protean man." As my stress is upon change and flux, I shall not speak much of "character" and "personality," both of which suggest fixity and permanence. Erikson's concept of identity has been, among other things, an effort to get away from this principle of fixity; and I have been using the term self-process to convey still more specifically the idea of flow. For it is quite possible that even the image of personal identity, in so far as it suggests inner stability and sameness, is derived from a vision of a traditional culture in which man's relationship to his institutions and symbols are still relatively intact—which is hardly the case today. If we understand the self to be the person's symbol of his own organism, then self-process refers to the continuous psychic re-creation of that symbol.

I came to this emphasis through work in cultures far removed from my own, studies of young (and not so young) Chinese and Japanese. Observations I was able to make in America, between and following these East Asian investigations, led me to the conviction that a very general process was taking place. I do not mean to suggest that everybody is becoming the same, or that a totally new "world-self" is taking shape. But I am convinced that a universally shared style of self-process is emerging. Considering once more the three-way interplay responsible for the behavior of human groups—universal psychobiological potential, specific cultural emphasis, and prevailing historical forces—my thesis is that the last factor plays an increasingly important part in shaping self-process.

In work done in Hong Kong (in connection with a study of the process of "thought reform"—or "brainwashing"—as conducted on the mainland), I found that Chinese intellectuals of varying ages had gone through an extraordinary array of what I then called identity fragments—of combinations of belief and emotional involvement—each of which they could readily abandon in favor of another. I remember particularly the profound impression made upon me by the extraordinary psychohistorical journey of one young man in particular: beginning as a "filial son" or "young master," that elite status of an only son in an upper-class Chinese family, with all it meant within the traditional social structure; then feeling himself an abandoned and betrayed victim, as traditional cultural forms collapsed midst civil war and general chaos, and his father, for whom he was always to long, was taken from him by political and military duties; then a "student activist" in militant rebellion against the traditional cultural structures in which he had been so recently immersed (as well as against a Nationalist regime whose abuses he had personally experienced); which led him to Marxism and to strong emotional involvement in the Communist movement; then, because of remaining "imperfections," becoming a participant in a thought reform program which pressed toward a more thoroughgoing ideological conversion; but which, in his case, had the opposite effect, as he was alienated by the process, came into conflict with the reformers, and fled the country; then, in Hong Kong, struggling to establish himself as an "anti-Communist writer"; after a variety of difficulties, finding solace and significance in becoming a Protestant convert; and following that, still just thirty, apparently poised for some new internal (and perhaps external) move.

Even more dramatic were the shifts in self-process of young Japanese whom I interviewed in Tokyo and Kyoto from 1960 to 1962, and then again in 1967. I need only mention those depicted in the young Japanese businessman I refer to in the first essay as Kondo, all of which took place before he was 25.*

There are, of course, important differences between the protean life styles of the two young men, and between them and their American counterparts—differences which have to do with cultural emphases and which contribute to what is generally called national character. But such is the intensity of the shared aspects of historical experience that contemporary Chinese, Japanese, and American self-process turn out to have striking points of convergence.

I would stress two general historical developments as having special importance for creating protean man. The first is the worldwide sense of what I have called *historical* (or *psychohistorical*) *dislocation*, the break in the sense of connection which men have long felt with the vital and nourishing symbols of their cultural tradition— symbols revolving around family, idea-systems, religions, and the life cycle in general. In our contemporary world one perceives these traditional symbols (as I have suggested elsewhere, using the Japanese as a paradigm) as irrelevant, burdensome, or inactivating, and yet one cannot avoid carrying them within or having one's self-process profoundly affected by them. The second large historical tendency is the *flooding of imagery* produced by the extraordinary flow of post-modern cultural influences over mass-communication networks. These cross readily over local and national boundaries, and permit each individual to be touched by everything, but at the same time cause him to be overwhelmed by superficial messages and undigested cultural elements, by headlines and by endless partial alternatives in every sphere of life. These alternatives, moreover, are universally and simultaneously shared—if not as courses of action, at least in the form of significant inner imagery.

We know from Greek mythology that Proteus was able to change his shape with relative ease—from wild boar

---

* See Chapter 1, pp. 32–38. The same version of Kondo's life history was included in the original Protean Man essay.

to lion to dragon to fire to flood. But what he did find difficult, and would not do unless seized and chained, was to
commit himself to a single form, a form most his own, and
carry out his function of prophecy. We can say the same
of protean man, but we must keep in mind his possibilities
as well as his difficulties.

The protean style of self-process, then, is characterized
by an interminable series of experiments and explorations—some shallow, some profound—each of which may
be readily abandoned in favor of still new psychological
quests. The pattern in many ways resembles what Erik
Erikson has called "identity diffusion" or "identity confusion," and the impaired psychological functioning which
those terms suggest can be very much present. But I would
stress that the protean style is by no means pathological
as such, and in fact may well be one of the functional
patterns of our day. It extends to all areas of human experience—to political as well as sexual behavior, to the
holding and promulgating of ideas, and to the general
organization of lives.

I would like to suggest a few illustrations of the protean style, as expressed in America and Europe, drawn
both from psychotherapeutic work with patients and
from observations on various forms of literature and art.

One patient of mine, a gifted young teacher, spoke of
himself in this way:

> I have an extraordinary number of masks I can put on or
> take off. The question is: Is there, or should there be, one
> face which should be authentic? I'm not sure that there
> is one for me. I can think of other parallels to this, espe-
> cially in literature. There are representations of every kind
> of crime, every kind of sin. For me, there is not a single
> act I cannot imagine myself committing.

He went on to compare himself to an actor on the stage
who "performs with a certain kind of polymorphous versatility"—and here he was referring, slightly mockingly,
to Freud's term, "polymorphous perversity" for diffusely
inclusive (also protean) infantile sexuality. And he asked:

> Which is the real person, so far as an actor is concerned?
> Is he more real when performing on the stage—or when
> he is at home? I tend to think that for people who have
> these many, many masks, there is no home. Is it a futile
> gesture for the actor to try to find his real face?

My patient was by no means a happy man, but neither was
he incapacitated. And although we can see the strain
with which he carries his "polymorphous versatility," it
could also be said that, as a teacher and a thinker, and in
some ways as a man, he was well served by it.

In contemporary American literature Saul Bellow is
notable for the protean men he has created. In *The Adventures of Augie March*, one of his earlier novels, we meet a
picaresque hero with a notable talent for adapting himself to divergent social worlds. Augie himself says "I
touched all sides, and nobody knew where I belonged. I
had no good idea of that myself." And a perceptive young
English critic, Tony Tanner, tells us, "Augie indeed celebrates the self, but he can find nothing to do with it." Tanner goes on to describe Bellow's more recent protean hero,
Herzog, as "a representative modern intelligence, swamped
with ideas, metaphysics, and values, and surrounded by
messy facts. It labors to cope with them all."

A distinguished French literary spokesman for the protean style—in his life and in his work—is, of course, Jean-
Paul Sartre. Indeed, I believe that it is precisely because of
these protean traits that Sartre strikes us as such an embodiment of twentieth-century man. An American critic,
Theodore Solotaroff, speaks of Sartre's fundamental assumption that "there is no such thing as even a relatively
fixed sense of self, ego, or identity—rather there is only
the subjective mind in motion in relationship to that which
it confronts."[1] And Sartre himself refers to human consciousness as "a sheer activity transcending toward objects," and "a great emptiness, a wind blowing toward
objects." Both Sartre and Solotaroff may be guilty of over-
statement, but I doubt that either could have written as he
did prior to the last thirty years or so. Solotaroff further
characterizes Sartre as

constantly on the go, hurrying from point to point, subject to subject; fiercely intentional, his thought occupies, fills, and distends its material as he endeavors to lose and find himself in his encounters with other lives, disciplines, books, and situations.

This image of repeated, autonomously willed death and rebirth of the self, so central to the protean style, becomes associated with the themes of fatherlessness—as Sartre goes on to tell us in his autobiography with his characteristic tone of serious self-mockery:

> There is no good father, that's the rule. Don't lay the blame on men but on the bond of paternity, which is rotten. To beget children, nothing better; To have them, what iniquity! Had my father lived, he would have lain on me at full length, and would have crushed me. Amidst Aeneas and his fellows who carry their Anchises on their backs, I move from shore to shore, alone and hating those invisible begetters who bestraddle their sons all their life long. I left behind me a young man who did not have time to be my father and who could now be my son. Was it a good thing or bad? I don't know. But I readily subscribed to the verdict of an eminent psychoanalyst: I have no superego.[2]

We note Sartre's image of interchangeability of father and son, of "a young man who did not have time to be my father and who could now be my son"—which in a literal sense refers to the age of his father's death, but symbolically suggests an extension of the protean style to intimate family relationships. And such reversals indeed become necessary in a rapidly changing world in which the sons must constantly "carry their fathers on their backs," teach them new things which they, as older people, cannot possibly know. The judgment of the absent superego, however, may be misleading, especially if we equate superego with susceptibility to guilt. What has actually disappeared —in Sartre and in protean man in general—is the *classical* superego, the internalization of clearly defined criteria of right and wrong transmitted within a particular culture by parents to their children. Protean man requires freedom from precisely that kind of superego—he requires a symbolic fatherlessness—in order to carry out his explorations. But we shall see that, rather than being free of guilt, his guilt takes on a different form from that of his predecessors.

There are many other representations of protean man among contemporary novelists: in the constant internal and external motion of "beat generation" writings, such as Jack Kerouac's *On the Road;* in the novels of a gifted successor to that generation, J. P. Donleavy, particularly *The Ginger Man;* and of course in the work of European novelists such as Günter Grass, whose *The Tin Drum* is a breathtaking evocation of prewar Polish-German, wartime German, and postwar German environments, in which the protagonist combines protean adaptability with a kind of perpetual physical-mental "strike" against any change at all.

In the visual arts, perhaps the most important of postwar movement has been aptly named "Action Painting" to convey its stress upon process rather than fixed completion. And a more recent and related movement in sculpture, called Kinetic Art, goes further. According to Jean Tinguely, one of its leading practitioners, "Artists are putting themselves in rhythm with their time, in contact with their epic, especially with permanent and perpetual movement." As revolutionary as any style of approach is the stress upon innovation per se which now dominates painting. I have frequently heard artists, themselves considered radical innovators, complain bitterly of the current standards dictating that "innovation is all," and of a turnover in art movements so rapid as to discourage the idea of holding still long enough to develop a particular style.

We also learn much from film stars. Marcello Mastroianni, when asked whether he agreed with *Time*'s characterization of him as "the neocapitalist hero," gave the following answer:

In many ways, yes. But I don't think I'm any kind of hero, neocapitalist or otherwise. If anything, I am an *anti*-hero or at most a *non*-hero. *Time* said I had the frightened, characteristically twentieth-century look, with a spine made of plastic napkin rings. I accepted this—because modern man is that way; and being a product of my time and an artist, I can represent him. If humanity were all one piece, I would be considered a weakling.

Mastroianni accepts his destiny as protean man; he seems to realize that there are certain advantages to having a spine made of plastic napkin rings, or at least that it is an appropriate kind of spine to have these days.

John Cage, the composer, is an extreme exponent of the protean style, both in his music and in his sense of all of us as listeners. He concluded a recent letter to *The Village Voice* with the sentence "Nowadays, everything happens at once and our souls are conveniently electronic, omni-attentive." The comment is McLuhan-like, but what I wish to stress particularly is the idea of omniattention—the sense of contemporary man as having the possibility of "receiving" and "taking in" everything. In attending, as in being, nothing is "off limits."

To be sure, one can observe in contemporary man a tendency which seems to be precisely the opposite of the protean style. I refer to the closing-off of identity or constriction of self-process, to a straight-and-narrow specialization in psychological as well as in intellectual life, and to a reluctance to let in any "extraneous" influences. But I would emphasize that where this kind of constricted or "one-dimensional" self-process exists, it has an essentially reactive and compensatory quality. In this it differs from earlier characterlogical styles it may seem to resemble (such as the "inner-directed" man described by Riesman, and still earlier patterns in traditional society). For these were direct outgrowths of societies which then existed, and in harmony with those societies, while at the present time a constricted self-process requires continuous psychological work to fend off protean influences which are always abroad.

Protean man has a particular relationship to the holding of ideas which has, I believe, great significance for the politics, religion, and general intellectual life of the future. For just as elements of the self can be experimented with and readily altered, so can idea systems and ideologies be embraced, modified, let go of, and re-embraced, all with a new ease that stands in sharp contrast to the inner struggle we have in the past associated with these shifts. Until relatively recently, no more than one major ideological shift was likely to occur in a lifetime, and that one would be long remembered as a significant individual turning-point accompanied by profound soul-searching and conflict. But today it is not unusual to encounter several such shifts, accomplished relatively painlessly, within a year or even a month; and among many groups, the rarity is a man who has gone through life holding firmly to a single ideological vision.

In one sense, this tendency is related to "the end of ideology" spoken of by Daniel Bell, since protean man is incapable of enduring an unquestioning allegiance to the large ideologies and utopian thought of the nineteenth and early twentieth centuries. One must be cautious about speaking of the end of anything, however, especially ideology, and one also encounters in protean man what I would call strong ideological hunger. He is starved for ideas and feelings that can give coherence to his world, but here too his taste is toward new combinations. While he is by no means without yearning for the absolute, what he finds most acceptable are images of a more fragmentary nature than those of the ideologies of the past; and these images, although limited and often fleeting, can have great influence upon his psychological life. Thus political and religious movements, as they confront protean man, are likely to experience less difficulty convincing him to alter previous convictions than they do providing him a set of beliefs which can command his allegiance for more than a brief experimental interlude.

Intimately bound up with his flux in emotions and beliefs is a profound inner sense of absurdity, which finds expression in a tone of mockery. The sense and the tone are related to a perception of surrounding activities and beliefs as profoundly strange and inappropriate. They stem from a breakdown in the relationship between inner and outer worlds—that is, in the sense of symbolic integrity—and are part of the pattern of psychohistorical dislocation I mentioned earlier. For if we view man as primarily a symbol-forming organism, we must recognize that he has constant need of a meaningful inner formulation of self and world in which his own actions, and even his impulses, have some kind of "fit" with the "outside" as he perceives it.

The sense of absurdity, of course, has a considerable modern tradition, and has been discussed by such writers as Camus as a function of man's spiritual homelessness and inability to find any meaning in traditional belief systems. But absurdity and mockery have taken much more extreme form in the post-World War II world, and have in fact become a prominent part of a universal life-style.

In American life absurdity and mockery are everywhere. Perhaps their most vivid expression can be found in such areas as pop art and the more general burgeoning of "pop culture." Important here is the complex stance of the pop artist toward the objects he depicts. On the one hand he embraces the materials of the everyday world, celebrates and even exalts them—boldly asserting his creative return to representational art (in active rebellion against the previously reigning nonobjective school), and his psychological return to the "real world" of *things*. On the other hand, everything he touches he mocks. "Thingness" is pressed to the point of caricature. He is indeed artistically reborn as he moves freely among the physical and symbolic materials of his environment, but mockery is his birth certificate and his passport. This kind of duality of approach is formalized in the stated "duplicity" of Camp, an ill-defined aesthetic in which all varieties of mockery converge under the guiding influence of the homosexual's subversion of a heterosexual world.

Also relevant is a group of expressions in current

slang, some of them derived originally from jazz. The "dry mock" has replaced the dry wit; one refers to a segment of life experience as a "bit," "bag," "caper," "game" (or "con game"), "scene," "show," or "scenario"; and one seeks to "make the scene" (or "make it"), "beat the system," or "pull it off"—or else one "cools it" ("plays it cool") or "cops out." The thing to be experienced, in other words, is too absurd to be taken at its face value; one must either keep most of the self aloof from it, or if not, one must lubricate the encounter with mockery.

A similar spirit seems to pervade literature and social action alike. What is best termed a "literature of mockery" has come to dominate fiction and other forms of writing on an international scale. Again Günter Grass's *The Tin Drum* comes to mind, and is probably the greatest single example of this literature—a work, I believe, which will eventually be appreciated as much as a general evocation of contemporary man as of the particular German experience with Nazism. In this country the divergent group of novelists known as "black humorists" also fit into the general category—related as they are to a trend in the American literary consciousness which R. W. B. Lewis has called a "savagely comical apocalypse" or a "new kind of ironic literary form and disturbing vision, the joining of the dark thread of apocalypse with the nervous detonations of satiric laughter." For it is precisely death itself, and particularly threats of the contemporary apocalypse, that protean man ultimately mocks.

The relationship of mockery to political and social action has been less apparent, but is, I would claim, equally significant. There is more than coincidence in the fact that the largest American student uprising of recent decades, the Berkeley Free Speech Movement of 1964, was followed immediately by a "Filthy Speech Movement." While the object of the Filthy Speech Movement—achieving free expression of forbidden language, particularly of four-letter words—can be viewed as a serious one, the predominant effect, even in the matter of names, was that of a mocking caricature of the movement which preceded

it. But if mockery can undermine protest, it can also en-
liven it. There have been signs of craving for it in major
American expressions of protest such as the rebellion of
the blacks and the opposition to the war in Vietnam. In the
former a certain chord can be struck by the comedian Dick
Gregory, and in the latter by the use of satirical skits and
parodies, that revives the flagging attention of protesters
becoming gradually bored with the repetition of their
"straight" slogans and goals. And on an international scale,
I would say that, during the past decade, Russian intellectual life has been enriched by a leavening spirit of
mockery—against which the Chinese leaders are now, in
pressing ahead with their Cultural Revolution, fighting a
vigorous but ultimately losing battle.

Closely related to the sense of absurdity and the spirit
of mockery is another characteristic of protean man which
I call "suspicion of counterfeit nurturance." Involved here
is a severe conflict of dependency, a core problem of protean man. I originally thought of the concept several
years ago while working with survivors of the atomic bomb
in Hiroshima. I found that these survivors both felt themselves in need of special help, and resented whatever help
was offered them because they equated it with weakness
and inferiority. In considering the matter more generally, I found that this equation of nurturance with a
threat to autonomy was a major theme of contemporary
life. The increased dependency needs resulting from the
breakdown of traditional institutions lead protean man to
seek out replacements wherever he can find them. The
large organizations (government, business, academic,
etc.) to which he turns, and which contemporary society
increasingly holds out as a substitute for traditional institutions, present an ambivalent threat to his autonomy in
one way; and the intense individual relationships in which
he seeks to anchor himself in another. Both are therefore
likely to be perceived as counterfeit. But the obverse
of this tendency is an expanding sensitivity to the inauthentic, which may be just beginning to exert its general
creative force on man's behalf.

Technology (and technique in general), together with science, have special significance for protean man. Technical achievement of any kind can be strongly embraced to combat inner tendencies toward diffusion, and to transcend feelings of absurdity and conflicts over counterfeit nurturance. The image of science itself, however, as the ultimate power behind technology and, to a considerable extent, behind contemporary thought in general, becomes much more difficult to cope with. Only in certain underdeveloped countries can one find, in relatively pure form, those expectations of scientific-utopian deliverance from all human want and conflict, which were characteristic of eighteenth- and nineteenth-century Western thought. Protean man retains much of this utopian imagery, but he finds it increasingly undermined by massive disillusionment. More and more he calls forth the other side of the God-devil polarity generally applied to science, and sees it as a purveyor of total destructiveness. This kind of profound ambivalence creates for him the most extreme psychic paradox: the very force he still feels to be his liberator from the heavy burdens of past irrationality also threatens him with absolute annihilation, even extinction. But this paradox may well be—in fact, I believe, already has been—the source of imaginative efforts to achieve new relationships between science and man, and indeed, new visions of science itself.

I suggested before that protean man was not free of guilt. He indeed suffers from it considerably, but often without awareness of what is causing his suffering. For his is a form of hidden guilt: a vague but persistent kind of self-condemnation related to the symbolic disharmonies I have described, a sense of having no outlet for his loyalties and no symbolic structure for his achievements. This is the guilt of social breakdown, and it includes various forms of historical and racial guilt experienced by whole nations and peoples, both by the privileged and the abused. Rather than a clear feeling of evil or sinfulness, it takes the form of a nagging sense of unworthiness all the more troublesome for its lack of clear origin.

Protean man experiences similarly vague constellations of anxiety and resentment. These too have origin in symbolic impairments and are particularly tied in with suspicion of counterfeit nurturance. Often feeling himself uncared for, even abandoned, protean man responds with diffuse fear and anger. But he can find neither a good cause for the former, nor a consistent target for the latter. He nonetheless cultivates his anger because he finds it more serviceable than anxiety, because there are plenty of targets of one kind or another beckoning, and because even moving targets are better than none. His difficulty is that focused indignation is as hard for him to sustain as is any single identification or conviction.

Involved in all of these patterns is a profound psychic struggle with the idea of change itself. For here too protean man finds himself ambivalent in the extreme. He is profoundly attracted to the idea of making all things, including himself, totally new—to what I have elsewhere called the "mode of transformation." But he is equally drawn to an image of a mythical past of perfect harmony and prescientific wholeness, to the "mode of restoration." Moreover, beneath his transformationism is nostalgia, and beneath his restorationism is his fascinated attraction to contemporary forms and symbols. Constantly balancing these elements midst the extraordinarily rapid change surrounding his own life, the nostalgia is pervasive, and can be one of his most explosive and dangerous emotions. This longing for a "Golden Age" of absolute oneness, prior to individual and cultural separation or delineation, not only sets the tone for the restorationism of the politically Rightist antagonists of history: the still-extant Emperor-worshipping assassins in Japan, the *colons* in France, and the John Birchites and Ku Klux Klanners in America. It also, in more disguised form, energizes that transformationist totalism of the Left which courts violence, and is even willing to risk nuclear violence, in a similarly elusive quest.

Following upon all that I have said are radical impairments to the symbolism of transition within the life cycle—the *rites de passage* surrounding birth, entry into adulthood, marriage, and death. Whatever rites remain seem shallow, inappropriate, fragmentary. Protean man cannot take them seriously, and often seeks to improvise new ones with whatever contemporary materials he has available, including cars and drugs. Perhaps the central impairment here is that of symbolic immortality—of the universal need for imagery of connection, antedating and extending beyond the individual life span, whether the idiom of this immortality is biological (living on through children and grandchildren), theological (through a life after death), natural (*in* nature itself which outlasts all), or creative (through what man makes and does). I have suggested that this sense of immortality is a fundamental component of ordinary psychic life, and that it is now being profoundly threatened: by simple historical velocity, which subverts the idioms (notably the theological) in which it has traditionally been maintained; and, of particular importance to protean man, by the existence of nuclear weapons, which, even without being used, call into question all modes of immortality. (Who can be certain of living on through children and grandchildren, through teachings or kindnesses?)

Protean man is left with two paths to symbolic immortality which he tries to cultivate, sometimes pleasurably and sometimes desperately. One is the natural mode we have mentioned. His attraction to nature and concern over its desecration have to do with an unconscious sense that, in whatever holocaust, at least nature will endure—though such are the dimensions of our present weapons that he cannot be absolutely certain even of this. His second path is that of "experiential transcendence"—of seeking a sense of immortality in the way that mystics always have, through psychic experience of such great intensity that time and death are, in effect, eliminated. This, I believe, is the larger meaning of the "drug revolution," of protean man's hunger for chemical aids to "expanded consciousness." And indeed all revolutions may be thought of, at bottom, as innovations in the struggle for immortality, as new combinations of old modes.

We have seen that young adults individually, and youth movements collectively, express most vividly the psychological themes of protean man. And although it is true that these themes make contact with what we sometimes call the "psychology of adolescence," we err badly if we overlook their expression in all age groups and dismiss them as "mere adolescent phenomena." Rather, protean man's affinity for the young—his being metaphorically and psychologically so young in spirit—has to do with his never-ceasing quest for imagery of rebirth. He seeks such imagery from all sources: from ideas, techniques, religious and political systems, mass movements, and drugs; or from special individuals of his own kind whom he sees as possessing that problematic gift of his namesake, the gift of prophecy. The dangers inherent in the quest seem hardly to require emphasis. What perhaps needs most to be kept in mind is the general principle that renewal on a large scale is impossible to achieve without forays into danger, destruction, and negativity. The principle of "death and rebirth" is as valid psychohistorically as it is mythologically. However misguided many of his forays may be, protean man also carries with him an extraordinary range of possibility for man's betterment, or more important, for his survival.

# THE YOUNG AND
# THE OLD—NOTES ON
# A NEW HISTORY

## 16

*This piece represents a kind of culmination—not in the sense of being the end of anything (other than the book itself), but of bringing together most of the themes dealt with in the preceding essays, and in fact throughout my work. It is particularly speculative and digressive —so much so that its seven sections could be considered separate statements about a single general phenomenon. In pulling together disparate observations and varying levels of individual and collective experience, it is concerned less with any particular youth rebellion than with what youth rebellions seek and reflect. Many of the events it draws upon, such as the Columbia and Paris uprisings, were hardly over when I wrote about them; I write this commentary just a few months after the essay itself was completed; the whole enterprise is, in the truest sense, process. It does have a structure which, I believe, stops events at least momentarily in time—holds them together—even if the essay strains at its own structure.*

*Like the previous essay (which it draws upon), it is rendered provocative by its receptivity to what one might call the "psychohistorical logic" of the young. All the more so when that "logic," in relationship to culture and to his-*

*tory, becomes revolutionary. Inevitably, it has angered a few colleagues who, by the tone of their comments, all too clearly confirmed one of the themes of the essay: the two-way explosiveness in the encounters between the old and the young, between what I call the old and the New History.*

*To express this kind of empathy for the young is to open oneself not only to their revolutionary stirrings, cultural and otherwise, but to one's own as well. And in this sense the writing of the essay has been what is these days called a radicalizing experience. Yet I would see it as also having a conservative cast. For it returns repeatedly to the principle of historical connection, as again expressed by Collingwood in his emphasis upon "historical knowledge," upon "the knowledge of what mind has done in the past and . . . the perpetuation of past acts in the present"; and by Genovese in his equally conservative formulation of the revolutionary task of intellectuals, quoted earlier ("not to invent myths, but to teach each people its own particular contradictory truth"). There is similar "revolutionary conservatism" in the essay's psychological stance: while rejecting Freud's vision of individual and collective history as essential recurrence or "return of the repressed," it adheres to the Freudian-Eriksonian principle of the central significance of the past for all innovation.*

*My stress upon the pitfalls of romantic totalism is related to my own earlier work, to Camus' "philosophy of limits," and perhaps also to a vast modern tradition of antipathy not to romanticism as such but to its excesses. This kind of stress, along with the principle of historical connection just stated, could well evoke criticism from the other side, that is, from some of the more militantly antihistorical among the young. Ultimately, though, it would be very wrong to view reactions to it (or to anything else) in purely generational terms. I have been struck by an increasing awareness in many of the radical young of the problem of totalism (they at times even use the word) within their own movements. And by the existence of an expanding group of people over forty, many of them in*

*positions of authority, intent upon opening themselves
to the logic of the young. The generational divide can be
symbolic no less than biological; one must continue to explore its historical significance, but not with the idea of
"explaining history" around it.*

*The essay attempts to illustrate the principle of investi-
gative radicalism suggested in the Introduction to this volume. The sequence of its concerns—from the idea of a
New History, to the innovations therein (whether concerning ideology or father-son symbolism), to a more or
less autonomous description of pitfalls—tries to depict the
special intensity of antagonistic possibilities inherent in
our situation. I take seriously the kinds of themes that are
ordinarily ignored or else considered no more than
amusing (if not irritating or maddening) oddities—such
as the nature of the mockery contained in the "Up Against
the Wall, Motherfucker!" slogan of the Columbia students.
But there is a related theme I do not take up, though it has
great importance for the events I describe: that of public
drama and theatricality.*

*Consider for a moment two judgments: "Much of the
American student movement today is not concerned
with injustices, but with theater." And: "The [French]
students played the parts of revolutionaries. It was beautiful—the most magnificent theater I have ever seen." The
first judgment was made by David Riesman (in a letter to
me, in which he critically contrasted present student
trends with earlier civil rights and antiwar protests). The
second was made by Julian Beck (director of the Living
Theater at a seminar held at the Yale Drama School). The
two men, though of opposite views, were commenting on
the phenomenon of the breakdown of boundaries between
theater and revolution, between artistic imagination and
historically actuality.*

*To be sure, all creative imagination takes place within
the historical process; and history itself—as written, read,
and generally perceived—is an expression of the human
imagination, of what Martin Buber called "imagining the
real." Moreover, great historical events have always been*

*infused with elements of performance and drama. Yet
the traditional separation of these two great strands of
human experience is more than a minor convenience. The
separation has been in the service of protecting the autonomy of the imagination from the enveloping matrix of history (and I include, as part of history, the rituals of
theology and of secular ideology); and equally, of setting
standards for responsibility to specific events and people,
as opposed to the responsibilities of the creative imagination, which are elsewhere. One can well understand how
the breakdown of this distinction could be viewed with
alarm by as keen a student of society as David Riesman,
aware as he is of the fragility of social bonds (especially
in America) and of the depth of existing confusion in social commitments. From this standpoint there is surely
more than a little intellectual and ethical fuzzing in
Beck's cheerful equation of theater and revolution.*

*Yet might it not be true that here, as in so many other
ways, young rebels are straining at boundaries, and in the
process taking huge risks as they press toward still inchoate visions of transformation? What I am suggesting
is that the young are struggling to set new standards for
history and theater in order to alter significantly the over-
all historical drama. Since the latter is fundamentally concerned with man's struggle for eternal continuity in the
face of his biological mortality, we may suspect that here
too we are dealing with efforts to create the new combinations in symbolic immortality that can define and give
substance to a New History.*

*The etymology of the words "drama" and "theater" is
highly suggestive: the former originating in verbs meaning "to do," "to make," or "to be ready to do," and the latter in verbs meaning "to see" or "to view." One thinks of
Teilhard de Chardin's equation of "deeper vision" and
"fuller being," and of their relationship to doing and
making. One may speak of a reaching back to prehistory—
to a state in which imagined and actual events could not
be distinguished—in order to reassemble symbolic elements that might revitalize both imagination and history.*

*Should the effort fail—that is, fall prey to totalistic assumptions that there need not be distinctions of any kind between the two—imagination could become unfocused (and therefore blunted) and history suffocating. But as investigators of, and participants in, this vast effort to create new human forms, are we not all called upon to see further, to do and be more?*

✻         ✻         ✻

What is a New History? And why do the young seek one? I raise these questions to introduce the idea of a particular New History—ours—and to suggest certain ways in which we can begin to understand it.

Let us define a New History as a radical and widely shared re-creation of the forms of human culture—biological, experiential, institutional, technological, aesthetic, and interpretive. The newness of these cultural forms derives not from their spontaneous generation, but from extensions and transformations of what already exists; that which is most genuinely revolutionary makes psychological use of the past for its plunge into the future. Of special importance is the reassertion of the symbolic sense of immortality man requires as he struggles to perpetuate himself biologically and communally, through his works, in his tie to nature, and through transcendent forms of psychic experience.

The shapers of a New History—political revolutionaries, revolutionary thinkers, extreme holocausts, and technological breakthroughs—also express the death of the old. This has been true of the American, French, Russian, and Chinese revolutions; the ideas of Copernicus, Darwin, and Freud; the mutilations of the two World Wars; and, most pertinent to us, the technological revolution which produced Auschwitz and Hiroshima, as well as the postmodern automated and electronic society. Each of these has been associated with "the end of an era," with the devitalization, or symbolic death, of forms and images defining the world-view and life-patterns of large numbers of people over long periods of time.

Great events and new ideas can thus, in different ways,

cause, reflect, or symbolize historical shifts. The combination of Nazi genocide and the American atomic bombings of two Japanese cities terminated man's sense of limits concerning his self-destructive potential, and thereby inaugurated an era in which he is devoid of assurance of living on eternally as a species. It has taken almost twenty-five years for formulations of the significance of these events to begin to emerge—formulations which cannot be separated from the technological developments of this same quarter-century, or from the increasing sense of a universal world-society that has accompanied them.

The New History, then, is built upon the ultimate paradox of two competing, and closely related, images: that of the extinction of history by technology, and that of man's evolving awareness of himself as a single species. It may be more correct to speak of just one image, extraordinarily divided. And whatever the difficulties in evaluating the human consequences of this image, psychologists and historians who ignore it cease to relate themselves to contemporary experience.

The celebrated 1962 "Port Huron Statement" of the Students for a Democratic Society, which is still something of a manifesto for the American New Left, contains the assertion: "Our work is guided by the sense that we may be the last generation in the experiment with living." I think we should take this seriously, just as many of us took seriously Albert Camus' declaration that, in contrast with every generation's tendency to see itself as "charged with remaking the world," his own had a task "perhaps even greater, for it consists in keeping the world from destroying itself." What I wish to stress is the overriding significance for each generation after Hiroshima (and the SDS leaders, though twenty-five years younger than Camus, made their statement just five years after he made his) of precisely this threat of historical extinction. In seeking new beginnings, men are now haunted by an image of the end of everything.

Do the young feel this most strongly? They often say just the opposite. When I discuss Hiroshima with students, they are likely to point to a disparity between my (and Camus') specific concern about nuclear weapons and their generation's feeling that these weapons are just another among the horrors of the world bequeathed to them. Our two "histories" contrast significantly: my (over forty) generation's shocked "survival" of Hiroshima and continuing need to differentiate the pre-Hiroshima world we knew from the world of nuclear weapons in which we now live; their (under twenty-five) generation's experience of growing up in a world in which nuclear weapons have always been part of the landscape. This gradual adaptation, as opposed to original shock, is of great importance. Man is psychologically flexible enough to come to terms with almost anything, so long as it is presented to him as an ordained element of his environment.

But such adaptation is achieved at a price, and achieved only partially at that. The inner knowledge on the part of the young that their world has always been capable of exterminating itself creates an undercurrent of anxiety against which they must constantly defend themselves— anxiety related not so much to death as to a fundamental terror of premature death and unfulfilled life, and to high uncertainty about all forms of human continuity. Their frequent insistence that nuclear weapons are "nothing special" is their form of emotional desensitization, or what I call psychic numbing (as opposed to other forms called forth by their elders). But the young must do a great deal of continuous psychological work to maintain their nuclear "cool." And this in turn may make them unusually responsive to possibilities of breaking out of such numbing, and of altering the world which has imposed it upon them.

All perceptions of threatening historical developments must occur through what Ernst Cassirer called the "symbolic net"—that special area of psychic re-creation characteristic of man, the only creature who "instead of dealing with . . . things themselves . . . . constantly converses . . . with himself." In these internal (and often unconscious) dialogues, anxieties about technological annihilation merge with various perceptions of more symbolic forms of death. That is, Hiroshima and Auschwitz become inwardly associated with the worldwide sense of profound historical dislocation: with the disintegration of formerly vital and nourishing symbols revolving around family, religion, principles of community, and the life cycle in general; and with the inability of the massive and impersonal postmodern institutions (of government, education, and finance) to replace psychologically that which has been lost. They become associated also with the confusions of the knowledge-revolution, and the unprecedented dissemination of half-knowledge through media whose psychological impact has barely begun to be discerned. There is a very real sense in which the world itself has become a "total environment"—a closed psychic chamber with continuous reverberations, bouncing about chaotically and dangerously. The symbolic death perceived, then, is this combination of formlessness and totality, of the inadequacy of existing forms and imprisonment within them. And the young are exquisitely sensitive to such "historical death," whatever their capacity (which we shall return to later) for resisting an awareness of the biological kind.

The young are struck by the fact that most of mankind simply goes about its business as if these extreme dislocations did not exist—as if there were no such thing as ultimate technological violence or existence rendered absurd. The war in Vietnam did not create these murderous incongruities, but it does epitomize them, and it consumes the American youth in them. No wonder, then, that in their "conversations with themselves," so many of the young everywhere seem to be asking: How can we bring the world—and ourselves—back to life,

In referring to the young and their quests, my examples are drawn mostly from the more radical among them; and what I say refers more to those who are white, educated, and of middle-class origin, than to blacks, uneducated youth, or those of working-class backgrounds. The same is true concerning my references to my own genera-

tion. In neither case can the people I describe be anything more than a very small minority within their age
group, their country, or, for that matter, their university.
But in both cases they seem to me to exemplify certain
shared themes, psychological and historical, that in one
way or another affect all people in our era and are likely
to take on increasing importance over the next few decades
and beyond.

II

Students of revolution and rebellion have recognized
the close relationship of both to death symbolism, and to
visions of transcending death by achieving an eternal
historical imprint. Hannah Arendt speaks of revolution as
containing an "all-pervasive preoccupation with permanence, with a 'perpetual state' . . . for . . . 'posterity.' "[1] And
Albert Camus describes insurrection, "in its exalted and
tragic forms," as "a prolonged protest against death, a
violent accusation against the universal death penalty,"
and as "the desire for immortality and for clarity." But
Camus also stressed the rebel's "appeal to the essence of
being," his quest "not . . . for life, but for reasons for
living."[2] And this brings us to an all-important question
concerning mental participation in revolution: What is the
place of ideology, and of images and ideas, and of the self
in relationship to all three?

Men have always pursued immortalizing visions. But
most of the revolutionary ideologies of the past two centuries have provided elaborate blueprints for individual
and collective immortality—specifications of ultimate
cause and ultimate effect, theological in tone and scientific in claim. When present-day revolutionaries reject these
Cartesian litanies they are taking seriously some of the
important psychological and historical insights of the last
few decades. For they are rejecting an oppressive ideological totalism—with its demand for control of all communication within a milieu, its imposed guilt and cult of purity
and confession, its loading of the language, and its

principles of doctrine over person and even of the dispensing of existence itself (in the sense that sharp lines are drawn between those whose right to exist can be recognized and those who possess no such right). This rejection represents, at its best, a quest by the young for a new kind of revolution—one perhaps no less enduring in historical impact, but devoid of the claim to omniscience and of the catastrophic chain of human manipulations stemming from that claim.

It is, of course, quite possible that the anti-ideological stance of today's young will turn out to be a transitory phenomenon, a version of the euphoric denial of dogma that so frequently appears during the early moments of revolution, only to be overwhelmed by absolutist doctrine and suffocating organization in the name of revolutionary discipline. Yet there is reason for believing that the present antipathy to ideology is something more, that it is an expression of a powerful and highly appropriate contemporary style. The shift we are witnessing from fixed, all-encompassing forms of ideology to more fluid *ideological fragments* approaches Camus' inspiring vision of continuously decongealing rebellion, as opposed to dogmatically congealed, all-or-none revolution. I would also see it as an expression of contemporary, or what I call "protean," psychological style—post-Freudian and postmodern, characterized by interminable exploration and flux, and by relatively easy shifts in identification and belief.* Protean man as rebel, then, seeks to remain open, while in the midst of rebellion, to the extraordinarily rich, confusing, liberating, and threatening array of contemporary historical possibilities.

His specific talent for fluidity greatly enhances his

---

* Related psychological styles have undoubtedly emerged during such earlier periods of historical dislocation as the Renaissance in the West or the Meiji Restoration in Japan. But the extremity of recent technological change, the contemporary loss of a sense that society is still "there," and the flooding of imagery of limitless choices by the mass media—these have combined to create, if not a world of shape-shifters, one in which rapid shifts in external commitments and inner forms have become part of a functional pattern of living. (See Chapter 15.)

tactical leverage. For instance, Daniel Cohn-Bendit, the leader of the French student uprisings of May, 1968, in an interesting dialogue with Jean-Paul Sartre insisted that the classical Marxist-Leninist principle of the omniscient revolutionary vanguard (the working class, as represented by the Communist Party) be replaced with "a much simpler and more honorable one: the theory of an active minority acting, you might say, as a permanent ferment, pushing forward without trying to control events." Cohn-Bendit went on to characterize this process as "uncontrollable spontaneity" and as "disorder which allows people to speak freely and will later result in some form of 'self-organization.'" He rejected as "the wrong solution" an alternate approach (urged upon him by many among the Old Left) of formulating an attainable program and drawing up realizable demands. While this was "bound to happen at some point," he was convinced it would "have a crippling effect." In the same spirit are the warnings of Tom Hayden, a key figure in the American New Left, to his SDS colleagues and followers, against "fixed leaders"; and his insistence upon "participatory democracy," as well as upon ideology of a kind that is secondary to, and largely achieved through, revolutionary action. So widespread has this approach been that the American New Left has been characterized as more a process than a program.

I would suggest that the general principle of "uncontrollable spontaneity" represents a meeting ground between tactic and deeper psychological inclination. The underlying inclination consists precisely of the protean style of multiple identifications, shifting beliefs, and constant search for new combinations. Whatever its pitfalls, this style of revolutionary behavior is an attempt on the part of the young to mobilize the fluidity of the twentieth century as a weapon against what they perceive to be two kinds of stagnation: the old, unresponsive institutions (universities, governments, families) and newly emerging but fixed technological visions (people "programmed" by computers in a "technetronic society"). A central feature of his attempt is the stress upon the communal spirit and the creation of actual new communities. And here too we observe an alternation between conservative images of stable and intimate group ties, and images of transforming society itself in order to make such ties more possible than is now the case.

The process, and the underlying psychological tendencies, moreover, seem to be universal. Observing the nearly simultaneous student uprisings in America, France, Japan, Brazil, Germany, Italy, Mexico, South Africa, Czechoslovakia, Chile, Yugoslavia, and Spain, one can view them all as parts of a large single tendency, occurring within a single worldwide human and technical system. Here the planet's instant communications network is of enormous importance, as is the process of psychological contagion. To recognize the striking congruence in these rebellions, one need not deny the great differences in, say, Czech students rebelling against Stalinism, Spanish students against Falangism, and American, French, and Italian students against the Vietnam war, the consumer society, and academic injustices.

In every case the young seek active involvement in the institutional decisions governing their lives, new alternatives to consuming and being consumed, and liberated styles of individual and community existence. Unspecific and ephemeral as these goals may seem, they are early expressions of a quest for historical rebirth, for reattachment to the Great Chain of Being, for reassertion of symbolic immortality.

The French example is again revealing (though not unique), especially in its extraordinary flowering of graffiti. Here one must take note of the prominence of the genre—of the informal slogan-on-the-wall virtually replacing formal revolutionary doctrine, no less than the content. But one is struck by the stress of many of the slogans, sometimes to the point of intentional absurdity, upon enlarging the individual life space, on saying "yes" to more and "no" to less. Characteristic were "Think of your desires as realities," "Prohibiting is forbidden" (a play on words in which the ubiquitous "Défense d'afficher" is converted to "Défense d'interdire"), and, of course, the two most famous: "Imagination in power" and "Imagination is revolution." Sartre was referring to the over-all spirit of these graffiti, but perhaps most to the revolutionary acts themselves, when he commented (in the same dialogue mentioned before): "I would like to describe what you have done as extending the field of possibilities."

Precisely such "extending [of] the field of possibilities" is at the heart of the worldwide youth rebellion—for hippies no less than political radicals—and at the heart of the protean insistence upon continuous psychic re-creation of the self. Around this image of unlimited extension and perpetual re-creation, as projected into a dimly imagined future, the young seek to create a new mode of revolutionary immortality.

### III

Of enormous importance for these rebellions is another basic component of the protean style, the spirit of mockery. While young rebels are by no means immune from the most pedantic and humorless discourse, they come alive to others and themselves only when giving way to—or seizing upon—their very strong inclination toward mockery. The mocking political rebel merges with the hippie and with a variety of exponents of pop culture to "put on"—that is mislead or deceive by means of some form of mockery or absurdity—his uncomprehending cohorts, his elders, or anyone in authority. (Despite important differences, there has always been a fundamental unity in the rebellions of hippies and young radicals which is perhaps just now becoming fully manifest.) In dress, hair, and general social and sexual style the mocking rebel is not only "extending the field of possibilities," but making telling commentary—teasing, ironic, contemptuous—on the absurd folkways of "the others." The mockery can be gentle and even loving, or it can be bitter and provocative in the extreme. *

---

* A classic example of the mocking put-on was Yippie leader Jerry Rubin's appearance at the House Un-American Activities Committee

Here the Columbia rebellion is illuminating. What it lacked in graffiti it more than made up for in its already classic slogan, "Up Against the Wall, Motherfucker!" I make no claim to full understanding of the complete psychological and cultural journey this phrase has undergone—indeed, a truly comprehensive account of that journey would teach us a good deal about contemporary America, and much more. But let me at least sketch in a few steps along the way:

(1) The emergence of the word "motherfucker" (increasingly unhyphenated) to designate (let us say now) a form of extreme transgression. The word might well have originated within the black American subculture, and certainly has been given fullest expression there and used with great nuance to express not only contempt but also awe or even admiration (though an equivalent can probably be found in virtually every culture).

(2) The use of the word in contemptuous command by white policemen when ordering black (and perhaps other) suspects to take their places in the police lineup, thereby creating the full phrase "Up against the wall, motherfucker!" The mockery here was that of dehumanization, and use of the phrase was at times accompanied by beatings and other forms of humiliation.

(3) LeRoi Jones's reclaiming of the phrase for black victims—and, in the process, achieving a classic victim-

---

hearing on possible Communist involvement in the Chicago street demonstrations during the Democratic National Convention. *The New York Times* reporter, noting that Rubin wore a "bandolier of live cartridges," painted a vivid scene: "Bearded, beaded, barefooted and barechested, Mr. Rubin waved aloft what he called 'an M-16 rifle.' It turned out to be a toy. Later, stripped of his bullets, but still carrying his toy weapon, he was allowed into the hearing room where he spent much of the day jingling bells attached to his wrists, popping bubble gum and burning tiny sticks of incense." Here the put-on includes a dramatization of the most lurid fantasies of the adversary, together with little rituals so radically "out of place" in the particular setting that either they or the setting itself must be viewed as absurd. In contrast, the testimony of a staff investigator for the subcommittee that (again as reported by *The Times*) "the demonstrations were in line with 'the policies of Hanoi, Peking and Moscow,'" was a straight form of accusation and not, at least by intention, a put-on.

izer-victim turnabout—by means of the simple expedient of adding to it, in a poem, the line, "This is a stick-up."

(4) The appearance of an East Village Yippie (Youth International Party) style group (now becoming national) which embraced Jones's reversal to the point of naming themselves the "Up-Against-The-Wall-Motherfuckers."

(5) The attraction of Columbia SDS leaders to this East Village group ("mostly because we liked their style," Mark Rudd said on one occasion); and the use of part of the phrase (Up against the wall!) for the title of a pre-uprising one-issue newspaper, and all of the phrase, including Jones's addition, to express contempt for Grayson Kirk in Mark Rudd's open letter to him published in that same newspaper. (The threatening chant "To the wall!" or "Up against the wall!"—borrowed by young American radicals from the Cuban Revolution—might also have figured in this sequence.)

(6) The slogan's full flowering during the course of the Columbia strike, both in abbreviated and complete form, in shouted student chorus, for confronting just about all representatives of what was considered negative authority—police, city officials, administrators, and faculty. Rudd has claimed that his group adopted the slogan "in order to demonstrate our solidarity with the blacks and our understanding of the oppression they have been subjected to." But other student-strikers told me this was "a public explanation." They attributed the slogan's popularity to the students' general mood and feelings about their adversaries; and also to the presence of a few members of the East Village group. One, known as "John Motherfucker," was constantly in view, wearing his "club jacket" with the organization's name lettered on it, and advocating even greater militancy. He became an object of both humor (other students thought his ideas "crazy") and affection.

(7) The arrested students' renewed encounter with the police version of the shorter phrase ("Up against the wall!") when *they* were called to the police lineup ("I can't get over how they really do use the term," wrote

"Simon James" (James Simon Kunen) in his *New York Magazine* article).

(8) Finally, Lionel Trilling's pun, in characterizing the striking students (not without affection) as "Alma-Mater-fuckers"—a witty example of an important principle: the mocking of mockery.

In evaluating the significance of the phrase and its vicissitudes, the classical psychoanalytic approach would, immediately and definitively, stress the Oedipus complex. After all, who but *fathers* are mother-fuckers? And who but sons yearn to replace them in this activity? Moreover, the authorities at whom the Columbia students aimed the phrase could certainly qualify, in one way or another, as father-substitutes. And there was much additional evidence throughout the student rebellions of a totem-and-taboo-like attack upon the father—as exemplified, mockingly and playfully, by another bit of French graffiti, "Daddy stinks" (*Papa pue*); and, mockingly and nastily, by Columbia students reported to have shouted at their faculty elders, "Why don't you go and die!"

But one does well to move beyond this kind of psycho-analytic explanation—to take it as at most a beginning of, rather than an end to, understanding. For if we assume that the mother in question is, so to speak, the fucker's own, we are dealing with an image of the ultimate violation of the ultimate incest taboo. Now, it has been said that this taboo is society's last inviolate principle—the only psycho-moral barricade which contemporary rebels have not yet stormed. Whether or not this is true, the bandying about of the phrase "Up Against the Wall, Motherfuckers!" is a way of playing with an image of ultimate violation, and of retribution for that violation. The tone could be menacing and hateful, but on the whole (at least among the students) less one of irreconcilable rage than of taunting ridicule and mimicry. And the continuous reversals characterizing the whole sequence—the switches between victimizer and victim, accuser and accused—ultimately mock not only the whole social order and its linguistic and sexual taboos; like Trilling's pun, they mock the mocking phrase itself.

The tone of mockery can be a source of great unifying power. One could argue, for instance, that mockery provided the necessary continuity in the evolution, metaphorically speaking, from hippie (socially withdrawn experiments in feeling) to Yippie (activist assaults upon social institutions); as well as the psychological style around which elements of student-radical and hippie cultures could come to coexist within individual minds. In the Columbia rebellion the spirit of mockery was able to unite, if not in political action, at least in a measure of shared feeling, such disparate groups as hippies, Yippies, white student radicals and moderates, and some blacks (the police could also be included, but from across the barricades). And one can add to the list the distinguished professor whose pun I quoted, many of his faculty colleagues, a large number of Columbia students not involved in the strike, the writer of this essay, and probably most of its readers. For mockery is central to the contemporary style, confronting as it does the sense of absurd incongruity in the relationship of self to society, and ultimately of death to life, which we all share. There are moments when this incongruity can be dealt with only by the combinations of humor, taunt, mimicry, derision, and ridicule contained within the style of mockery. For when historical dislocation is sufficiently profound, mockery can become the only inwardly authentic tone for expressing what people feel about their relationships to the institutions of their world. And in this sense young rebels express what a great many other people—from conservative Wall Street broker to liberal college professor to black militant to anti-black Wallaceite—in one way or another inwardly experience.

On the border of mockery are such slogans of the French students as "We are all undesirables!" and the much more powerful "We are all German Jews!" The slogans refer directly to the origins of Cohn-Bendit, the student leader, but their significance extends much further. They mock not only anti-Semitism and national-racial chauvinism, but the over-all process of victimization itself, and the "old history" for harboring such victimization. The method by which this was done is worth noting: a vast open-air cha-

rade with thousands of students who, by shouting in unison, "We are all German Jews!", momentarily became
classical European victims, thereby rendering ridiculous
the very categories of victim and victimizer. At this affirm-
ative border of mockery, then, and at the far reaches of the
protean style, is a call for man to cease his folly in divid-
ing himself into what Erik Erikson has called pseudo-
species, and to see himself as the single species he is.

One can observe a related if much more confusing impulse toward inclusiveness, though, in the diversity of
ideological fragments young rebels embrace. Thus hippies,
for their experiments with the self, draw upon Eastern and
Western mysticism, chemically induced ecstasy, and various traditions, new and old, of polymorphous sexuality.
Young radicals may incorporate any of these aspects of
hippie culture, and combine them with ideas and images
drawn from many different revolutionary experiences
(pre-Marxist utopians, anarchists, Marx, Trotsky, Lenin,
Rosa Luxemburg, Mao, Castro, Guevara, Debray, Ho,
Gandhi, Fanon, Malcolm X, Martin Luther King, Stokely
Carmichael, and H. Rap Brown); from recent psychological and social theorists (Sartre, Camus, C. Wright Mills,
Herbert Marcuse, Norman O. Brown, Erik Erikson, Abra-
ham Maslow, and Paul Goodman); and from just about
any kind of evolving cultural style (derived from jazz or
black power or "soul," from the small-group movement
and the Esalen-type stress upon Joy, or from camp-mock-
ery of Victorian or other retrospectively amusing periods),
including all of the revolutionary and intellectual traditions just mentioned.

Moreover, the emphasis upon the experiential—upon
the way a man and his ideas *feel* to one right now, rather
than upon precise theory—encourages inclusiveness and
fits in with the focus upon images and fragments. Details
of intellectual history may be neglected, and even revered
figures are often greatly misunderstood. But the over-all
process can be seen as a revolutionary equivalent to the
artist's inclination to borrow freely, selectively, impres-
sionistically, and distortingly from predecessors and contemporaries as a means of finding his own way.

Of enormous importance as models are heroic images of men whose lives can be viewed as continuously revolutionary. The extraordinary lives of Mao, Castro, and especially Guevara can combine with romantic mythology of many kinds, including that of perpetual revolution. In a sense Castro and Guevara are transitional figures between the total ideologies of the past and the more fragmentary and experiential ones of the New History. (I shall comment later upon the particular dilemmas Mao presents for the new rebels.) But heroes and models tend to be easily discarded and replaced, or else retained with a looseness and flexibility that permits the strangest of revolutionary bedfellows. In lives as in ideologies, the young seek not the entire package but those fragments which contribute to their own struggle to formulate and change their world, to their own sense of wholeness. Their constant search for new forms becomes a form in itself.

To dismiss all this as a "style revolution" is to miss the point—unless one is aware of the sense in which style is everything. One does better to speak of a *revolution of forms*, of a quest for images of rebirth which reassert feelings of connection and re-establish the sense of immortality; and of a *process revolution*, consistent with the principles of action painting and kinetic sculpture, in which active rebelling both expresses and creates the basic images of rebellion. The novelist Donald Barthelme's statement that "Fragments are the only form I trust" has ramifications far beyond the literary. However severe the problems posed by such a principle for social and especially political revolution, we deceive ourselves unless we learn to focus upon these shifting forms—to recognize new styles of life and new relations to institutions and to ideas. Indeed, we require a little revolutionizing of our psychological assumptions, so that both the young and the old can be understood, not as bound by static behavioral categories, but as in continuous historical motion.

## IV

Let us, for instance, turn to the extremely important symbolism surrounding fathers and sons. Here the theme of fatherlessness is prominent—but it does not necessarily include a search for a "substitute father."

In addition to his biological and familial relationship to his children, we may speak of the father as one who mediates between prevailing social images on the one hand and the developmental thrusts of his children (biological or symbolic) on the other. Because the father is clearly not a simple conduit, and imposes a strong personal imprint (his "personality") upon the child, we tend to fall into the lazy psychoanalytic habit of seeing every authoritative man or group coming into subsequent contact with the child from the larger society as a "substitute" for the father, as a "father figure." Yet considering the enormous part played by general historical forces in shaping what the father transmits (or fails to transmit), one might just as well say that he is a "substitute" for history, a "history figure." The analogy is admittedly a bit far-fetched—a flesh-and-blood father, and not "history," conceives the child, teaches him things, and tells him off—but so is the tendency toward indiscriminate labeling of one person as a "substitute" for another. We do better, especially during periods of rapid change, to see fathers and sons as bound up in a shifting psychological equilibrium, each influencing the other, both enmeshed in forms specific to their family and their historical epoch. (Mothers and daughters are, of course, very much part of all this. But the mother's "mediation," for biological and cultural reasons, tends to be more heavily infused with nurturing; her way of representing forms of social authority tends to be more indirect, complex, and organically rooted. And revolutionary daughters, like their mothers, deserve an evaluation of their own, quite beyond the scope of this essay.) A son's developing image (or images) of the world should not be attributed to a single cause, nor considered a replacement for an earlier imprint.

Nor is the father by any means a pure representative of the past. Rather he is a molder of compromise between the history he has known and the newer one in which the life of his family is immersed. During periods like the present he is, psychologically speaking, by no means a clear spokesman for stability and "order." He is more of a troubled negotiator, caught between the relatively orderly images he can retain (or reach back for) from his own experience, and the relatively disorderly ones anticipating the new shape of things. While likely to be more on the side of the former than the latter, in the midst of a revolution of forms his allegiances may not be too clear. He finds himself suspended in time, weakened by the diminishing power of old forms, and by his inability to relate himself significantly to (or even comprehend) the new.

During earlier revolutions (the French Revolution or the social revolution of the Renaissance) the old history under attack, however vulnerable, was still part of a coherent formulation of the world—theological, political, and social. One suspects that this formulation provided the fathers of the time with psychic ammunition sufficient at least to confront, and oppose directly, their rebellious sons. But the old history now being attacked, reflecting as it does more than two hundred years of erosion of traditional forms of every kind, permits fathers no such symbolic strength, no such capacity for confrontation. Instead we find a characteristic father-son pattern emerging in families in various parts of the world—among young American radicals (as reported by Kenneth Keniston), middle-class Germans (described by Alexander Mitscherlich), Japanese *Zengakuren* student-activists (whom I interviewed), and, very likely, among many young French student-rebels. The pattern is this: The son, fortified and recurrently exhilarated by his radical convictions, and by his sense of being ethically and historically *right*, pities rather than hates his father for the latter's "sellout" to evil social forces. Whether kindly or contemptuous in this judgment, he views his father as one who has erred and been misled, as a man in need of patient re-education (if he is to be salvaged at all) rather than total denunciation. And the father himself, inwardly, cannot help but share many of these judgments, however he may try to attribute them to his son's immaturity and youthful excess. This is the sense in which fathers no longer exercise ethical—or formative—authority over their sons. They have lost their capacity to guide their offspring (rather than be guided by them) through the shifting forms of their common world. They can be fathers but not mentors.

This loss of mentorship is what we generally call "the absence of male authority." Its large-scale occurrence reflects the *historical* absence of a meaningful set of inner images of what one should value, how one should live. But it is experienced by the individual as a profound sense of fatherlessness. Sons feel abandoned by their fathers and perceive the world as devoid of strong men who know how things are and how they should be. They experience the hunger for new forms—and especially imagery of rebirth—that I have described as characteristic of contemporary man.

But precisely this kind of symbolic fatherlessness, as I have also suggested, makes possible every variety of experiment and innovation. Just as the young lack the nurturing comfort of fixed social forms, so are they free of the restricting demands of these forms. Since nothing is psychologically certain, everything is possible. And there emerges what might be called an "unencumbered generation" (if we may give it still one more name), in politics as well as in everyday life.

Unencumbered rebellion can include every variety of tactical and ideological foray into present-day existence—as expressed in this country's "new politics" (the young radicals' politics of confrontation, the Yippies' "politics of ecstasy," and the more staid but still politically unconventional and youth-influenced campaigns of Eugene McCarthy and Robert Kennedy); and especially in contemporary novels (such as the nightmare version depicted by Sol Yurick in *The Bag*). This potential for innovation is perhaps the least understood dimension of the new rebels. It particularly confuses members of the Old Left, and provokes them either to reassert older judgments about how radicals should behave, or to attempt (often with considerable sympathy) to subsume the new rebellion under a traditional ideological label. "Anarchism" is the most tempting, because of its stress upon human relations in autonomous communities and opposition to centralized power, and because of what George Woodcock has referred to as "its cult of the spontaneous . . . [and] striking protean fluidity in adapting its approach and methods to special historical circumstances." But even Woodcock speaks of "a new manifestation of the idea"; and the young themselves tend to alternate between accepting the anarchist label as one of their ideological fragments, and expressing wariness toward it as still another potential ideological trap. Perhaps Sartre was wiser in his characterization of the phenomenon to Cohn-Bendit: "You have many more ideas than your fathers had. . . . Your imagination is far richer."

The formative fathers of the young rebels are the middle-aged members of the intellectual Left. (I recently heard one articulate young rebel say as much to an audience made up mostly of university professors: "We are your children. You taught us what American society is like.") And the encounter between formative fathers and sons takes on special importance. On the one hand the young rebels seize upon their innovative freedom and seek to live out both the classical revolutionary myth of making all things new, and the contemporary protean myth (if I may call it that) of infinite shape-shifting to the point of rendering the past totally "irrelevant." They may thus view their formative fathers as no more than rickety impediments. But on the other hand, they give the impression of constantly seeking *something* from this group of their elders: confirmation in radicalism, adult-dispensed legitimation (psychological and ethical), authoritative support and at times even guidance (but never direction) concerning theory and tactics. (One must keep in mind the origins of many of the ideological fragments of the young rebels in older-generation thought, such as that of Herbert Marcuse and C. Wright Mills, without viewing these origins as determining everything.) The young, then, do seek connection, but a connection that does not suffocate or even restrict. The connection may be essen-

tially negative—the young may contrast their own ac-
tivism, flexibility, and moral intensity with their elders'
passivity, fixity, and shameful compromise—but even this
can be a form of connection.

The "fathers" involved also crave connection. As long-
standing advocates of liberal or radical programs, now
puzzled or even terrified by their intellectual offspring,
they too ask themselves where they can link up with what
is happening. But nothing for these formative fathers is
clear-cut. They do not live in a time (Confucian or Bibli-
cal) in which sons are expected to honor, and seek to become like, their fathers. Nor do the young bring to them
the kind of total negation expressed in a three-sentence
commentary by a member of Hell's Angels: "I don't like
nothin'. I don't like nobody. Fuck everything." Instead,
the middle-aged Left-intellectual finds the encounter to
be replete with ambiguity. He is likely to be alternately
attracted, repulsed, impressed, bedazzled, jarred, and
bemused by young rebels and their behavior—his historical sense and paternal impulse combining to tell him
he should *do* something, but what?

He at times responds by reviving his own radicalism—
possibly an awakening from a long political sleep—which
can in turn take the form of either a serious re-examination of his world, or of an uncritical psychological identification with the young almost to the point of near total
self-surrender. Or he may have the opposite response of
angry and unyielding dissociation from the young, sometimes with searching criticism of their programs, but all
too often with a petulant and willfully uncomprehending declaration of generational warfare. A third response,
a favorite of postmodern intellectuals in times of crisis, is
that of escape into technical and professionalized preoccupations—though the allergy of the young to this stance
is making it more and more difficult to maintain. There
are, of course, other kinds of responses, as I shall soon suggest. But here I want to stress the very real psychological
—actually psychohistorical—problems faced by these
members of the "older generation."

For instance, they experience severe feelings of guilt

over reminders of never-quite-abandoned ideals and never-quite-comfortable accommodations; over not doing more to embrace the young and their movement, or if they do embrace them, over the possibility of repeating their own past political mistakes in response to a new call to revolution. They feel rage toward the young because of the severe threat they represent (sometimes accompanied by envy of the strength and conviction behind that threat), as well as rage toward themselves because of their own sense of impotence. Most of all, they perceive a fundamental threat to over-all integrity, to whatever degree of wholeness they have been able to achieve in their own blend of individual and historical forms, in their decent liberalism, ordered radicalism, professional autonomy, and personal privacy—that is, a threat to the entire structure of their lives. And even those who, like Sartre, wish to acknowledge the superior imagination of their "sons," must sense that as older models, they are likely to be rather quickly "used up," and either discarded or retained condescendingly (as is to some extent already the case with Marcuse), in order to make way for new imaginative forays. It could be argued that the young have bypassed fathers for formative grandfathers, such as the seventy-year-old Marcuse and the seventy-five-year-old Mao, a pattern frequently resorted to when rapid historical change weakens the former and renders the latter in various ways more heroic. But I would see this as only one among many patterns, and point to younger models such as Guevara and Castro, as well as to such "old" young radicals as Tom Hayden. In any case, formative fathers risk inner agreement with the young's accusatory chant of "irrelevance" until they can discover their own relationship to unprecedented events.

## v

Formative fathers and sons meet at the university. There has been much discussion about young rebels' selection of the university as a primary target for recent upheavals. Many distinguished commentators (David Riesman,

Christopher Lasch, Stephen Spender, Herbert Marcuse, Lionel Trilling, and Noam Chomsky, among others) have cautioned students about the dangers of confusing the vulnerable centers of learning they attack, and for periods of time "bring down," with society at large. Spender put the matter eloquently when he said that "however much the university needs a revolution, and the society needs a revolution, it would be disastrous . . . not to keep the two revolutions apart." He went on to point out, as have others also, that the university is "an arsenal from which [student-rebels] can draw the arms from which they can change society"; and that "To say, 'I won't have a university until society has a revolution,' is as though Karl Marx were to say 'I won't go to the reading room of the British Museum until it has a revolution.'" Yet wise as these cautionary thoughts undoubtedly are, one also has to consider the ways in which the university's special symbolic significance makes it all too logical (if unfortunate) a target for would-be revolutionaries.

What makes universities unique is the extent to which, within them, the prevailing concepts of a society are at the same time presented, imposed, examined, and criticized. The university is indeed a training ground for available occupational slots in society, as young rebels are quick to point out; it can at its worst approach a technical instrument in the hands of the military-industrial complex. But it can also be precisely the opposite, a training ground for undermining social institutions, as Spender suggests, and as the young rebels themselves attest by the extent to which they are campus products. In most cases the university is a great many things in between. It provides for students four years of crucial personal transition—a *rite de passage* from relatively unformed adolescence to a relatively formed adulthood. And the fact that many are likely to move through continuing protean explorations during the post-university years renders especially important whatever initial adult "formation" the university makes possible. For these reasons, and because both groups are there, the university is the logical place for the rebellious young to confront their ostensible mentors, and thereby both define themselves and make a statement about society at large.

The statement they make has to do not only with social inequities and outmoded institutions, but with the general historical dislocations of everyone. And in this sense the target of the young is not so much the university, or the older generation, as the continuing commitment of both to the discredited past. But the university provides unique opportunities for the young to reverse the father-son mentorship—and, moreover, to do so *in action*. The reversal may be confused and temporary, with student and teacher moving back and forth between leadership and followership, but in the process the young can assert their advanced position in the shaping of what is to come. Though the "generation gap" seems at times to be increasing beyond redemption, there is also a sense in which the gap narrows as the young engage their elders as they never have before, and the university becomes a place of unprecedented intellectual and emotional contact between the generations. And what happens at one university can be repeated, with many variations, at any other university throughout the world. Universities everywhere share a central position in the susceptibility to new currents, and tend also to present students with very real grievances; the global communications network provides not only the necessary contagion but instant instruction in the art of university rebellion. Specific actions and reactions then give way to a general historical process.

We learn more about the university in the midst of militant social disorder by turning to the greatest of recent national upheavals, the Chinese Cultural Revolution. More than is generally realized, universities were the focus of much that took place during that extraordinary movement. Not only were they a major source of Red Guard activists but within them a series of public denunciations of senior professors and administrators by students and young faculty members preceded—and in a sense set off —the Cultural Revolution as a whole. These denunciations originated at Peking University, which was the scene of many such upheavals both before the Communist victory in China and during the subsequent campaigns of "thought reform" that have become a trademark of the Chinese Communist regime. The Cultural Revolution, the most extreme of these campaigns, contrasted with more recent student rebellions elsewhere in one very important respect: the young were called forth by their elders (Mao and the Maoists) to fight the latter's old revolutionary battles, and to combat the newly threatening impurities associated with revisionism. But from the beginning there was probably a considerable amount of self-assertion and spontaneity among Red Guard leaders and followers. And over the course of the Cultural Revolution, overzealous Red Guard groups became more and more difficult for anyone to control, especially as they split into contending factions, each claiming to be the most authentically revolutionary and Maoist. And during the summer of 1968 reports of jousts, fights, and pitched battles among them, also taking place at Peking University, revealed how within two years that institution had shifted in its function from provider of the spark of the Cultural Revolution to receptacle for its ashes. Significantly, members of the Red Guard were then demoted to the status of "intellectuals" who required the tutelage of workers and especially peasants (and the control of the Army). But Peking and other universities continued to preoccupy the regime as places in need of fundamental reform.

Indeed, the remolding of educational institutions has been greatly stressed over the course of the Cultural Revolution. And the extraordinary step of closing all schools throughout China for more than a year was both a means of mobilizing students for militant political struggles beyond the campuses, and revamping (however chaotically) the nation's educational process. In *Revolutionary Immortality*, I described the Cultural Revolution as a quest for a symbolic form of immortality, a means of eternalizing Mao's revolutionary works in the face of his anticipated biological death and the feared "death of the revolution."

The university was perceived throughout as both an arena of fearful dangers (revisionist ideas), and as what might be called an immortalizing agent (for the promulgation at the highest cultural levels of the most complete Maoist thought).

In its own fashion, the Cultural Revolution was a response to the New History, which in China's case includes not only Russian and Eastern European revisionism but early manifestations of proteanism. Chinese universities, however, have been forced to flee from contemporary confusions into what is most simple and pure in that country's Old Revolutionary History; this is in contrast to the more open-ended plunge into a threatening but more open-ended future being taken by universities throughout the rest of the world. Yet these issues are far from decided. Universities everywhere, China included, are likely to experience powerful pressures from the young for "restructuring." While this hardly guarantees equivalent restructuring of national governments, it may well be a prelude to fundamental changes in almost every aspect of human experience.

## VI

One can hardly speak of definitive conclusions about something just beginning. Nor would I claim a position of omniscient detachment from the events of the New History—I have in no way been immune from the combinations of feelings about them I have described for my generation of Left-intellectuals, and have here and there contributed to dialogues on them. But having earlier in this essay affirmed the significance of the New History, I wish now to suggest some of its pitfalls, and then, finally, present-day potentialities for avoiding them.

From the standpoint of the young, these pitfalls are related to what is best called romantic totalism. I refer to a post-Cartesian absolutism, to a new quest for old feelings. Its controlling image, at whatever level of consciousness, is that of *replacing history with experience.*

This is, to a considerable extent, the romanticism of the "youth movement." I have heard a number of thoughtful European-born intellectuals tell, with some anxiety, how the tone and atmosphere now emanating from young American rebels is reminiscent of that of the German youth movement of the late Weimar Republic (and the Hitler Youth into which it was so readily converted). What they find common to both is a cult of feeling and a disdain for restraint and reason. While I would emphasize the differences between the two groups much more than any similarities, there is a current in contemporary youth movements that is more Nietzschean than Marxist-Leninist. It consists of a stress upon what I call experiential transcendence, upon the cultivation of states of feeling so intense and so absorbing that time and death cease to exist. (Drugs are of great importance here but as part of a general quest.) The pattern becomes totalistic when it begins to tamper with history to the extent of victimizing opponents in order to reinforce these feelings, and a danger signal is the absolute denial of the principle of historical continuity.

The replacement of history with experience—with totally liberated feeling—is by no means a new idea, and has long found expression in classical forms of mysticism and ecstasy. But it has reappeared with considerable force in the present-day drug revolution, and in the writings of a number of articulate contemporary spokesmen such as Norman O. Brown. This general focus upon the transcendent psychic experience would seem to be related to impairments in other modes of symbolic immortality. That is, the modern decline of theological concepts of immortality, on the one hand, and the threat posed by present weapons (nuclear, bacterial, and chemical) to man's biological and cultural continuity, on the other, have radically undermined symbolism of death and transcendence. In the absence of intact images of biological and cultural immortality, man's anxiety about both his death and his manner of life is profoundly intensified. One response to this anxiety, and simultaneous quest for new forms, is the unique contemporary blending of experiential transcendence with social and political revolution.

We have already noted that political revolution has its own transformationist myth of making all things new. When this combines with the experiential myth (of eliminating time and death), two extreme positions can result. One of these is the condemnation and negation of an entire historical tradition: the attempt by some of the young to sever totally their relationship to the West by means of an impossibly absolute identity replacement, whether the new identity is that of the Oriental mystic or that of the Asian or African victim of colonialism or slavery. And a second consequence of this dismissal of history can be the emergence of a single criterion of judgment: what feels revolutionary is good, what does not is counter-revolutionary.

A related, equally romantic pitfall might be called "generational totalism." The problem is not so much the slogan "Don't trust anyone over thirty" as the unconscious assumption that can be behind it: that "youth power" knows no limits because youth equals immortality. To be sure, it is part of being young to believe that one will never die, that such things happen only to other people, old people. But this conviction ordinarily lives side by side with a realization—at first preconscious, but over the years increasingly a matter of awareness—that life is, after all, finite. And a more symbolic sense of immortality, through works and connections outlasting one's individual life span, takes hold and permits one to depend a little less upon the fantasy that one will live forever.

Under extreme historical conditions, however, certain groups—in this case, youth groups—feel the need to cling to the omnipotence provided by a more literal image of immortality, which they in turn contrast with the death-tainted lives of others. When this happens, we encounter a version of the victimizing process: the young "victimize" the old (or older) by equating age with individual or historical "exhaustion" and death; and the "victim," under duress, may indeed feel himself to be "as if dead," and

collude in his victimization. Conversely, the older generation has its need to victimize, sometimes (but not always)
in the form of counterattack, and may feel compelled to
view every innovative action of the young as destructive
or "deadly." Indeed, the larger significance and greatest
potential danger of what we call the "generation gap"
reside in these questions of broken historical connection
and impaired sense of immortality.

The recent slogan of French students, "The young
make love, the old make obscene gestures," is patroniz-
ing rather than totalistic, and its mocking blend of truth
and absurdity permits a chuckle all around. But when the
same students refer to older critics as "people who do not
exist," or when young American radicals label everyone
and everything either "relevant" ("revolutionary") or
"irrelevant" ("counter-revolutionary") on the basis of
whether or not the person, idea, or event is consistent or
inconsistent with their own point of view—then we are
dealing with something more potentially malignant, with
the drawing of sharp lines between people and nonpeo-
ple.

Perhaps the ultimate expression of generational totalism
was that of an early group of Russian revolutionaries
who advocated the suppression and even annihilation
of everyone over the age of twenty-five because they
were felt to be too contaminated with that era's old
history to be able to absorb the correct principles of the
New. I have heard no recent political suggestions of
this kind; but there have certainly been indications (aside
from the Hollywood version of youth suppressing age in
the film *Wild in the Streets*) that young radicals at times
have felt a similar impulse; and that some of their antagonists in the older generations have felt a related urge to
eliminate or incarcerate everyone *under* twenty-five.

I have stressed the promiscuous use of the word "relevant." Beyond its dictionary meanings, its Latin origin,
*relevare*, to raise up, is suggestive of its current meaning.
What is considered relevant is that which "raises up" a
particular version of the New History—whether that of

the young rebels or of the slightly older technocrats (such as Zbigniew Brzezinski) who are also fond of the word. Correspondingly, everything else must be "put down"— not only criticized and defeated but denied existence.

Such existential negation is, of course, an old story: one need only recall Trotsky's famous reference to the "dustbin of history." But the young, paradoxically, call it forth in relationship to the very images and fragments we spoke of before as protean alternatives to totalism. An example is the all-encompassing image of the "Establishment": taken over from British rebels, it has come to mean everything from the American (or Russian, or just about any other) political and bureaucratic leadership, to American businessmen (from influential tycoons to salaried executives to storekeepers), to university administrators (whether reactionary or liberal presidents or simple organization men), and even to many of the student and youth leaders who are themselves very much at odds with people in these other categories. And just as Establishment becomes a devil-image, so do other terms—such as (in different ways) "confrontation" and "youth"—become god-images. It is true that these god- and devil-images can illuminate many situations, as did such analogous Old Left expressions as "the proletarian standpoint," "the exploiting classes," and "bourgeois remnants," these last three in association with a more structured ideology. What is at issue, however, is the degree to which a particular image is given a transcendent status and is then uncritically applied to the most complex situations in a way that makes it the start and finish of any ethical judgment or conceptual analysis.

This image-focused totalism enters into the ultimate romanticization, that of death and immortality. While the *sense* of immortality—of unending historical continuity—is central to ordinary psychological experience, *romantic totalism tends to confuse death with immortality, and even to equate them.* Here one recalls Robespierre's famous dictum, "Death is the beginning of immortality," which Hannah Arendt has called "the briefest and most grandiose definition . . . [of] the specifically modern emphasis on politics, evidenced in the revolutions." Robespierre's phrase still resonates for us, partly because it captures an elusive truth about individual death as a *rite de passage* for the community, a transition between a man's biological life and the continuing life of his works. But within the phrase there also lurks the romantic temptation to court death in the service of immortality—to view dying, and in some cases even killing, as the only true avenues to immortality.

The great majority of today's radical young embrace no such imagery—they are in fact intent upon exploring the fullest possibilities of life. But some can at times be prone to a glorification of life-and-death gestures, and to all-or-none "revolutionary tactics," even in petty disputes hardly worthy of these cosmic images. In such situations their sense of mockery, and especially self-mockery, deserts them. For these and the related sense of absurdity can, at least at their most creative, deflate claims to omniscience and provide a contemporary equivalent to the classical mode of tragedy. Like tragedy, mockery conveys man's sense of limitation before death and before the natural universe, but it does so now in a world divested of more "straight" ways to cope with mortality. Those young rebels who reject this dimension, and insist instead upon unwavering militant rectitude, move toward romanticized death and the more destructive quests for immortality.

The theme of militant rectitude brings us back once more to the Chinese experience—and to Maoism as the quintessential expression of romantic totalism. For we may see in Mao a paradigm of the pitfalls of a noble vision, a paradigm which has great bearing on the struggles of youth throughout the world quite apart from whatever attraction they may feel toward this extraordinary leader. Mao's unparalleled accomplishments make him perhaps the greatest of all revolutionaries. If one studies his writings, one is impressed by his tone of transcendence, his continuous insistence upon all-or-none confrontation with death in the service of revitalizing the Chinese people, so much so that I have described him as "a death-conquering hero who became the embodiment of Chinese immortality." Young rebels throughout the world can perceive something of this aura, however limited their knowledge of the concrete details of Mao's life. They can, moreover, make psychological use of his Chineseness to reinforce their condemnation of Western cultural tradition, while also viewing him as the leader of "the external proletariat" (a new, post-Marxist term for the people of the Third World, seen as possessing a vanguard revolutionary role).

Further, young rebels respond to Mao's militant opposition not only to Russia and America but to the "world establishment" dominated by these two great powers. And even more to his deep distrust of bureaucracies which culminated in his remarkable assault during the Cultural Revolution upon the organizational structure of his own party and regime. (Several student-radicals I asked about Mao gave as their first reason for admiring him: "He's against institutions." Though it should be added that many others find fault with him, and sometimes mock both Mao's celebrated Thought and what they regard as equally stereotyped American attitudes toward the man and his ideas.) Add to this Mao's achievements in guerrilla warfare, his affinity for the great Chinese outlaws, and his sentimental but often moving poetry with its stress upon immortality through revolution—and one can understand why even Chinese Communist spokesmen themselves have referred to him as a "romantic revolutionary."

Yet Mao's very romanticism—his glorification of the revolutionary spirit and urge to inundate all minds with that spirit—has given rise to what is perhaps the most extensive program of human manipulation known to history. And during the Cultural Revolution he has become the center of an equally unprecedented immortalization of words and personal deification that has offended even admirers of long standing. Young rebels who embrace from afar Mao's version of "permanent revolution" may too easily overlook the consequences of the recent cam-

paign on behalf of that principle: irreparable national
dissension, convoluted and meaningless forms of violence,
and extreme confusion and disillusionment among Chinese youth (as well as their elders), perhaps especially
among those who initially responded most enthusiastically to the call for national transformation. Nor are
young rebels in the West aware of the extent to which the
Maoist vision has had to be modified and in some ways
abandoned in response to the deep-seated opposition it
encountered throughout China.

Intrinsic to Mao's romantic-totalistic conduct of the
Cultural Revolution is a pattern I call "psychism"—a confusion between mind and its material products, an attempt to control the external world and achieve strongly
desired technological goals by means of mental exercises
and assertions of revolutionary will. Now the radical
young in more affluent societies have a very different relationship to technology; rather than desperately seeking
it, they feel trapped and suffocated by it (though they
also feel its attraction). But they too can succumb to a
similar kind of confusion, which in their case takes the
form of mistaking a rewarding inner sense of group solidarity with mastery of the larger human and technological world "outside." The recent Maoist experience can find
its counterpart in a sequence of experiences of young rebels in the West: deep inner satisfaction accompanying
bold collective action, disillusionment at the limited effects achieved, and more reckless and ineffective action
with even greater group solidarity. This is not to say that
all or most behavior of young rebels falls into this category—to the contrary, their political confrontations have
achieved a number of striking successes largely because
they were *not* merely assertions of will but could also
mobilize a wide radius of opposition to outmoded and destructive academic and national policies. Yet the enormous impact of high technology in the postmodern
world, and the universal tendency to surround it with vast
impersonal organizations, present an ever increasing
temptation to transcend the whole system (or "bag") by

means of romantic worship of the will as such, and especially the revolutionary will.

Whatever their admiration of Mao, many young rebels find themselves in tactical conflict with pure Maoists who view Mao's sayings as transcendent truths, and insist upon apocalyptic violence as the only form of authentic revolutionary action. Such pure Maoists were depicted, one might say caricatured, by Godard in his film *La Chinoise*, and they have had their counterparts in the American student movement. As advocates of Maoism from a distance who lack their mentor's pragmatism and flexibility, they are somewhat reminiscent of the non-Russian Stalinists of the 1930s. But for most young rebels, Mao and Maoism are perceived less as demarcated historical person and program than as a constellation of heroic, and above all anti-bureaucratic, revolutionary images. The problem for these young rebels is to recover the historical Mao in all of his complexity—which means understanding his tragic transition from great revolutionary leader to despot. To come to terms with their own Maoism, they must sort out the various elements of the original—on the one hand its call for continuous militant action on behalf of the deprived, and its opposition to stagnant institutions, exhilarating principles which are consistent with evolving forms of the New History; on the other, its apocalyptic totalism, psychism, and desperate rear-guard assault upon the openness of contemporary man.

## VII

Yet precisely the openness of the young may help them to avoid definitive commitments to these self-defeating patterns. They need not be bound by the excesses of either Cartesian rationalism or the contemporary cult of experience which feeds romantic totalism. Indeed, though the latter is a response to and ostensibly a replacement for the former, there is a sense in which each is a one-dimensional mirror-image of the other. Today's young have available for their formulations of self and world the great twentieth-century insights which liberate man from the senseless exclusions of the opposition between emphasis on "experience" and on the "rational." I refer to the principles of symbolic thought, as expressed in the work of such people as Cassirer and Langer, and of Freud and Erikson. One can never know the exact effect of great insights upon the historical process, but it is quite possible that, with the decline of the total ideologies of the old history, ideas as such will become more important than ever in the shaping of the New. Having available an unprecedented variety of ideas and images, the young are likely to attempt more than did previous generations and perhaps make more mistakes, but also to show greater capacity to extricate themselves from a particular course and revise tactics, beliefs, and styles—all in the service of contributing to embryonic social forms.

These forms are likely to be highly fluid, but need not by any means consist exclusively of shape-shifting. Rather, they can come to combine flux with elements of connectedness and consistency, and to do so in new ways and with new kinds of equilibria. Any New History worthy of that name not only pits itself against, but draws actively upon, the old. Only through such continuity can the young bring a measure of sure-footedness to their continuous movement. And to draw upon the old history means to look both ways: to deepen the collective awareness of Auschwitz and Hiroshima and what they signify, and at the same time to carve out a future that remains open rather than bound by absolute assumptions about a "technetronic society" or by equally absolute polarities of "revolution" and "counter-revolution."

It is possible (though hardly guaranteed) that man's two most desperately pressing problems—nuclear weapons and world population—may contribute to the overcoming of totalism and psychism. In *The Broken Connection*, and more briefly in the National Book Award acceptance statement at the end of this volume, I speak of the pattern of nuclearism, the deification of nuclear weapons and of a false dependency upon them for the attainment of political and social goals. This "nuclearism" tends to go hand in hand with a specific form of psychism, the calling-forth of various psychological and political constructs in order to deny the technological destructiveness of these weapons. Nuclear illusions have been rampant in both America and China. There are impressive parallels between certain Pentagon nuclear policies (grotesquely expressed in the John Foster Dulles doctrine of "massive retaliation"), on the one hand, and the joyous Chinese embrace of nuclear weapons as further confirmation of the Maoist view of world revolution, on the other. Similarly, Pentagon (and early Herman Kahn) projections of the ease of recovery from nuclear attack—of what I have called the nuclear afterlife—bear some resemblance to the Maoist view of the weapons not only as "paper tigers" but even as a potential source of a more beautiful socialist order rising from the nuclear ashes. Now, I think that young rebels, with their frequent combination of flexibility and inclusiveness, are capable of understanding these matters. They have yet to confront the issues fully, but have begun to show inclinations toward denouncing nuclearism and nuclear psychism as they occur not only in this country but among the other Great Powers. Insights about nuclear weapons are of the utmost importance to the younger generation—for preventing nuclear war, and for creating social forms which take into account man's radically changed relationship to his world because of the potentially terminal revolution associated with these weapons.

To the problem of world population young rebels are capable of bringing a pragmatism which recognizes both the imperative of technical programs on behalf of control and the bankruptcy of an exclusively technical approach. Looking once more at China, we find that a country with one of the world's greatest population problems has approached the matter of control ambivalently and insufficiently—mainly because of a Maoist form of psychism which insisted that there could never be too many workers in a truly socialist-revolutionary state. Yet this position has been modified, and there is much to suggest that the inevitable Chinese confrontation with the actualities of population has in itself been a factor in undermining more general (and widely disastrous) patterns of psychism. Young radicals elsewhere are capable of the same lessons—about population, about Maoist contradictions and post-Maoist possibilities, and about psychism per se.

Are these not formidable problems for youngsters somewhere between their late teens and mid-twenties? They are indeed. As the young approach the ultimate dilemmas that so baffle their elders, they seem to be poised between the ignorance of inexperience, and the wisdom of a direct relationship to the New History. Similarly, in terms of the life cycle, they bring both the dangers of zealous youthful self-surrender to forms they do not understand, and the invigorating energy of those just discovering both self and history—energy so desperately needed for a historical foray into the unknown.

As for the "older generation"—those middle-aged Left-intellectuals I spoke of—the problem is a little different. For them (us) one of the great struggles is to retain (or achieve) protean openness to the possibilities latent in the New History, and to respond to that noble slogan of the French students, "Imagination in power." But at the same time this generation does well to be its age, to call upon the experience specific to the lives of those who comprise it. It must tread the tenuous path of neither feeding upon its formative sons nor rejecting their capacity for innovative historical imagination. This is much more difficult than it may seem, because it requires that those now in their forties and fifties come to terms with the extremely painful history they have known, neither to deny that history nor to be blindly bound by it. Yet however they may feel shunted aside by the young, there is special need for their own more seasoned, if now historically vulnerable, imaginations.

For both the intellectual young and old—together with society at large—are threatened by a violent counter-reaction to the New History, by a restorationist impulse often centered in the lower middle classes but not confined to any class or country. This impulse includes an urge to eliminate troublesome young rebels along with their liberal radical "fathers," and to return to a mythical past in which all was harmonious and no such disturbers of the historical peace existed. For what is too often forgotten by the educated of all ages, preoccupied as they are with their own historical dislocations, is the extent to which such dislocations in others produce the very opposite kind of ideological inclination—in this case a compensatory, strongly anti-protean embrace of the simple purities of the old history—personal rectitude, law and order, rampant militarism, and narrow nationalism.

If man is successful in creating the New History he must create if he is to have any history at all, then the formative fathers and sons I have spoken of must pool their resources and succeed together. Should this not happen, the failure too will be shared—whether in the form of stagnation and suffering or of shared annihilation. Like most other things in our world, the issue remains open. There is nothing absolute or inevitable about the New History—except perhaps the need to bring it into being.

# APPENDIX:
## ACCEPTANCE SPEECH FOR
### The 1969 National Book Award in the Sciences (For <u>Death in Life: Survivors of Hiroshima</u>)

I am grateful for this occasion. But Hiroshima permits no awards. It does require, though seldom receives, unflinching recognition. This recognition is important for the survivors of atomic bombing, because it conveys to them the sense that their experience has significance for the world, and for themselves. But it is even more important for the rest of us. We need Hiroshima to give substance to our terror—however inadequately that city can represent what would happen now if thermonuclear weapons were to be used on human populations. As a way of recognizing Hiroshima, I shall forward one half of the monetary award to a Special Fund for Survivors; and the other half, equally divided, to two American groups: The Council for a Livable World, and Physicians for Social Responsibility —groups which refuse to allow us to deceive ourselves about nuclear and biological weapons, and insist that we pursue science to promote life, and medicine to promote healing.

Nuclear weapons have already damaged us more than we know. They have created within us an image of historical extinction, and caused us to feel severed from both past and future. They also impose upon us every variety of psychic numbing—of emotional and intellectual anesthesia—so that we need not feel and cannot grasp their brutalizing effects upon human beings. This numbing not only interferes with our capacity to cope with the weapons themselves, but extends into all of our perceptions of living and dying. Rather than an age of anxiety, we live in an age of numbing.

Still worse, the weapons create in us an aura of worship. They become grotesque technological deities for a debased religion of nuclearism—gods sought by everybody as part of an all-too-human tendency to confuse the power of apocalyptic destruction with the capacity to protect, or even create, life. We then speak of nuclear stockpiles, nuclear arsenals; of a beneficent nuclear umbrella or of an equally beneficent system of anti-ballistic missiles. We perpetuate an illusion of security by means of step-by-step logic—but this is the logic of madness.

Are we inexorably condemned to live out our image of historical extinction—or rather, to die out in accordance with that image? Had I thought so, I would not have attempted to say anything at all about Hiroshima. Both haunting and true is a phrase of Theodore Roethke: "In a dark time the eyes can see." The kind of vision needed for us to keep going as a species includes full confrontation with the weapons themselves—with what they do, cause, and mean. Through such Faustian immersion into our particular purgatory, we may not only be able to cleanse ourselves but to understand our predicament and act upon it. Here and there have emerged the beginnings of such a vision—on the part of older generations who have lived through Hiroshima, and younger ones who, without yet focusing upon the specific nature of the weapons, have been trying to tell us that a world dominated by these weapons is not the only kind of world we need have. Hiroshima makes clear that our dilemmas are ultimate ones: that we are equally capable of destroying or renewing ourselves.

# NOTES

## 1. YOUTH AND HISTORY

1. Erik H. Erikson, "The Dream Specimen of Psychoanalysis," *Journal of the American Psychoanalytic Association* (1954), 2:5–56.

2. *Growing Up Absurd* (New York: Random House, 1960).

3. Ryusaku Tsunoda, William Theodore de Bary, and Donald Keene, *Sources of Japanese Tradition* (New York: Columbia University Press, 1958), pp. 592, 606.

4. See Ruth Benedict's discussions "Clearing One's Name" and "The Dilemma of Virtue," in *The Chrysanthemum and the Sword* (Boston: Houghton Mifflin, 1946).

5. For discussions of *kokutai*, see Masao Maruyama, "Chōkokka-shugi no Ronri to Shinri" (Theory and Psychology of Ultranationalism), in *Gendai Seiji no Shisō to Kōdō* (Thought and Action in Current Politics) (Tokyo, 1956); Tsunoda, de Bary, and Keene, 597–598; Richard Storry, *The Double Patriots* (Boston: Houghton Mifflin, 1957), p. 5; and Ivan Morris, *Nationalism and the Right Wing in Japan* (London: Oxford University

Press, 1960). I am also indebted to Professor Maruyama for personal discussions of *kokutai* and *shutaisei*.

6. José Ortega y Gasset, *What is Philosophy?* (New York: Norton, 1960), pp. 32–39.

7. Takeyoshi Kawashima, "Giri," *Shisō* (Thought) (September, 1951), as quoted in Nobutaka Ike, *Japanese Politics* (New York: Alfred A. Knopf, 1957), p. 29.

8. Fukuzawa Yukichi, as quoted by Masao Maruyama, "Kaikoku" (The Opening of the Country), in *Kōza Gendai Rinri* (Modern Ethics) (Tokyo: Chikuma Shobō, 1959).

9. Much of the following discussion is based upon Hajime Nakamura, *The Ways of Thinking of Eastern Peoples* (Tokyo: Japanese National Commission for UNESCO, 1960), pp. 304–433.

10. *Ibid.*, p. 307.

11. L. Takeo Doi, "Jibun to Amaeru no Seishin Byōri" (The Psychopathology of the Self and Amaeru), *Seishin Shinkei Gaku Zasshi* (Journal of Neuropsychiatry) (1960), 61: 149–162; and "*Amae*—A Key Concept for Understanding Japanese Personality Structure" (unpublished manuscript). Dr. Doi emphasizes correctly, I believe, that the emotions surrounding *amaeru* are by no means unique to the Japanese but are particularly intense in them.

12. *Philosophy in a New Key* (New York: Mentor, 1948), p. 111.

13. "An Approach to the Dynamics of Growth in Adolescence," *Psychiatry* (1961) 24: 18–31.

14. Tsunoda, de Bary, and Keene, p. 533.

15. Nakamura, p. 471.

16. Shunsuke Tsurumi, as quoted and summarized in Morris, Appendix I, pp. 427–428.

17. Nakamura, p. 465.

18. Langer, pp. 75–94. I would stress that this is a *relative*

difference in emphasis between Japanese and Western patterns of symbolization.

19.  New York: Norton, 1958. See also Zevedei Barbu, *Problems of Historical Psychology* (London: Routledge & Kegan Paul, 1960).

20.  Nakamura, and Kojiro, Yoshikawa, "The Introduction of Chinese Culture," *Japan Quarterly* (1961) 8: 160–169.

21.  I have discussed this tendency at greater length in *Thought Reform and the Psychology of Totalism: A Study of "Brainwashing" in China* (New York: Norton, 1961).

## 2.  IMAGES OF TIME

1.  Benedict, L. Takeo Doi, *"Giri-Ninjō*; An Interpretation" (unpublished manuscript).

2.  *Civilization and Its Discontents, Standard Edition of the Complete Psychological Works* (London: The Hogarth Press, 1961), pp. 64–65.

3.  Albert M. Craig, *Chōshū in the Meiji Restoration* (Cambridge, Massachusetts: Harvard University Press, 1961), and Marius B. Jansen, *Sakamoto Ryōma and the Meiji Restoration* (Princeton: Princeton University Press, 1961). See also the review article on these books by Thomas C. Smith, *The Journal of Asian Studies* (1962) 21: 215–219.

4.  *Thought Reform.* . . . See especially Chapter 22.

5.  Norman O. Brown, *Life Against Death* (Middletown, Connecticut: Wesleyan University Press, 1959), p. 93. While I strongly concur with Brown's focus upon the past (he stresses the individual past) as a prime mover of history, I would emphasize the interplay of time symbols, rather than his principle that "repression and the repetition-compulsion generate historical time."

6.  See Erik H. Erikson, *Young Man Luther* (New York, Norton, 1958) for a brilliant exposition of the interplay

between individual psychology (in this case the psychological struggles of a great man) and historical change.

7. *Thought Reform.* . . .

8. See Margaret Mead and Theodore Schwartz, "The Cult as a Condensed Social Process," in Bertram Schaffner (Ed.), *Group Processes* (Transactions of the Fifth Conference) (New York: Josiah Macy, Jr., Foundation, 1958); Margaret Mead, *New Lives for Old* (New York: Morrow, 1956); and Peter Worsley, *The Trumpet Shall Sound: a Study of "Cargo" Cults in Melanesia* (London: MacGibbon and Kee, 1957).

## 3. YOUNG DEMONSTRATORS

1. For an authoritative evaluation of this whole series of events, see George R. Packard III, *Protest in Tokyo: The Security Treaty Crisis of 1960* (Princeton, New Jersey: Princeton University Press, 1966).

## 5. THE HIROSHIMA BOMB

1. Much of the extensive literature on radiation effects has been summarized in the following: Ashley W. Oughterson and Shields Warren, *Medical Effects of the Atomic Bomb in Japan* (New York: McGraw-Hill, 1956); J. W. Hollingsworth, "Delayed Radiation Effects in Survivors of the Atomic Bombings," *New England Journal of Medicine* (September 8, 1960) 263: 381–487; "Bibliography of Publications Concerning the Effects of Nuclear Explosions," *Journal of the Hiroshima Medical Association*, Vol. 14, No. 10 (1961); and in the series of Technical Reports of the Atomic Bomb Casualty Commission (ABCC) and the various issues of the *Proceedings of the Research Institute for Medicine and Biology* of Hiroshima University, and of the *Hiroshima Journal of Medical Sciences*.

2. There has, however, been some preliminary sociological and psychological research in these areas. See S. Nakano, "Genbaku Eikyo no Shakaigakuteki Chōsa" (Sociologi-

cal Study of Atomic Bomb Effects), *Daigakujinkai Kenkyuronshu I, Betsuzuri* (April, 1954), and "Genbaku to Hiroshima," (The Atomic Bomb and Hiroshima), in *Shinshu Hiroshima Shi-shi* (Newly Revised History of Hiroshima City) (Hiroshima Shiyakusho, 1951); Y. Kubo, "Data about the Suffering and Opinion of the A-bomb Sufferers," *Psychologia* (March, 1961) 4: 56–59 (in English); and "A Study of A-bomb Sufferers' Behavior in Hiroshima: A Socio-psychological Research on A-bomb and A-energy," *Japanese Journal of Psychology* (1952) 22: 103–110 (English abstract); T. Misao, "Characteristics in Abnormalities Observed in Atom-bombed Survivors," *Journal of Radiation Research* (September, 1961) 2: 85–97 (in English), in which various psychosomatic factors are dealt with; Irving L. Janis, *Air War and Emotional Stress* (New York: McGraw-Hill, 1951), particularly Chapters 1–3. Additional studies of social aspects of the atomic bomb problem, under the direction of K. Shimizu, are now under way at the Hiroshima University Research Institute for Nuclear Medicine and Biology.

3. See Chapters 1 and 2.

4. *Thought Reform. . . .*

5. See "Genbaku Iryōhō no Kaise Jishi ni tsuite" (Concerning the Enforcement of the Revision of the Atomic Bomb Medical Treatment Law of August 1, 1960), published by the Hiroshima City Office.

6. For corroborating published accounts, see, for instance: M. Hachiya (Warner Wells, Ed., Trans.), *Hiroshima Diary* (Chapel Hill: University of North Carolina Press, 1955); T. Nagai, *We of Nagasaki* (New York: Duell, Sloan and Pearce, 1951); H. Agawa, *Devil's Heritage* (Tokyo: Hokuseido Press, 1957); Arata Osada (compiler), *Children of the A-Bomb* (New York: Putnam, 1963); Robert Jungk, *Children of the Ashes* (New York: Harcourt, Brace & World, 1961); John Hersey, *Hiroshima* (New York: Bantam, 1959); Robert Trumbull, *Nine Who Survived Hiroshima and Nagasaki* (Tokyo and

Rutland, Vermont: Charles E. Tuttle, 1957); S. Imahori, *Gensuibaku Jidai* (The Age of the A- and H-bomb) (Hiroshima: 1959); Y. Matsuzaka (Ed.), *Hiroshima Genbaku Iryō-shi* (Medical History of the Hiroshima A-Bomb) (Hiroshima, 1961); Yoko Ota, *Shikabane no Machi* (Town of Corpses) (Tokyo: Kawade Shobō, 1955); and the large number of back issues of the *Chugoku Shimbun*, Hiroshima's leading newspaper, which include accounts of personal A-bomb experiences.

7.    For estimates of damage, casualties, and mortality, see Oughterson and Warren; *Hiroshima Genbaku Iryō-shi*; M. Ishida and I. Matsubayashi, "An Analysis of Early Mortality Rates Following the Atomic Bomb—Hiroshima," ABCC Technical Report 20–61, Hiroshima and Nagasaki (n.d.); S. Nagaoka, *Hiroshima Under Atomic Bomb Attack* (Peace Memorial Museum, Hiroshima, n.d.); and "Hiroshima: Official Brochure Produced by Hiroshima City Hall" (based largely upon previously mentioned sources). Concerning mortality, Oughterson and Warren estimate 64,000, believed to be accurate within ± 10 per cent; K. Shimizu (in *Hiroshima Genbaku Iryō-shi*) estimates "more than 200,000," the figure which is accepted by the City of Hiroshima; Nagaoka estimates "more than 240,000"; the official estimate is usually given as 78,150; and one frequently sees estimates of "more than 100,000." Contributing to this great divergence in figures are such things as varying techniques of calculation, differing estimates of the number of people in Hiroshima at the moment the bomb fell, the manner in which military fatalities are included, how long afterward (and after which census count) the estimate was made, and undoubtedly other human factors outside the realm of statistical science. The obvious conclusion is that no one really knows, nor, considering the degree of disorganization interfering with collection of accurate population data, is the problem ever likely to be fully solved.

8.    See note 21.

9.    See Oughterson and Warren, as well as other sources mentioned in note 1.

10. See Hollingsworth and other sources mentioned in note 1 for discussions of delayed radiation effects and bibliographies of work done on the subject. Concerning the problem of leukemia, see also A. B. Brill, M. Tomonaga, and R. M. Heyssel, "Leukemia in Man Following Exposure to Ionizing Radiation," *Annals of Internal Medicine* (1962) 56: 590–609, and S. Watanabe, "On the Incidence of Leukemias in Hiroshima During the Past Fifteen Years From 1946–1960," *Journal of Radiation Research* (1961) 2: 131–140 (in English).

11. The most extensive work on these genetic problems has been done by James V. Neel and W. O. Schull. See their "Radiation and Sex Ratio in Man: Sex Ratio among Children of Atomic Bombings Suggests Induced Sex-Linked Lethal Mutations," *Science* (1958) 128: 343–348; and *The Effect of Exposure to the Atomic Bomb on Pregnancy Termination in Hiroshima and Nagasaki* (Washington, D. C., National Academy of Sciences—National Research Council; U. S. Government Printing Office, 1956). Belief in the possibility of an increase in various forms of congenital malformations in offspring of survivors has been stimulated by the work of I. Hayashi at Nagasaki University, reported in his paper "Pathological Research on Influences of Atomic Bomb Exposure upon Fetal Development," *Research in the Effects and Influences of the Nuclear Bomb Test Explosions* (in English, n.d.), though Dr. Hayashi, in summarizing his material, cautions that "one hesitates to give any concrete statement about the effect of the atomic bomb radiation [upon] the growth of fetal life, based on the data available in this paper."

12. Misao.

13. Especially "Genbaku Iryōhō no Kaise. . . ."

14. See the later (October 6 to December 7, 1959) series of articles in the *Chugoku Shimbun* on the history of postwar Hiroshima literature; Imahori; Jungk.

15. Nakano, "Genbaku to Hiroshima"; see also Imahori, Jungk.

16.   For Japanese attitudes about purity, see Chapter 1; and for relationship of attitudes toward death and purity, see Robert N. Bellah, *Tokugawa Religion* (Glencoe, Illinois: The Free Press, 1957).

17.   Compilations of the general literature on disaster are to be found in: George W. Baker and Dwight W. Chapmen, *Man and Society in Disaster* (New York: Basic Books, 1962); Martha Wolfenstein, *Disaster* (Glencoe, Illinois: The Free Press, 1957); "Human Behavior in Disaster: A New Field of Social Research," *The Journal of Social Issues*, Volume 10, No. 3; *Field Studies of Disaster Behavior, An Inventory* (Disaster Research Group, National Academy of Sciences—National Research Council, Washington, D. C., 1961); and L. Bates, C. W. Fogleman, and Vernon J. Parenton, *The Social and Psychological Consequences of a National Disaster: A Longitudinal Study of Hurricane Audrey* (National Academy of Sciences—National Research Council, Washington, D. C., 1963).

18.   See, for instance, Bates *et al.*

19.   The psychiatric and psychological literature leaves much to be desired in its treatment of the subject of death, but recent studies that have made significant contributions to this most difficult of areas include: Herman Feifel (Ed.), *The Meaning of Death* (New York: McGraw-Hill, 1959); K. R. Eissler, *The Psychiatrist and the Dying Patient* (New York: International Universities Press, 1955); and Brown. Two interesting reports of work in progress are: Thomas P. Hackett and Avery D. Weisman, "Human Reactions to the Imminence of Death," and Claus B. Bahnson, "Emotional Reactions to Internally and Externally Derived Threat of Annihilation"; both were presented at the Symposium on Human Reactions to the Threat of Impending Disaster at the 1962 Annual Meeting of the American Association for the Advancement of Science in Philadelphia. There has also been an expanding literature on the psychological barriers, mostly concerned with death, which impair approaches to nuclear problems. See, for instance: *Some*

*Socio-Psychiatric Aspects of the Prevention of Nuclear War* (forthcoming report of the Committee on Social Issues of the Group for the Advancement of Psychiatry); Jerome D. Frank, "Breaking the Thought Barrier: Psychological Challenges of the Nuclear Age," *Psychiatry* (1960) 23: 245–266; and Lester Grinspoon, "The Unacceptability of Disquieting Facts," presented at the AAAS Symposium on Human Reactions, etc., Philadelphia, 1962.

20. For discussions of symbolization of the self see Robert E. Nixon, "An Approach to the Dynamics of Growth in Adolescence," *Psychiatry* (1961) 24: 18–31; and Langer, p. 111. For the relevance of shame to this kind of process, see Helen M. Lynd, *On Shame and the Search for Identity* (New York: Harcourt, Brace, 1958).

21. "Guilt and Guilt Feelings," *Psychiatry* (1957) 20: 120. In attributing guilt feelings to Japanese, here and elsewhere in this article, I am following recent critiques of the concept of "shame cultures" and "guilt cultures": Gerhart Piers and Milton B. Singer, *Shame and Guilt* (Springfield: Charles C. Thomas, 1953); and more specifically in relationship to Japan, George DeVos, "The Relation of Guilt Toward Parents to Achievement and Arranged Marriage Among Japanese," *Psychiatry* (1960) 23: 287–301. See also Erik H. Erikson, *Childhood and Society* (New York: Norton, 1950), pp. 222–226.

6. ON DEATH AND DEATH SYMBOLISM

1. See particularly Oughterson and Warren for detailed studies of early mortality. Other sources for over-all mortality estimates are listed in Chapter 5, note 7. Without here attempting to enter into the complexities of mortality estimates, one may say that it is significant that Japanese estimates are consistently higher than American ones.

2. Ota, p. 63.

3. This concept of self follows that of Nixon, who states

that ". . . *self* is the person's symbol for his organism" (p. 29). Also relevant is Susanne Langer's idea that "The conception of 'self' . . . may possibly depend on this process of symbolically epitomizing our feelings" (p. 111).

4.  See, for instance, Rollo May's discussion on this concept in *Existence: A New Dimension in Psychiatry and Psychology*, Rollo May, Ernest Angel, and Henri F. Ellenberger (Eds.) (New York: Basic Books, 1958), pp. 55–61.

5.  Harold F. Searles, *The Nonhuman Environment* (New York: International Universities Press, 1960).

6.  See Erik H. Erikson, "The Problem of Ego Identity," *Journal of the American Psychoanalytic Association* (1956) 4: 56–121; and also Martin Grotjahn, "Ego Identity and the Fear of Death and Dying," *Journal of the Hillside Hospital* (1960) 9: 147–155.

7.  See, respectively, Gert Heilbrunn, "The Basic Fear," *Journal of the American Psychoanalytic Association* (1955) 3: 447–466; and William James, *The Varieties of Religious Experience* (London: Longmans, Green, 1952).

8.  *Young Man Luther*, p. 111.

9.  *Thought Reform . . .* , pp. 69–72.

10. For an interesting discussion of the significance of the end-of-the-world fantasy in the history of psychoanalysis, see Sheldon T. Selesnick, "C. G. Jung's Contributions to Psychoanalysis," *American Journal of Psychiatry* (1963) 120: 350–356.

11. Shoji Inoguchi, "Funerals," in Vol. 4, *Nihon Minzoku Gakutaikei* (An Outline of the Ethnological Study of Japan), Oma Chitomi *et al.* (Eds.) (Tokyo: Heibonsha, 1959).

12. See note 2.

13. Betty Jean Lifton, "A Thousand Cranes," *The Horn Book Magazine* (April, 1963); Robert Jungk, pp. 289–290.

14. "The Problems of the Survivor: Part I, Some Remarks on the Psychiatric Evaluation of Emotional Disorders in Survivors of Nazi Persecution," *Journal of the Hillside Hospital* (1961) 10: 233–247.

15. See Bruno Bettelheim, *The Informed Heart: Anatomy in a Mass Age* (Glencoe, Illinois: The Free Press, 1960).

16. Among recent psychiatric and psychological studies of death and death symbolism, see Eissler; Feifel (Ed.); Brown. In addition, a good deal of research is now in progress. See, for instance, Avery Weisman and Thomas P. Hackett, "Predilection to Death: Death and Dying as a Psychiatric Problem," *Psychosomatic Medicine* (1961) 23: 232–256; and Edwin S. Shneidman, "Orientations Toward Death: A Vital Aspect of the Study of Lives," in Robert W. White (Ed.), *The Study of Lives* (New York: Atherton, 1963).

17. Sigmund Freud, "Thoughts for the Times on War and Death," *Standard Edition of the Complete Psychological Works*, 14: 275–300 (London: Hogarth, 1957), p. 289. The editor of this edition, James Strachey, states (p. 274) that the two essays contained in the paper were written "round about March and April, 1915." Eissler (see Chapter 5, note 19; pp. 24–25) dates them "at the end of 1914 or at the beginning of 1915," emphasizing that they were not written after exhausting years of despair and horror but were "a rather quick response to the very evident fact . . . that there is more aggression in man than one would have thought from his behavior in peacetime and that man's attitude toward death is usually the outcome of the mechanism of denial, so long as he does not face death as a reality which may befall him or his loved ones at any moment." Ernest Jones (*The Life and Work of Sigmund Freud*; New York: Basic Books, 1955; Vol. 2, pp. 367–368) points out that the essays were written in response to a request from the publisher (Hugo Heller) of the psychological periodical *Imago*, though he adds that Heller probably did not suggest the theme and that Freud, in writing them, must have been "like all highly civilized people . . . not only greatly

distressed, but also bewildered, by the frightful happenings at the onset of the first World War, when so many things took place of which no living person had any experience or any expectation." Jones adds that these two essays "may be regarded as an effort to clear his mind about the most useful attitude to adopt to the current events." In any case it seems clear that with this paper, more than with most of his writings, Freud was responding to the stimulus of a great and highly threatening historical event; it is also significant that while his private reactions to the war were at times impulsive and quite variable, his public statement contained only a controlled series of ideas growing directly out of his previous concepts.

18. *Phénoménologie de la Perception*; pp. 249–250, as quoted and translated by Arleen Beberman in "Death and My Life," *Review of Metaphysics* (1963) 17: 18–32, p. 31.

19. In developing his ideas on the "inherited image," Joseph Campbell (*The Masks of God: Primitive Mythology*; New York: Viking, 1959; pp. 30–49, 461–472) follows Adolf Bastian and C. G. Jung. Otto Rank (*Beyond Psychology*; New York: Dover, 1958; pp. 62–101) develops his concepts of man's quest for immortality through the literary and psychological concept of "The Double as Immortal Self." While I do not agree with all that Rank and Campbell say on these issues (I would, in fact, take issue with certain Jungian concepts Campbell puts forward), their points of view at least serve to open up an important psychological perspective which sees the quest for immortality as inherent in human psychology and human life.

20. Huxley and Père Teilhard, of course, go further, and visualize the development of a unifying, more or less transcendent idea-system around this tendency. Huxley refers to this as "evolutionary humanism" (*The Humanist Frame*, Julian Huxley, Ed.; New York: Harper, 1961; pp. 11–48) and Père Teilhard speaks of the "Omega point," at which a "hyperpersonal" level of advanced human consciousness may be attained (*The*

*Phenomenon of Man*; New York: Harper, 1959; pp. 257–263).

21. The *Hagakure*, the classical eighteenth-century compilation of principles of *Bushidō* (The Way of the Samurai), contains the famous phrase: "The essence of *Bushidō* lies in the act of dying." And another passage, originally from the *Manyōshū*, a poetic anthology of the eighth century: "'He who dies for the sake of his Lord does not die in vain, whether he goes to the sea and his corpse is left in a watery grave, or whether he goes to the mountain and the only shroud for his lifeless body is the mountain grass.' This is the way of loyalty." (Bellah, pp. 90–98.)

22. Weisman and Hackett, "Predilection to Death," p. 254.

23. Leo Tolstoy, *The Death of Ivan Ilyich and Other Stories* (New York: Signet Classics, 1960). The quotations that follow are from pp. 97, 138, 152, and 156.

24. Weisman and Hackett, "Human Reactions. . . ."

25. Lifton, "Youth and History."

26. See Leslie H. Farber, "Despair and the Life of Suicide," *Review of Existential Psychology* (1962) 2: 125–139; and "The Therapeutic Despair," *Psychiatry* (1958) 21: 7–20.

27. Sigmund Freud, "Beyond the Pleasure Principle," *Standard Edition of the Complete Psychological Works* 18: 55–56 (London: Hogarth, 1955). Maryse Choisy (*Sigmund Freud: A New Appraisal*; New York: Philosophical Library, 1963) has pointed out that Freud (and presumably Barbara Low), in employing this terminology, misunderstood the actual significance of Nirvana —to which I would add that Nirvana (whether the ideal state or the quest for that state) probably involves various kinds of indirect activity and sense of movement, and not simply ultimate stillness.

28. See, for instance, Langer; Campbell; Kenneth Boulding, *The Image: Knowledge in Life and Society* (Ann Arbor,

Michigan: University of Michigan Press, 1956); S. A. Barnett, "'Instinct,'" *Daedalus* (1963) 92: 564–580; and Adolf Portmann, *New Paths in Biology* (New York: Harper, 1964). What Freud refers to as the death instinct may well be "imagery" prefiguring of death, which the organism contains from birth, which becomes in the course of life further elaborated into various forms of conscious knowledge, fear, and denial; and which interacts with other forms of innate imagery relating to life-enhancement (sexual function, self-preservation, and development) as well as to mastery. From this perspective, the need to transcend death involves the interrelationship of all three of these forms of imagery, with that of mastery of great importance.

29. For a discussion of psychological and historical aspects of ideology, and particularly of ideological extremism, see *Thought Reform . . .* , Chapter 22.

30. See, for instance, Hans J. Morgenthau, "Death in the Nuclear Age," *Commentary* (September, 1961). Among psychological studies, see Frank, "Breaking the Thought Barrier . . ."; *Some Socio-Psychiatric Aspects of the Prevention of Nuclear War*; and Grinspoon.

31. Eissler (pp. 65–67) notes the frequently observed psychological relationship between suicide and murder, and goes on to speak of suicide as "the result of a rebellion against death," since "for most suicides the act does not mean really dying" but is rather a means of active defiance of, rather than passive submission to, death.

32. *Thought Reform . . .* , Preface to Norton Library (paperback) edition (1963).

### 7.   ATOMIC-BOMBED CHILDREN

1. Osada, *Children of the A-Bomb.*

### 8.   JEWS AS SURVIVORS

1. See Erik Erikson, "Psychological Reality and Historical

Actuality," in *Insight and Responsibility*, pp. 159–215; and Sigmund Freud, "Fragment of an Analysis of a Case of Hysteria" [1905], *Standard Edition of the Complete Psychological Works*, 7: 3–122 (London: Hogarth, 1953).

2. *Treblinka* (New York: Simon & Schuster, 1968).

## 9. AMERICA IN VIETNAM—THE COUNTERFEIT FRIEND

1. See Betty Jean Lifton, "Waiting for the Herky Bird," *The New Journal* (February 4, 1968), and also her "An Outsider at Someone Else's Feast," *The New Journal* (May 12, 1968), for recollections of what it was like when Ho Chi Minh marched into Hanoi in 1954.

## 10. REASON, REARMAMENT, AND PEACE

1. *Deadly Logic: The Theory of Nuclear Deterrence* (Columbus, Ohio: Ohio State University Press, 1966).

2. "Rearmament and Japan: Thoughts on a Familiar Bogey," *Asian Survey* (September, 1961), pp. 10–15.

## 11. WHAT AILS MAN?

1. *On Aggression* (New York: Harcourt, Brace & World, 1966).

2. *Human Aggression* (New York: Atheneum, 1968), p. 121.

3. Vintage, 1964.

4. Pantheon, 1969.

5. Arthur Koestler, *The Ghost in the Machine* (New York: Macmillan, 1968).

6. *Philosophy in a New Key*, p. 45.

## 12. WOMAN AS KNOWER

1. *The Woman in America* (Boston: Houghton Mifflin, 1965).

2. Ivan Morris, *The World of the Shining Prince: Court*

*Life in Ancient Japan* (New York: Alfred A. Knopf, 1964). Subsequent quotations concerning women writers in the Heian period, in this and the next two paragraphs (including the quotation from Arthur Waley), are from Morris' book.

3.   Sigmund Freud, "On the Universal Tendency to Debasement in the Sphere of Love (Contributions to the Psychology of Love II)," *Standard Edition of the Complete Psychological Works*, 11: 177–190 (London: The Hogarth Press and The Institute of Psycho-analysis, 1957).

4.   See Erik H. Erikson, "Inner and Outer Space: Reflections on Womanhood," in *The Woman in America*, for a discussion of these psychobiological distinctions—particularly that between feminine "inner space" and masculine "outer space"—and their appearance early in life.

5.   Michael Polanyi, *Personal Knowledge* (Chicago: University of Chicago Press, 1958), pp. 300–303.

6.   I have discussed some of these issues at length in *Thought Reform . . .* , and other related matters in Chapter 1.

7.   Charles Haldeman, *The Sun's Attendant* (New York: Simon & Schuster, 1964), p. 256; his italics.

8.   See Chapter 2 for a discussion of these ways of psychologically symbolizing time; Chapter 1 deals with some of the observations on Japanese students that follow.

9.   Kenneth Keniston, "Inburn, an American Ishmael," in Robert W. White (Ed.), *The Study of Lives* (New York: Atherton, 1963), and *The Uncommitted* (New York: Harcourt, Brace & World, 1965). See also, Ellen and Kenneth Keniston, "An American Anachronism: The Image of Women and Work," *American Scholar* (1964) 33: 355–375.

10.  Edna Rostow, "Conflict and Accommodation," in *The Woman in America*.

11.  Vincent Sheean, *Dorothy and Red* (Boston: Houghton Mifflin, 1963), p. 340.

12. Diana Trilling, "The Image of Women in Contemporary Literature," in *The Woman in America*.

13. New York: Norton, 1963.

14. For this and subsequent references to Bowlby, see his "The Nature of the Child's Tie to his Mother," *International Journal of Psycho-analysis* (1958) 39: 350–373; and "Separation Anxiety," *International Journal of Psycho-analysis* (1960) 41: 1–25.

15. See Chapter 6.

16. W. K. C. Guthrie, *The Greeks and Their Gods* (Boston: Beacon Press Paperback Series, 1955), pp. 284, 286.


## 13.   PSYCHOANALYSIS AND HISTORY

1. *Psychoanalysis and History* (Englewood Cliffs, New Jersey: Prentice-Hall, 1963).


## 14.   COMMENTS ON METHOD

1. For the rest of the exchange I refer the interested reader to Frederick Wyatt, "In Quest of Change: Comments on Robert J. Lifton's 'Individual Patterns and Historical Change,'" *Comparative Studies in Society and History* (1964) 6: 384–392; and Kenneth Keniston, "Accounting for Change," *Comparative Studies in Society and History* (1965) 7: 117–126.


## 15.   PROTEAN MAN

1. All Solotaroff quotations are from a review essay on Sartre in *Bookweek*, April 25, 1963.

2. *The Words* (New York: Braziller, 1964), p. 19.


## 16.   THE YOUNG AND THE OLD—NOTES ON A NEW HISTORY

1. *On Revolution* (New York: Viking, 1963), p. 232.

2. *The Rebel* (New York: Alfred A. Knopf, 1954), pp. 72–3.

# INDEX

A bomb, *see* Nuclear weapons
A-bomb disease, 130-43, 166-69, 171n
  death from, 131-34, 137-38, 140-41, 146, 168
  spiritual feature of, 140
"A-bomb Dome" (Hiroshima), 148-49
"A-bomb neurosis," 138, 168
A-bomb Hospital (Hiroshima), 141
"A-bomb literature," 206
Absurdity, 157, 340, 344-45, 364, 366
  protean sense of, 313, 315, 324-28
Accommodationism, 58, 71-76, 78-79, 85
  defined, 71
  interchangeable nature of, 76
Action painting, 322, 351
Aesthetics, *see* Beauty
Africa, 306, 344, 363
  underdeveloped areas of, 39, 78-79
Age differences, *see* Generation gap; Older generations; Youth
Alexander, Franz, 14
All Japan Federation of Student Self-Governing Societies, *see* Zengakuren
*Amaeru*, 44-45, 144
America, United States of (U.S.), 9, 17-20, 57, 100, 117n, 167, 201, 301, 337, 367
  Japanese attitudes toward, 83, 193-94
    ambivalent, 33-36, 74, 89, 96
    American military presence, 68, 85, 89
    anti-American demonstrations, 87-89, 92, 94-95
    critical, 41
    hostility, 147-48, 194
    Oi's attitude, 240, 242
  McCarthy epoch of, 33-34
  mass demonstrations in, 84, 326-27, 332, 334, 346-49
  nuclear weapons of, 371
    weapons detonated, 121, 147-48, 166, 223, 338
  protean style in, 311, 318-19, 325-26
  restorationism in, 306
  in Vietnam War, 20, 85, 210-37, 248n, 253, 327
    resentment of U.S. presence, 211, 219, 225-30, 250

*See also* Japanese-American Security Treaty; Negroes
American Academy of Arts and Sciences, 256
American accommodationism, 79
American Embassy (Saigon), 231
American Embassy (Tokyo), 81-82
American interventionism, 20, 250
American psychiatry, 12-14, 19
American universities, 10, 15, 17-18, 332, 334, 346-49
American Western films, 41, 101-2, 104-10
American women, 256-58, 260, 265, 276-84
  as vanguard group, 277-78
American youth, 26, 28, 272
  family relations of, 276, 353-54
  Goodman on, 30n
  identity of, 37-38
  New History of, 332, 334, 346-49, 353-54, 362, 365, 369
  New Leftist, 338, 343; *see also* SDS; Yippies
Annihilation, anticipation of, 161-62
Anxiety, *see* Fear
Apple, R. W., Jr., 212
Arendt, Hannah, 199, 341, 365-66
*Asahi Evening News*, 102
*Asahi Graphic*, 140n
Asian countries, 92, 98, 242-43, 363
  East, 9, 16, 18, 83, 174, 179-80, 185, 261, 276-78
  underdeveloped, 39-40, 78-79
  World War II in, 121
  *See also* China; Japan; Vietnam
*Asian Survey* (periodical), 102
Atomic-bomb disease, *see* A-bomb disease
"Atomic bomb maidens," 144
Atomic weapons, *see* Nuclear weapons
Attachment behavior, 252, 285-86

Baldwin, James, 290
Baron, Salo W., 292
Beauty (aesthetics), 325
  Japanese sense of, 131
    among the young, 26, 30, 32, 46-52, 64, 131
Beck, Julian, 334-35
Bell, Daniel, 324
Bellow, Saul, 102, 320
Benedict, Ruth, 63n
Biosocial continuity, 174, 177, 182-83, 253
Bowlby, John, 285-86

ROBERT JAY LIFTON holds the Foundation's Fund for Research in Psychiatry professorship at Yale University. He has been particularly concerned with the relationship between individual psychology and historical change—in China, Japan, and the United States—and with the problems surrounding the extreme historical situations of our era. He has spent almost seven years in the Far East, including an extensive stay from 1960 to 1962, during which he carried out a study of psychological patterns of Japanese youth as an investigation of the psychological effects of the atomic bomb in Hiroshima. He has played a prominent part in the creation of a new approach known as "psychohistory." Dr. Lifton has recently been involved in writing, speaking, and giving public testimony concerning the psychological state contributing to American atrocities in Vietnam.

Dr. Lifton was born in New York City in 1926. From 1956 to 1961, he taught and did research at Harvard, where he was associated with the Center for East Asian Studies as well as the Department of Psychiatry. He lives in Woodbridge, Connecticut, with his wife, a writer, and their two small children.

He is the author of *History and Human Survival; Death in Life: Survivors of Hiroshima* (for which he received the National Book Award in Sciences in April of 1969); *Revolutionary Immortality: Mao Tse-tung and the Chinese Cultural Revolution; Thought Reform and the Psychology of Totalism: A Study of "Brainwashing" in China; Boundaries: Psychological Man in Revolution;* and is the editor of *The Woman in America* and *America and the Asian Revolutions.* In addition, his writings have appeared in *Partisan Review, The Atlantic Monthly, The American Scholar, The New Republic* and *Daedalus,* as well as in various East Asian, psychiatric, and psychological journals. His new book, *Crimes of War: After Songmy,* co-edited with Richard Falk and Gabriel Kolko, was published by Random House in 1971.

# VINTAGE WORKS OF SCIENCE
## AND PSYCHOLOGY